Price Analysis of China's Carbon Emissions

This book explores the determination of China's carbon emission targets, especially with regard to the allocation of responsibility of China's import and export carbon emissions, and carbon emission quota allocations across different time periods, industries, and regions.

Research outside of China tends to focus on methods and approaches of carbon emission reduction policies and the impact of their implementation. Instead, within China, the focus has been on discussion of the necessity and conditions for China's development of a low-carbon economy as well as its introduction as a concept in the light of overseas comparisons. This book utilizes game theory, mechanism design, input-output theory, econometric theory, and other methods to scrutinize China's carbon emissions and carbon emissions targets across different periods, industries, and regions. The result is a detailed theoretical and empirical investigation of carbon emission issues in the Chinese context.

The book will be essential reading for students and scholars of economics, especially those with a focus on Chinese economic development and policymakers in the low-carbon economy sphere.

Wenju Wang is president and professor of Beijing Wuzi University, China, doctoral supervisor in Quantitative Economics at Capital University of Economics and Business, China. He serves as vice president of China Federation of Logistics Purchasing, vice president of China Society of Quantitative Economics, and vice chairman of Teaching Steering Committee of Economics and Trade of Ministry of Education. He has been engaged in the research and teaching of game theory and quantitative economics for a long time.

Price Analysis of China's Carbon Emissions

Wenju Wang

Routledge
Taylor & Francis Group
LONDON AND NEW YORK

首都经济贸易大学出版社
Capital University of Economics and Business Press

First published 2023
by Routledge
4 Park Square, Milton Park, Abingdon, Oxon OX14 4RN

and by Routledge
605 Third Avenue, New York, NY 10158

Routledge is an imprint of the Taylor & Francis Group, an informa business

Translated by Hongyan Du

British Library Cataloguing-in-Publication Data
A catalogue record for this book is available from the British Library

ISBN: 978-1-032-48328-3 (hbk)
ISBN: 978-1-032-48329-0 (pbk)
ISBN: 978-1-003-38850-0 (ebk)

DOI: 10.4324/9781003388500

Typeset in Times New Roman
by codeMantra

Contents

Figures

Tables

Preface

Low-carbon economy has become a global development trend and concern. In China, the pursuit of low-carbon economy and reducing carbon emissions is the only choice to implement scientific outlook on development, transform economic growth model, and enhance economic restructuring for a sound and fast development.

Studies on carbon emissions in China and abroad are increasing. Overseas studies focus on analyzing the realization effect, methods, and approaches of carbon emission reduction policies, while domestic studies mainly focus on the statements of necessities and requirements to develop a low-carbon economy in China, the concept of a low-carbon economy, and the introduction to overseas experiences. However, studies on key issues such as the determination of China's carbon emission targets especially on the responsibility allocation of China's import and export carbon emissions, and carbon emission quota allocation in different time periods, industries, and regions are still limited. Meanwhile, most of the current studies are qualitative; the quantitative studies using game theory and dynamic modeling are still limited. In fact, developing a low-carbon economy will have a profound influence on the central government, local governments, industries, enterprises, and consumers, and will inevitably form a new game theory pattern, which needs to be analyzed and evaluated. The game theory and dynamic modeling approaches can provide a better analysis and evaluation.

This book is the fruits of two projects: one is "Comprehensive Study on the Determination of China's Total Carbon Emissions, Index Allocation, and Mechanism Design of the Realization Path" from the key project of the National Philosophy and Social Science Foundation (Project No. 10AJY002); the other is "Carbon Emissions and Game Measurement Research" from the project of the Great Wall Program for the Introduction and Training of High-Level Talents in Beijing Higher Education Institutions (Project No. CIT & TCD 20140321). This book uses game theory, mechanism design theory, input-output theory, econometric theory, computable general equilibrium, and other methods to study the determination of China's total carbon emissions, index allocation among different periods, industries, and regions, and mechanism design for the realization path of carbon emission targets. In addition, the book conducts simulation studies by the dynamic simulation method, which provides guidance and reference for the development of low-carbon economy in China.

The innovations of the research methods in this book are mainly reflected in the following two aspects:

First, a systematic game analysis framework for carbon emission reduction behavior is constructed.

With local governments deemed as the players in this part, we establish a static game model, a signal game model, and an evolutionary game model for the dilemma of carbon emission reduction, and provide the "static game—dynamic game—evolutionary game" model, a more systematic game analysis framework for carbon emission reduction dilemma in China. This not only complements the current research on the carbon emission reduction game among local governments but also improves the research on the long-term interaction and evolution of carbon emission reduction initiatives among local governments.

Second, a dynamic input-output model for total carbon emissions accounting is constructed.

A dynamic input-output model for industrial restructuring is established based on the final demand in the input-output relationship with the national economic system as a whole. Under the premise of rigid consumption and export product mix, the dynamic input-output model for industrial restructuring is established with investment as objects. The model not only estimates the potential total carbon emissions at equilibrium economic growth but also provides basis for decision-making and data support to achieve China's carbon emissions reduction targets.

The outstanding features of this book are as follows: based on game theory and mechanism design theory, it conducts systematic and extensive research on the relevant carbon emission issues in China, and provides a basis and reference for the index allocation of carbon emissions and mechanism of design for a path to achieve carbon emissions targets in China. Among them, the main game models constructed include the cooperative game model for sharing the carbon emissions responsibility of the imports and exports in China; the static game model, a signal game model, and an evolutionary game model for the dilemma of carbon emission reduction among local governments; the game model of initial allocation of carbon emission rights in China; the bargaining game model formed by the trading price of carbon emission rights in China; the auction model of the first-price sealed-bid auction of carbon emission rights trading in China; and so on.

The main achievements of this book include the following aspects:

First, the study on the accounting and responsibility allocation of carbon emissions embodied in international trade. The study concludes that responsibility allocation for international carbon emissions should be taken by "producers" and "consumers" by distinguishing between scale effect, structural effect, pure technical effect, and exchange rate effect. This method is more equitable than the simple "producer responsibility" or "consumer responsibility" and can avoid "carbon leakage" from developed countries to developing countries through trade.

Second, an assessment of China's industrial restructuring and its potential for energy saving and emission reduction. The results show that if the energy structure and the energy consumption per unit of product of each sector remain at the level of 2005, then industrial structuring alone can reduce energy consumption by 1.8 billion to 2.5 billion tonnes of standard coal in 2020. Carbon dioxide emissions can be reduced by 3.9 billion to 5.6 billion tonnes of standard coal and the production energy intensity and carbon intensity can be reduced by 26% to 31%. The industrial restructuring can contribute up to about 60% to achieving China's carbon intensity target.

Third, the fairness research on the selection of international carbon emission accounting standards. The results show that the results of fairness measures vary greatly under different accounting standards. Taking cumulative carbon emissions per capita as an accounting standard, the G8 has a high relative deprivation coefficient for the other two country subgroups. However, with the carbon emissions per unit of GDP as the accounting standard, the situation is just the other way around. The accounting standard based on the adjustment of carbon emissions embodied in international trade can better reflect the principle of "common but differentiated responsibilities". It will be more equitable to develop global emission reduction programs based on carbon emissions embodied in international trade.

The academic values and applications of this book mainly include:

First is academic values. This book employs game theory, mechanism design theory, input-output theory, econometric theory, computable general equilibrium, and other methods to study the determination of China's total carbon emissions, index allocation among different periods, industries and regions, and mechanism design for the realization path of carbon emission targets. It has achieved academic success and has been widely recognized by the academic community. According to the query results of CNKI's on April 14, 2016, "Accounting and Responsibility Allocation of Carbon Emissions Embodied in International Trade" has been downloaded 1,753 times and cited 42 times in total.

Second is applications. Providing support for government decision-making is the goal of this study. From the perspective of index allocation of carbon emissions and the mechanism design to achieve carbon emission target in China, this book puts forward a total of nearly 100 countermeasures and suggestions, which are served as important applications and references to achieve China's carbon emission targets and develop low-carbon economic development policy. Among them, some of the results have been used as the reference for the government to formulate energy-saving and emission-reduction policies.

Wenju Wang

Acknowledgment

Dr. Wenju Wang is the leader of this research group. He is president and professor of Beijing Wuzi University, China, doctoral supervisor in Quantitative Economics at Capital University of Economics and Business, China. He serves as vice president of China Federation of Logistics Purchasing, vice president of China Society of Quantitative Economics, and vice chairman of Teaching Steering Committee of Economics and Trade of Ministry of Education. He has been engaged in the research and teaching of game theory and quantitative economics for a long time. The other members of the research group are Dr. Qifeng Xiang, professor at the School of Statistics and mathematics, Yunnan University of Finance and Economics; Dr. Feng Li, lecturer at the School of Business Administration, Capital University of Economics and Business; and Dr. Li Nie , associate professor at the School of Statistics, Capital University of Economics and Business. Members of the research group published a number of research results with joint efforts and close collaboration, which laid a firm foundation for the completion of this project. This book is the result of the hard work of all the members of the research group!

The authorship of this book is as follows: Chapters 1, 2, 3, 5, 6, 7, 8, and 9 were written by Wenju Wang and Qifeng Xiang; Chapters 4, 10, and 11 were written by Wenju Wang and Feng Li ; and Chapters 12, 13, 14, and 15 were written by Li Nie and Wenju Wang. The project leader designed the framework of the project, pointed out the difficulties, and provided methods for project breakthroughs. The leader organized project research, reviewed project results, revised, and wrote the final report about the project. Doctoral students Fei Teng, Qifeng Xiang, Feng Li, Qili Xu, Yongjie Tian, Lan Shen, Hanbing Xue and others did extensive editing, typesetting, and proofreading. Any bias, deficiencies, or errors that may appear in the report shall be the responsibility of the project leader.

Part I

Determination of total carbon emissions in China

Under the background of global warming and frequent extreme weather events, low-carbon economy has become a global development trend and concern. In China, the pursuit of low-carbon economy and reduced carbon emissions is the only choice to implement scientific outlook on development, transform economic growth model, and enhance economic restructure for a sound and fast development.

The carbon emission right is a country's right to development. Since 2012, the competition for carbon emission rights has intensified among countries in the world. This part first examines and compares the initiative emission rights allocated to China from international and domestic carbon emission allocation schemes respectively in terms of rationality and implementability. Second, it analyzes pros and cons of "producer principle" and "consumer principle" under the carbon emission accounting principle, pointing out that calculation of carbon footprint embodied in international trade and its responsibility allocation are key to solve the accounting problem. According to the relevant data in 2005, this part provides a reasonable calculation method of embodied carbon emissions in trade based on the input-output model. The result shows that international trade has a significant impact on carbon emissions, and gives rise to a large number of carbon leakage, a major cause to the growing greenhouse gas emissions in China, where a great portion of carbon emissions are to meet the production and living needs of developed countries, that is, through a large amount of cheap products exported from China. Therefore, China is not the only party responsible for carbon emission reduction.

As for trade embodied carbon responsibility allocation, it can be divided into four parts by LMDI decomposition of the net transfer of embodied carbon in international trade (net carbon export), namely scale effect, structural effect, pure technical effect, and exchange rate effect. For the first time, the consumers are responsible for the carbon emission reduction related to scale effect, structural effect, and exchange rate effect, and the producers and consumers are jointly responsible for the reduction involving pure technical effect. The result of quantitative analysis of the international carbon emission accounting standard with relative deprivation coefficient demonstrates that it is the most equitable method of responsibility allocation of trade carbon emissions till now.

DOI: 10.4324/9781003388500-1

1 Carbon emission rights and carbon emission reduction target

1.1 Background of carbon emissions

1.1.1 Carbon emissions and low-carbon economy

Under the background of global warming and frequent extreme weather events, low carbon economy has become a global development trend and concern. In China, to develop a low carbon economy and reduce carbon emissions is the only choice to implement scientific outlook on development, transform economic growth model, and enhance economic restructure for a sound and fast development.

There are many studies abroad on carbon emission reduction and low carbon economy. Nicholas (2006) assessed the potential for low carbon economy transitions and adaptive approaches in the context of climate change and analyzed the impact of climate change on the economy of the UK and other countries. Johnston et al. (2005) and Treffers et al. (2005), respectively, explored the technical feasibility of carbon emission reduction in the UK and Germany, and believed that it is possible to achieve both robust economic growth and greenhouse gas emission reduction through relevant policy measures. Gottinger (1998) used Computable General Equilibrium (CGE) models to simulate the impact of unilateral and multilateral policy tools of major EU member states on greenhouse gas emission reduction. Kemfert and Welsch (2000) used CGE models to study the economic effect of carbon emission reduction policies in different countries.

In recent years, Chinese scholars have also started to pay attention to the research on carbon emission reduction and low carbon economy. Pengfei Gao and Wenying Chen (2002) studied the effects of a carbon tax on China's carbon emissions and macro-economy. Juhuang He et al. (2002) established a static CGE model to analyze the effects of a carbon tax on the national economy. Can Wang et al. (2005) used a dynamic CGE model to analyze the economic effect of carbon emission reduction policies in China. Qunwei Wang et al. (2010) measured the carbon emission performance of 28 provinces, municipalities, and autonomous regions in China from 1996 to 2007. Qirong Zhu (2010) used the input-output model to calculate the

DOI: 10.4324/9781003388500-2

total carbon emissions generated by China's export trade activities in 2002 and 2007. Feng Wang et al. (2010) studied 11 driving factors for the carbon emission growth from energy consumption in China and their contribution rates. Gang Fan et al. (2010) studied the determination of carbon emission responsibility in different countries under the influence of international trade. Xiaoping Li and Xianxiang Lu (2010) made an empirical test with environmental input-output models and net export consumption index methods to see whether international trade made China a "paradise of polluting industries" in developed countries.

In conclusion, studies on carbon emissions in China and abroad are increasing. Overseas studies focus on analyzing the realization effect, methods, and approaches of carbon emission reduction policies, while domestic studies mainly focus on the statements of necessities and requirements to develop a low carbon economy in China, the concept of a low carbon economy, and the introduction to overseas experiences. However, studies on key issues such as the determination of China's carbon emission targets, especially on the responsibility allocation of China's import and export carbon emissions, and carbon emission quota allocation in different time periods, industries, and regions are still limited. Meanwhile, most of the current studies are qualitative, the quantitative studies using game theory and dynamic modeling are still limited. In fact, developing a low carbon economy will have a profound influence on the central government, local governments, industries, enterprises, and consumers, and will inevitably form a new game theory pattern, which needs to be analyzed and evaluated. The game theory and dynamic modeling approaches can provide a better analysis and evaluation.

1.1.2 Current research in total carbon emissions

1.1.2.1 Carbon emission rights

In response to global warming, the United Nations Framework Convention on Climate Change (UNFCCC) set a long-term goal, namely stabilization of greenhouse gas concentrations in the atmosphere at a level that "would prevent dangerous anthropogenic interference with the climate system", and a specific goal of "limiting the maximum global average temperature increase to no more than 2 degrees Celsius above pre-industrial levels" was proposed at the Copenhagen Climate Change Conference in 2009. Therefore, the atmospheric concentration of increased carbon dioxide is supposed to be very limited from 2005 to 2050, merely 191.33 GtC (total of 701.61 Gt CO_2, 1 Gt = 1 billion tonne; 1 tonne of carbon dioxide contains 12/44 tonnes of carbon) according to Zhongli Ding's estimation (2009). In this case, in order to balance the interests of all countries and encourage carbon dioxide emission reduction, the Kyoto Protocol, which came into force in 2005, offered the world an "emission reduction mechanism": each developed country was assigned an "emission allowance" and countries short of allowance were allowed to buy "emission indicator" from countries with excessive or unrestricted allowances. Since then, the atmosphere layer has become a kind of quasi-public goods due to the carbon emission mechanism. Mingyuan Wang (2010) discussed the quasi-property rights and development rights of carbon emission rights from the legal perspective. Of course, after all, the carbon emission right is a right to development (Zewei Yang , 2011).

Since the carbon emission right is a right to development, the competition for carbon emission rights is to compete for economic development opportunity. Therefore, the focus of climate negotiations among countries actually falls on the initial allocation of carbon emission rights. In terms of allocation methods, over 20 popular allocation schemes, including the Intergovernmental Panel on Climate Change (IPCC) scheme, the G8 scheme, the United Nations Development Programme (UNDP) scheme, the Organisation of Economic Cooperation and Development (OECD) scheme, the Garnaut scheme, the convergence scheme, the GCI contraction and convergence allocation model, the increasing participation methodology of RIVM, the multi-stage participation methodology of RIVM, the Triptych approach, the multi-sector convergence approach, the US alternative scheme based on decreased carbon emission intensity, the binary intensity targets, and the South Africa SD-PAMs approach have been proposed worldwide. Representatives of the developed countries favored convergence in per capita emissions, whereas developing countries led by Brazil, India, and China proposed to allocate emissions rights by history, per capita, and final consumption. Jingjing Zeng et al. (2009) compared the allocation schemes and concluded that specific emission reduction amounts and measures varied significantly in spite of consistent GHG (greenhouse gases) control targets. Yi Wang and Yu Huang (2011) argued that all allocation schemes were divergent in understanding the principle of fairness, and would lead to uncertain ecological and economic impacts if performed.

Domestic scholars put forward their own views on the initial allocation of carbon emission rights. Gang Fan et al. (2010) argued that each country's share of carbon emissions should be measured based on the final consumption from the perspective of fairness and welfare. Weizhong Wang et al. (2002) argued that developing countries should adhere to equal per capita emission quotas, and the emission reduction responsibilities undertaken by developed countries were still insufficient. Jiankun He et al. (2009) argued that the principle of convergence in per capita emissions evaded the historical responsibility of developed countries. Junyong Qiu (2011) evaluated fairness of cumulative carbon dioxide emissions and found that Gini coefficients of National Land areas, population, ecologically productive land area, and currently proven fossil fuel reserves are all in unfair and very unfair state. Wenying Chen et al. (2005) argued that the "two convergences" approach conforms to the principle of fair, common but differentiated responsibilities and sustainable development. Kaisheng Li (2012) suggested to allocate carbon emission rights with John Rawls's theory of justice. Tongjin Yang (2010) analyzed the rationality and limitations of history baseline principle, historical responsibility principle, the principle of utilitarianism, and the principle of egalitarianism, and concluded that the combination of the advantages of these four principles would contribute to an ideal ethical principle. In terms of empirical evidence, Zhongli Ding et al. (2009) modeled the seven global carbon dioxide reduction schemes, including IPCC, UNDP, and OECD schemes, and found that these schemes took sides with developed countries in the future allocation of carbon emission rights without considering their historical responsibilities. He believed that "cumulative emission per capita" is the only indicator reflecting the principle of "common but differentiated responsibilities" and the principles of justice and equity. Currently, Zhongli Ding's view has been acknowledged by many scholars in China.

As for the allocation principles of carbon emission rights, there is a huge divergence between developed countries and developing countries, and a consensus is impossible in the short term. The allocation principle based on history, per capita, and final consumption proposed by domestic scholars is undoubtedly the most favorable for our country. However, the final allocation principle depends on the climate negotiation outcomes among interest groups.

1.1.2.2 Carbon emissions accounting methods

Carbon emission allocation schemes based on historical responsibilities involve historical emissions in all countries; therefore, many scholars have begun to study the accounting of the historical emissions in all countries. Jiangling Zhu et al. (2010) calculated the cumulative emissions and cumulative emissions per capita of major countries and China during 1850–2008 based on the carbon emissions data of the Carbon Dioxide Information Center of the Oak Ridge National Laboratory in the US from the perspective of producer emissions. The results showed that developed countries, with both historical cumulative emissions and cumulative emissions per capita much higher than those in developing countries, are main contributors to the growing carbon dioxide concentration. China's historical cumulative emissions and cumulative emissions per capita are much lower than those of developed countries, in spite of an increasingly high per capita emissions and total carbon emissions in recent years. Gang Fan et al. (2010) calculated the cumulative consumption emissions and the cumulative consumption emissions per capita of the major countries in the world during1850–2005 from the perspective of final consumption. The results showed that China's cumulative emission actuals accounted for 10.19% of the total cumulative carbon emissions worldwide, but its cumulative consumption emissions accounted for only 6.84%–8.76% of that worldwide, while in most developed countries, the cumulative consumption emissions are greater than cumulative emission actuals.

Scholars in China estimated and allocated the future carbon emission rights under the principle of historical responsibility. The Development Research Center project group of the State Council (2009, 2011) built a theoretical framework to define the historical and future emission rights of each country with property rights theory and externality theory. On this basis, the group designed an open and inclusive framework of country-specific emission accounts that feature optimal allocation of emission space, carbon emission reduction, and technological progress, accounted the initial allocation of global carbon emission budgets among countries in a fair manner under the principle of equal per capita emissions and accounted current available budgets of each country based on the available data. Among these countries, the initial emission budget remained about 394.94 Gt in China after the portion for cumulative emissions was deducted, while such figure was a negative value for most developed countries. Shengmin Wang et al. (2010) simulated the results of allocation by historical per capita cumulative emissions under four possible scenarios of population dynamics, confirmed operability of the scheme, and estimated that China's disposable carbon budgets during 2013–2050 would remain 28 Gt. Zhongli Ding et al. (2009) calculated the emission quotas of each country during 2006–2050 under the principle of equal per capita cumulative emissions rights, and found that most G8 countries had used up their quotas by 2005 and ended up with emission deficits. China, although with over 30% of global emission quotas in 2006–2050, still had to reduce its emissions for a balanced result.

In addition, scholars have also estimated China's future carbon emissions under various scenarios. Jianmin Zhang (2011) predicted China's primary energy demand and carbon emissions in 2015 and 2020 using 2005 as the base year and estimated that China's carbon dioxide emissions in 2015 and 2020 would reach 1.998 billion tonnes and 2.424 billion tonnes, and the carbon dioxide emissions per capita would reach 1.45 tonnes and 1.72 tonnes, respectively. Yi Wang (2012) incorporated environmental regulation factors into Kaya's equation to construct an improved decomposition equation for carbon emissions per capita, and projections for future scenarios during 2010–2020 showed that China's carbon emissions per capita would be 13.0–18.1 tonnes. Zheng Wang et al. (2010) made a more comprehensive estimate of China's future carbon emissions from the aspects of energy consumption, cement production, and forest carbon sinks, and argued that China's carbon emissions from energy consumption would reach a peak of 2 637 MtC in 2031 and net carbon emissions would reach a peak of 2 748 MtC in 2033. Chao Yue et al. (2010) predicted China's carbon emissions in 2050, and concluded that the best possible range of China's carbon emissions in 2050 might be 2.4–3.3 PgC/a and carbon emission per capita might be 1.7–2.3 tC; the carbon emissions under the premise of the best possible upper limit would be expected to reach a peak in 2035, the peak carbon emissions would be 4.4 PgC/a, and the peak carbon emission per capita would be 3.0 tC. During 2006–2050, the best possible range of China's cumulative carbon emissions would be 102–156 PgC and the cumulative emissions per capita would be 71–109 tC, with a best prediction upper limit lower than that of the US in the same period and not far from that of the developed countries in the same period.[1]

1.1.2.3 The carbon emissions embodied in trade and emission reduction responsibilities

As early as the late 20th century, the impact of international trade on the utilization of natural resources and environmental changes has attracted extensive attention from scholars. Many scholars began to measure the carbon emissions embodied in international trade, and emphasized that attention should be paid to the impact of international trade on carbon dioxide emissions in a country and worldwide. These scholars conducted research with the input-output method. Among them, Munksgaard and Pedersen (2001) measured carbon dioxide emissions of Denmark in 1989–1994 under the principles of producer responsibility and consumer responsibility, respectively, based on Denmark input-output tables. The results showed that the increasing carbon dioxide emissions resulted from foreign demands made it even more difficult for Denmark to meet its emission targets. Peters and Hertwich (2008) calculated the trade-embodied emissions of 87 countries and regions in 2001 using GTAP Data Base and multi-regional input-output (MRIO) models, and found that the trade-embodied carbon emissions already accounted for 1/4 of the global carbon emissions. Among them, China's carbon emissions from exported goods accounted for 24% of domestic carbon emission actuals, while this figure was 7% for imported goods. Xin Zhou (2010) calculated the carbon emissions embodied in international trade of ten countries or regions including China using multi-regional input-output analysis under the principles of "consumer responsibility for pollution" and "shared producer and consumer responsibility", retested the greenhouse gas emissions in each country or region. The results showed that the US was the largest net importer of trade-embodied carbon emissions, followed by Japan, and China was the largest net exporters.

As a major trading country in the world, China has ranked among top three of total import and export trade volume in the world since 2004. In 2007, China's merchandise export volume amounted to USD 1.218 trillion, which accounted for 8.8% of global merchandise export. With the rapid growth of China's export volume, the issue of the trade-embodied carbon emissions has also attracted widespread attention from domestic academics. Many scholars in China calculated trade-embodied carbon emissions in China's import and export trade. According to the calculation of Yanmei Li and Jiafeng Fu (2010), the carbon emissions embodied in China's export trade in 1997 and 2007 reaching 290.61Mt and 940.69 Mt, respectively, accounting for 28.47% and 45.53% of China's total carbon emissions from production activities, respectively. Qirong Zhu (2010) calculated the carbon dioxide emissions from China's export trade in 2002 and 2007, and found a mushrooming trend as well as a shift of some high carbon products to exporting industries in China. Xiaoping Li et al. (2010) calculated the embodied carbon dioxide emissions in China's foreign trade, and found that the proportion of embodied carbon dioxide of domestic inputs in export products was decreasing, while the proportion of carbon dioxide embodied in imported intermediate products was increasing. Shuzhong Ma and Ying Chen (2010) estimated China's embodied carbon emissions during 2000–2009 using single region input-output model with domestic consumption activities as a standard and found the results were lower than the international statistics.

The current debate on the responsibility allocation for carbon emissions embodied in international trade falls on the subject of responsibility. The producer and the consumer are deemed the two main subjects responsible for the carbon emissions. Manfred Lenzen et al. (2007) discussed the theory and practice of producers and consumers jointly responsible for the carbon emissions embodied in international trade, and pointed out the existing difficulties. Benyong Wei et al. (2010) proposed to extend national greenhouse gas accounting across national borders and redefine the emission responsibility from the perspective of consumption of goods or services in the future international negotiations. Liping Li et al. (2008) argued that greenhouse gas emissions, including carbon dioxide emissions, due to trade surplus increased significantly in China, and consumer demand in western countries accelerated China's carbon emissions increase. "Global consumers, especially those in developed countries had responsibilities for China's increasing ecological impacts overseas, China was not the only one responsible for its ecological footprint".[2] Yuhshan Ji and Hongliang Zhao (2010) argued that the current accounting of national emissions and reductions were based mainly on national borders rather than final consumers, resulting in a large amount of "carbon leakage" in developing countries, while developed countries benefiting from the cheap products provided by developing countries required developing countries to take responsibility for carbon emission reductions. It was against the principle of interpersonal fairness.

In general, the above studies have limitations. Most studies, with only one country as the study objective, calculate carbon emission of import trade based on the carbon emission intensity of similar goods or services within the country rather than that of imported goods. Although Peters and Hertwich (2001) addressed the issues well using GTAP Data Base and MRIO models, it was an old story. Zhou Xin's MRIO analysis is also a good approach. However, it can barely reflect the global situations as it focuses on the flow of carbon dioxide among ten countries or regions, including China. In terms of responsibilities in embodied carbon emission reductions, although scholars abroad begin to advocate joint responsibilities of producers and consumers, specific allocations still need to be discussed. Domestic scholars have insisted on consumer responsibility and longed for a reasonable method to quantify "common but differentiated responsibilities" of each country according to the stages of economic development, energy endowment, and natural environment.

1.2 Carbon emission rights and China's carbon emission reduction targets

1.2.1 Emergence and current situation of carbon emission rights

For a long time, the atmospheric space as a vital factor to human being and typical public goods has been free of property rights. Human's production activities have little impact on the atmosphere and hardly pose any threat. In recent years, with global warming, environmental degradation, and frequent climate disasters, human beings have become aware that changes of the global climate system due to their uncontrolled carbon dioxide emissions have led to a huge disaster for them. Therefore, in May 1992, at the headquarters of the UN, the intergovernmental negotiating committee reached a convention on climate change for the first time, namely UNFCCC (United Nations Framework Convention on Climate Change); to fully control emissions of greenhouse gas, including carbon dioxide and address the adverse effects of global warming on human society.

However, the property lessens and externalities of carbon dioxide emission space have made atmospheric layers "public commons". At this stage, energy is one of the most important inputs for economic growth, and it is impossible to fully control the greenhouse gas emissions through voluntary emission reductions by each country. Therefore, the Kyoto Protocol was adopted in December 1997 at the third session of the parties to the UNFCCC based on the principles and provisions of the UNFCCC. The Kyoto Protocol sets the targets for greenhouse gas reductions of each country during the first commitment period (2008–2012). Among them, countries listed in Annex I (mainly developed countries and regions) are assigned mandatory emission-reduction targets, while countries in Annex II may conduct voluntary emission reductions according to their conditions. In Annex I countries, the EU member states are required to reduce emissions of six greenhouse gases by 8%, the US by 7%, and Japan by 6%, with a total of greenhouse gas emissions of these countries 5.2% below 1990 levels. However, after the US President Bush took office, he refused to sign the Kyoto Protocols on the pretext of America's economic development and the uncertainty of climate change, which prevented the Kyoto Protocol from coming into effect. The Kyoto Protocol came into effect in February 2005 as scheduled, thanks to Russian President Vladimir Putin's signature.

In order to balance the interests of all countries and encourage carbon dioxide emission reduction, the Kyoto Protocol offers the world an "emission reduction mechanism": each developed country is assigned an "emission allowance" and countries short of allowance are allowed to buy "emission indicator" from countries with excessive or unrestricted allowances. Since then, people could trade emission indicators of carbon dioxide in the exchange just like buying and selling stocks. This is the emergence of the concept of carbon emission rights.

As the Kyoto Protocol terminated in 2012, each country started a new round of political game on climate issues to compete for a larger carbon emission space. Their focus was on the amount of carbon dioxide that a country could discharge into the atmosphere for free in the coming period, namely the initial allocation of carbon emission rights.

Among the allocation principles of carbon dioxide emission rights, countries have a biggest divergence in the historical principle. From the preindustrial 1751–2009, the cumulative carbon dioxide emissions from fossil fuel combustion and cement production exceeded 1.3 trillion tonnes, among which the cumulative emissions only accounted for 0.35% before 1850 and 16.71% during 1850–1949, and 46.39% of the global accumulative emissions during 1950–1991. Cumulative effect of the carbon dioxide, which remains in the atmosphere for quite a long period, causes global warming. Therefore, the UNFCCC states clearly in its preamble that "common but differentiated responsibilities", "Noting that the largest share of historical and current global emissions of greenhouse gases has originated in developed countries, that per capita emissions in developing countries are still relatively low and that the share of global emissions originating in developing countries will grow to meet their social and development needs". Therefore, the cornerstone of the allocation of carbon emission rights is "common but differentiated responsibilities".

1.2.2 China's future carbon emission rights

Over 20 allocation schemes of carbon emission rights have been proposed on the basis of "common but differentiated responsibilities" under principles of efficiency and fairness. For those schemes, Zhongli Ding, a member of the Chinese Academy of Sciences, evaluated seven most influential schemes worldwide and analyzed their differences in per capita emission rights of each country. The chapter lists China's future carbon emission rights under the seven schemes according to Zhongli Ding's conclusion.

The first scheme is the IPCC scheme, which sets a medium- to long-term global emission reduction target of limiting global temperature change to well below 2°C from the industrial revolution to the end of the 20th century. Among them, Annex I countries are required to reduce emissions by 80%–95% below 1990 levels by 2050 and non-Annex I countries to reduce emissions significantly below baseline levels. In the medium term (2020), Annex I countries are required to reduce emissions by 25%–40% below 1990 levels and non-Annex I countries, including those in Latin America, the Middle East, East Asia, and Central Planned economies in Asia, are required to reduce emissions significantly below baseline levels. Zhongli

Ding calculated the total carbon emissions and carbon emissions per capita of China during 2006–2050, based on the population in 2005.

The second scheme was proposed by the Group of Eight (the US, the UK, France, Germany, Italy, Canada, Japan and Russia) in 2009, with a target of reducing carbon dioxide emissions from fossil energy and cement production by 50% globally and by 80% in developed countries by 2050. With 1990 as the base year and 445 ppmv of carbon dioxide concentrations in 2050 as a control target, Ding calculated carbon emission rights of developed countries (about 84.23 GtC) and allocated the remaining 146.98 GtC of carbon emission rights to Annex II countries based on the population in 2005. Calculation showed that the carbon emission right of China during 2006–2050 would reach about 127.862 billion tonnes of carbon dioxide.[3]

The third scheme is proposed by the UNDP, which calls for controlling the carbon dioxide concentration in the air at around 445 ppmv in 2050. Under the target, 50% emission reductions in 2050 and peak carbon emissions in 2020 are required. For developing countries and regions, their carbon emissions in 2020 are permitted to be 80% higher than current level. With 2005 as the base year, China's carbon emission rights in 2020 will reach 2.842 GtC or 10.422 billion tonnes of carbon dioxide.[4]

The fourth scheme, namely the OECD scheme, is proposed by the OECD with a target of 3% global emission reductions in 2030 on the basis of the 2000 level. Among them, OECD countries should reduce emissions by18%, other countries could increase emissions by 7%; by 2050, carbon emission reduction should reach 55% in OECD countries, 25% in other countries, and 41% worldwide on the basis of the 2000 level. On these grounds, according to relevant calculations, China's carbon emission right during 2006–2050 is about 103.004 billion tonnes of carbon dioxide.

The fifth scheme is proposed by Garnaut, an Australian. According to this scheme, with 2001 as the base year, if the carbon emission reduction begins in 2005, the global carbon emissions could increase by 29% by 2020 and reduce by 50% by 2050. This scheme also specifies China's carbon emission reduction target in 2020, which is 195% higher than that in 2001. On these grounds, China's cumulative carbon emission right should be 295.23 billion tonnes of carbon dioxide by 2050, and 10.281 billion tonnes of carbon dioxide in 2020.

The sixth scheme is jointly proposed by Chakravarty et al., scientists from the US, the Netherlands, and Italy, known as the CCCPST scheme, which requires to reduce global greenhouse gas emissions to 8.18 GtC by 2050 and to reach a peak emission of 9.03 GtC in 2020. According to the carbon emission rights allocated to China, China's cumulative carbon emission rights should be 191.857 billion tonnes of carbon dioxide by 2050, and 2.32 GtC, or 8.507 billion tonnes of carbon dioxide by 2020.

The seventh scheme, known as the Sorensen scheme, was proposed by Sorensen, a Danish, in 2008. The scheme calculated the carbon emission space of 13 major countries under the principle of "convergence in future emissions per capita". Among them, China's total carbon emission space was about 250 Gt of carbon dioxide, allowing China to discharge carbon dioxide for another 64 years at the 2007 emission level, provided that carbon dioxide emissions were reduced to zero thereafter. At the 2007 emission level, China's carbon emission rights in 2020 were about 6.792 billion tonnes of carbon dioxide according to this scheme.

For the above seven allocation schemes, Zhongli Ding demonstrated their unfairness in terms of the distinctive differences in emission rights per capita. None of the seven schemes mentioned the historical emissions, and they also allocated more carbon emission rights per capita to developed countries and regions in the future, which would be barely accepted by developing countries and regions.

After 2008, China, India, and Germany successively proposed the "carbon budget" scheme. The Chinese Academy of Social Sciences proposed to create a carbon emission account for each country and to deduct historical emissions while allocating carbon emission rights under the principle of "equal per capita historical cumulative emission rights". According to their calculations, with 1850–2050 as the budget period, the global annual carbon emissions per capita based on population in 2005 were 2.33 tonnes of CO_2/(person·year). China's current account balance is 394.94–481.94 billion tonnes of CO_2, which is basically consistent with the carbon emission allowance of 403.027 billion tonnes of CO_2 during 2006–2050 calculated by Zhongli Ding, a member of Chinese Academy of Sciences, under the principle of "equal per capita historical cumulative emission rights".

The Indian scheme allocates "carbon budget" by the stage of carbon emission trajectory. With 1970–2009 as the historical emission stage, 2009–2050 as the future emission budget stage I, and 2050–2100 as the future emission budget stage II, carbon budgets allocated to stage I, II, and III are 223 Gt, 1440 Gt, and 225 Gt carbon dioxide, respectively. Based on the population in 2009, this scheme offers global carbon emission budget per capita in the future: not exceeding seven tonnes of carbon dioxide/ (person·year) during 2009–2020, not exceeding four tonnes of carbon dioxide/(person·year) during 2020–2040, and not exceeding two tonnes of carbon dioxide/(person·year) after 2040.

The "carbon budget" allocation scheme proposed in 2009 by the German Advisory Council on Global Change (WBGU) is based on the population in 2010.With the target of 750 Gt of carbon dioxide emitted in 2010–2050, calculations are made under the principle of equal future emission rights per capita, and results show that the carbon emissions per capita during 2011–2050 is 2.7 tonnes of carbon dioxide/(person·year). For historical emissions during 1990–2009 (about 500 Gt of carbon dioxide), the scheme suggests that countries with high carbon emission per capita compensate countries with low carbon emissions per capita through financial and technological means according to the per capita emissions gap.

The "carbon budget" schemes in China, India, and Germany are all based on the equal emission rights per capita, and have considered historical responsibility for emissions. Although the results of carbon budgets vary greatly due to the different measurement standards in the historical emission period, such schemes reflect the "interpersonal fairness of carbon emission rights" at least. The historical period begins from 1900 in China's scheme, from 1970 in India's scheme, and from 1990 in Germany's scheme. The shorter the historical period, the more unfair the historical responsibility would be.

According to the carbon emission rights allocated to China under various schemes, excluding the emissions before 2010 (among them, the data of carbon emissions during 2001–2009 are from the Carbon Dioxide Information Center of the Oak Ridge National Laboratory in the US, and the carbon dioxide emissions in 2010 are estimated according to energy consumption), China's carbon emission rights during 2011–2050 are listed in Table 1.1.

As shown in the table, except for China's own scheme, carbon emission rights allocated to China under other schemes are quite few. The Garnaut scheme offers the most allowance to China, reaching 260.768 billion tonnes; while the OECD scheme offers the least allowance, reaching only 68.542 billion tonnes. They are all far from the counterpart (about 370 billion tonnes) calculated by China under the principle of "equal historical cumulative emissions per capita".

1.2.3 China's international and domestic targets for carbon emission reduction by 2020

According to scholars' research on carbon emission laws, China's carbon emissions will continue to rise, and are expected to reach a peak in 2035 and decline thereafter. Taking China's estimated carbon dioxide emissions (8 billion tonnes) from fossil combustion in 2011 as a starting point, its

Table 1.1 Estimation of China's future carbon emission rights (billion tonnes of carbon dioxide)

Allocation scheme	*Period*	*Cumulative carbon dioxide emissions*	*Carbon dioxide emissions after 2011*
IPCC	2006–2050	140.584–159.955	106.122–125.493
G8	2006–2050	127.862	93.400
UNDP	2020	10.422	——
OECD	2006–2050	103.004	68.542
Garnaut	2006–2050	295.230	260.768
CCCPST	2004–2030	191.857	146.695
Sorensen	2000–2100	250	193.319
Chinese Academy of Social Sciences	2006–2050	394.940–481.940	360.478–447.478
Ding Zhongli	2006–2050	403.027	368.565
India	2010–2050	236.206	228.515
Germany	2011–2050	144.818	144.543

carbon emissions in 2035 are expected to be at least eight billion tonnes, and the cumulative carbon dioxide emissions during 2011–2035 will be no less than 200 billion tonnes. As shown in Table 1.1, China cannot meet the emission reduction targets under the IPCC scheme, the G8 scheme, the OECD scheme, the CCCPST scheme, the Sorensen scheme, and the Germany scheme, or those under the Garnaut scheme and India scheme.

In the remaining schemes, the UNDP directly offers China's carbon emissions in 2020, which is about 10.422 billion tonnes of carbon dioxide. According to the "carbon budget" balance of the Chinese Academy of Social Sciences, China's average annual carbon dioxide emission rights are about 11.187 billion tonnes during 2011–2050. While according to Zhongli Ding's allocation scheme, this figure is about 9.214 billion tonnes. Except for the scheme proposed by domestic scholars, the UNDP scheme is the most favorable one for us, with relatively reasonable carbon emission rights (about 10.422 billion tonnes) between the Zhongli Ding's scheme and the scheme of Chinese Academy of Social Sciences. In addition, the carbon dioxide emission right in 2020 under the Garnaut scheme is about 10.281 billion tonnes, which is also relatively close to the above-mentioned figure.

The carbon emission reduction has become an uncertain target of each country since 2013, as there has been no binding international convention on carbon emission reduction following the Kyoto Protocol. The current studies on carbon emissions in China are based on the relative reduction target announce by Premier Jiabao Wen at the government work conference in 2009, which is lowering carbon dioxide emissions per unit of GDP by 40%–45% in 2020 compared to 2005. Since China's carbon emission intensity in 2005 was 3.062 tonnes of carbon dioxide/CNY 10,000, it is estimated that the carbon dioxide emissions per unit of GDP should be controlled below 1.837 tonnes of carbon dioxide/CNY 10,000 in 2020. With the GDP in 2011 as the baseline and calculated at constant prices in 2005, if China's economy continues to grow at a rate of 6.5%–8.5%, its GDP will reach CNY 60.60–71.65 trillion in 2020, and the corresponding total carbon dioxide emissions are required to be controlled below 11.034–13.164 billion tonnes. Even with the 11.194 billion tonnes of carbon dioxide rights under the scheme of the Chinese Academy of Social Sciences, it is impossible to achieve completely free emissions. Therefore, the carbon emission reduction target set by Chinese government is lower than that required by the international community.

Notes

1 The units of carbon measurement in different literatures vary. Some are Gt, some Mt, and some Pg. The correlation is: 1 Gt = 1 Pg = 1,000 Mt = 1 billion ton. Therefore, GtC represents 1 billion tonnes of carbon, PgC also represents 1 billion tonnes of carbon, MtC represents 1 million tonnes of carbon, tC represents 1 tonne of carbon. Generally, GtC represents 1 billion tonnes of carbon, PgC also represents 1 billion tonnes of carbon, MtC represents 1 million tonnes of carbon. In addition, PgC/a represents 1 billion tonnes of carbon per year.

2 A survey released by the World Wide Fund for Nature in April 2007.
3 A unit of concentration for carbon dioxide, ppmv (parts per million by volume). It is literally translated as one share out of a million shares, which represents the milliliters of carbon dioxide in per cubic meter of air.
4 Different units for carbon calculation are used in different literatures. Some are tonnes of carbon dioxide (tCO2), and some are tonnes of carbon (tC). The correlation between them is: tonnes of carbon dioxide = [molecular weight of carbon dioxide (12+2×16)/ molecular weight of carbon (12)] tonnes of carbon = 3.67 tonnes of carbon.

References

Chen Wenying, Wu Zongxin, He Jiankun. Two-convergence approach for future global carbon permit allocation. *Journal of Tsinghua University (Science and Technology)*, 2005, 45 (6): 850–853.

Ding Zhongli, Duan Xiaonan, Ge Quansheng, et al. Control of atmospheric carbon dioxide concentration in 2050: calculation of carbon emission rights in each country. *Scientia Sinica (Terrae)*, 2009 (8): 1009–1027.

Fan Gang, Su Ming, Cao Jing. An economic analysis of consumption and carbon emission responsibility. *Economic Research Journal*, 2010 (01): 4–14.

Gao Pengfei, Chen Wenying. Carbon tax and carbon emission. *Journal of Tsinghua University (Science and Technology)*, 2002, 42 (10): 1335–1338.

Gottinger, H.W. Greenhouse gas economics and computable general equilibrium. *Journal of Policy Modeling*, 1998, 20 (5): 537–580.

He Jiankun, Chen Wenying, Teng Fei, et al. Long-term climate change mitigation target and carbon permit allocation. *Climate Change Research*, 2009, 5 (6): 362–368.

He Juhuang, Shen Keting, Xu Songling. Carbon taxation and CGE model of carbon dioxide mitigation. *The Journal of Quantitative and Technical Economics*, 2002, 19 (10): 39–47.

Ji Yushan, Zhao Hongliang. Analysis of China's carbon emission responsibility from the perspective of the right to development. *Comprehensive Competition*, 2010, 4: 84–88.

Johnston, D., Lowe, R, Bell, M. An exploration of the technical feasibility of achieving CO_2 emission reductions in excess of 60% within the UK housing stock by the year 2050. *Energy Policy*, 2005, 33: 1643–1659.

Kemfert C., Welsch H. Energy-capital-labor substitution and the economic effects of CO_2 abatement: evidence for Germany. *Journal of Policy Modeling*, 2000, 22 (6): 641–660.

Li Kaisheng. Rawls's theory of justice and the global burden sharing of greenhouse gas emission. *World Economics and Politics*, 2012 (3): 39–56.

Li Liping, Ren Yong, Tian Chunxiu. Analysis of China's carbon emission responsibility from the perspective of international trade. *Environmental Protection*, 2008 (6): 62–64.

Li Xiaoping, Lu Xianxiang. International Trade, Transfer of polluting industry and China's industrial of carbon dioxide emissions. *Economic Research Journal*, 2010 (1): 15–26.

Li Yanmei, Fu Jiafeng. Structural decomposition analysis on carbon emissions growth embodied in exports in China. *Chinese Journal of Population, Resources and Environment*, 2010 (8): 53–57.

Ma Shuzhong, Chen Ying. The influence of international trade to China's embodied carbon emissions during 2000–2009: based on consumption and SRIO model. *Finance and Trade Economics*, 2010 (12): 82–89.

Manfred Lenzen, Joy Murray, Fabian sack Thomas Wiedmann. Shared producer and consumer responsibility—Theory and practice. *Ecological Economics*, 2007, 61: 27–42.

Munksgaard, J., Pedersen, K.A. CO_2 accounts for open economies: producer or consumer responsibility?. *Energy Policy*, 2001, 29: 327–334.

Nicholas Sturn. The stern review on the economic effects of climate change. *Population and Development Review*, 2006, 32: 793–798.

Peters, G.P., Hertwich, E.G. CO_2 embodied in international trade with implications for global climate policy, 2008, 42(5): 1401–1407.

Qiu Junyong, Zhong Dingsheng, Yu Qiaocui, et al. Equity analysis of global CO_2 emissions based on Gini coefficient. *China Soft Science*, 2011 (4): 14–21.

Treffers, T., Faaij, A.P., CvSparkman, J., et al. Exploring the possibilities for setting up sustainable energy systems for the long term: two visions for the Dutch energy system in 2050. *Energy Policy*, 2005, 33: 1723–1743.

Wang Can, Chen Jining, Zou Ji. Impact assessment of CO_2 mitigation on China economy based on a CGE model. *Journal of Tsinghua University (Science and Technology)*, 2005, 45 (12): 1621–1624.

Wang Feng, Wu Lihua, Yang Chao. Driving factors for growth of carbon dioxide emissions during economic development in China. *Economic Research Journal*, 2010, 45 (2): 23–29.

Wang Mingyuan. On carbon emission right's dual-nature. *China Legal Science*, 2010 (6): 92–99.

Wang Qunwei, Zhou Peng, Zhou Dequn. Research on dynamic carbon dioxide emissions performance, regional disparity and affecting factors in China. *China Industrial Economics*, 2010 (1): 45–54.

Wang Shengmin, Gao Xiang, Zhai Lihua, Ma Cuimei. Research on operational definition and allocation scheme of historical cumulative emission rights per capita. *Advances in Climate Change Research*, 2010, 6(06): 456–460.

Wang Weizhong, Chen Bin, Lu Chuanyi, et al. The Koyto protocol and allocation of carbon emission permits. *Journal of Tsinghua University (Philosophy and Social Sciences)*, 2002 (10): 18–21.

Wang Yi. China's carbon emissions scenario prediction-based on the perspective of environmental regulation. *Economy and Management*, 2012, 4.

Wang Yi, Huang Yu. Equity and uncertainty: the key problems for the allocation of world carbon emissions. *Chinese Journal of Population, Resources and Environment*, 2011 (S1): 501–504.

Wang Zheng, Zhu Yongbin, Liu Changxin, et al. Integrated projection of carbon emission for China under the optimal economic growth path. *Acta Geographica Sinica*, 2010, 65 (12): 1562–1571.

Wei Benyong, Wang Yuan, Yang Huimin, et al. Advances on carbon emissions embodied in international trade. *World Regional Studies*, 2010, 19 (2):138–147.

Yang Tongjin. Global justice: ethical principle of distributing greenhouse gas emissions. *Journal of Renmin University of China*, 2010 (2):1–10.

Yang Zewei. The right to carbon emission: a new right to development. *Journal of Zhejiang University (Humanities and Social Sciences)*, 2011 (3): 40–49.

Yue Chao, Wang Shaopeng, Zhu Jiangling, et al. 2050 carbon emissions projection for China (carbon emissions and social development, Ⅳ). *Acta Scientiarum Naturalism Universitatis Pekinensis*, 2010 (4): 517–524.

Zeng Jingjing, Qu Jiansheng, Zhang Zhiqiang. Review of the international greenhouse gas emission reduction scenario programs. *Advances in Earth Science*, 2008, 23 (1): 47–54.

Zhang Jianmin. China energy demand from 2005 to 2020 and international comparative study on carbon emissions. *Energy of China*, 2011 (1): 33–37.

Zhou Xin. Accounting of carbon embodied Emissions in international trade and national greenhouse gas emissions after trade adjustment. *Management Review*, 2010, 22(6): 17–24.

Zhu Jiangling, Yue Chao, Wang Shaopeng, et al. Carbon emissions in China and major countries from 1850 to 2008 (carbon emissions and social development, Ⅰ). *Acta Scientiarum Naturalism Universitatis Pekinensis*, 2010(4):497–504.

Zhu Qirong. Research on the CO_2 emissions produced by China's exports. *China Industrial Economy* 2010, 262 (1): 55–64.

2 Carbon emission accounting in China

2.1 Principles of carbon emission accounting

2.1.1 Producer principle and consumer principle

The "producer principle", also known as the "polluter pays principle", upholds that those who produce pollution should bear the cost of managing it. For a long time, the international community has measured carbon emissions by the producer principle; also, a polluter pays principle based on territorial responsibilities, under which pollutions produced in a country are accounted directly. This method of accounting has no disputes for a closed economy, where producers are consumers, and production emissions are equal to consumption emissions. However, in the current open international environment, the producer principle has brought a series of disputes on carbon emission reductions.

In this increasingly open world, economic globalization leads to global resource allocation based on capital. A product may be produced in a country and sold in others, and producers and consumers are no longer the same. In cross-border product flow, developed countries and regions transfer pollution emissions to other countries by exporting capital and raw materials to developing countries and regions for processing and production, and then shipping back semi-finished and finished products. They reduce their own carbon emissions and escape the constraints of carbon emission reduction in this way. Developing countries and regions, with a relatively low level of technology, are temporarily exempt from carbon emission reduction regulations, which, instead, increases global carbon emissions and results in "carbon leakage".

The consumer principle is therefore put forward. It holds that consumers should be responsible for the entire ecological impact in the production process and greenhouse gas (GHG) emissions associated with this process. Munksgaard and Pedersen (2001) calculated the production-based carbon emissions and consumption-based carbon emissions in Denmark in 1994, respectively, and found that the production-based carbon emissions were 7.8 million tonnes less than consumption-based carbon emissions, which

DOI: 10.4324/9781003388500-3

proved transfer of carbon emissions in international trade. Ahmad and Wyckoff (2003) calculated the production-based carbon emissions and consumption-based carbon emissions of OECD members in 1995 through the input-output model, and found that the consumption-based carbon emissions of OECD members were 0.55 billion tonnes higher than the production-based carbon emissions, which proved the "carbon leakage" from developed countries and regions to developing countries and regions through trade. Therefore, they suggested adopting consumer principle for accounting of carbon dioxide emissions, so as to effectively avoid carbon leakage in international trade and ultimately reduce the global carbon dioxide emissions.

However, some scholars have questioned the effectiveness of global carbon emission reductions under the consumer principle. They believe that if consumers are solely responsible for the carbon emissions in the production process, then producers will not initiate to reduce carbon emissions, which may reduce incentives for developing countries to create cleaner and more efficient production process. Although consumers can choose producers who are motivated to reduce GHG emissions, they may neglect their environmental responsibility due to information asymmetry and lack of incentives and policy constraints (Benyong Wei et al., 2010).

The "producer responsibility" and the "consumer responsibility" have a mere disagreement over the embodied carbon in international trade. Therefore, as long as the accounting and responsibility allocation of embodied carbon in international trade are resolved, there will be no dispute over the responsibility attribution of carbon emissions.

2.1.2 Total carbon emissions determined by the producer principle

Accounting of total carbon emissions shall serve as the basis for the allocation of carbon emission rights, regardless of the allocation scheme. The per capita carbon dioxide emissions of major countries and regions worldwide in 2009 and the cumulative emissions during 1850–2009 are briefly calculated, according to the data of carbon emissions from the Carbon Dioxide Information Center of the Oak Ridge National Laboratory in the US. The results are shown in Tables 2.1 and 2.2.

As shown in Table 2.1, China had the largest emission of carbon dioxide (7.6871 billion tonnes) in the world in 2009, 2.3875 billion tonnes more than the second place, the US. The top 24 countries and regions discharged a total of 24.6651 billion tonnes of carbon dioxide, accounting for 81.33% of global emissions. Annex I countries and regions emitted 12.9126 billion tonnes of carbon dioxide, accounting for 42.58% of global emissions. Australia had the largest per capita carbon dioxide emission in 2009 (18.262 tonnes per person), followed by the US (17.015 tonnes per person). Despite a large number of carbon emissions, China had a low per capita carbon emission, which was 5.757 tonnes of carbon dioxide, one third of the US level.

Table 2.1 Total and per capita carbon emissions by country and region in 2009

No.	*Country and region*	*Total carbon emissions*	*Proportion in global carbon emissions*	*Per capita carbon emissions*
		(billion tonnes of carbon dioxide)	*(%)*	*(tonnes of carbon dioxide/person)*
1	China[a]	76.871	25.35	5.757
2	US	52.996	17.48	17.015
3	India	19.794	6.53	1.650
4	Russia	15.744	5.19	11.001
5	Japan	11.011	3.63	8.691
6	Germany	7.346	2.42	8.911
7	Canada	5.139	1.69	15.255
8	South Korea	5.094	1.68	10.634
9	South Africa	4.99	1.65	10.048
10	UK	4.746	1.56	7.664
11	Indonesia	4.518	1.49	1.907
12	Mexico	4.462	1.47	3.997
13	Italy	4.008	1.32	6.637
14	Australia	4.002	1.32	18.262
15	Brazil	3.671	1.21	1.907
16	France	3.634	1.20	5.831
17	Poland	2.989	0.99	7.811
18	Spain	2.882	0.95	6.307
19	Turkey	2.778	0.92	3.850
20	Thailand	2.717	0.90	3.960
21	Taiwan, China	2.391	0.79	10.341
22	Argentina	1.747	0.58	4.364
23	The Netherlands	1.697	0.56	7.407
24	Vietnam	1.423	0.47	1.650
25	Total	246.651	81.33	—
26	Annex I	129.126	42.58	—
27	Global	303.254	100.00	4.4748

Source: Demographic data is from the World Bank database: http://data.worldbank.org/.
[a]Taiwan's carbon emission is counted separately.

In terms of the cumulative carbon emissions by country and region during 1850–2009, the US ranks first (349.6791 billion tonnes of carbon dioxide), accounting for 26.91% of global emissions in the same period; followed by Russia with 142.8446 billion tonnes of carbon dioxide, accounting for 10.99% of global emissions, and China with 124.2742 billion tonnes of carbon dioxide, accounting for 9.56% of global emissions. In terms of phased emissions, China's carbon emissions are concentrated in 1992–2009, accounting for 64.1% of its cumulative emissions, while the US had the most carbon emissions in the second phase, accounting for almost half of the total cumulative emissions. Russia had the largest share of carbon emissions in the second phase, accounting for about 71.7% of its total cumulative emissions. In general, developed countries, such as France and Japan,

Table 2.2 Phased and cumulative carbon emissions by country and region during 1850–2009 (billion tonnes of carbon dioxide)

No.	*Country and region*	*1850–1949*	*1950–1991*	*1992–2009*	*1850–2009*	*Cumulative share (%)*
1	China[a]	17.943	428.36	796.438	1,242.742	9.56
2	US	883.562	1,621.909	991.32	3,496.791	26.91
3	India	22.378	112.716	221.412	356.506	2.74
4	Russia	103.377	1024.604	300.465	1428.446	10.99
5	Japan	41.006	268.627	215.212	524.845	4.04
6	Germany	285.913	391.079	153.021	830.014	6.39
7	Canada	43.564	130.56	91.771	265.896	2.05
8	South Korea	0.052	34.101	76.346	110.499	0.85
9	South Africa	14.943	75.63	69.092	159.665	1.23
10	UK	358.999	246.205	98.332	703.536	5.41
11	Indonesia	3.177	25.023	52.445	80.646	0.62
12	Mexico	4.743	65.307	70.826	140.875	1.08
13	Italy	16.517	106.956	79.711	203.184	1.56
14	Australia	14.416	65.507	61.598	141.521	1.09
15	Brazil	3.356	46.44	57.301	107.096	0.82
16	France	114.942	156.584	69.143	340.67	2.62
17	Poland	53.986	127.581	58.115	239.681	1.84
18	Spain	11.323	53.468	52.964	117.754	0.91
19	Turkey	1.745	23.956	38.604	64.305	0.49
20	Thailand	0.006	10.88	39.668	50.553	0.39
21	Taiwan, China	1.542	19.161	39.526	60.23	0.46
22	Argentine	5.266	32.655	26.286	64.207	0.49
23	The Netherlands	18.118	50.253	31.043	99.413	0.76
24	Vietnam	1.341	6.19	12.138	19.669	0.15
25	Total	2,022.215	5,123.753	3,702.777	10,848.744	83.47
26	Global	2,179.665	6,050.403	4,766.587	12,996.655	

[a]Taiwan's carbon emission is counted separately.

had relatively more cumulative carbon emissions in the second phase, while developing countries, such as China, Brazil, and Vietnam, had cumulative carbon emissions concentrated in the third phase due to the faster increase of carbon emissions in the third phase.

2.1.3 Accounting methods of final consumption emissions

Since the introduction of the consumer principle, the consumption-based accounting of emissions has been a research object for scholars from all countries. In terms of production-based emissions, there is no doubt that the existing studies are generally based on the data of carbon emissions from the Carbon Dioxide Information Center of the Oak Ridge National Laboratory in the US. Consumption-based emissions involve accounting difficulties and disputes due to the embodied carbon emissions in international trade, especially in historical trade.

In terms of the embodied carbon emissions in international trade, many scholars have accounted the embodied carbon emissions using national or interregional input-output models. But due to a lack of historical data, this method cannot be used to account the cumulative consumption-based emissions of each country.

Gang Fan, a Chinese scholar, calculated the cumulative consumption-based carbon emissions of the major countries in the world during 1950–2005, and provided a range of possible values for the cumulative consumption-based emissions of each country from the perspective of final consumption, according to the final consumption data of each country (Gang Fan et al., 2010). Those are under the two hypotheses: the consumption patterns and products of each country are the same and the carbon emission intensity per unit of consumption in each country differs.

When the Development Research Center project group of the State Council (2011) proposed national accounts for "carbon budget", it also provided an approach to deal with the carbon transfer embodied in historical trade: estimate shadow price of carbon emissions and other products through the general equilibrium model and the shadow trade pattern under its shadow price system, then take the shadow trade pattern as a benchmark, deduct the embodied carbon emissions in exports that exceed the benchmark from the actual emissions in exports, and treat importing countries symmetrically. However, we have not seen any results of this accounting approach so far.

In fact, the attribution of embodied carbon in trade is the responsibility allocation of such carbon. If the embodied carbon in international trade can be accounted and the producer responsibility and consumer responsibility of embodied carbon can be distinguished, then the producer's final consumption emissions are the sum of producer emissions from which those responsible by foreign consumers are excluded and those responsible by domestic consumers.

2.2 China's carbon emissions from energy consumption

The carbon dioxide emissions from fossil energy consumption are the main component of carbon emissions from human activities. China's carbon dioxide emissions from fossil energy consumption account for 91% of carbon dioxide emissions from human activities. Therefore, the amount of carbon dioxide emissions is mainly determined by the amount of energy consumption and energy consumption structure.

2.2.1 Analysis of China's current energy consumption

Energy resources are indispensable and vital for human survival and social development. They are directly related to a country's economic lifeline and national defense. As China's economy takes off, China's demand for energy has increased dramatically. After the reform and opening up, China's economic development has entered the fast lane, with its gross domestic product (GDP) growing at double-digit rates for 30 consecutive years. The energy consumption has also grown rapidly at the same time, with an average annual growth rate at 5.2%. Today, China is the second-largest energy producer and second-largest energy consumer worldwide. In 2010, China's total primary energy consumption was 3.249 billion tonnes of standard coal, accounting for about 20.3% of global energy consumption.

Changes to China's energy consumption trend can be divided into four stages. The first stage is before 1997. At this stage, the total energy consumption grew slowly and entered a relatively stable stage. In the second stage (1997–2002), the domestic economic growth slowed down due to the Asian financial crisis. At the same time, the State Council shut down a number of enterprises with high levels of energy consumption, material consumption, and pollution, which reduced energy consumption, lead to a sharp decline or even zero growth in energy consumption growth. The third stage (2002–2007) witnessed global economic slowdown. Affected by international trade, China's new round of economic growth featured heavy industrialization, resulting in a faster energy consumption growth at more than 10% rate for several consecutive years, which even exceeded the economic growth rate in certain years. In the fourth stage, on the one hand, the 2008 global financial crisis and the global economy downturn led to a sharp decline in China's export trade. On the other hand, with the great pressure in domestic economic slowdown, climate change, and environmental pollution, the energy conservation and emission reduction were incorporated into the management system as a government assessment indicator, and the growth rate of energy consumption was back to about 5%.

2.2.2 China's structure of primary energy consumption

The *Encyclopaedia of Science and Technology* classifies energy resources into two categories by form: the primary energy and the secondary energy. Primary energy refers to nonrenewable energy such as coal, oil, and natural gas; secondary energy refers to energy transformed from primary energy such as heat power and electric power. Usually, the energy structure of a country refers to the composition of coal, oil, natural gas, and clean energy in primary energy. With the development of China's energy industry, China's energy structure has changed significantly and become more diversified. The share of coal in the conventional energy consumption has decreased to 68% in 2010, according to the method of coal consumption for electricity generation. Although the share of oil once exceeded 20%, it has declined slightly in recent years. In 2010, oil accounted for 19% of primary energy consumption. The share of clean energy has increased in recent years (Figure 2.1): the share of hydroelectric power, nuclear power, and wind power has reached 8.6% and the share of natural gas has exceeded 4%. China's energy structure is becoming cleaner and more diversified.

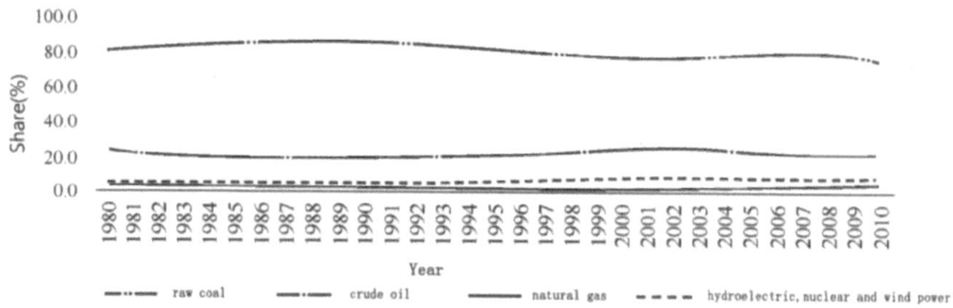

Figure 2.1 Changes to the structure of China's primary energy consumption

Although China's energy consumption structure has targeted cleaner energy, it is a long process in general. Figure 2.1 shows the changes to the shares of four primary energy consumptions in 1980–2010. It can be seen that China's energy consumption pattern dominated by coal has remained basically unchanged, with the share of coal remaining at around 70% and oil remaining at around 20%. Although the share of cleaner energy such as natural gas and hydropower has gradually increased in recent years, it is difficult to dramatically increase the share of natural gas and clean energy in the short term due to the supply capacity uncertainty. China's energy reserves, which feature "rich coal, deficient oil, and lean gas", determine that the energy consumption structure can only be dominated by coal in the long term.

The coal-based energy consumption is not only inefficient in energy utilization and economic benefits, but also highly polluting. On the one hand, coal mining results in environmental damage in coal mining areas, such as the vegetation deterioration, soil erosion, and soil collapse, and brings ecologic and environmental damage. On the other hand, the processing and use of coal have released large amounts of carbon dioxide and sulfur dioxide, resulting in the greenhouse effect, acid rain, acid fog, etc., which are the main causes of air quality deterioration in some regions of China.

Facing the huge impact of global climate change, people have realized that the environmental issues such as global warming and air pollution caused by GHG emissions are threatening production, life, and health of human beings. In response to the United Nations Framework Convention on Climate Change or in consideration of our own long-term development for better living environment, we must change the coal-based energy consumption pattern and optimize the energy structure.

2.2.3 China's current energy-related carbon emissions

It has become a consensus that GHG emissions cause global warming, resulting in climate catastrophes. The greenhouse traps solar radiation and heats the air inside, while GHG warms the earth's surface. This warming effect is called the "greenhouse effect". Strictly speaking, carbon dioxide (CO_2) is not the only GHG; water vapor (H_2O), nitrous oxide (N_2O), methane (CH_4), and ozone (O_3) are also primary GHGs in the earth's atmosphere. The Kyoto Protocol lists six GHGs: carbon dioxide (CO_2), methane (CH_4), nitrous oxide (N_2O), hydrofluorocarbons (HFCs), perfluorocarbons (PFCs) and sulphurhexafluoride (SF_6). Although water vapor is the most dominant GHG which may double the greenhouse effect, studies have shown that the greenhouse effect is primarily caused by carbon dioxide. Carbon dioxide accounts for the largest share (about 80%) of GHG emissions from human activities. Therefore, the control over GHG emissions mainly depends on carbon dioxide emissions.

There are two ways to calculate carbon dioxide emissions: one is to calculate the mass of carbon dioxide, which is expressed in units of 100 million tonnes of carbon dioxide, gigatonnes of carbon dioxide ($GtCO_2$) or tonnes of carbon dioxide (tCO_2); the other is to calculate the mass of carbon in carbon dioxide, which is expressed in units of gigatonnes of carbon (GtC) or tonnes of carbon (tC). The mass of carbon dioxide is 3.667 times that of the corresponding carbon element (i.e., molecular weight ratio of carbon dioxide and carbon is 44/12). Carbon emissions usually refer to carbon dioxide emissions, regardless of the unit of measurement. Carbon emissions in this book refer to the mass of carbon dioxide emissions unless stated otherwise, which is expressed in units of tonnes of carbon dioxide (tCO_2), 100 million tonnes of carbon dioxide or gigatonnes of carbon dioxide ($GtCO_2$).

The growth of China's carbon dioxide emissions and energy consumption is almost synchronized. As shown in Figure 2.2, the growth of carbon dioxide emissions was relatively slow before 2002, ranging from 1.552 billion tonnes in 1980 to 3.698 billion tonnes in 2002, with an average annual growth rate of 4.03%. However, carbon dioxide emissions grew at a faster rate after 2002; the average annual growth rate has exceeded 9% by 2010. At present, China has overtaken the US as the world's largest carbon emitter. It is estimated that China's carbon emissions from fossil energy combustion in 2010 was close to 7.412 billion tonnes of carbon dioxide, accounting for about 22.1% of the world's total carbon emission in the same period.

Although China's total carbon emissions have been growing rapidly, the carbon emission intensity has been declining. Judging from China's carbon emission intensity in 1980–2010, carbon emission intensity measured by GDP has decreased rapidly from 32.277 tonnes/CNY 10,000 in 1980 to 2.066 tonnes/CNY 10,000 in 2010, with an average annual decline of 9.6%. However, China's carbon emission intensity has decreased by only 5.694 tonnes/CNY 10,000 over the 30 years, with an average annual decline rate of 3.76%, irrespective of the price factor. Calculated at constant price in 2005, carbon emission intensity during 1980–2000 dropped from 8.337 tonnes/CNY 10,000 to 2.954 tonnes/CNY 10,000, with an average annual decrease of 5.06%. However, the decline rate of carbon emission intensity in the first decade of 2000 has slowed down significantly, and the carbon emission

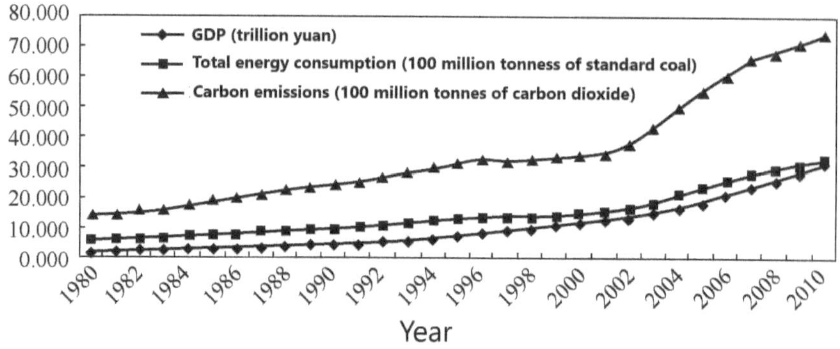

Figure 2.2 China's GDP, total energy consumption, and carbon emissions by year

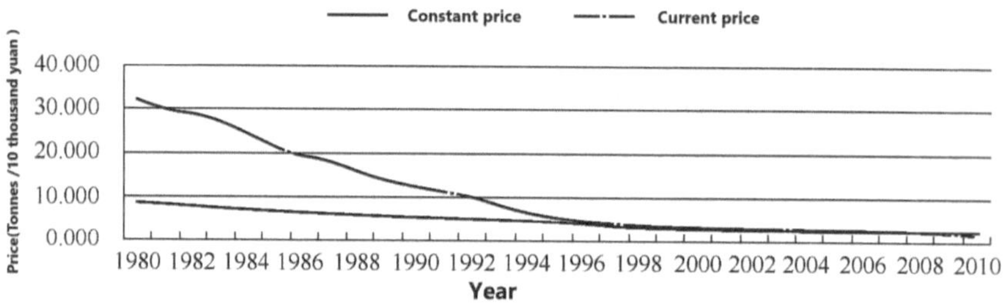

Figure 2.3 Trend of China's carbon emission intensity in 1980–2010

Sources: Data of carbon dioxide emissions are from the World Bank database (http://data.worldbank.org.cn/), GDP data are from *China Statistical Yearbook* (2011) and have been converted at 2005 constant price.

intensity has only dropped by 0.310 tonnes/CNY 10,000, with an average annual decrease of 1.1%. Such intensity even increased in 2003 and 2004, indicating a bottleneck for China's carbon emission reduction and narrowing emission reduction potentials, as shown in Figure 2.3.

References

Fan Gang, Su Ming, Cao Jing. An economic analysis of consumption and carbon emission responsibility. *Economic Research Journal*, 2010 (01): 4–14.

Munksgaard, J., Pedersen K.A. CO_2 accounts for open economies: producer or consumer responsibility?. *Energy Policy*, 2001, 29: 327–334.

Wei Benyong, Wang Yuan, Yang Huimin, et al. Advances on carbon emissions embodied in international trade. *World Regional Studies*, 2010, 19 (2): 138–147.

3 Accounting and responsibility allocation of embodied carbon in international trade

3.1 Accounting of embodied carbon in international trade

Accounting of embodied carbon emissions in international trade is a key for a country to account its carbon emissions under consumer principle. Due to limited data, the chapter only offers a method to account and allocate embodied carbon emissions in international trade, using the data from 2005 as an example. The accounting of cumulative final consumption-based emissions still needs to be discussed.

3.1.1 Accounting principles and methods

3.1.1.1 Accounting framework

According to input-output tables, the total input includes two parts: domestic intermediate input and imported intermediate input; total output goes in three directions: fixed assets and inventories, domestic consumption, and exports. In addition, some imported products are directly supplied for domestic consumption. Among them, imported intermediate input and imported consumption are produced abroad, with the corresponding carbon emissions generated abroad. Of the final products produced in domestic country, those exported are consumed by citizens of other countries with the carbon emissions generated in the domestic country. Fixed assets, inventories, and domestic consumption together constitute domestic demands for the year. Given the G_k^D as domestic emission demands of country k, G_k^{OUT}, G_k^{EX}, and G_k^{IM} as emissions from domestic combustion, embodied emissions of exported products and embodied emissions of imported products of country k, respectively, then:

$$G_k^D = G_k^{OUT} - G_k^{EX} + G_k^{IM} \tag{3.1}$$

Depending on the structures of imported and exported products in each country, it is assumed that there are n sectors in total. G_{kj}^{IM} and G_{kj}^{EX} are,

DOI: 10.4324/9781003388500-4

respectively, import- and export-embodied emissions of the sector j of country k; IM_{kj} and EX_{kj} are, respectively, import and export volumes of sector j of country k; Q_{kj} and P_{kj} are, respectively, the unit emission intensity of imported and exported products in sector j of country k, then:

$$G_k^{IM} = \sum_{j=1}^{n} G_{kj}^{IM} = \sum_{j=1}^{n} IM_{kj} \cdot Q_{kj}, \quad G_k^{EX} = \sum_{j=1}^{n} G_{kj}^{EX} = \sum_{j=1}^{n} EX_{kj} \cdot P_{kj} \tag{3.2}$$

3.1.1.2 Accounting of carbon emission intensity of exported products in each sector

Due to the lack of energy consumption data or CO_2 emissions data in each country's sub-sectors, such CO_2 emissions can be measured only based on input-output tables and CO_2 emissions from fossil fuels. Take one country as an example. Given that sector s in the input-output tables produces coal, sector t produces oil and gas, G_1 is the CO_2 emissions from coal combustion in the country, and G_2 is the CO_2 emissions from oil and gas combustion in the country. According to the input-output principle, the CO_2 emissions in each sector are proportional to its consumption of fossil energy. Therefore, the CO_2 emissions of the country can be allocated by proportion of coal, oil, and gas consumed in each sector on the basis of the input-output coefficient. With X as the total output vector in the country, Y the final product vector, and A the Leontief Matrix, the input-output model is as follows:

$$x_{i1} + x_{i2} + \cdots + x_{in} + y_{i1} + y_{i2} + y_{i3} + y_{i4} = X_i \tag{3.3}$$

Wherein x_{ij} is the quantity of products in sector i consumed by sector j; y_{i1}, y_{i2}, y_{i3}, and y_{i4}, respectively, represent the quantities of final products in sector i used for domestic consumption, fixed asset formation, inventory increase, and export, and X_i represents the total products produced by sector i in the year.

G_1 is generated from $X_s - y_{s3} - y_{s4}$ (the increased energy inventory is not emitted in the current year and the energy exported is emitted abroad), the energy consumed by sector j is x_{sj}, and relevant items of sector t are calculated in the same manner. Thus, the CO_2 emission in sector j can be calculated as follows:

$$G_j = \frac{x_{sj}}{X_s - y_{s3} - y_{s4}} \cdot G_1 + \frac{x_{tj}}{X_t - y_{t3} - y_{t4}} \cdot G_2 \quad j = 1,2,\ldots,n; \tag{3.4}$$

Therefore, the direct carbon emission coefficient in sector j is:

$$C_j = G_j / X_j, \quad j = 1,\ldots,n; \tag{3.5}$$

From $Y = (I - A)^{-1} X$, we can get the complete carbon emission coefficient, which is the carbon emission intensity of the exported products of each industrial sector of the country:

$$P_j = C_j \cdot (I - A)^{-1}, \quad j = 1,\ldots,n; \tag{3.6}$$

3.1.1.3 Calculation of carbon emission intensity of imported products in each sector

Since it is difficult to distinguish the country of origin of imported goods by sector, according to the existing data in international trade, most researchers resort to carbon emission intensity of similar domestic goods or services when calculate the carbon emission intensity of imports. It is feasible. However, due to the lack of actual pollution flows in trade, the embodied carbon emissions in imports may be overestimated or underestimated, which eventually leads to the imbalance of global import- and export-embodied carbon emissions. In this chapter, the carbon emission intensity of imported products is calculated according to the average export carbon emission intensity of such products in major countries (m). There are two advantages in this regard. First, it can ensure that the world's import- and export-embodied carbon emissions are roughly balanced. Second, it is fair and convenient to calculate and easy to compare the technology levels among countries. Therefore, sector j of each country shares the same carbon emission intensity of imported products, and it is expressed in the equation:

$$Q_j = \sum_{k=1}^{m} G_{kj} \Big/ \sum_{k=1}^{m} EX_{kj}, \quad j = 1,\ldots,n \tag{3.7}$$

3.1.2 Data source

In this chapter, 28 countries and regions,[1] which have larger amount of carbon dioxide emissions and OECD input-output tables, were selected for accounting carbon dioxide emissions in 2005. Among them, input-output tables of most countries and regions are for 2005 and a few near 2005, such as Russia (2000), India (2003–2004), Australia (2004–2005), Mexico (2003), Turkey (2002), and Vietnam (2000). Since the input-output relationship changes little in consecutive years, an allocation method based on input-output proportion is not affected by the year during accounting of carbon emissions demanded or exported by a country or a region, therefore an adjustment is unnecessary. When accounting the embodied carbon emissions of imported products, we have to adjust the volume of imported and exported products in major countries and regions, according to the data of international trade in 2005,[2] on the basis of the input-output relationship.

Table 3.1 Total carbon dioxide emissions by country and region in 2005 (million tonnes)

Region and country	*Total carbon dioxide emissions*	*Carbon dioxide emissions from coal*	*Carbon dioxide emissions from oil*	*Carbon dioxide emission from natural gas*
US	5,994.29	2,162.38	2,614.79	1,217.12
China[a]	5,429.30	4,448.99	888.58	91.73
Russia	1,698.56	450.79	383.03	864.74
Japan	1,249.62	427.33	641.48	180.81
India	1,194.01	808.34	314.15	71.52
Germany	852.57	318.67	346.37	187.53
Canada	632.01	142.00	301.10	188.90
UK	584.65	145.31	246.10	193.24
South Korea	496.64	194.14	238.60	63.90
Italy	472.78	61.95	245.48	165.35
South Africa	437.76	356.47	76.70	4.59
Australia	416.89	236.30	126.28	54.31
France	414.36	49.66	264.88	99.81
Mexico	406.53	36.19	266.65	103.69
Spain	384.04	83.54	232.39	68.10
Brazil	370.55	41.75	288.07	40.73
Indonesia	323.51	55.34	183.61	84.57
Taiwan, China	290.41	153.19	115.66	21.55
Poland	289.80	202.91	58.21	28.68
Netherlands	272.69	48.18	141.63	82.89
Thailand	242.68	46.22	136.85	59.60
Turkey	231.23	96.17	81.71	53.35
Belgium	151.11	19.37	97.76	33.98
Czech Republic	114.84	69.43	27.41	18.00
Greece	105.28	35.36	64.41	5.51
Romania	98.30	33.35	30.98	33.96
Vietnam	82.07	37.21	36.46	8.40
Austria	79.43	16.79	43.30	19.34

Source: http://www.eia.doe.gov/emeu/international/carbondioxide.html.
[a]Taiwan's carbon emission is counted separately.

The carbon dioxide emission data for each country and region is from the US Energy Information Administration's website and the carbon dioxide emissions are classified into those from coal, oil, and natural gas, but not from cement production. Therefore, it is slightly different from the carbon dioxide data of the World Bank database and the Carbon Dioxide Information Center of the Oak Ridge National Laboratory in the United States. The total carbon dioxide emission data of major countries and regions in 2005 are shown in Table 3.1 (unit: million tonnes or Mt).

The total carbon dioxide emissions of these 28 countries and regions account for 81.85% of the global carbon dioxide emissions in 2005. Other countries and regions with larger carbon dioxide emissions include Iran (445.77 Mt), Saudi Arabia (405.44 Mt), Ukraine (349.85 Mt), Kazakhstan (203.30 Mt), Egypt (161.22 Mt), Malaysia (160.24 Mt), and Argentina (151.93

Mt), and the total carbon dioxide emissions of these countries and regions account for 6.6% of the global carbon dioxide emissions. However, no accounting has been done due to the lack of input-output tables for corresponding countries and regions.

3.1.3 Accounting results of embodied carbon emissions in international trade

3.1.3.1 Unit carbon emission intensity of final products in major countries and regions

The unit carbon emission intensity of final product for each country and region as well as the unit carbon emission intensity of final products demanded and exported domestically and regionally can be calculated according to the input-output tables for each country and region. The OECD input-output tables for 48 sectors, prepared in local and regional currency units, are converted at the market exchange rates and purchasing power parity (PPP) exchange rates of the corresponding years for comparison. The data are shown in Table 3.2.

As shown in Table 3.2, the carbon emission intensity of the unit final product in each country and region varies significantly due to the great differences in energy distribution, product mix, and technology. Moreover, the unit carbon emission intensity converted at the two exchange rates differs greatly. Russia has the highest unit of carbon emission intensity, which reaches 4.4527 tonnes/USD 1,000 if measured at market exchange rates and 2.0050 tonnes/USD 1,000 if measured at PPP exchange rate. This is closely related to Russia's production structures mainly dominated by energy-intensive sectors such as energy, machinery, and non-ferrous metals. France has the lowest unit carbon emission intensity, which reaches only 0.1116 tonnes/USD 1,000 if measured at market exchange rates. The carbon emission intensity measured at PPP exchange rate is much lower than that measured at the market exchange rate in most developing countries and regions,[3] while developed countries have slightly higher carbon emission intensity measured at PPP exchange rate than that measured at the market exchange rate.

3.1.3.2 Emission demands and import- and export-embodied carbon emissions in major countries and regions

As shown in Table 3.3, import and export trade has a great impact on carbon dioxide emissions in a country or region. China has the largest export-embodied carbon emissions (1563.90 Mt), accounting for 28.8% of the total domestic carbon emissions, followed by Russia with 758.93 Mt, accounting for 44.68% of the total domestic carbon emissions. The Netherlands has the highest share of export-embodied carbon emissions in the total domestic

Table 3.2 Unit carbon emission intensity for final products by country and region (tonnes/USD 1,000)

Country and region	*Conversion at market exchange rate*			*Conversion at purchasing power parity exchange rate*		
	Final product	*Domestic demand*	*Exported product*	*Final product*	*Domestic demand*	*Exported product*
US	0.3173	0.3173	0.3807	0.3173	0.3173	0.3807
China[a]	1.7068	1.7068	1.8424	0.7181	0.7181	0.7752
Russia	4.4527	4.4527	7.0356	2.0050	2.0050	3.1680
Japan	0.2002	0.2002	0.2944	0.2353	0.2353	0.3460
India	0.1596	0.1596	0.1960	0.0529	0.0529	0.0649
Germany	0.1565	0.1565	0.2387	0.1687	0.1687	0.2573
Canada	0.2956	0.2956	0.3611	0.2961	0.2961	0.3617
UK	0.1327	0.1327	0.1519	0.1535	0.1535	0.1757
South Korea	0.3116	0.3116	0.5311	0.2400	0.2400	0.4091
Italy	0.1528	0.1528	0.1923	0.1647	0.1647	0.2073
South Africa	1.3249	1.3249	1.7964	0.8067	0.8067	1.0938
Australia	0.3909	0.3909	0.8067	0.4080	0.4080	0.8420
France	0.1116	0.1116	0.1610	0.1281	0.1281	0.1849
Mexico	0.3740	0.3740	0.2392	0.2446	0.2446	0.1564
Spain	0.2026	0.2026	0.3980	0.1927	0.1927	0.3786
Brazil	0.2872	0.2872	0.5006	0.1601	0.1601	0.2790
Indonesia	0.7615	0.7615	0.7139	0.3087	0.3087	0.2894
Taiwan, China	0.3390	0.3390	0.6063	0.2000	0.2000	0.3576
Poland	0.6013	0.6013	0.6158	0.3474	0.3474	0.3557
Netherlands	0.1536	0.1536	0.3874	0.1712	0.1712	0.4317
Thailand	0.5919	0.5919	0.5724	0.2345	0.2345	0.2267
Turkey	0.7461	0.7461	0.8608	0.4613	0.4613	0.5322
Belgium	0.1536	0.1536	0.2661	0.1718	0.1718	0.2977
Czech Republic	0.5662	0.5662	0.4677	0.3383	0.3383	0.2795
Greece	0.2514	0.2514	0.5982	0.2232	0.2232	0.5312
Romania	0.2739	0.2739	0.4341	0.1338	0.1338	0.2120
Vietnam	1.7762	1.7762	1.5937	0.5280	0.5280	0.4737
Austria	0.1313	0.1313	0.1547	0.1447	0.1447	0.1705

Note: OECD provides input-output tables in units of local currency and million US dollars. However, the unit of million US dollars is applicable to quite a few sectors in the input-output tables. Therefore, the corresponding exchange rate (approximately equal to the market exchange rate for the same year) can be converted based on the two tables of the same country.

[a]Taiwan's carbon emission is counted separately.

emissions, which reaches 60.29%. The US has the largest import-embodied carbon emissions, which reaches 1200.40 Mt, accounting for 20.03% of the total domestic carbon emissions in the same year, followed by Germany with 530.62 Mt, accounting for 62.24% of the total domestic carbon emissions in the same year. Belgium has the highest share of import-embodied carbon emissions in the total domestic emissions, which reaches 156.57%.

International trade has a huge impact on carbon emissions, which leads to a large amount of "carbon leakage". China is the largest net importer of

Table 3.3 Emission demands and import- and export-embodied carbon emissions by country and region

Country and region	*Carbon dioxide emissions in demand* (*Mt*)	*Carbon dioxide emissions from exported products* (*Mt*)	*Share of export emissions* (*%*)	*Carbon dioxide emissions from imported products* (*Mt*)	*Share of import emissions* (*%*)	*Net transfer of carbon dioxide emissions* (*Mt*)
US	5,573.60	420.69	7.02	1,200.40	20.03	−779.71
China[a]	3,865.40	1,563.90	28.80	440.28	8.11	1,123.62
Russia	939.63	758.93	44.68	88.95	5.24	669.98
Japan	1,068.60	181.04	14.49	368.06	29.45	−187.02
India	1,016.50	177.55	14.87	97.69	8.18	79.86
Germany	598.83	253.72	29.76	530.62	62.24	−276.90
Canada	470.77	161.24	25.51	177.61	28.10	−16.37
UK	498.72	85.93	14.70	316.13	54.07	−230.20
South Korea	315.59	181.05	36.45	181.14	36.47	−0.09
Italy	394.94	77.85	16.47	247.33	52.31	−169.48
South Africa	339.34	98.42	22.48	54.32	12.41	44.10
Australia	315.94	100.95	24.21	76.42	18.33	24.53
France	334.41	79.95	19.29	326.24	78.73	−246.29
Mexico	370.95	38.58	9.42	139.47	34.31	−100.89
Spain	290.76	93.27	24.29	191.50	49.86	−98.23
Brazil	300.98	69.57	18.78	49.13	13.26	20.44
Indonesia	252.37	71.15	21.99	50.10	15.49	21.05
Taiwan, China	135.57	154.84	53.32	120.34	41.44	34.50
Poland	223.89	65.91	22.74	72.00	24.84	−6.09
Netherlands	108.28	164.41	60.29	199.19	73.05	−34.78
Thailand	166.56	76.11	31.37	76.65	31.58	−0.54
Turkey	197.66	33.56	14.52	92.94	40.19	−59.38
Belgium	76.63	74.48	49.29	236.59	156.57	−162.11
Czech Republic	74.25	40.59	35.35	50.95	44.37	−10.36
Greece	81.81	23.48	22.30	37.19	35.32	-13.71
Romania	83.73	14.56	14.81	26.23	26.68	−11.67
Vietnam	57.77	24.29	29.60	32.59	39.71	−8.30
Austria	57.33	22.10	27.83	83.81	105.51	−61.71

[a]Taiwan's carbon emission is counted separately.

carbon dioxide (1123.62 Mt), while the US is the largest net carbon dioxide exporter (779.71 Mt). It indicates that China has emitted 1123.62 Mt of carbon dioxide for consumers in other countries, while other countries have emitted 779.71 Mt of carbon dioxide for consumers in the US through international trade. Countries and regions with net carbon dioxide imports also include Russia, India, and South Africa, which are either rich in resources or backward in technology levels. Major developed countries, such as Japan, Germany, the UK, Italy, France, Mexico, and Belgium, all have over 100 Mt net export of carbon dioxide. In general, developed countries and regions

Table 3.4 Per capita emission demands by country and region in 2005

Country and region	*Total emission demands (Mt)*	*Population (10,000)*	*Per capita emissions (tonnes/person)*	*Country and region*	*Total emission demands (Mt)*	*Population (10,000)*	*Per capita emissions (tonnes/person)*
US	6,774.00	29,575.30	22.90	Spain	482.26	4,339.82	11.11
China[a]	4,305.68	130,372.00	3.30	Brazil	350.11	18607.46	1.88
Russia	1028.58	14,315.00	7.19	Indonesia	302.47	21,921.03	1.38
Japan	1,436.66	12,777.30	11.24	Taiwan, China	255.91	2,277.10	11.24
India	1,114.19	109,458.30	1.02	Poland	295.89	3,816.55	7.75
Germany	1,129.45	8,246.94	13.70	Netherlands	307.47	1,631.99	18.84
Canada	648.38	3,231.20	20.07	Thailand	243.21	6,594.57	3.69
UK	814.85	6,022.65	13.53	Turkey	290.60	7,116.90	4.08
South Korea	496.73	4,813.80	10.32	Belgium	313.22	1,047.87	29.89
Italy	642.27	5,860.71	10.96	Czech Republic	125.20	1,023.58	12.23
South Africa	393.66	4,719.85	8.34	Greece	119.00	1,110.40	10.72
Australia	392.36	2,039.48	19.24	Romania	109.96	2,163.44	5.08
France	660.65	6,087.30	10.85	Vietnam	90.36	8,310.63	1.09
Mexico	510.42	10,308.91	4.95	Austria	141.14	823.33	17.14

[a]Taiwan's carbon emission is counted separately.

are mainly net exporters, while developing countries and regions are mainly net importers of carbon dioxide. Developed countries and regions transfer pollution-intensive, energy-intensive, and resource-based industries to developing countries and regions through export trade and then import semi-finished and finished products. In this way, their own carbon emissions are reduced, but carbon emissions in developing countries and the world are increased. Therefore, international trade is a major cause of the surging greenhouse gas emissions in China, where a great portion of greenhouse gas emissions are produced to satisfy the production and living needs of developed countries and regions. That is, China, which exports a large number of cheap products to developed countries and regions, is not the only responsible party for carbon reduction.

3.1.3.3 Per capita emission demand in 2005

The total domestic or regional emission demand can be calculated based on the final emission demand and emissions of imported products in a country or region. The total demand divided by the domestic or regional population[4] equals the per capita emission demand of the country or region in 2005, as shown in Table 3.4.

As shown in Table 3.4, the per capita emission demands in developing countries and regions are significantly lower than those of developed countries and regions. The annual per capita emission demands are over 10 tonnes in developed countries and regions, and even more than 20 tonnes in a few countries and regions, while in most developing countries and regions this figure is less than 10 tonnes, or even less than 5 tonnes in some countries and regions. The country with the smallest per capita emission demand is India, with an annual per capita emission of 1.02 tonnes. The country with the largest annual per capita emissions is Belgium (29.89 tonnes). The US has the second-largest annual per capita emission (22.9 tonnes); China's annual per capita emission is 3.30 tonnes, which is about one-seventh of that of the US.

3.2 Responsibility allocation of embodied carbon in international trade

3.2.1 Logarithmic Mean Divisia Index decomposition of carbon dioxide net transfer

The embodied carbon emissions from a country's exports and imports are generally different, resulting in the net transfer of carbon dioxide. When the carbon embodied in a country's exported products is greater than that in its imported products, the country must have emitted carbon dioxide for consumers abroad, resulting in the net transfer-in of carbon dioxide. Otherwise, other countries must have emitted carbon dioxide for consumers of the very country, resulting in the net transfer-out of carbon dioxide.

The LMDI method (Logarithmic Mean Divisia Index) is a decomposition method of energy consumption proposed by Sun (1998), Ang & Choi (1997), Ang & Liu (2001), and Albrecht et al. (2002). It is used to objectively measure the influence of economic growth, industrial structure changes, and energy saving and consumption reduction measures on total energy consumption and unit energy consumption, respectively. With reference to the decomposition of energy consumption, we can use the LMDI method to decompose the net transfer of carbon dioxide in international trade.

With EX_k and IM_k as the total export and import volumes of country k, respectively, $SE_{kj} = EX_{kj} / EX_k$ and $SI_{kj} = IM_{kj} / IM_k$ as the proportion of export and import volumes of the sector j in total export and import volumes, respectively, in conjunction with Equation (3.2), we have $w_{kj} = \frac{G_{kj}^{EX} - G_{kj}^{IM}}{LnG_{kj}^{EX} - LnG_{kj}^{IM}}$ and:

$$G_k^{EX} - G_k^{IM} = \sum_{j=1}^{n} w_{kj} \cdot Ln\frac{EX_k}{IM_k} + \sum_{j=1}^{n} w_{kj} \cdot Ln\frac{SE_{kj}}{SI_{kj}} + \sum_{j=1}^{n} w_{kj} \cdot Ln\frac{P_{kj}}{Q_{kj}} \quad (3.8)$$

Wherein the first part is scale effect. If a country has a large trade scale or surplus, the net emission transfers of CO_2 will be large. The second part is caused by the structure inconsistency of import and export products, which is regarded as structural effect. The third part is caused by the difference of unit carbon emission intensity of import and export products, which is regarded as technical effect.

The carbon emission intensity of a country measured at US dollars is necessarily in relation to its exchange rates against the US dollars. The OECD offers two exchange rates: the market rate and the PPP. Broadly speaking, the more developed a country is (as measured by real GDP per capita), the closer its PPP is to market exchange rates, while for developing countries, market exchange rates are generally underestimated. Since market exchange rates reflect only the price conversion relationship between tradable goods and services rather than the proportion of prices of goods and services that are not traded on international markets, PPP exchange rates may be more appropriate than market exchange rates in calculating carbon emission intensity. In the LMDI decomposition equation of net carbon dioxide transfer (3.8), we still have the carbon emission intensity converted at market exchange rates, according to international conventions. In fact, the technical effect in Equation (3.8) is a combination of pure technical effect and exchange rates effect.

With Q'_{kj} and P'_{kj} as the unit carbon emission intensity of import and export products in sector j of country k measured at PPP, respectively, and T_k as the conversion factor of the PPP of country k (T_k = PPP exchange rate/market exchange rate), then:

$$P'_{kj} = P_{kj} \cdot T_k, \quad Q'_{kj} = Q_{kj} \cdot \sum_{k=1}^{m} EX_{kj} \bigg/ \sum_{k=1}^{m} \left(EX_{kj} / T_k \right) \tag{3.9}$$

$$\sum_{j=1}^{n} w_{kj} \cdot \ln \frac{P_{kj}}{Q_{kj}} = \sum_{j=1}^{n} w_{kj} \cdot \ln \frac{P'_{kj}}{Q'_{kj}} + \sum_{j=1}^{n} w_{kj} \cdot \ln \left[\left(\sum_{k=1}^{m} EX_{kj} \right) / T_k \bigg/ \sum_{k=1}^{m} \left(EX_{kj} / T_k \right) \right] \tag{3.10}$$

Wherein the first item reflects the difference in carbon emission intensity of import and export products converted at PPP exchange rate, which is regarded as the pure technical effect. The second item can be regarded as the net carbon dioxide transfers caused by exchange rate (conversion factor), which is called exchange rate effect.

3.2.2 Decomposition results of net transfer of emissions

The net transfer of carbon dioxide in major countries and region can be decomposed by the LMDI method. The results are shown in Table 3.5.

As shown in Table 3.5, the net transfer of carbon dioxide of a country or region is influenced first by trade scale and net exports. In terms of scale effect, the larger the net export, the larger the net transfer of carbon dioxide. Net export in a positive value represents net carbon dioxide transfer-in, while net export in a negative value represents net carbon dioxide transfer-out. With the largest trade deficit in the world, the US has the largest scale effect, and the net carbon dioxide transfer-out due to the trade deficit is as high as 415.34 Mt. Countries with large trade surplus, such as Germany, Russia, China, and Japan, have a large amount of net carbon dioxide transfer-in.

The mix of imported and exported products has a non-negligible impact on the net transfer of carbon dioxide in a country or region. When the imports are dominated by high-carbon products and exports are dominated by low-carbon products in a country or region, carbon dioxide emissions are transferred out; otherwise, carbon dioxide emissions are transferred in. The US and Russia, as two countries with the largest structural effects, are typical of these two scenarios, respectively.

Technological advancement is one of the main drivers of carbon reduction. The major developed countries worldwide utilize advanced energy conservation and emission reduction technologies and develop clean and renewable energy to keep the carbon emission intensity of domestic products below the average carbon emission intensity of the similar products in the world. Consequently, the pure technical effect is less than zero with net carbon dioxide transfer-out in developed countries. The country with the largest amount of net carbon dioxide transfer-out due to technical effect is Germany (191.96 Mt), followed by France, Belgium, Italy, and the UK. These Western European countries have been developing clean energy such

Table 3.5 Decomposition of net transfer of carbon dioxide by country and region (million tonnes)

Country and region	*Net transfer of carbon dioxide*	*Scale effect*	*Structural effect*	*Pure technical effect*	*Exchange rate effect*
US	−779.71	−415.34	−162.37	−44.87	−157.12
China[a]	1123.62	117.40	44.62	503.50	458.06
Russia	669.98	139.37	497.37	−45.02	78.26
Japan	−187.02	29.34	−71.78	−60.93	−83.66
India	79.86	−28.04	10.53	8.77	88.60
Germany	−276.90	78.96	−56.39	−191.96	−107.51
Canada	−16.37	22.44	28.06	−26.96	−39.90
UK	−230.20	−46.66	−20.38	−101.21	−61.95
South Korea	−0.09	13.11	9.36	−26.65	4.10
Italy	−169.48	−3.00	−1.45	−121.07	−43.96
South Africa	44.10	−11.05	−6.69	45.37	16.48
Australia	24.53	−8.53	17.77	37.74	−22.45
France	−246.29	−14.43	−1.19	−170.92	−59.75
Mexico	−100.89	−2.31	−21.87	−85.71	9.00
Spain	−98.23	−50.55	9.78	−34.30	−23.16
Brazil	20.44	25.90	4.84	−27.63	17.34
Indonesia	21.05	20.32	7.61	−39.29	32.41
Taiwan, China	34.50	10.33	7.77	−15.92	32.32
Poland	−6.09	−7.76	−0.62	−15.59	17.88
Netherlands	−34.78	19.10	47.06	−45.70	−55.24
Thailand	−0.54	−3.54	22.85	−51.89	32.04
Turkey	−59.38	−22.54	−8.89	−37.71	9.77
Belgium	−162.11	5.47	15.06	−131.13	−51.51
Czech Republic	−10.36	0.94	−6.10	−16.84	11.65
Greece	−13.71	−22.87	8.54	3.09	−2.47
Romania	−11.67	−6.49	3.93	−17.19	7.62
Vietnam	−8.30	−2.30	−0.23	−22.39	16.62
Austria	−61.71	−0.81	−5.52	−40.44	−14.93

[a]Taiwan's carbon emission is counted separately.

as nuclear, solar, and wind power due to their natural resources constraints and have achieved good effect over the years. The largest amount of net carbon dioxide transfer-in due to technical effect occurs mainly in developing countries and regions. Among them, China has the largest amount of carbon dioxide transfer-in due to technical effect (503.50 Mt), followed by South Africa (45.37 Mt).

Exchange rate difference also has a great impact on the net transfer of carbon dioxide. Most developing countries and regions often choose an export-oriented development pattern to boost domestic economic growth and severely underestimate market exchange rates. In the end, they have to bear the carbon emissions obligation of exported products while selling large quantities of cheap products. China has the largest effects of exchange rates, where the PPP exchange rate in 2005 only accounted for 42% of the market exchange rate, resulting in net transfer-in of 458.06 Mt of carbon dioxide in the same year. Countries with a lower conversion factor (PPP exchange rates/market exchange rates) such as Russia and India have similar situations. In general, the PPP exchange rates in developed countries and regions are close to or even slightly higher than market exchange rates. Therefore, the effect of exchange rates in developed countries usually results in net carbon dioxide transfer-out. The US has the largest amount of net carbon dioxide transfer-out (157.12 Mt) due to effects of exchange rates, followed by Germany (107.51 Mt).

3.2.3 Embodied carbon responsibility allocation

The accounting results of embodied carbon emissions indicate that trade produces a large number of "carbon leakages". Developed countries and regions transfer pollution-intensive, energy-intensive, and resource-based industries to developing countries and regions through export trade and then import semi-finished and finished products. In this way, their own carbon emissions are reduced, but carbon emissions in developing countries and the world are increased. If embodied carbon emission responsibilities in trade are not shared well, then "carbon leakage" could exacerbate global climate change.

China is the largest embodied carbon exporter in the world, where carbon emissions increase dramatically to satisfy the production and living needs of developed countries and regions, that is, for the purpose of exporting a large number of cheap products. Therefore, consumers in developed countries have inescapable responsibilities for carbon emissions.

According to the per capita emission demand data in 2005, the annual average per capita emissions in developed countries and regions are much higher than those of developing countries. Carbon emissions are luxury emissions in developed countries and regions, and also essential emissions to meet basic survival needs in developing countries and regions. It is against the principle of interpersonal fairness to require developing countries and developed countries to undertake equal carbon emission reduction obligations.

In order to find a fair and reasonable allocation scheme for responsibilities of embodied carbon emissions that is acceptable to most countries, we need not only accurately measure the amount of embodied carbon emissions in international trade, but also to distinguish producer responsibility from consumer responsibility based on the composition of embodied carbon emissions. The decomposition of the net carbon dioxide transfer in trade shows that the net export volume, product mix, technology level, and exchange rate are all factors affecting the amount of net carbon dioxide transfer. In terms of scale effects and effects of exchange rates, the author believes that consumer responsibilities are reasonable. Consumers have benefited from a number of cheap products provided by producers, so they should be responsible for the resulting ecological effects. As for structural effects, the author also holds the viewpoint of consumer responsibility. Structural effects reflect the difference between imported and exported products. Usually, countries export products that they are rich in and import products that they lack. Imported products make up for the shortage of domestic resources, and importers gain more benefits from exporting than exporters. Therefore, consumers should be responsible for the structural effects. As for technical effects, the author believes that the producers and consumers should take the responsibility jointly. First, consumer demand is the cause of emissions; second, from historical perspective, low emission technologies of developed countries and regions are based on years of development and emissions. Therefore, developed countries and regions have the obligation to help developing countries and regions in technology improvement, energy conservation, and emission reduction. Finally, producers have the obligation to reduce their own emissions. The "shared responsibility" principle for the technical effect will facilitate producers and consumer work together for a clean environment.

Notes

1 Data source: http://comtrade.un.org/.
2 Data source: http://comtrade.un.org/.
3 The developed countries and regions in this chapter are from the *World Economic Outlook* issued by the International Monetary Fund in April 2007, which are slightly different from the OECD standard. There are 29 developed economies in this chapter: the US, Germany, France, Italy, Spain, the Netherlands, Belgium, Austria, Finland, Greece, Portugal, Ireland, Luxemburg, Japan, the UK, Canada, South Korea, Australia, Taiwan province of China, Sweden, Switzerland, Hong Kong Special Administrative Region of People's Republic of China, Denmark, Norway, Israel, Singapore, New Zealand, Cyprus, and Iceland. The rest are considered developing countries and regions.
4 Source: http://data.worldbank.org/.

References

Albrecht J, Francois D, Schoors K. Decomposition of Carbon Emissions Without Residuals[J]. Energy Policy, 2002, 30(9): 727–736.

Ang, B.W., Choi, K.H. Decomposition of aggregate energy and gas emission intensities for industry: a refined Divisia index method. *Energy Journal*, 1997, 18(3): 59–73.

Ang, B.W., Liu, F.L. A new energy decomposition method: perfect in decomposition and consistent in aggregation. *Energy*, 2001, 26(6): 537–548.

Sun J. W. Changes in energy consumption and energy intensity: A complete decomposition model[J]. Energy Economics, 2002, 20(1): 85–100.

4 Fairness in the selection of international carbon emission accounting standards

4.1 Fairness measures for the selection of international carbon emission accounting standards

4.1.1 International carbon emission accounting standards and its principle of fairness

Since the United Nations ratified the negotiation on United Nations Framework Convention on Climate Change (UNFCCC) in December 1990, almost all countries have joined the game of international carbon emissions. Although the 18th Session of the Conference of the Parties to the UNFCCC and the 8th Session of the Conference of the Parties to the Kyoto Protocol ended in Doha, Qatar, all Parties will never stop striving for more reasonable and equitable carbon emission rights for their countries. Solutions to comprehensively reflect the real carbon emissions of each country, to fairly allocate the carbon emission rights of each country, and to effectively ensure the effective implementation of the carbon emission reduction mechanism are still under discussion. The selection of the international carbon emission accounting standards and the interpretation of fairness of the standards throughout the solution of these three questions are also emerging and evolving. As shown in Table 4.1, the initial international carbon emission accounting standard is the carbon emissions of each country in the current year.[1] Later in 2001, after withdrawing from the Kyoto Protocol, the US announced the Clear Skies and Global Climate Change Action, which combined carbon emission activities with economic development and made carbon emissions per unit of gross domestic product (GDP) known as an accounting standard. Brazil proposed to consider the historical responsibility for carbon emissions of each country in its Brazil's Climate Pledge submitted to the UN Climate Change Conference in 2002, in which cumulative carbon emissions were debated as an accounting standard. According to the "contraction and convergence" scheme proposed by Global Commons Institute in 2004 and *Breaking the Climate Deadlock: A Global Deal for Our Low Carbon Future* written by Nicholas Stern, former Chief Economist of World Bank in 2008, per capita carbon emissions based on equal human rights

DOI: 10.4324/9781003388500-5

Table 4.1 Accounting standards of embodied carbon emissions and corresponding principle of fairness in various international emission reduction schemes

No.	*Scheme*	*Designer*	*Year*	*Accounting standards*	*Principle of fairness*
1	The United Nations Framework Convention on Climate Change and the Kyoto Protocol	The United Nations Climate Change Conference	1992/1997	Carbon emissions in current year	Consider current responsibility
2	The Clear Skies and Global Climate Change Action	The US government	2001	Carbon emissions per unit of GDP	Consider economic development
3	Brazil's climate pledge	The government of Brazil	2002	Cumulative carbon emissions	Consider historical responsibility
4	"Contraction and convergence" scheme and Nicholas Stern scheme	Global Commons Institute and Nicholas Stern	2004/2008	Per capita carbon emissions	Consider equal human rights
5	Carbon budget scheme	Chinese Academy of Social Sciences	2007	Cumulative carbon emissions per capita	Consider equal human rights, historical responsibility, and future demand
6	Greenhouse Gas Development Rights Program	Stockholm Environment Institute (SEI)	2008	Cumulative carbon emissions per unit of GDP	Consider population size, economic capability, and historical responsibility

Sources: Compiled from the relevant discussions of Zhiqiang Zhang et al. (2008), Jiahua Pane t al. (2009), and websites of the UN Climate Change (http://www.un.org/zh/climatechange/) and the Intergovernmental Panel on Climate Change (IPCC) (http://www.ipcc.ch/index.htm).

are valued as an accounting standard. The above accounting standards are based on a single principle of fairness. Jiahua Pan and Ying Chen (2010) of Chinese Academy of Social Sciences proposed to consider the cumulative carbon emissions per capita based on various principles of fairness such as equal human rights and historical responsibility as an accounting standard in their "carbon budget" scheme submitted to the United Nations Climate Change Conference in 2007. The Greenhouse Gas Development Rights

Program proposed by the Stockholm Environment Institute in Sweden in 2008 advocates overall consideration of multiple principles of fairness in population size, economic capability, and historical responsibility, and the "responsibility-capability" index can also be interpreted as an accounting standard based on cumulative carbon emissions per unit of GDP. In addition, the report *Who Owns China's Carbon Emissions* issued by the Tyndall Centre for Climate Change Research in 2007 facilitates exploring the accounting of the carbon emissions embodied in international trade and revising the carbon emissions of each country under the above accounting standards, so as to better reflect the principle of "common but differentiated responsibilities" as stated in Article IV of the United Nations Framework Convention on Climate Change (1992).

International carbon emission accounting standards, which serve as the basis to reflect the carbon emissions, determine the carbon emission rights and build an effective carbon emission reduction mechanism of each country, may lead to different judgments and interpretations of fairness. Despite a lot of argumentations and long-term debates, above accounting standards still fail in reaching any consensus and definitive conclusion and related studies tend to have obvious country-specific biases. In China, Zhiqiang Zhang et al. (2008), and Yan Zheng and Fan Liang (2011) explored carbon emission accounting standards suitable for China based on the analysis of the above accounting standards and their principles of fairness. In addition, the measurement for the fairness of global carbon emissions under the established accounting standards is also an important area for research and exploration, which provides an important quantitative basis for the selection of accounting standards and the interpretation of their principles of fairness. When selecting the measurement methods and indicators, foreign studies mainly adopt the Gini coefficient and the Theil index. The former is used by scholars, including Heil and Wodon (1997) and Padilla and Serrano (2006), and the latter by scholars, including Duro and Padilla (2006). There are few relevant studies in China and only a few Chinese scholars have measured the fairness of global carbon emissions based on the Gini coefficient (Junyong Qiu et al, 2011). It is worth mentioning that there have been many meaningful explorations on the differences and fairness of carbon emissions among regions in China based on the Gini coefficient and the Theil index. In addition to the Gini coefficient and the Theil index, Clarke et al. used a coefficient of variation for overall measurement of the fairness of China's interprovincial carbon emissions.

There are two main limitations in the above studies. One is about the selection of accounting standards and the interpretation of principles of fairness. The existing literature focuses mainly on normative research, without any quantitative analysis or comprehensive comparison. The other is about the measurement of the fairness of international carbon emissions under the established accounting standards. First, as for the selection of accounting standards, the existing foreign literature mainly uses carbon emissions per unit of GDP, which is partial to developed Western countries represented by the US, while the accounting standards based on cumulative carbon emissions per capita which are beneficial to developing countries are rarely considered. Second, as for the selection of study objects, the existing literature mainly takes certain number of countries as a whole in the study. Although some literatures classify study objects by levels of affluence for group comparison, none of them reflect the form of developed countries or developing countries which has been adopted in the United Nations Climate Change Conference. Finally, as for the fairness measure and indicators, although the existing literature mainly focuses on the Gini coefficient and the Theil index, in decomposition of the group disparity, the Theil index decomposition method only considers the difference of subsamples rather than subsample distribution within the group, while the Gini coefficient decomposition method fails to provide a convictive explanation of the economic logic.

4.1.2 Fairness measure—relative deprivation of international carbon emissions

The Gini coefficient is one of the most widely used measures of inequality or fairness in all areas of society. Since its introduction by Italian scholar Gini in the early 20th century, the Gini coefficient has gone through nearly a century of research and development. In the early days of its development, researchers focused on inequality measures within groups. However, since the 1960s, inequality between groups has received increasing attention. Many scholars have worked together to promote the development and continuous enrichment of Gini coefficient's subgroup decomposition. However, as noted by Xingjian Hong (2008), the subgroup decomposition of any inequality index requires the construction of inequality measurement between groups, according to the connotation of the index. Among them, according to Runciman (1996), relative deprivation is an inequality measure with realistic connotations, which can express individual's feelings of being treated unfairly more directly. Later, Yitzhaki (1979) studied the relation between relative deprivation and the Gini coefficient and claimed that Gini coefficient can be interpreted by relative deprivation. Hey and Lambert provided a more general formula of relative deprivation on this basis. In China, Xingjian Hong (2008) provided an overview of the above theories, and Guoqiang Ren and Jinyan Shang (2011) further made a comprehensive analysis and arguments for subgroup decomposition of the Gini coefficient based on relative deprivation theory. This chapter, which focuses on the fairness measure of international carbon emissions with single country and country subgroup as study objects, is also applicable to the subgroup decomposition of the Gini coefficient based on relative deprivation theory. However, it emphasizes more on the measurement of relative deprivation of international carbon emissions rather than decomposition of the Gini coefficient. Based on the studies of Xingjian Hong (2008) and Guoqiang Ren and Jinyan Shang (2011), studies of this chapter start from the following aspects.

4.1.2.1 Measures of intra-country relative deprivation

Assuming that there are n homogeneous countries, each country is assigned a carbon emission target x_i (i = 1, 2, ..., n), according to any of the above six accounting standards, and is measured by feelings of fairness in comparison to other countries. Relative deprivation is used to measure feelings of fairness of each country in comparison of allocated carbon emissions among countries. A country will not feel unfair or relatively deprived when allocated higher carbon emission index than other countries. However, for a country allocated with lower carbon emission index, this would be another story. The relative deprivation of country i to country j or the country j to country i can be expressed as:

$$d_{ij} = \begin{cases} x_j - x_i, & \text{if} \quad x_i < x_j \\ 0, & \text{if} \quad x_i \geq x_j \end{cases} \tag{4.1}$$

Similarly, the average relative deprivation of country i to all of n homogeneous countries can be expressed as:

$$d_i = \sum_{j=1}^{n} d_{ij} / n \tag{4.2}$$

4.1.2.2 Relative deprivation measures among country subgroups

Assuming that the above n countries are divided into s subgroups, the kth subgroup is Ω_k (k = 1, ..., s), and there are n_k countries in this subgroup. The average relative deprivation of country i in subgroup Ω_k can be decomposed as:

$$\begin{aligned} d_i &= \frac{\sum_{j=1}^{n} d_{ij}}{n} = \frac{\sum_{j \in \Omega_1} d_{ij} + \sum_{j \in \Omega_2} d_{ij} + \cdots + \sum_{j \in \Omega_s} d_{ij}}{n} \\ &= \frac{n_1}{n} \frac{\sum_{j \in \Omega_1} d_{ij}}{n_1} + \frac{n_2}{n} \frac{\sum_{j \in \Omega_2} d_{ij}}{n_2} + \cdots + \frac{n_s}{n} \frac{\sum_{j \in \Omega_s} d_{ij}}{n_s} \end{aligned} \tag{4.3}$$

Wherein $\sum_{j \in \Omega_k} d_{ij} / n_k$ is the average relative deprivation of country i compared to other countries in its sub-group.

When $i \in \Omega_k$, $j \in \Omega_l$, and $k \neq l$, $\sum_{j \in \Omega_1} d_{ij} / n_1$ represents the average relative deprivation of country i compared to all countries in another subgroup Ω_l. Then the average relative deprivation d_{kl} of subgroup Ω_k compared to subgroup Ω_l and the average relative deprivation d_{kk} within subgroup Ω_k can be expressed below respectively:

$$d_{kl} = \frac{\sum_{i \in \Omega_k} \left(\sum_{j \in \Omega_l} d_{ij} / n_l \right)}{n_k} = \sum_{i \in \Omega_k} \sum_{j \in \Omega_l} d_{ij} / n_k n_l \tag{4.4}$$

$$d_{kk} = \frac{\sum_{i \in \Omega_k} \left(\sum_{j \in \Omega_k} d_{ij} / n_k \right)}{n_k} = \frac{\sum_{i \in \Omega_k} \sum_{j \in \Omega_k} d_{ij}}{n_k n_k} \tag{4.5}$$

Similarly, the average relative deprivation d_{lk} of subgroup Ω_l compared to subgroup Ω_k can be calculated. d_{kl} and d_{lk} are often confused. In fact, these two items are often not equal and their connotations are completely different. The former measures the perceived unfairness of subgroup Ω_k compared to subgroup Ω_l, which focuses on the average perceived unfairness of subgroup Ω_k, while the latter is just the opposite.

4.1.2.3 Relative deprivation coefficient

The above calculations of the relative deprivations are in absolute values, making it difficult to compare the relative deprivations among single countries or country subgroups. For the convenience of the study, we change the absolute values of obtained relative deprivations into ratios. We divide the absolute values of the relative deprivation of a single country by its corresponding carbon emissions allowance and divide the absolute values of the average relative deprivations of each subgroup by the mean of the carbon emissions allowance of each country within the subgroup. This practice is consistent with the core connotation of relative deprivation, that is, to measure the subjective dissatisfaction and perceived unfairness when people compare their positions to others. On this basis, the relative deprivation coefficient d_{if} of a single country i, the relative deprivation coefficient d_{klf} of subgroup Ω_k compared to subgroup Ω_l, and the relative deprivation coefficient d_{kkf} within subgroup Ω_k can be expressed as follows:

$$d_{if} = \sum_{j=1}^{n} d_{ij} / n x_i$$

$$d_{klf} = \frac{\sum_{i \in \Omega_k, j \in \Omega_l} d_{ij} / n_k n_l}{\sum_{i=1}^{n_k} x_i / n_k} = \sum_{i \in \Omega_k} \sum_{j \in \Omega_l} d_{ij} / n_l \sum_{i=1}^{n_k} x_i \tag{4.7}$$

$$d_{kkf} = \frac{\sum_{i \in \Omega_k} \sum_{j \in \Omega_k} d_{ij} / n_k n_k}{\sum_{i=1}^{n_k} x_i / n_k} = \frac{\sum_{i \in \Omega_k} \sum_{j \in \Omega_k} d_{ij}}{n_k \sum_{i=1}^{n_k} x_i} \tag{4.8}$$

d_{klf} and d_{kkf} are often referred to the Gini coefficients that measure the unfairness among and within subgroups. Unlike the Gini coefficients, the relative deprivation coefficients that reflect the unfairness among individual countries or country subgroups have a value range of $(0 + \infty)$. The larger the relative deprivation coefficient, the higher the degree of perceived unfairness. In measuring the history and status quo, the larger the relative deprivation coefficient of a country or a subgroup of countries is, the less responsibility for emission reductions will be allocated, and the fairer the emission reduction scheme will be.

4.1.3 The impacts of international trade on relative deprivation coefficients of carbon emissions

As stated in the report issued by the Tyndall Centre for Climate Change Research, it is more reasonable to consider the impact of international trade when accounting international carbon emissions. According to Equations (4.6)–(4.8), we can calculate the impact of international trade on relative deprivation coefficients for carbon emissions among individual countries or country subgroups. Similarly, assuming there are two countries, country i and country j, and their carbon emissions are x_i and x_j, respectively, irrespective of the impact of international trade. The carbon emissions of country j are greater than those of country i, i.e., $x_j > x_i$. There is international trade as well as difference in the carbon emissions embodied in the exports and imports between the two countries. International trade leads to the transfer of carbon emissions between the two countries. For one country, if the carbon emissions embodied in exports are greater than those embodied in imports, then it surely has burdened carbon emissions for the other, which can be called net carbon emission transfer-in. Whereas if the carbon emissions embodied in imports are greater than those embodied in exports, then the other country surely has burdened the carbon emissions for the country, which can be called net carbon emission transfer-out. In this regard, considering the international transfer of carbon emissions during international trade, measuring the relative deprivation coefficients of carbon emissions among individual countries or country subgroups involves the following two scenarios.

Scenario 1: If the net carbon emission transfer from country j to country i is Δt, then the relative deprivation coefficient for carbon emissions of country j to country i after the adjustment for the impact of international trade is:

$$\begin{aligned} d_{ij} &= \left[\left(x_j + \Delta t\right) - \left(x_i - \Delta t\right)\right] / \left(x_i - \Delta t\right) \\ &= \left(x_j - x_i\right) / \left(x_i - \Delta t\right) + 2\Delta t / \left(x_i - \Delta t\right) \end{aligned} \tag{4.9}$$

Scenario 2: If the net carbon emission transfer from country i to country j is Δt, then the relative deprivation coefficient for carbon emissions of country j to country i after the adjustment for the impact of international trade is:

$$\begin{aligned} d_{ij} &= \left[\left(x_j - \Delta t\right) - \left(x_i + \Delta t\right)\right] / \left(x_i + \Delta t\right) \\ &= \left(x_j - x_i\right) / \left(x_i + \Delta t\right) - 2\Delta t / \left(x_i + \Delta t\right) \end{aligned} \tag{4.10}$$

Comparison between Equations (4.9) and (4.10) shows that adjusting the impact of international carbon emission transfer has strong asymmetrical impacts on calculating the relative deprivation coefficients of international carbon emissions. Due to the constant Δt in both scenarios, the increase in relative deprivation coefficient in scenario 1 is much greater than that in scenario 2. That is, in addition to $2\Delta t / \left(x_i - \Delta t\right)$ being much greater than $2\Delta t / \left(x_i + \Delta t\right)$, $\left(x_j - x_i\right) / \left(x_i - \Delta t\right) - \left(x_j - x_i\right) / x_i$ is also greater than $\left(x_j - x_i\right) / x_i - \left(x_j - x_i\right) / \left(x_i + \Delta t\right)$.

The accounting standard of carbon emissions in the current year is the basis for the calculation of other accounting standards, and the international transfer of carbon emissions in the current year during international trade will also affect the calculation of other accounting standards. The above analysis also applies to the measurement and analysis of impacts of international trade on the relative deprivation coefficients of carbon emissions among individual countries or country subgroups under other accounting standards.

4.2 International carbon emission accounting with different standards

4.2.1 Analysis objects and data source

In consideration of current international climate negotiations between developed and developing countries, in this chapter, the G20 member states are selected as the analysis objects, including eight industrialized nations (the US, Japan, Germany, France, the UK, Italy, Canada, and Russia, also known as the Group of Eight or G8), four developing countries (China, India, Brazil, and South Africa, also known as BASIC countries or B4), and seven newly industrialized countries (Argentina, Australia, Indonesia, Mexico, Saudi Arabia, South Korea, and Turkey, also known as N7). Since the European Union consists of many countries, including some of the G8 countries, it is not included in the study. In order to measure the cumulative carbon emissions of industrialized countries more comprehensively, the carbon emission data in this chapter are from the Carbon Dioxide Information Analysis Center of the Oak Ridge National Laboratory in the US,[2] and the data of carbon emissions from fossil fuel by country date back to 1751. The starting years of the carbon emission data for the above countries are: 1800 for the US, 1751 for the UK, 1868 for Japan, 1792 for Germany, 1802 for France, 1860 for Italy, 1785 for Canada, 1992 for Russia, 1899 for China, 1858 for India, 1901 for Brazil, 1884 for South Africa, 1851 for Australia, 1945 for South Korea, 1887 for Argentina, 1865 for Turkey, 1891 for Mexico, 1889 for Indonesia, and 1935 for Saudi Arabia. In addition, the carbon emission data provided mainly include carbon emissions from solid fuels, liquid fuels, and gaseous fuels, cement production, exhaust gas combustion, and the total amount of carbon emissions in these categories. The data in this chapter is the total amount of carbon emissions in these categories as of 2011. To ensure the uniformity and comparability of data sources of each country, the data on GDP and population size are from the World Bank website.[3] The preliminary statistics show that in 2011, carbon emissions of the above 19 countries accounted for 74.88% of the global carbon emissions, of which the G8 accounted for 30.92%, the B4 accounted for 35.45%, and the N7 accounted for 8.51%; the GDP of the above 19 countries accounted for 76.89% of the global GDP, of which the G8 accounted for 50.68%, the B4 accounted for 17.22%, and the N7 accounted for 8.99%; the population of the above 19 countries accounted for 61.53% of the global population, of which the G8 accounted for 12.71%, the B4 accounted for 40.62%, and the N7 accounted for 8.20%. Therefore, the selection and classification of the above countries are highly representative.

4.2.2 Comparison of international carbon emissions under different accounting standards

The results of fairness measures vary with the starting point and considerations of various accounting standards. Table 4.2 shows the descriptive statistics of carbon emissions by country and country subgroup under different accounting standards in 2011.

As shown in Table 4.2, with the carbon emissions in the current year as an accounting standard, China has the largest emission in the world (2.485 billion tonnes), which is nearly 70% higher than that of the runner-up, namely the US. However, considering the population size and historical

Table 4.2 Carbon emissions by country and country subgroup under different accounting standards in 2011

	Carbon emissions of current year (1,000 tons)	*Cumulative carbon emissions (1,000 tons)*	*Per capita carbon emissions (tons/person)*	*Cumulative carbon emissions per capita (tons/person)*	*Carbon emissions per unit of GDP (tons/USD 1,000)*	*Cumulative carbon emissions per unit of GDP (tons/USD 1,000*
US	1,473,381	98,375,259	4.73	315.72	0.98	65.62
UK	124,886	20,416,763	1.99	325.93	0.51	83.49
Japan	320,838	14,945,980	2.51	116.93	0.55	25.47
Germany	202,056	23,111,715	2.47	282.80	0.56	64.18
France	93,848	9,572,509	1.43	146.29	0.34	34.52
Italy	108,976	5,765,671	1.79	94.88	0.50	26.28
Canada	145,961	75,629,75	4.23	219.33	0.84	43.56
Russia	458,108	9,047,544	3.23	63.75	2.47	48.7
China[a]	2,484,812	38,636,558	1.85	28.74	3.4	52.79
India	615,500	10,926,665	0.50	8.80	3.33	59.13
Brazil	115,737	3,125,834	0.59	15.9	0.47	12.62
South Africa	141,624	4,651,396	2.80	91.95	3.47	113.94
Australia	106,947	4,062,938	4.73	179.61	0.78	29.45
South Korea	157,565	3,334,501	3.17	66.99	1.41	29.87
Argentina	53,334	1,839,613	1.31	45.13	1.20	41.24
Turkey	84,451	1,906,415	1.15	25.89	1.09	24.6
Mexico	125,325	4,063,799	1.09	35.4	1.09	35.23
Indonesia	141,459	2,494,137	0.58	10.29	1.67	29.45
Saudi Arabia	137,256	2,786,406	4.89	99.22	2.38	48.31
Mean of G8 countries (1)	366,007	23,599,802	2.80	195.7	0.84	48.98
Mean of B4 countries (2)	839,418	14,335,113	1.43	36.35	2.67	59.62
Mean of N7 countries (3)	115,191	2,926,830	2.42	66.08	1.37	34.02
(2)/(1)(%)	229.35	60.74	51.2	18.57	316.24	121.72
(3)/(1)(%)	31.47	12.4	86.31	33.76	162.85	69.46

Source: calculated by the author from the data in the website of Carbon Dioxide Information Analysis Center of the Oak Ridge National Laboratory in the US (http://cdiac.ornl.gov/) and the World Bank website (http://www.worldbank.org.cn/).

Note: All carbon emission indicators unlabeled with "cumulative" in this chapter are calculated from the data in the current year.

[a]Taiwan's carbon emission is counted separately.

responsibility, with cumulative carbon emissions per capita as an accounting standard, China ranks only 15th among the above 19 countries and has emissions less than 10% of that of the US. Likewise, if only the cumulative carbon emissions are taken as an accounting standard, the US has the largest emission (98.375 billion tonnes), which is 2.5 times that of the runner-up, namely China. In consideration of economic development only with carbon emissions per unit of GDP as an accounting standard, the US ranks 11th among the above 19 countries and has emissions less than 30% of that of China. In summary, the international community has different judgments on the fairness and rationality of carbon emissions of each country under different accounting standards. That's why countries propose accounting standards and emission reduction schemes that are beneficial to their selves.

As shown in Table 4.2, there are also huge differences in the results of fairness measurements for carbon emissions among country subgroups under different accounting standards. For example, with the carbon emissions in the current year as the accounting standard, the average carbon emissions of the G8 are more than three times those of the N7, but less than half of those of the B4. However, with the cumulative carbon emissions as an accounting standard, the average carbon emissions of the G8 are more than eight times those of the N7, and 1.6 times those of the B4. In addition, with the current year's carbon emissions, per capita carbon emissions and carbon emissions per unit of GDP as accounting standards, the gap between the G8 and the N7 is relatively small. While with the cumulative carbon emissions per capita as an accounting standard, the gap between the B4 and the N7 is relatively small. The difference in carbon emission allowances among country subgroups under different accounting standards provides an important quantitative basis for cooperation among country subgroups in international climate negotiations.

None of the above analysis takes into account the transfer of international carbon emissions in international trade. With the development of international trade, the increasing carbon emissions embodied in trade have a greater and greater impact on the accounting of international carbon emissions. Due to space limitations, please refer to related papers of Wenju Wang and Qifeng Xiang (2011) for details.

4.3 Fairness analysis of international carbon emission accounting standards

4.3.1 Static analysis of relative deprivation coefficients

4.3.1.1 Single country scenario

According to Equation (4.6), we can calculate the relative deprivation coefficients of the above 19 countries in 2011 under different accounting standards, as shown in Table 4.3. As mentioned above, different relative deprivation coefficients imply different carbon emission reduction responsibilities. The higher the relative deprivation coefficient of a country, the more unfair the country perceives itself to be, and the less emission reduction responsibility it has to take to better reflect the fairness in allocation of emission reduction responsibilities. Therefore, according to the relative deprivation coefficient, we can also calculate rankings of the emission reduction responsibilities of the above 19 countries under different accounting standards (Table 4.3). According to Table 4.3, there are different relative deprivation coefficients and emission reduction responsibility rankings for the same country under different accounting standards. Taking the US as an example, with carbon emissions per unit of GDP as an accounting standard, its relative deprivation coefficient is 0.62, and it ranks only 11th in terms of the corresponding emission reduction responsibilities; however, as cumulative carbon emissions or per capita carbon emissions as the accounting standard, its relative deprivation coefficient tends to be zero, and it is among top three in the ranking of emission reduction responsibility. That's a major reason why the US initially advocates taking carbon emissions per unit of GDP as an accounting standard. Likewise, with carbon emissions in the current year and carbon emissions per unit of GDP as accounting standards, China's relative deprivation coefficient tends to be zero, and the corresponding emission reduction responsibilities are also among top three. However, with cumulative carbon emissions per unit of GDP, per capita carbon emissions, and cumulative carbon emissions per capita as accounting standards, China's relative deprivation coefficients increase significantly, and it ranks sixth, 11th, and 15th, respectively, in terms of the corresponding emission reduction responsibility.

Table 4.3 also shows that the relative deprivation coefficients of the sample countries as a whole vary greatly under different accounting standards. For example, with the cumulative carbon emissions per capita as the accounting standard, the mean, standard deviation, and coefficient of variation for the overall relative deprivation coefficient are the largest, indicating that the sense of overall unfairness is the strongest under this accounting standard, and the disparity in the senses of unfairness is also the largest among different countries. With the cumulative carbon emissions per unit of GDP as the accounting standard, the mean and standard deviation for the overall relative deprivation coefficient are the smallest, indicating that the sense of overall unfairness is the weakest under this accounting standard. With the carbon emissions of the current year as the accounting standard, the coefficient of variation for the overall relative deprivation coefficient is the smallest, indicating a smallest disparity in the senses of unfairness among countries under this accounting standard. It is worth noting that the strength of the sense of overall unfairness is not the basis for selecting the accounting standards. If the aim is to reduce overall unfairness, the accounting standard that best reflects the overall unfairness deserves more attention.

Table 4.3 Relative deprivation coefficients by country under different accounting standards in 2011

	Carbon emissions in current year		*Cumulative carbon emissions*		*Per capita carbon emissions*		*Cumulative carbon emissions per capita*		*Carbon emissiosn per unit of GDP*		*Cumulative carbon emissions per unit of GDP*	
	Respon-sibility ranking	*Coef-ficient value*	*Respon-sibility ranking*	*Coef-ficient value*	*Respon-sibility ranking*	*Coef-ficient value*	*Respon-sibility ranking*	*Coef-ficient value*	*Respon-sibility ranking*	*Coef-ficient value*	*Respon-sibility ranking*	*Coef-ficient value*
US	2	0.04	1	0	2	0	2	0	11	0.62	3	0.05
UK	13	2.07	4	0.25	10	0.39	1	0	16	1.81	2	0.02
Japan	5	0.61	5	0.43	8	0.21	7	0.35	15	1.64	17	0.82
Germany	6	1.13	3	0.21	9	0.22	3	0.01	14	1.58	4	0.06
France	17	3.01	7	0.82	13	0.78	6	0.21	19	3.2	12	0.42
Italy	15	2.47	10	1.65	12	0.5	9	0.51	17	1.88	16	0.77
Canada	8	1.69	9	1.14	4	0.02	4	0.06	12	0.83	9	0.23
Russia	4	0.37	8	0.89	5	0.09	12	1.02	4	0.06	7	0.16
China	1	0	2	0.08	11	0.46	15	3.08	2	0	6	0.12
India	3	0.23	6	0.68	19	3.78	19	12	3	0	5	0.08
Brazil	14	2.28	15	3.55	18	3.04	17	6.24	18	2.06	19	2.62
South Africa	9	1.76	11	2.17	7	0.15	10	0.55	1	0	1	0
Australia	16	2.53	13	2.57	3	0	5	0.12	13	0.95	14	0.6
South Korea	7	1.54	14	3.28	6	0.10	11	0.95	7	0.31	13	0.58
Argentina	19	6	19	6.63	14	0.92	13	1.7	8	0.43	10	0.27
Turkey	18	3.44	18	6.36	15	1.15	16	3.51	9	0.51	18	0.88
Mexico	12	2.06	12	2.57	16	1.25	14	2.36	10	0.51	11	0.4
Indonesia	10	1.76	17	4.65	17	1.64	18	10.12	6	0.21	15	0.6
Saudi Arabia	11	1.83	16	4.08	1	0	8	0.47	5	0.07	8	0.16
Mean	——	1.83	——	2.21	——	0.77	——	2.28	——	0.88	——	0.47
Standard deviation	——	1.37	——	2.02	——	1.02	——	3.4	——	0.88	——	0.58
Coefficient of variation	——	0.75	——	0.91	——	1.32	——	1.49	——	1	——	1.24

Source: Calculated by the author according to equations.

4.3.1.2 About the subgroup of countries

As shown in Table 4.4, we can calculate the relative deprivation coefficients of the three subgroups of the G8, the B4, and the N7 in 2011 under different accounting standards based on Equations (4.7) and (4.8). And the relative deprivation coefficients vary with subgroups of countries under different accounting standards. Taking the G8 and the B4 as examples, regardless of the accounting standard (the cumulative carbon emissions, per capita carbon emissions, or the cumulative carbon emissions per capita), the G8 has a high relative deprivation coefficient to the B4 and therefore should take more responsibilities for emission reduction. In particular, with the cumulative carbon emissions per capita as the accounting standard, the relative deprivation coefficient of the G8 to the B4 is as high as 4.41, which reflects the carbon emission pressure of the B4 from population and the historical responsibility of the G8 for their industrialization. However, with the carbon emissions per unit of GDP as the accounting standard, the situation is just the other way around. The B4 has a higher relative deprivation coefficient to the G8 and therefore should take more responsibilities for emissions reduction. This is because the G8 has been industrialized and the carbon emissions per unit of GDP have been decreasing on the basis of the technological progress, while developing countries still rely on high energy consumption to promote economic development. In addition, with the carbon emissions in the current year, cumulative carbon emissions and carbon emissions per unit of GDP as accounting standards, there is an obvious relative deprivation to each other between the G8 and the B4, indicating an obvious overlap in carbon emissions between the two subgroups, under the above accounting standards, as well as blurred disparity in carbon emissions in terms of population and technology, which is where the limitation of the above accounting standards lies.

As shown in Table 4.4, the relative deprivation coefficient within is smaller than that between country subgroups, which reflects that the competition of interests between the groups of developing and developed countries in international negotiations on emission reduction is stronger than that within the groups of different countries. If the newly industrialized countries are considered as cooperation partners that developed and developing countries actively strive for in the negotiations, we can also conclude from Table 4.4 that, with carbon emissions in the current year, cumulative carbon emissions, cumulative carbon emissions per capita, and cumulative carbon emissions per unit of GDP as accounting standards, the G8 has a higher relative deprivation coefficient to the N7, while with carbon emissions per unit of GDP as the accounting standard, the N7 has a higher relative deprivation coefficient to the G8. With the carbon emissions in the current year, cumulative carbon emissions, carbon emissions per unit of GDP, and cumulative carbon emissions per unit of GDP as accounting standards, the B4 has a higher relative deprivation coefficient to the N7, while with the per capita

Table 4.4 Relative deprivation coefficient by country subgroup under different accounting standards in 2011

	Carbon emissions in current year	*Cumulative carbon emissions*	*Per capita carbon emissions*	*Cumulative carbon emissions per capita*	*Carbon emissions per unit of GDP*	*Cumulative carbon emissions per unit of GDP*
Relative deprivation coefficient within the G8 group	0.51	0.51	0.22	0.28	0.34	0.22
Relative deprivation coefficient within the B4 group	0.56	0.49	0.36	0.45	0.21	0.33
Relative deprivation coefficient within the N7 group	0.16	0.16	0.38	0.42	0.19	0.12
Relative deprivation coefficient of the G8 group to the B4 group	0.18	1.06	1.05	4.41	0.04	0.2
Relative deprivation coefficient of the B4 group to the G8 group	1.7	0.25	0.05	0	2.28	0.46
Relative deprivation coefficient of the N7 group to the B4 group	0	0.01	0.94	1.12	0.08	0.09
Relative deprivation coefficient of the B4 group to the N7 group	6.32	3.92	0.15	0.16	1.11	0.91
Relative deprivation coefficient of the G8 group to the N7 group	2.24	7.06	0.44	2.05	0.10	0.51
Relative deprivation coefficient of the N7 group to the G8 group	0.02	0	0.24	0.03	0.80	0.05

Source: Calculated by the author according to equations.

carbon emission and cumulative carbon emissions per capita as accounting standards, the N7 has a higher relative deprivation coefficient to the B4. We can conclude from international negotiations on emission reduction that when cumulative carbon emissions per capita are used as the accounting standard, it is more possible for the B4 to cooperate with the N7.

4.3.2 Dynamic analysis of relative deprivation coefficient

4.3.2.1 Among subgroups of countries

In the analysis of relative deprivation coefficient of carbon emissions among subgroups of countries in 2011, we can conclude that when the cumulative carbon emissions per capita is used as the accounting standard, the G8 has the highest relative deprivation coefficient to the B4, while when the carbon emissions per unit of GDP is used as the accounting standard, the B4 has the highest relative deprivation coefficient to the G8. Table 4.5 shows the dynamic changes of relative deprivation coefficients among different subgroups of countries under the two accounting standards from the conclusion of the UNFCCC during 1992–2011.

We can conclude from Table 4.5 that there are large differences in the changes to relative deprivation coefficients among different subgroups of countries under different accounting standards. With cumulative carbon emissions per capita as the accounting standard, the relative deprivation coefficient of the G8 to the B4 and to the N7 shows a downward trend year by year and the relative deprivation coefficient of the N7 to the B4 is stable. Among them, the relative deprivation coefficient of the G8 to the B4 has dropped by 23.04% in 20 years and the relative deprivation coefficient of the G8 to the N7 has dropped by 31.89% in 20 years, which is mainly due to the rising carbon emissions driven by the faster economic growth of the B4 and the N7 than the G8. With the carbon emissions per unit of GDP as the accounting standard, the relative deprivation coefficient of the B4 to the G8 shows a "first descend then rise" trend. Such coefficient rose when the US proposed carbon emissions per unit of GDP as the accounting standard and Western developed countries began to pay attention to the carbon emission intensity control in the process of economic development. The change of relative deprivation coefficients of the N7 to the G8 shows a more obvious upward trend, which reflects the relatively weak carbon emission control of newly industrialized countries in the process of rapid economic growth, while the decreasing relative deprivation coefficient of the B4 to the N7 reflects that developing countries such as China have begun to pay more attention to the control of carbon emission intensity in the process of economic growth. We can also conclude from Table 4.5 that although the relative deprivation coefficient of the G8 to the B4 and the N7 shows a downward trend year by year with cumulative carbon emissions per capita

Table 4.5 Dynamic changes of relative deprivation coefficients among subgroups of countries under two accounting standards during 1992–2011

Year	*With cumulative carbon emissions per capita as the accounting standard*			*With carbon emissions per unit of GDP as the accounting standard*		
	Relative deprivation coefficient of the G8 group to the B4 group	*Relative deprivation coefficient of the G8 group to the N7 group*	*Relative deprivation coefficient of the N7 group to the B4 group*	*Relative deprivation coefficient of the B4 group to the G8 group*	*Relative deprivation coefficient of the N7 group to the G8 group*	*Relative deprivation coefficient of the B4 group to the N7 group*
1992	5.73	3.01	1.14	2.24	0.53	1.87
1993	5.66	2.92	1.15	2.33	0.53	1.94
1994	5.6	2.84	1.17	2.13	0.58	1.65
1995	5.55	2.77	1.18	1.92	0.52	1.61
1996	5.51	2.70	1.19	1.84	0.51	1.57
1997	5.47	2.64	1.2	1.82	0.50	1.53
1998	5.44	2.58	1.21	1.43	0.52	1.20
1999	5.41	2.53	1.22	1.16	0.37	1.34
2000	5.4	2.48	1.24	1.34	0.42	1.35
2001	5.36	2.44	1.24	1.5	0.53	1.20
2002	5.31	2.40	1.24	1.65	0.64	1.08
2003	5.24	2.37	1.23	1.71	0.64	1.11
2004	5.14	2.32	1.23	1.99	0.78	1.08
2005	5.05	2.28	1.22	2.06	0.74	1.15
2006	4.96	2.24	1.2	2.26	0.76	1.23
2007	4.86	2.21	1.19	2.30	0.78	1.18
2008	4.75	2.17	1.17	2.66	0.81	1.32
2009	4.63	2.14	1.15	2.39	0.92	1.08
2010	4.52	2.1	1.13	2.13	0.79	1.04
2011	4.41	2.05	1.12	2.28	0.80	1.11

Source: Calculated by the author according to equations.

as the accounting standard, such coefficient under this accounting standard is still much higher than the relative deprivation coefficients of the B4 and the N7 to the G8 under the accounting standard of carbon emissions per unit of GDP, and under the latter accounting standard, the relative deprivation coefficient of the N7 to the G8 shows an upward trend, while the relative deprivation coefficient of the B4 to the N7 shows a downward trend. We can conclude that the N7 will be in a more disadvantaged position in the international climate negotiations among these three subgroups of countries under the accounting standard of carbon emissions per unit of GDP, while in international climate negotiations under the accounting standard of cumulative carbon emissions per capita, there is a stronger interest convergence between the B4 and the N7, and the G8 needs to take more responsibilities for emission reduction.

4.3.2.2 Within subgroups of countries

The relative deprivation coefficient within is smaller than that between subgroups of countries, which reflects that the competition of interests between is stronger than that within subgroups of countries. However, the relative deprivation coefficient within subgroups of countries, as a measure of feelings of internal fairness within subgroups of countries, can reflect not only the degree of interest competition within subgroups of countries, but also the consistency of external interest competition within subgroups of countries. Higher relative deprivation coefficient within subgroups of countries indicates stronger interest competition for carbon emissions within the subgroups and weaker consistency of external interest competition. Table 4.6 shows the dynamic changes of relative deprivation coefficients within subgroups of countries with the cumulative carbon emissions per capita and carbon emissions per unit of GDP as accounting standards during 1992–2011.

As can been seen from Table 4.6, the changes to relative deprivation coefficient within subgroups of countries are quite different under different accounting standards. With cumulative carbon emissions per capita as the accounting standard, relative deprivation coefficients of the G8, the B4 and the N7 all show a downward trend year by year, including a largest reduction by 24.32% in the G8 during 1992–2011, followed by 15.09% in the B4, and 12.5% in the N7.

With carbon emissions per unit of GDP as the accounting standard, although the relative deprivation coefficients within the G8, the B4, and the N7 show a downward trend on the whole, the trend is much less stable than that with the cumulative carbon emissions per capita as the accounting standard. For example, the relative deprivation coefficient within the G8 increased significantly in 1998 and went back to the pre-1998 level until 2004. The relative deprivation coefficient in the B4 shows an upward trend during 2000–2007 and a downward trend again after 2008. The relative deprivation coefficient in the N7 fluctuates around 0.2. This indicates that the uncertainty of economic development also brings about the uncertainty in calculating relative deprivation coefficients under the accounting standard of carbon emissions per unit of GDP. Table 4.6 also shows that with the cumulative carbon emissions per capita as the accounting standard, the relative deprivation coefficient in the B4 is the largest, followed by the relative deprivation coefficient in the N7, and the relative deprivation coefficient in the G8 is the smallest; while with the carbon emissions per unit of GDP as the accounting standard, the relative deprivation coefficient in the G8 is the largest, followed by the relative deprivation coefficient in the B4, and the relative deprivation coefficient in the N7 is the smallest. This indicates that with the cumulative carbon emissions per capita as the accounting standard, the G8 has

Table 4.6 Dynamic changes of relative deprivation coefficient within each subgroup of countries under two accounting standards during 1992–2011

Year	*With cumulative carbon emissions per capita as the accounting standard*			*With carbon emissions per unit of GDP as the accounting standard*		
	Relative deprivation coefficient within the G8 group	*Relative deprivation coefficient within the B4 group*	*Relative deprivation coefficient within the N7 group*	*Relative deprivation coefficient within the G8 group*	*Relative deprivation coefficient within the B4 group*	*Relative deprivation coefficient within the N7 group*
1992	0.37	0.53	0.48	0.53	0.36	0.22
1993	0.36	0.52	0.48	0.52	0.36	0.25
1994	0.36	0.52	0.47	0.53	0.34	0.25
1995	0.35	0.52	0.47	0.54	0.33	0.19
1996	0.35	0.51	0.47	0.53	0.30	0.19
1997	0.34	0.51	0.46	0.51	0.28	0.17
1998	0.34	0.50	0.46	0.58	0.25	0.25
1999	0.33	0.50	0.46	0.65	0.22	0.20
2000	0.33	0.49	0.46	0.6	0.21	0.22
2001	0.32	0.49	0.45	0.56	0.22	0.24
2002	0.32	0.48	0.45	0.55	0.22	0.20
2003	0.31	0.48	0.45	0.53	0.22	0.19
2004	0.31	0.48	0.45	0.49	0.24	0.23
2005	0.31	0.47	0.44	0.45	0.26	0.21
2006	0.30	0.47	0.44	0.41	0.26	0.20
2007	0.30	0.47	0.44	0.38	0.26	0.18
2008	0.29	0.46	0.43	0.35	0.23	0.18
2009	0.29	0.46	0.43	0.39	0.24	0.19
2010	0.28	0.46	0.43	0.35	0.22	0.21
2011	0.28	0.45	0.42	0.34	0.21	0.19

Source: Calculated by the author according to equations.

the strongest feelings of internal fairness and the strongest consistency in the external competition of interests. While with the carbon emission per unit of GDP as the accounting standard, the B4 and the N7 have the strongest feelings of internal fairness and the strongest consistency in the external competition of interests. We can conclude that in terms of trend stability, the accounting standard based on cumulative carbon emissions per capita is better than that based on carbon emissions per unit of GDP. And in terms of alleviating the feelings of unfairness within subgroups of countries and enhancing the consistency in the external competition of interests within subgroups of countries, the subgroups of the G8 should use cumulative carbon emissions per capita as the accounting standard, while the subgroups of the B4 and the N7 should use carbon emissions per unit of GDP as the accounting standard.

4.3.3 Fairness analysis of carbon embodied in international trade after adjustment

4.3.3.1 Analysis of relative deprivation coefficient considering the impact of international trade

Due to the large variety of products and services in international trade, there is no complete database based on transfer of international carbon emissions at home and abroad. This chapter calculates the relative deprivation coefficient of each country under the adjustment of the international transfer of carbon emissions in 2005, with the study of Wenju Wang and Qifeng Xiang (2011) as the basis, the G8 and the B4 as study objects, and the carbon emissions in the current year as the accounting standard, as shown in Table 4.7.

As can be seen from Table 4.7, most countries of the G8 group (except Russia) have the net export of carbon emissions to the B4 group. The B4 group has relative deprivation to the G8 without considering impacts of international trade. However, when such impacts are considered, except for the US and Russia, relative deprivation coefficients of carbon emissions in the other six countries of the G8 group have decreased dramatically, and

Table 4.7 Impact of international trade adjustment on relative deprivation coefficient of each country in 2005

Country	*Carbon emissions before adjustment (million tonnes)*	*Carbon emissions transfer-out in international trade (million tonnes)*	*Rate of carbon emissions transfer-out (%)*	*Relative deprivation coefficients before adjustment*	*Relative deprivation coefficients after adjustment*	*Decline rate of relative deprivation coefficients (%)*
US	1307.31	212.63	16.26	0	0	—
UK	73.23	62.78	85.73	3.86	1.68	-56.4
Japan	240.41	51.00	21.21	0.85	0.57	-32.79
Germany	87.79	75.51	86.01	3.09	1.32	-57.42
France	24.03	67.16	279.49	13.6	2.85	-79.06
Italy	61.48	46.22	75.17	4.76	2.29	-51.76
Canada	123.92	4.46	3.6	2.04	1.82	-10.72
Russia	438.94	-182.71	-41.62	0.34	0.69	102.67
China	1360.52	-306.41	-22.52	0	0.04	—
India	298.98	-21.78	-7.28	0.62	0.61	-0.73
Brazil	87.65	-5.57	-6.36	3.10	3.26	5.28
South Africa	104.57	-12.03	-11.5	2.50	2.79	11.51

Source: Calculated by the author according to the study of Wenju Wang and Qifeng Xiang (2011).

Note: The carbon emissions are obtained by dividing the cited carbon dioxide emissions by 3.667 (the ratio of carbon dioxide molecular weight to carbon molecular weight).

the relative deprivation coefficient of France has dropped by nearly 80%. In contrast, the increase in relative deprivation coefficients for the four developing countries in this regard is small, and South Africa has the largest increase in relative deprivation coefficient (only 11.51%). Therefore, the adjustment of international carbon emission transfer caused by international trade has strong asymmetrical impacts on relative deprivation coefficients of international carbon emissions, which causes a dramatic drop of relative deprivation coefficients of developed countries while slightly increasing relative deprivation coefficients of developing countries.

4.3.3.2 Analysis of relative deprivation coefficients among subgroups of countries under the impact of international trade

Similarly, we also calculate the relative deprivation coefficient among subgroups of countries after the adjustment of the international transfer of carbon emissions in 2005, as shown in Table 4.8. It can been seen from Table 4.8 that the relative deprivation coefficient within each subgroup of countries decreases to different degrees after the adjustment of the international transfer of carbon emissions, indicating that such adjustment can reduce the feelings of unfairness toward carbon emissions within each subgroup of countries. In addition, while reducing the relative deprivation coefficient of carbon emissions of the B4 to the G8, the adjustment also increases the relative deprivation coefficient of carbon emissions of the G8 to the B4, and the decrease of the former is smaller than the increase of the latter. This indicates that with the carbon emissions in the current year as the accounting standard, the adjustment of international trade can reduce the relative deprivation coefficient of the G8 and thus reduce the responsibility for emission

Table 4.8 Impact of international trade adjustment on relative deprivation coefficient of each country subgroup in 2005

	Before international trade adjustment	*After international trade adjustment*	*Change of rate (%)*
Relative deprivation coefficients within the G8	0.6	0.53	–13.10
Relative deprivation coefficients within the B4	0.54	0.51	–4.99
Relative deprivation coefficients of the B4 to the G8	1.06	0.65	–38.79
Relative deprivation coefficients of the G8 to the B4	0.31	0.47	52.76
Overall relative deprivation coefficients	0.59	0.54	–9.39

Source: Calculated by the author according to the study of Wenju Wang and Qifeng Xiang (2011).

reduction of the B4, and at the same time, increase the relative deprivation coefficient of the B4 as well as the responsibility for emissions reduction of the G8. Therefore, the adjustment of international trade is much fairer and can better reflect the principle of "common but differentiated responsibilities" in the allocation of international carbon emission reduction responsibilities.

Due to data limitations, only carbon emissions in the current year are used as the accounting standard for analysis. However, in terms of the equation for calculating the relative deprivation coefficient after the adjustment of international trade, the above analysis is also applicable to the analysis under other accounting standards and data sources, and generality of the conclusion can be guaranteed.

4.4 Conclusions and suggestions for the selection of international carbon emission accounting standards

This chapter measures the fairness of six accounting standards of international carbon emissions based on the relative deprivation coefficient. The results show that the relative deprivation coefficient of each country and the allocation suggestions for the embodied international emission reduction responsibilities vary with the accounting standard. With the carbon emissions in the current year as an accounting standard, major countries such as China, the US, and India have higher relative deprivation coefficients to other countries, and thus are supposed to take more responsibilities for emissions reduction. However, if historical responsibility is taken into account, i.e., with the cumulative carbon emissions as an accounting standard, countries with early industrialization such as the US, the UK, and Germany have higher relative deprivation coefficients to other countries, and thus are supposed to take more responsibilities for emissions reduction. If only population size is taken into account, i.e., with the per capita carbon emissions as the accounting standard, major vast and sparsely populated countries such as the US, Canada, and Russia have higher relative deprivation coefficients to other countries, and thus are supposed to take more responsibilities for emissions reduction; however, if only economic development is taken into account, i.e., with the carbon emissions per unit of GDP as an accounting standard, developing countries such as China, India, and South Africa have higher relative deprivation coefficients to other countries, and thus are supposed to take more responsibilities for emissions reduction. If both population size and historical responsibilities are taken into account, i.e., with the cumulative carbon emissions per capita as an accounting standard, countries such as the US, the UK, and Germany have higher relative deprivation coefficients to other countries, and thus are supposed to take more responsibilities for emissions reduction; if both economic development and historical responsibilities are taken into account, i.e., with the cumulative carbon emissions per unit of GDP as an accounting standard, countries such as South Africa, the UK, and the US have higher relative deprivation coefficients to other countries, and thus are supposed to take more responsibilities for emissions reduction. The proposed allocation of emission reduction responsibilities embodied in different accounting standards will also push countries to make efforts to promote accounting standards that are more beneficial to themselves. Since the signing of the UNFCCC in 1992, international accounting standards for carbon emissions have gone through a series of evolutions, and accounting standards which consider more factors of fairness are becoming dominant in this regard.

Another major reason for this trend is that in the current international climate negotiations, it has become a norm that both developing and developed countries appear in groups. For example, the B4 group and the N7 group are representatives of developing countries and the European Union and the G8 group are representatives of developed countries. The differences among the group members will definitely be considered in selection of accounting standards for the country groups. Static studies show that relative deprivation coefficients among subgroups of countries and their proposed allocation of embodied carbon emissions reduction responsibilities vary with the accounting standard. With cumulative carbon emissions, per capita carbon emissions, and cumulative carbon emissions per capita as accounting standards, the G8 group has higher relative deprivation coefficients to the B4 group and the N7 group, and thus is supposed to take more responsibilities for emissions reduction; however, with carbon emissions per unit of GDP as an accounting standard, the B4 group and the N7 group have higher relative deprivation coefficients to the G8 group, and thus are supposed to take more responsibilities for emissions reduction; with carbon emissions in the current year and cumulative carbon emissions per unit of GDP as the accounting standard, the B4 group has higher relative deprivation coefficient to the G8 group and the N7 group, and is supposed to take more responsibilities for emissions reduction. Therefore, the accounting standard based on carbon emissions per unit of GDP is more beneficial to developed countries such as the US in the allocation of emission reduction responsibilities, while the accounting standard based on cumulative carbon emission per capita is more beneficial to developing countries and newly industrialized countries such as China. The dynamic analysis shows that with carbon emissions per unit of GDP as the accounting standard, the newly industrialized countries will be in a more disadvantaged position in international negotiations on carbon emissions due to their rising relative deprivation coefficients to the developed countries, while with cumulative carbon emissions per capita as the accounting standard, the developing countries and the newly industrialized countries have a stronger interest convergence and larger space of cooperation. In terms of the stability of relative deprivation coefficient, the accounting standard based on cumulative carbon emissions per capita is better than the one based on carbon emissions per unit of GDP. It is worth noting that the relative deprivation coefficient within is smaller than that between subgroups of countries, which indicates that the subgroups of countries focus more on their external interests than their internal interests. The relative deprivation coefficients within the subgroups of countries reflect not only the intensity of competition for interests within the subgroups of countries, but also the consistency of the competition for external interests among countries within the subgroups of countries. From the perspective of alleviating the feelings of unfairness and enhancing the external consistency within subgroups of countries, when actively advocating carbon emissions per unit of GDP as the accounting standard, the G8 group should also promote the accounting standard based on cumulative carbon emissions per capita within its member states, while the B4 group and the N7 group should also promote the accounting standard based on carbon emissions per unit of GDP within its member states when actively advocating cumulative carbon emissions per capita as the accounting standard.

For the accounting standard based on cumulative carbon emission per capita or carbon emissions per unit of GDP, the starting point and basic logic are still based on the domestic carbon emissions rather than the unfair treatment to developing countries as some of emission reduction responsibilities have been transferred from developed countries to developing countries through international trade. Based on studies of Wenju Wang and Qifeng Xiang (2011), the adjustment in international carbon emission transfer can reduce the relative deprivation coefficients within subgroups of developed and developing countries and cause a significant asymmetrical change in the relative deprivation coefficients between subgroups of developed and developing countries. This indicates that the accounting standard based on the adjustment of carbon emissions embodied in international trade can better reflect the fairness of international carbon emissions and the principle of "common but differentiated responsibilities". This also requires us to reexamine the existing accounting standards, establish a set of accounting standards based on carbon emissions embodied in international trade, complete the historical data of embodied carbon emissions in the international trade of each country, and track their future changes.

According to World Bank statistics, China, as the world's largest developing country, has surpassed the US in carbon emission and become the largest carbon emitter in the world. In order to better safeguard national interests and obtain more favorable carbon emission rights and fairer emission reduction responsibilities in future climate negotiations, China needs to pay attention to the carbon emission accounting standards adopted by the international community and the explanation to their fairness, and should actively develop accounting standards that facilitate economic development and better reflect the principle of "common but differentiated responsibilities" and the explanation to their fairness under the increasing pressure from international public opinion, so as to seek more positive and fairer comments from the international community. Based on the ideas of Wenju Wang and Qifeng Xiang (2011), the study in this chapter supports the accounting standard of cumulative carbon emissions per capita based on the adjustment of carbon emissions embodied in international trade. We believe that with the improvement of data, there will be a larger sphere of study in this field, and corresponding study results will be of increasingly great guiding significance.

Notes

1 See the United Nations Framework Convention on Climate Change (1992) and the Kyoto Protocol (1997).
2 Data source: http://cdiac.ornl.gov/.
3 Data source: http: //www.worldbank.org.on.

References

Duro, J.A., Padilla, E. International inequalities in per capital CO_2 emissions: a decomposition methodology by Kaya factors. *Energy Economics*, 2006, 28(2): 170–187.

Heil, M.T., Wodon, Q.T. Inequality in CO_2 emissions between poor and rich countries. *The Journal of Environmental and Development*, 1997 (6): 426–452.

Hong Xingjian. A new subgroup decomposition of the Gini coefficient. *China Economic Quarterly*, 2008, 8(1).

Padilla, E., Serrano, A. Inequality in CO_2 emissions across countries and its relationship with income inequality: a distributive approach. *Energy Policy*, 2006, 34 (14): 1762–1772.

Pan Jiahua, Chen Ying. Carbon budget proposal: a framework for an equitable and sustainable international climate regime. *Social Sciences in China*, 2010 (1): 6–3.

Qiu Junyong, Zhong Dingsheng, Yu Qiaocui, et al. Equity analysis of global CO_2 emissions based on Gini coefficient. *China Soft Science*, 2011 (4): 14–21.

Ren Guoqiang, Shang Jinyan. The research on Gini index's subgroup decomposition method based on relative deprivation theory. *The Journal of Quantitative and Technical Economics*, 2011 (8): 103–114.

Runciman, W. *Relative deprivation and social justice: a study of attitudes to social inequality in twentieth-century England.* Berkeley and Los Angeles: University of California Press, 1966.

Wang Wenju, Xiang Qifeng. Accounting and responsibility analysis on carbon emissions embodied in international trade. *China Industrial Economics*, 2011 (10): 56–64.

Yitzhaki, S. Relative deprivation and the Gini coefficient. *The Quarterly Journal of Economics*, 1979, 93 (2): 321–324.

Zhang Zhiqiang, Qu Jiansheng, Zeng Jingjing. A quantitative comparison and analytical study on the assessment indicators of greenhouse gases emissions. *Acta Geographica Sinica*, 2008, 18 (4): 387–399.

Zheng Yan, Liang Fan. Principles of climate justice and the construction of international climate regime. *World Economics and Politics*, 2011 (6): 69–90.

Part II

Inter-industry indicator allocation of carbon emissions

The industrial restructuring is one of the three major approaches for energy conservation and emission reduction, but its potential in this regard has not been quantitatively evaluated. The study on the relationship between industrial structure and carbon emissions can be divided into three aspects: significant differences in the carbon emission intensity of different industries; impacts of industrial structure change on energy consumption and energy efficiency; and impacts of industrial structure change on carbon emissions and carbon emission intensity.

Changes in industrial structure have a positive impact on energy consumption and carbon emissions, and this conclusion is basically confirmed. However, the specific potential of industrial restructuring in energy conservation and emission reduction varies with the study object and study method according to scholars due to the lack of a quantitative research on the potential for energy conservation and emission reduction nationwide. In this part, a dynamic input-output model for industrial restructuring is established and the capital coefficient matrix K is estimated based on the final demand in the input-output relationship with the national economic system as a whole. The regression analysis and optimization techniques are adopted to predict the consumer product mix in 2020, and to provide the balanced economy growth rates and the corresponding balanced industrial structure under different combinations of consumption and export rates in conjunction with the forecast of export product mix. Carbon emissions in 2020 under high, medium, and low GDP targets are calculated based on the balanced industrial structure. Under the premise of rigid consumption and export product mix, a dynamic input-output model for industrial restructuring is established with investment as objects. Through investment adjustments, the allocation structure of final demand is changed, and the potential for energy conservation and emission reduction in balanced economic growth is estimated. The results show that if the energy structure and unit energy consumption of all sectors remain at the 2005 level, industrial restructuring alone could reduce the production energy consumption and production carbon emissions by 25.6%–31% in 2020, and industrial restructuring could contribute up to about 60% to the carbon emission intensity target of China.

DOI: 10.4324/9781003388500-6

On the basis of industrial restructuring, in conjunction with China's energy supply and supply structure forecast in 2020, energy production function of each sector is estimated by the transcendental logarithmic production function. The output elasticity of coal, oil, natural gas, heat, and electricity in all sectors are calculated. The optimization model for the minimum carbon emissions under energy supply and substitution constraints is established. Energy restructuring schemes for all subsectors are given and the potential for energy conservation and emission reduction of energy restructuring are calculated. We found that energy restructuring can reduce energy consumption by 20.17%–24.87% and carbon emissions by 27.12%–32.08%.

Finally, on the basis of the added values, total energy consumption, and energy structure of all sectors after industrial restructuring, the carbon emission intensity of all sectors are calculated, and the total carbon emission indicators and carbon emission intensity indicators for all sectors are provided, and corresponding suggestions for carbon emission targets are offered.

5 Industrial differences in carbon emissions

5.1 Impacts of industrial structure on carbon emissions

5.1.1 Industrial structure and carbon emissions

5.1.1.1 Theoretical research on industrial structure and carbon emissions

As one of the most important material input factors in production, energy is of great importance to economic growth. However, energy plays a different role in different stages of economic development. The relationship between energy consumption and economic development depends on the industrial structure at the stage of economic development. According to the theory of economic development, the history of economic development can be divided into four stages. The first stage is an agriculture-dominated stage, in which agriculture has a dominant position in the national economy, and the industry dominated by handicrafts transits to light and textile industry gradually. Since agriculture itself does not require much energy, the economic growth of agriculture has a low demand for energy. Therefore, a constraint on energy in regard to the economic growth of agriculture does not appear. The second stage is dominated by light and textile industry. At this stage, the economic growth has a higher demand for energy. Therefore, energy has become an important factor in production. The third stage is dominated by heavy and chemical industry. At this stage, the energy demand for economic growth and the demand for energy as raw materials increase sharply. The economy is heavily dependent on energy. The fourth stage is dominated by high-tech industries. At his stage, due to technology progress and emerging industries, energy efficiency increases significantly. The energy demand for economic growth has begun to decline and tends to be stable gradually.

At the first stage of economic development, industrialization has not begun. With a large proportion of the primary industry and limited demands on the energy, carbon dioxide emissions are very little and human impacts on the natural environment are minimal. Since the first industrial

DOI: 10.4324/9781003388500-7

revolution, human beings entered the industrial age gradually. At the same time, demands for energy have gradually increased, resulting in an increase in carbon dioxide emissions each year. However, the carbon dioxide emissions during this period have not yet had a significant impact on the climate. With the second industrial revolution, fossil fuels began to be used more than before, and carbon dioxide emissions increased sharply. According to the data from the Carbon Dioxide Information Center of the Oak Ridge National Laboratory in the US, the cumulative carbon dioxide emissions from human activities were only 4.6 billion tonnes before 1850. In the 100 years from 1850 to 1949, this figure rose to 179.967 billion tonnes; while in the last 60 years from 1950 to 2009, this figure reached a staggering 1,081.7 billion tonnes.

Industrialization in China started late. Therefore, the cumulative carbon emissions are relatively small. However, carbon dioxide emissions have grown rapidly due to the total economy growth in China and China's industrial restructuring. As early as 1676, William Petty described the tendency of industrial restructuring. Since the income from industry is more than that from agriculture and the income from commerce is more than that from industry, the income gap in these sectors will surely attract labors to industry from agriculture and then from industry to commerce. This means that the human society must begin with an agricultural society and then transit from an industrial society to the one dominated by tertiary industries. Economist Clark summed up the above-mentioned laws, and his theory is called "Petty-Clark Theorem". After that, in 1932, Japanese economist Akamatsu Kaname (1974) pointed out the way for backward countries to catch up with developed countries in industrial restructuring, that is, the theory of "the flying geese pattern of development". According to this theory, in the catching-up process, the evolution of backward countries' industrial structure presents a flying geese pattern, that is, an "import-domestic production-export" industrial pattern. There are two variations of this pattern. One involves the sequence of industrial development, which is, generally speaking, a continuous advancing process from the industry for means of consumption to the industry for means of production, from agriculture to light industry, and then to heavy industry. The other involves diversified and advanced industrial structure, with products in the industry for means of consumption shifting from crude products to refined products and products in the industry for means of production shifting from daily necessities to production necessities. When the dominant industrial structure shifts from light industry to heavy industry, high pollution and high emissions are unavoidable.

In the 1990s, American economists Grossman and Krueger studied the relationship between environmental quality and economic growth and proposed the famous "Environmental Kuznets Curve", which believes that with economic development, pollution gradually increases and the environment deteriorates. When economic growth reaches a certain level, the pollution emissions reach a peak and environmental deterioration reaches the limit. Then, the pollution gradually decreases and the environmental quality improves. The relationship between the pollution and national income shows an inverted U-shaped curve. This is also the "pollute first, control later" path that developed countries have gone through in their own development.

Both the "Petty-Clark Theorem" and the "Environmental Kuznets Curve" demonstrate that in the process of economic development, there is bound to be a stage where pollution and emissions are rising. When the industrial structure has gone through the heavy industrialization stage, with the rising incomes, shift of consumption to tertiary industries, and progress in energy utilization technology, carbon emissions will surely decrease. So if we can continuously adjust and optimize the industrial structure according to the evolutionary law of industrial structure and actively guide the industrial structure to evolve in a more advanced direction, then we will be able to pass the inflection point of "Environmental Kuznets Curve" as soon as possible and step on the development path of low carbon economy.

5.1.1.2 Empirical studies on industrial structure and carbon emissions

The study on the relationship between industrial structure and carbon emissions can be divided into the following three aspects:

1 Carbon emission intensity varies greatly with industries
2 Changes in industrial structure will affect energy consumption and energy efficiency
3 Changes in industrial structure will ultimately affect the amount and intensity of carbon emissions

Lazhen Xiao and Yan Chen (2011) found in the Kruskal-Wallis test significant differences in the carbon emission intensity of eight industries. Among them, the production and supply industries for electricity, gas, and water have the highest emission intensity and agriculture, construction, wholesale, retail, catering, accommodation, and other industries have lower carbon emission intensity. Dafeng Xu (2011) also found in input-output analysis obvious industrial differences in carbon productivity in China.

The industrial structure first directly affects the total energy consumption. Zhengnan Lu (1999) and Zhijun Guo et al. (2003) confirmed in regression analysis that the total energy consumption is highly correlated with the industrial structure. Lei Zhang and Yuanxi Huang (2008) proved the accelerating effect of the economic structure dominated by the secondary industry on energy consumption demand using the "structural evolution-energy consumption" model and the "structural evolution-unit energy consumption" model. Shouli Chen and Liping Ma (2011) have slightly different conclusions. They found in the factor decomposition analysis that industrial restructuring reduced the total amount of energy consumption before 2002, and later promoted the energy consumption to some extent. Industrial structure also affects energy efficiency indirectly. Yihua Yu et al. (2011) proved the positive correlation between the proportion of secondary industry and carbon emission intensity through a panel data regression. Xiaqing Fang et al. (2008) believed that the decrease in energy intensity in China over the years is caused by the increased energy utilization efficiency of each industry. Therefore, the industrial structure has an important impact on energy utilization efficiency. Yuanyuan Zhang(2012) created a mathematical function with energy efficiency and industrial structure, and concluded basically the same as Lei Zhang in an empirical analysis on the correlation between industrial structure and energy efficiency in Shanxi province. Da Wang (2008) analyzed the impact of industrial restructuring on energy efficiency using Guangzhou city as a sample and concluded that technological progress is the root cause of energy efficiency improvement, while industrial restructuring can affect energy efficiency to a large extent. Guangtao Guo et al. (2008) developed a multi-objective optimization model of energy input and output based on the energy input-occupancy-output table in western China and found that when the GDP and labor compensation increase by more than 8% and technologies, product prices, and other conditions remain unchanged, the energy consumption per unit of GDP could be decreased by 2.7% through industrial restructuring alone. Ke Li (2010) developed a nonlinear threshold co-integration model based on the correlation between economic structure and energy efficiency, and corresponding test and estimation results showed that before 1976, changes in economic structure restrained the decrease in energy intensity, but the effect of economic structure on changes in energy intensity from 1977 to 2002 was just the opposite.

Scholars have also carried out relevant researches on the relationship between industrial structure and carbon emissions. Using energy and economy data from 1978 to 2008, Zuo Yu and Xianli Kong (2011) studied the relationship among China's industrial structure, economic growth, and coal consumption and found a long-term equilibrium between them. The existing industrial structure has large negative effects on economic growth, and it is not sustainable. Also, the excessive coal consumption leads to high carbon emissions. Changde Zheng and Shuai Liu (2011) conducted an empirical analysis of the relationship between industrial structure and carbon emissions in China's provinces using interprovincial panel data from 2000 to 2008.They found that economic growth is the main reason for the increase of carbon emissions in China. Specifically, for each industry, the secondary industry has the greatest impacts on carbon emissions, while the primary and tertiary industries have fewer impacts. Chaoxian Guo (2012) decomposed China's carbon emissions between 1996 and 2009 through the LMDI decomposition method and found that China's carbon dioxide emissions increased by 4.64678 billion tonnes during this period. Among them, 498.87 million tonnes were due to the effect of industrial structure, which contributed 10.7% to the growth of carbon emissions. Although the industrial structure is not the most important factor, industrial restructuring has definitely driven the growth of carbon emissions.

At the same time, scholars have also studied the emission reduction effects of industrial structure and got some useful conclusions. Lei Zhang et al. (2011) put forward the "energy structure-carbon emission" model on the basis of the original research and concluded that the high proportion of the secondary industry leads to the slowdown process of the "inverted U-shaped" unit energy consumption and the industrial structure could contribute 60% to the carbon emission reduction. Feiyan Tang and Wen Zhang (2011) verified and came to the same conclusion as Lei Zhang did with interprovincial panel data. Shuhui Wen et al. (2012) conducted an empirical analysis of energy consumption effect and carbon emission effect of industrial evolution in Yunnan province with the "industrial structure evolution – energy consumption correlation" model and the "industrial structure evolution – unit energy consumption correlation" model, and concluded that industrial restructuring is important for improving energy efficiency and reducing emissions. Honglei Niu and Keshen Jiang (2012) simulated the operation using the non-dominated sorting genetic algorithm with elite strategy and obtained the Pareto optimal solution set for Jiangsu province. The results showed that under the premise of stable growth and employment, industrial restructuring is still a means to reduce carbon emissions to a certain extent.

The relationship among industrial restructuring and total energy consumption, energy efficiency, carbon emissions, and carbon emissions intensity is considered relevant by most scholars, but there are disputes about whether the correlation is linear or nonlinear, positively or negatively related. This is due to differences in research methods and economic variables representing the industrial structure as well as differences in sampling periods. To conclude, industrial restructuring could affect energy consumption and energy intensity, which would, in turn, affect carbon emissions and carbon emission intensity.

5.1.2 The industrial structure and its revolutionary characteristics in China

Since the reform and opening up in 1978, China's industrial structure has gone through great changes. In general, among the three major industries, the proportion of the primary industry has been decreasing and its share in the national economy has dropped from about 30% at the beginning to 10%. The proportion of the secondary industry has been maintained between 40% and 50%. The tertiary industry has developed rapidly, with a proportion increasing from 20% at the beginning of the reform and opening up to 40% (Figure 5.1). China has shifted from an agricultural country to an

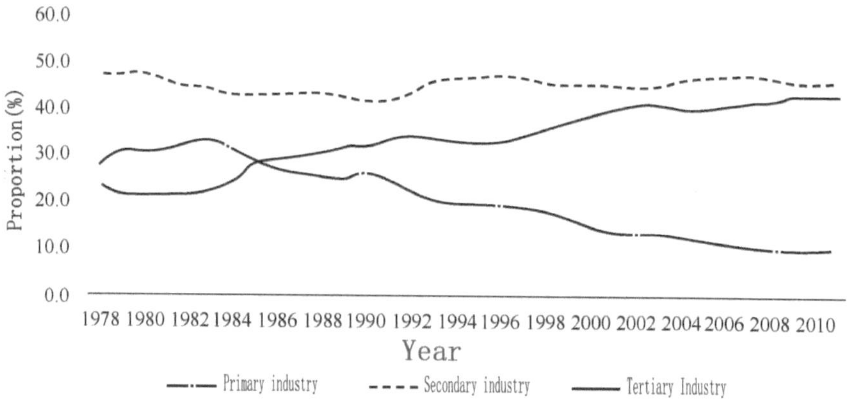

Figure 5.1 Changes to the proportion of China's three major industries in the national economy

industrial country and moving toward an industrial power. During this process, the proportional relationship of the three major industries has been improved greatly compared with the previous one and the industrial structure is becoming more rational. However, the development of the tertiary industry has relatively lagged behind. The degree of heavy industrialization has increased and the proportion of industry in the economy has increased in recent years, leading to serious environmental problems. The demand for industrial restructuring is urgent.

On the whole, the primary industry shows a downward trend. In the early 1980s, its proportion in the national economy remained at about 30% and reached the highest level in 1982 at 33.4%. After that, the proportion of the primary industries began to decrease year after year, especially in the 1990s. After 2000, the downward trend slowed down and the proportion of industries tended to be stable. In 2010, the proportion of the primary industry in GDP dropped to 10.1%. In terms of labor input, it is basically the same as the changes in industrial structure. The proportion of the labor force of the primary industry in the total labor force had been decreasing since the reform and opening up, from 70.5% in 1978 to 36.7% in 2010. However, problems, including the unbalanced development of agriculture, forestry, animal husbandry, and fishery industries, unreasonable internal structures, low agricultural productivity, and labor surplus, have been troubling the development of the primary industry.

The secondary industry is the lifeblood of the national economy and plays an important role. On the whole, the proportion of the secondary industry in GDP does not change significantly. It decreased from 48.2% in 1980 to 41.34% in 1990, then went through ups and downs, and finally rose to 48.0% in 2006 and dropped to 46.8% in 2010. The labor force absorbed by the secondary industry increased continuously from 17.3% in 1978 to 28.7% in 2010. However, the total labor forces absorbed are significantly less than those absorbed by primary and tertiary industries.

From the perspective of the internal structure of industry, China's industry has gone through three stages: light industry, light and heavy industry, and heavy industry. In the early 1980s, in order to adjust the unreasonable structure of light and heavy industries, the light and textile industry were given priority to develop. The proportion of light industry rapidly rose to 50%. From the mid-to-late 1980s to the early 1990s, the light and heavy industries were basically balanced and maintained a stable development trend. After 1992, China's industrial structure showed an obvious trend of heavy industrialization. By 1998, the value added of heavy industry has accounted for nearly 60% of the total industry. Since 1999, heavy industry has been developing rapidly and the industrial growth has been once again dominated by heavy industry. After 2002, the proportion of heavy industry in the value added of an industry had continued to rise and reached 71.36% by 2010. The gap between the proportion of light industry and heavy industry has widened significantly. Heavy industrialization has been increasingly prominent. Heavy industrialization has had a significant impact on China's economic development, making China go through an extensive growth phase with high energy consumption, high emissions, and high input.

The proportion of the tertiary industry in the economy shows an upward trend. In the early 1980s, the proportion of the tertiary industry in GDP remained at about 22%. Since 1983, the proportion of the tertiary industry had increased rapidly, and it exceeded 40% by 2001 for the first time. However, after 2002, the proportion of the tertiary industry began to decrease slightly, and it rose back to 43.4% in 2009. Similarly, the proportion of labor force absorbed by the tertiary industry rose from 12.2% to 34.6% in 2010. While the proportion of the tertiary industry in the national economy is increasing, the internal structure of the tertiary industry is also changing. After over 30 years of development, the focus of the tertiary industry has gradually shifted from traditional industries such as commerce, catering, resident services, transportation, and post and telecommunication services to emerging industries, including tourism, information, science and technology, education, culture, finance, and real estate. Although China's tertiary industry has developed rapidly, it still lags behind national economic development as well as the level of developed countries in the world.

5.1.3 Energy consumption characteristics and energy structure of each industry

There are significant industrial differences in energy consumption. Table 5.1 shows the total energy consumption and the energy consumption structure of the industry by end use energy consumption[1] in 2010. In 2010, the total energy consumption for all industries and household use was 3,050.096

Table 5.1 Energy consumption structure by industry in 2010

Sectors	*Total energy consumption (10,000 tonnes standard coal)*	*Coal (%)*	*Petroleum (%)*	*Natural gas (%)*	*Heat (%)*	*Electricity (%)*
Agriculture	6,477.3	20.5	31.16	0.1	0.05	48.19
Mining industry	15,040.9	37.31	1.1	9.23	1.11	41.24
Food, beverage, and tobacco products industry	5,437.8	38.09	6.02	1.44	8.16	46.28
Textile and leather products industry	7,316.9	19.35	3.73	0.36	10.23	66.32
Other manufacturing industries	7,275.7	29.34	4.08	0.65	7.66	58.27
Production and supply industries of electricity, heat, and water	13,592.6	17	1	0.08	1.71	80.2
Coking and petroleum processing industry	13,303.5	13.81	59.51	3.44	7.66	15.58
Chemical industry	35,489.9	30.79	14.28	6.96	7.17	40.8
Non-metallic mineral products industry	27,655.8	59.75	9.75	2.04	0.16	28.3
Metal products manufacturing industry	72,700.9	58.08	1.41	0.6	1.64	38.26
Machinery and equipment manufacturing sector	13,812.1	17.14	7.77	3.53	2.27	69.29
Construction industry	6,226.3	8.49	66.09	0.25	0.36	24.81
Transportation and post and telecommunication services	25,614.7	1.76	83.86	5	0.22	9.17
Wholesale, retail, accommodation, and catering sector	6,826.8	21.67	10.58	5.31	1.95	60.5
Other service industries	13,680.5	10.85	27.45	2.53	1.88	57.29
Household consumption	34,557.9	21.48	15.73	8.73	6.65	47.40

Source: Calculated by the author according to the data listed in the China Energy Statistical Yearbook (2011).

million tonnes of standard coal. Among them, the production energy consumption involved about 2,704.517 million tonnes of standard coal, accounting for 88.67% of the total energy consumption, while household energy consumption accounted for less than 12%. Among the production energy consumption, the primary industry consumed the least energy, accounting for only 2.12% of the total energy consumption. Followed by the tertiary industry, accounting for 15.12% of the total energy consumption, energy consumption is mainly concentrated in the secondary industry, accounting for more than 70% of the total energy consumption.

In the secondary industry, the majority energy consumption is from the industry. Since 1990, the proportion of China's industrial energy consumption has remained about 70%. During the period of the Tenth Five-Year Plan (2001–2005), the proportion of industrial energy consumption to total energy consumption showed an upward trend. The industrial energy consumption contributed more than 70% to the growth of total energy consumption. Therefore, the industrial sector is under the greatest pressure on energy conservation and emission reduction. Specifically, the metal manufactured product sector has the largest end use energy consumption. The energy consumption in 2010 exceeded 700 million tonnes of standard coal, accounting for more than 28% of the total energy consumption, followed by the chemical industry, which consumes 354.899 million tonnes of standard coal. In addition, industries such as transportation, warehousing, post and communications services, and non-metallic mineral products industry are also sectors with high energy consumption. In addition to the significant industrial differences in total energy consumption, there are also significant differences in the industrial energy structure. In terms of the energy structure of the sub-sectors, agricultural energy consumption is dominated by electricity and oil, which together account for more than 80% of the energy consumption in agricultural sector. In the tertiary industry, oil is the main source of the energy consumption in transportation, warehousing, post and communications services, accounting for 83.86%; the energy consumption in wholesale, retail, trade, accommodation, catering, and other industries is dominated by electricity, accounting for more than 55%; the household energy consumption is also dominated by electricity, accounting for 47.4%, while the consumption of coal and oil is relatively low, accounting for 21.48% and 15.73%, respectively.

There are also significant differences in the structure of energy consumption within the secondary industry. Sectors related to energy production and its conversion show different preferences for types of energy consumption. The energy consumption of the mining sector is dominated by electricity and coal, which together account for nearly 80%. The energy consumption of electricity, heat, and water production and supply industries is dominated by electricity, which accounts for 80.20% of the total energy consumption of the sector. Among the energy consumption in the petroleum and coking processing industry, petroleum has the largest share, accounting for 59.51%. Among the other industries, the energy structure of the non-metallic mineral products industry and metal products manufacturing industry is dominated by coal, accounting for nearly 60% of the total energy consumption. The construction industry is dominated by petroleum consumption, accounting for 60.09% of the energy consumption. In the remaining five industries (food, beverage, and tobacco products industry; textile and leather product industry; other manufacturing industries; and chemical industry and machinery and equipment manufacturing industry), the energy consumption is dominated by electricity and coal.

China's electricity production mainly relies on thermal power, and clean electricity accounts for only 15% of the total electricity consumption. It means that except for the industry of petroleum and coking processing, construction industry and transportation, warehousing and post and telecommunication services, other industries consume coal-based energy directly or indirectly. Natural gas, as clean energy, is mainly used in household consumption currently due to its small supply. Among other industries, the natural gas consumption in only three industries, including mining industry, chemical industry, and transportation, warehousing, and post and telecommunication services accounts for more than 5% of the total energy consumption.

5.2 Carbon emissions accounting by sector

5.2.1 Accounting methods for carbon dioxide emissions by industry

The statistics in China do not provide data on carbon dioxide emissions at the industrial and regional levels, so they can only be calculated based on energy consumption in industry and region. *China Energy Statistical Yearbook* provides two types of energy consumption data by industry: one is the total energy consumption data by industry, including coal, coke, crude oil, gasoline, kerosene, diesel, fuel oil, natural gas, and electricity; and the other is the end use energy consumption by industry. We can calculate the end use energy consumption of 20 kinds of energy in all 53 industries based on the end use energy consumption and energy balance sheet of industrial sectors.

In most of the existing studies, the first type of energy consumption data is used to calculate carbon dioxide emissions of the industry. Yanmei Li, Tao Yang (2011) and Peng Yuan et al. (2012) had the total energy consumption of each industry multiplied by the corresponding carbon dioxide emission coefficient, and obtained the carbon dioxide emissions of each industry. Although studies of Zhu Liu et al. (2011) on carbon emissions accounting for urban energy consumption showed that the carbon emissions calculated based on the energy balance sheet and total energy consumption have no great differences and are higher than those calculated based on the end use energy consumption, in terms of carbon dioxide emissions accounting in the industry, there are some problems in calculating carbon dioxide emissions by total energy consumption in sub-sectors. First, the total energy consumption by industry is the production energy of each industry rather than final consumption or final emissions. For non-energy producing sectors, the total energy consumption is the production consumption and also the final consumption, while for the energy producing sectors, the production energy consumption is much larger than the final consumption of the sector. Second, the total energy consumption by industry includes both primary energy and some secondary energy. Calculating the carbon dioxide emissions with the data multiplied by the corresponding carbon dioxide emission coefficient may involve omissions and double counting. For example, coke in secondary energy is produced by heating coal, which has been calculated. If the coke is calculated again, it is a double calculation. In petroleum products, in addition to gasoline, kerosene, diesel, and fuel oil, there are liquefied petroleum gases and refinery dry gases which are not provided in the total energy consumption data by industry. Thus, there are omissions in the calculation of carbon dioxide emissions.

In comparison, it seems more reasonable to calculate carbon dioxide emissions based on end use energy consumption of the sub-sectors. End use energy consumption is the final consumption of each industry. According to the relevant definitions of OECD or IEA, the end use energy consumption only measures the energy obtained from the inlet of end use energy-consumed equipment, which is equal to primary energy consumption minus the losses in energy processing, conversion and storage and transportation and energy used by the energy industry. However, in *China Energy Balance Sheet*, the end use energy consumption calculated by equivalent value only deducts losses in coal preparation, coking, oilfield, oil refining, and power transmission and distribution. Power generation losses and energy used in the energy industry are not deducted. Therefore, the calculated end use energy consumption in China is much higher than that calculated according to the international prevailing standards,[2] and it is close to the total energy consumption.

However, there are also problems to calculate carbon emissions based on end use energy consumption. First, the actual carbon dioxide emissions of the sector, which are not equal to the end use energy consumption emissions of the sector, are mainly related to heat and electricity in the secondary energy. Although heat and electricity are consumed by each sector, emissions from electricity generation and heat supply are in the electricity and heat producing sectors. Second, as for the accounting of electricity and heat emissions, the energy conversion efficiency varies from year to year due to the technological progress. Therefore, the emission coefficients of heat and electricity should also vary from year to year. In this chapter, when calculating the carbon dioxide emissions from electricity and heat, we need to calculate the total carbon dioxide emissions from electricity and heat production based on the fossil energy consumed for power generation and heat supply, then divide it by the total electricity and heat consumed for production and household activities to obtain the unit emission coefficient of electricity and heat, and then calculate the carbon dioxide emissions from electricity and heat in each sector. Since the use of heat and electricity does not produce emissions, the emissions are only indirect emissions of the sector. However, from the other perspective, demand is the root cause of production. According to the consumer responsibility principle, it is reasonable to attribute the electricity and heat emissions to the corresponding consumption sector. The calculated carbon dioxide emissions can be regarded as those from final consumption.

5.2.2 Carbon emission coefficients

To calculate the carbon emissions of each sector according to energy consumption, we need to calculate carbon emission coefficients of each energy. In the end use energy consumption, energy consumption is subdivided into 20 categories. All the energy sources, except heat and electricity, produce emissions during the usage. According to the carbon emission coefficients in the IPCC list and the average low calorific value of each energy source in the *China Energy Statistical Yearbook*, the carbon dioxide emission coefficients of each energy source can be calculated. Among them, some of the data of carbon oxidation rates are from the *Guidelines on Preparation of Provincial Greenhouse Gas Emission Inventory* (F.G.B.Q.H. [2011] No. 1041). The carbon oxidation rate of the remaining energy is the same as that of the same type of energy. Other coking products from coking and other petroleum products from petroleum refining are not included in the carbon dioxide emission coefficients of energy sources. Because "other coking products" mainly refer to products such as benzene and coal tar and "other petroleum products" mainly refer to lubricating oil, lubricating grease, naphtha, paraffin, petroleum asphalt, etc. (see the relevant descriptions in the *Energy Statistics Sheet*). These products are mainly used for non-combustion purposes and do not produce carbon dioxide emissions, so the corresponding emissions are not calculated (Zhu Liu et al., 2011). The other energy is energy sources other than fossil energy and electric heat energy, including biomass energy and solar energy, which also produce a small amount of carbon dioxide emissions. However, such emissions can be ignored since their emission coefficients are not available and their proportion in the total energy consumption is small. The carbon dioxide emission coefficients of the other 15 types of energy sources are shown in Table 5.2.

The emission coefficients of electricity and heat need to be calculated based on energy balance sheet. First, we need to obtain the amount of each energy source consumed by thermal power generation according to the energy balance sheet; then calculate the emissions from the consumption

Table 5.2 Carbon emission coefficients by energy source

Types of energy sources	*Average low calorific value (kJ/kg)*	*Converted standard coal coefficients (kgce/kg)*	*Carbon content per unit of calorific value*	*Carbon oxidation rates*	*Carbon dioxide emission coefficient (kg-CO/kg)*
Raw coal	20,908	0.7143	26.4	0.94	1.9003
Cleaned coal	26,344	0.9000	26.8	0.94	2.4336
Other cleaned coal	8,363	0.2857	26.6	0.94	0.7668
Briquette	15,910	0.5429	26.6	0.94	1.4588
Coke	28,435	0.9714	29.5	0.93	2.8604
Coke oven gas	17,354	0.5929	12.1	0.98	0.7546
Other coal gas	16,308	0.5571	12.1	0.98	0.7091
Crude oil	41,816	1.4286	20.1	0.98	3.0202
Gasoline	43,070	1.4714	18.9	0.98	2.9251
Kerosene	43,070	1.4714	19.5	0.98	3.0179
Diesel	42,652	1.4571	20.2	0.98	3.0959
Fuel oil	41,816	1.4286	21.1	0.98	3.1705
Liquefied petroleum gases	50,179	1.7143	17.2	0.98	3.1013
Refinery dry gases	46,055	1.5714	18.2	0.98	3.0119
Oilfield gas	38,931	1.3300	15.3	0.99	2.1622

of each energy source according to the carbon dioxide emission coefficient of each energy source; finally, add them up to obtain the carbon dioxide emissions from thermal power generation. In conjunction with the primary electrical energy (hydro, nuclear, and wind power) production and electricity transmission losses in the current year, we can obtain the final electricity consumption. On this basis, we can obtain the carbon dioxide emissions produced from per unit of the end use electricity consumption. The specific data are shown in Table 5.3. The carbon dioxide emission coefficients of thermal power can be calculated similarly, and the results are shown in Table 5.4.

Description: 1 Fuel with low calorific value equal to 29,307 kilojoules (kJ) is called one kilogram of standard coal (1 kgce).

2 The first two columns of data in the table are from General Principles for Calculation of the Comprehensive Energy Consumption (GB/T 2589-2008).

3 The last two columns of data in the table are from the Guidelines on Preparation of Provincial Greenhouse Gas Emission Inventory (F.G.B.Q.H. [2011] No. 1041).

Table 5.3 End use electricity emission coefficients in 1995–2005

Year	*Thermal power emissions (10,000 tonnes of carbon dioxide)*	*Thermal power generation (0.1 billion kW·h)*	*Carbon emission coefficients of thermal power (CO_2 kg/ kW·h)*	*Supply of other electricity (0.1 billion kW·h)*	*Losses (0.1 billion kW·h)*	*End use electricity emission coefficients (CO_2 kg/ kW·h)*
1995	86,260.71	8,043.16	1.0725	1,980.24	744.52	0.9296
1996	98,885.17	8,777.13	1.1266	1,987.16	769.45	0.9894
1997	97,316.47	9,240.70	1.0531	2,043.70	798.38	0.9281
1998	97,084.96	9,441.00	1.0283	2,157.43	790.93	0.8983
1999	102,598.59	10,257.04	1.0003	2,048.16	861.93	0.8966
2000	108,761.79	11,141.86	0.9762	2,330.82	936.71	0.8676
2001	116,389.92	11,834.25	0.9835	2,889.84	1,033.47	0.8501
2002	133,224.71	13,381.36	0.9956	3,084.60	L,168.66	0.8709
2003	158,985.42	15,803.61	1.0060	3,228.55	1,260.68	0.8946
2004	178,876.67	17,955.88	0.9962	4,016.46	1,420.60	0.8704
2005	199,779.14	20,473.36	0.9758	4,467.41	1,706.47	0.8598
2006	228,934.76	23,696.03	0.9661	4,892.41	1,859.30	0.8565
2007	250,379.38	27,229.33	0.9195	5,483.05	2,062.28	0.8169
2008	259,009.35	27,900.78	0.9283	6,640.02	2,137.33	0.7993
2009	275,402.91	29,827.80	0.9233	7,204.90	2,258.77	0.7920
2010	297,798.59	33,319.28	0.8938	8,617.18	2,570.21	0.7565

Table 5.4 Carbon dioxide emission coefficients of heat in 1995–2005

Year	*Heating emission (10,000 tonnes of carbon dioxide)*	*Heat supply (10,000 million kJ)*	*Losses (10,000 million kJ)*	*End use heat (10,000 million kJ)*	*End use heat emission coefficients (kg CO_2/10,000 kJ)*
1995	10,325.40	107,200.21	1,485.56	105,714.65	0.9767
1996	11,280.66	114,830.13	1,705.08	113,125.05	0.9972
1997	12,884.64	117,569.51	1,664.70	115,904.81	1.1117
1998	13,364.25	127,067.73	1,072.33	125,979.42	1.0608
1999	16,427.16	134,446.33	1,678.81	132,791.57	1.2371
2000	18,139.19	146,136.16	1,760.58	144,374.18	1.2564
2001	18,497.32	153,203.45	1,795.58	151,406.65	1.2217
2002	18,470.42	164,190.77	2,005.84	162,179.84	1.1389
2003	21,993.01	177,300.00	2,026.06	175,278.41	1.2547
2004	23,311.50	192,586.50	2,260.48	190,322.38	1.2248
2005	26,872.15	228,894.66	2,631.20	226,259.34	1.1877
2006	29,573.90	246,811.92	2,973.26	243,835.54	1.2129
2007	30,399.07	258,602.67	3,168.90	255,426.55	1.1901
2008	29,805.67	257,763.00	3,168.90	254,588.50	1.1707
2009	30,403.92	266,747.95	3,168.90	263,753.11	1.1527
2010	30,569.82	293,422.74	3,400.00	321,885.43	0.9497

4 Calculation of "carbon dioxide emission coefficient": take raw coal as an example, $1.9003 = 20{,}908 \times 10^{-9} \times 26.37 \times 0.94 \times 1{,}000 \times 3.667$.
5 The carbon emission coefficients of ten energy sources, such as raw coal, in the table are from Energy Management Contract website (http://www.emcsino.com/html/news_info.aspx? Id=9267), and the coefficients of the other five energy sources (cleaned coal, other cleaned coal, briquette, coke-oven gas, and other coal gas) are obtained based on the same calculation.
6 The unit of measurement for natural gas and coal gas is cubic meter.

5.2.3 Carbon emissions by sector

The total emissions of each sector can be calculated according to the end use energy consumption and emission coefficients of each sector. Since electricity and heat do not produce emissions during use, the corresponding emissions are indirect emissions of each sector. Without the indirect emissions, the remaining emissions are produced from the direct consumption of fossil energy of the sector, which should be called the direct emissions of the sector. Indirect emissions of all sectors are direct emissions from the production and supply of electricity, heat, and water (sector 6).

Table 5.5 lists the total and direct emissions of 15 sectors. In terms of total emissions, the metal manufactured products sector (sector 10) has the largest total emissions, which accounts for 21%–30% of the total emissions of end use energy, followed by the chemical industry (sector 8), and the non-metallic mineral products industry (sector 9). The sum of the emissions of these three sectors accounts for 47.7%–51.8% of the total emissions. In terms of direct emissions, if all indirect emissions are recorded as direct emissions from the production and supply of electricity, heat, and water, then such direct emissions are the largest, which account for 34.3%–46.4% of the total emissions. The direct emissions of the metal manufactured products sector, the non-metallic mineral products industry and the chemical industry are also large, with a sum accounting for 31.7%–37.5% of the total emissions. The production and supply of electricity, heat, and water, the metal manufactured products sector, the non-metallic mineral products industry, and the chemical industry are the four sectors with the largest direct emissions and also key sectors for emission reduction. The transportation, post and telecommunication services, (sector 13) and extractive industries (sector 2) also have large direct emissions, and are crucial sectors for emission reduction.

Table 5.5 Carbon dioxide emissions by sector (10,000 tonnes of CO_2)

	Sector	*Total emissions in 1995*	*Direct emissions in 1995*	*Total emissions in 2000*	*Direct emissions in 2000*	*Total emissions in 2005*	*Direct emissions in 2005*	*Total emissions in 2010*	*Direct emissions in 2010*
1	Agriculture, forestry, animal husbandry, and fishery industry	13,500.52	79,72.33	9,011.13	4,382.32	14,177.65	7,496.41	14,998.32	7,602.53
2	Extractive industries	17,632.05	9,705.83	20,586.51	11,074.84	29,792.21	16,262.98	35,660.38	20514.87
3	Food, beverage, and tobacco products industry	10,696.45	7,213.87	9,383.99	5,709.00	11,200.97	6,085.56	13,692.67	6,500.63
4	Textile and leather products industry	10,197.79	5,530.51	8,624.36	3,909.97	15,116.03	4,977.31	17,961.40	4,392.27
5	Other manufacturing industries	10,302.19	6,545.97	10,638.39	4,909.48	15,292.36	6,042.75	18,024.64	6,439.5
6	Production and supply industries of electricity, heat, and water	10,482.68	87,452.8	18,450.38	117,745.45	26,674.03	202,342.10	33,893.29	287,382.05
7	Coking and petroleum processing industry	7,697.95	4,227.87	11,849.37	6,147.17	14,592.18	8,236.43	16,043.62	8,962.72
8	Chemical industry	42,493.58	27,371.70	40,474.29	22,026.72	63,142.98	30,380.09	75,370.63	34,015.46
9	Non-metallic mineral products industry	32,987.28	27,363.3	34,277.86	27,505.15	49,470.34	37,191.19	62,152.38	43,502.96
10	Metal products manufacturing industry	55,556.36	40,837.99	60,076.89	40,158.61	28,211.20	86,506.06	190,032.85	120,879.31

11	Machinery and equipment manufacturing sector	12,845.97	7,665.41	12,156.82	5,393.63	20,451.52	7,244.37	33,045.99	9,522.13
12	Construction industry	3,100.10	1,607.1	3,560.33	2,157.12	5,058.83	2,992.22	7,582.77	3,864.21
13	Transportation and post and telecommunication services	12,473.47	10,770.39	23,394.99	20,861.86	38,399.26	34,573.07	53,988.06	48,275.78
14	Wholesale, retail, accommodation, and catering sector	4,769.66	2,910.23	7,215.07	3,446.39	11,519.24	4,788.78	15,897.41	5,752.84
15	Other service industries	10,336.11	7,896.88	12,865.66	7,138.32	21,377.51	9,356.99	31,174.76	1,911.91
Total		255,072.17	255,072.17	282,566.04	282,566.04	464,476.30	464,476.30	619,519.17	619,519.17

Notes

1 End use energy consumption refers to the amount of energy from inlet of the end use energy-consumed equipment, which is equal to the amount of primary energy consumption minus the losses in energy processing, conversion, storage, and transportation and the amount of energy used by the energy industry.
2 Source: http://baike.baidu.com/view/1486796.htm.

References

Akamatsu Kaname. *Scrap gold currency and international economy*. Tokyo: Toyo Keizai, 1974.

Chen Shouli, Ma Liping. The influence of industrial structure changes on energy consumption in China: statistical analysis based on factor decomposition. *China Statistics*, 2011, 49 (11): 52–53.

Fang Xiaqing, Wu Tianzu, Ou-Yang Zhongjian. A study of the influence of industrial structure on energy utilization efficiency in China. *Northern Economy*, 2008, 16 (20): 9–11.

Guo Chaoxian. Impact of industrial structure change on carbon emission in China. *China Population, Resources and Environment*, 2012, 22 (7): 15–20.

Guo Guangtao, Guo Juer, Xi Youmin, Meng Lei. Study on energy saving and consumption reduction effect of industrial structure adjustment in Western China and its realization strategy. *China Population, Resources and Environment*, 2008, 18 (4): 44–49.

Guo Zhifei, Li Fei, Qin Wei. Co-integration and analysis of China's industrial structure change on energy consumption. *Journal of Industrial Technological Economics*, 2007, 17 (11): 97–101.

Li Ke. Threshold effect analysis of China's economic restructuring on energy efficiency. *Proceedings of 2010 the 3rd International Conference on Power Electronics and Intelligent Transportation System* (Volume 5), Chengdu, Sichuan, 2010.

Li Yanmei, Yang Tao. Structural decomposition of China's CO_2 emission intensity decline: based on the input output analysis from 1997 to 2007. *Resource Science*, 2011, 35 (4): 605–611.

Liu Zhu, Geng Yong, Xue Bing, et al. A calculation method of CO_2 emission from urban energy consumption. *Resources Science*, 2011, 33 (7): 1325–1330.

Lu Zhengnan. Empirical analysis of the influence of industrial structure adjustment on energy consumption in China. *The Journal of Quantitative & Technical Economics*, 1999, 16 (12): 53–55.

Niu Honglei, Jiang Keshen. Low carbon effect measurement of industrial structure adjustment based on NSGA genetic algorithm. *Industrial Economics Research*, 2012, 11 (1): 62–69.

Tang Feiyan, Zhang Wen. Analysis of the carbon emission effect of china's industrial structure changes: an empirical study based on provincial data. *Economic Problem*, 2011, 33 (9): 32–35.

Wang Da. *A study of the influence of industrial structure change on energy efficiency*. Wuhan: Huazhong University of Science and Technology, 2008.

Wen Shuhui, Wang Haiting, Xuan Juneng. Analysis on energy consumption effect and carbon emission of industrial structure adjustment in Yunnan Province. *Academic Research*, 2012, 20 (3): 74–77.

Xiao Lazhen, Chen Yan. Industrial difference analysis of carbon emission in China. *Statistics and Decision*, 2011, 27 (2): 106–108.

Xu Dafeng. Carbon productivity, industrial relationship and low carbon economic structure adjustment: an empirical analysis based on Chinese input-output table. *Soft Science*, 1999, 16 (12): 53–55.

Yu Yihua, Zheng Xinye, Zhang Li. Economic development level, industrial structure and carbon emission intensity: an analysis of provincial panel data in China. *Economic Theory and Business Management*, 2011, 31 (3): 72–81.

Yu Zuo, Kong Xianli. Industrial structure, economic growth and Sustainable Utilization of coal resources in China. *Finance & Trade Economics*, 2011, 6: 129–135.

Yuan Peng, Cheng Shi, Liu Haiyang. The impact of international trade on the growth of China's CO_2 emissions: a decomposition method based on the combination of SDA and LMDI. *Economic Review*, 2012, 33 (1): 122–132.

Zhang Lei, Huang Yuanxi. Energy saving potential analysis of China's industrial structure. *China Soft Science*, 2008, 23 (5): 27–29, 32–34, 51.

Zhang Lei, Li Yanmei, HuangYuanxi, Wu Yingmei. Potential analysis of structural energy conservation and emission reduction in China, *China Soft Science*, 2011, 2: 42–51.

Zhang Yuanyuan. *Analysis of the influence of industrial structure change on energy efficiency in Shanxi Province*. Xi'an: Shanxi Normal University, 2012.

Zheng Changde, Liu Shuai. Industrial structure and carbon emissions: an empirical analysis based on China's provincial panel data. *Research on Development*, 2011, 2: 26–33.

6 Industrial restructuring and its potential to save energy and reduce emissions

6.1 The dynamic input-output model of industrial restructuring

6.1.1 Directions and basic hypotheses of industrial restructuring

6.1.1.1 Directions of industrial restructuring

In recent years, the contradiction in economic structure has become increasingly prominent due to the one-sided pursuit of economic growth. The heavy industrialization since 2002 has resulted in serious surplus of industrial products and production capacity, pollution, and a decrease in the proportion of tertiary industry. In the troika of economic growth, namely consumption, investment, and exports, consumption is seriously insufficient and its contribution to economic growth has dropped to a minimum. Exports have suffered major setbacks since the global financial crisis of 2008, making China's economic growth heavily reliant on investment. The overheating and surplus investments have exacerbated the trend of heavy industrialization. These changes, in turn, exacerbate the contradictions in the industrial structure. Therefore, only by promoting industrial restructuring, improving economic efficiency, and optimizing the ratio of investment and consumption can China expand employment opportunities and promote the development of low carbon economy and therefore enhance the transformation of China's economic growth pattern.

Due to the complex industrial linkages in economy systems, separate restructuring to a sector or several sectors, which contributes to the industrial restructuring and carbon emission reduction in the sector, may have a significant negative impact on the stability of China's economic growth. Therefore, the impact of industrial restructuring on economic growth, the impact of industries on carbon emissions, and the solution to maintain the stability of economic systems should be taken into account during industrial restructuring.

The input-output model, which studies the quantitative dependent relationships between the input and output of each sector in economic activities, reflects the direct and indirect relationship among sectors and the overall

DOI: 10.4324/9781003388500-8

balance of economic systems. Research on changes in industrial structure based on the input-output model can avoid the impact of single industrial restructuring on the stability of economic systems. What's more, according to economic growth theories, long-term economic growth is achieved through capital accumulation and technological progress, while short-term economic growth depends on demand growth. Growth in consumption, investment, and exports is the driver of short-term economic growth. Under certain final demand, different final demand structures correspond to different industrial structures and have different impacts on the national economy.

In the input-output model, end use, also known as final demand, can be divided into three major parts: final consumption *C*, capital formation *I*, and net exports *E*. Final consumption *C* includes household consumption and government consumption. The volume of final consumption *C* and its structural changes depend on changes in income and propensity to consume; capital formation *I* is determined by the propensity to invest and investment structure; and a country's net export *E* is determined by its economic development level, economic structure, and international trade environment.

As shown in Figure 6.1, when the total volume and structure of final consumption *C*, capital formation *I* and net export *E* are given, and the total volume of end use *Y* and its structure are also determined. When the input-output relationship remains unchanged, the total output *X* and the industrial structure are also determined. Therefore, industrial restructuring through adjusting the structure of final demand considers the complex industrial linkages in economic systems and will not have a large impact on the stability of economic growth, thus ensuring a steady and balanced economic growth. Generally speaking, the restructuring of final demand involves the ratio of consumption, investment, and net export in end use or the internal structure of consumption, investment, and net export. For a long term, the export-oriented economic growth based on investment and export has led to an unreasonable industrial structure and high carbon

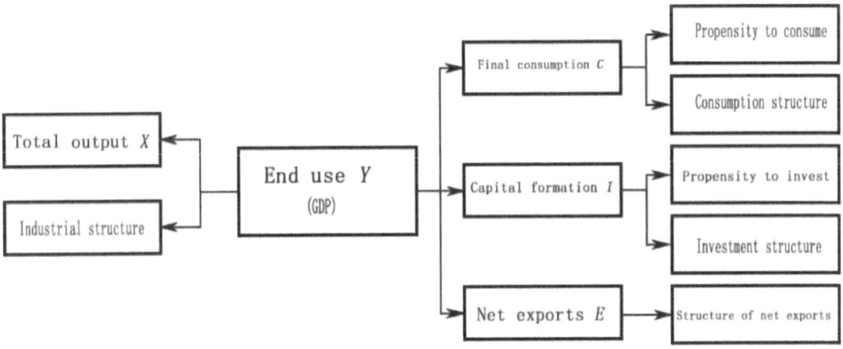

Figure 6.1 Principle of industrial structure adjustment

emissions per unit of GDP in China. Table 6.1 shows the carbon emissions per unit of final product in China calculated according to the domestic part of the input output table in 1995, 2000 and 2005 in conjunction with energy consumption data.

As shown in Table 6.1, in the end use, the emission per unit of product in the consumption sector is the lowest, the emission per unit of product in the export sector is the highest, and the emission per unit of product in the investment sector is close to that of the export sector. Therefore, a large ratio of investment and export in end use is unfavorable for emission reduction. In terms of the structure of China's final products in 1995, 2000, and 2005, the structural change is little before 2000; the ratio of consumption drops significantly to nearly 40% after 2000, while the ratio of export increases significantly to nearly 30%. The changes in the demand structure make the industry evolve toward high carbon emissions, thus making it difficult for China to reduce the carbon emission intensity during the period.

From this point of view, the industrial restructuring should start from demand to adjust the demand structure, increase the ratio of consumption, especially household consumption in the final demand, and reduce the ratio of net exports, shifting the entire national economy from investment- and export-driven to consumption-driven growth mode. Only in this way can the industrial structure evolve toward low carbon emissions.

6.1.1.2 Basic hypotheses of industrial restructuring

In the adjustment of the final product structure, the ratio of investment demand, consumption demand, and export demand should be adjusted first. Generally speaking, the ratio of consumption demand in total demand is determined by the distribution structure of the national economy. As long as the distribution structure is adjusted, the ratio of investment, consumption, and export in final demand can tend to be reasonable.

Table 6.1 Comparison of carbon intensity of consumption, investment, and exports and the structure of the final products

	1995		*2000*		*2005*	
	Emission per unit of product (tonnes/ CNY 10,000)	*The structure of the final product (%)*	*Emission per unit of product (tonnes/ CNY 10,000)*	*The structure of the final product (%)*	*Emission per unit of product (tonnes/ CNY 10,000)*	*The structure of the final product (%)*
Consumption	3.321	50.11	2.2400	50.19	1.4945	39.78
Investment	4.9072	30.74	3.2247	29.03	2.3565	31.27
Export	5.1481	19.15	3.3806	20.78	2.4405	28.95

Internal restructuring features long duration, high level of difficulty, and unobvious effect due to the strong rigidity of propensity to consume and consumption structure. The export product structure depends on the country's resources, technology level, labor costs, international economic environment, etc., which cannot be changed in the short term. In contrast, the propensity to invest and investment structure are greatly influenced by policies, so they are easier to be adjusted.

China's primary task is economic development at present as it is in the middle stage of industrialization, which features unwealthy people and relatively backward economy. Our current primary task is to develop economy. Therefore, the industrial restructuring goal in this chapter is not to reduce carbon emissions directly, but to achieve balanced and steady economic growth. However, the industrial restructuring can also reduce carbon emissions under the guidance of low carbon policy.

In order to better examine the impact of changes in industrial structure on carbon emissions, we make the following hypotheses:

(1) The input-output structure remains unchanged

(2) The energy consumption per unit of product in each sector remains unchanged

(3) The energy structure of each sector remains unchanged

(4) Consumption is rigid

Therefore, the propensity to consume and consumption structure evolve according to their own laws, that is, residents have different marginal propensities to consume products in each sector. However, such propensity remains unchanged within a certain period of time:

(5) The propensity to invest and investment structure can be changed by macro-control

(6) The export product structure remains unchanged in the short term

6.1.2 Dynamic input-output model of industrial restructuring

Compared with the static input-output model, the dynamic input-output model, which separates investment from end use and endogenizes it, is used to study and analyze the total investment and composition of the national economy in the forward period and quantitative relationship and internal relationship between the scale and structure of production in each economic sector in the subsequent period (Xikang Chen and Cuihong Yang, 2011).

Given the input-output model:

$$X - AX = Y = Y^C + Y^I + Y^E \qquad (6.1)$$

Wherein X is the total output vector, A is the direct consumption coefficient matrix, and Y is the end use vector. Y^C, Y^I, and Y^E are consumption, capital formation, and net exports in end use, respectively.

In order to remove the impact of the embodied carbon of import intermediate use products on the calculation of emission coefficients and carbon emissions, the input-output model and data in this chapter do not include the domestic part of import intermediate use and import end use. Therefore, A is actually the domestic direct consumption coefficient matrix A_d and Y^E are exports.

In terms of the total output X of the current period, AX is used for intermediate consumption, Y^C and Y^E are used for consumption and exports, respectively, and the remaining Y^I is used to expand reproduction. The increase in total output X is determined by the capital formation Y^I of the previous year. Therefore:

$$Y^I = K\left[X(t+1) - X(t)\right] \tag{6.2}$$

Wherein K is the capital coefficient matrix, $K = \left(k_{ij}\right)_{n \times n}$; $k_{ij} = \dfrac{\Delta S_{ij}}{\Delta x_j}$, ΔS_{ij} is the increase in the total output of sector j, $j$and Δx_j requires the products of sector i as newly added capital.

Substituting Equation (6.2) into Equation (6.1), then:

$$X(t) - AX(t) - K\left[X(t+1) - X(t)\right] = Y^C(t) + Y^E(t) \tag{6.3}$$

An ideal steady-state industrial structure involves all sectors growing continuously at a fixed growth rate. Such industrial structure is called a balanced-growth industrial structure, that is:

$$X(t+1) = (E+P)X(t) \tag{6.4}$$

Wherein E is the unit matrix; $P = \begin{bmatrix} p_1 & & \\ & \ddots & \\ & & p_n \end{bmatrix}$, and p_i is the growth rate of the total output of sector i.

According to Equations (6.3) and (6.4):

$$X(t) = (E - A - KP)^{-1}\left[Y^C(t) + Y^E(t)\right] \tag{6.5}$$

$$Y(t) = (E - A)(E - A - KP)^{-1}\left[Y^C(t) + Y^E(t)\right] \tag{6.6}$$

Then, set $C = \begin{bmatrix} C_1 \\ C_2 \\ \vdots \\ C_n \end{bmatrix}$ as consumer product structure; $E = \begin{bmatrix} E_1 \\ E_2 \\ \vdots \\ E_n \end{bmatrix}$ as export product structure; α as the share of consumption in final demand, namely consumption rate; β as the share of export in final demand, namely export rate; $y=\sum_{i=1}^{n} Y_i$ as the total final product; and then $Y^C=\alpha yC$, $Y^E=\beta yE$. Set $\mu^T=\begin{bmatrix} 1 & 1 & \cdots & 1 \end{bmatrix}$, with constant growth rate of the total output in each sector, that is $p_1 = p_2 = \cdots = p_n = p$. We can have the following equation:

$$\mu^T Y = \mu^T (E-A)(E-A-pEK)^{-1}(\alpha C+\beta E)y \tag{6.7}$$

Therefore:

$$\mu^T (E-A)(E-A-pEK)^{-1}(\alpha C+\beta E)=1 \tag{6.8}$$

Obviously, Equation (6.8) is a monadic equation for p, which may be solved to obtain p, which is the balanced growth rates of the total output under given consumption rate, export rate, consumption structure, and export structure.

The solution p of the balanced industrial structure is related to not only the proportion of consumption α and proportion of exports β in the final product, but also the internal structure C of consumption, the internal structure E of exports, and the capital coefficient K. In the following, C and E will be first predicted and then K will be estimated.

6.2 Prediction of consumer product structure and export product structure

Consumption is the driving force behind production as well as the purpose and end of production. The relationship between consumption structure and industrial structure is determined by the relationship between consumption and production. Consumption structure and industrial structure have the same identity and they are the premise of each other. Industrial structure determines consumption structure. Without changes in industrial structure, changes in consumption structure will have no material foundations. Consumption structure also determines industrial structure to some degree. The upgrading of consumption structure is the ultimate driving force behind production, while industrial structure must adapt to consumption structure (Jie Zhu, 2007).

Changes in consumer demand will inevitably lead to changes in market demand, which will promote development of related industries and cause changes in industrial structure. The upgrade of consumer demand will promote continuous innovation of industries, and at the same time, the potential consumer demand also provides a huge space for the adjustment and upgrading of industrial structure, indicating a cause relationship between the consumer demand structure and the industrial structure. As for the consumer demand, resident consumption demand, as the most important factor affecting industrial structure, has direct influence on industrial structure and guides changes in the industrial structure through income and prices. An increase in residents' income will cause changes in demand structure, which requires a corresponding adjustment in industrial structure to adapt to this change. Similarly, changes in commodity prices caused by changes in resident consumption demand will lead to a reallocation of production resources, thus realizing the industrial restructuring.

6.2.1 Prediction of urban and rural residents' consumption structure

In economics, means of consumption is divided into means of subsistence, means of enjoyment and means of development by their importance to people's life and the way people consume them, and further categorized into different consumption objects, including food, clothing, housing, goods, transportation, fuel, and services. Consumption structure refers to the proportion of each of these consumption objects in consumption expenditures. There are many factors that affect the consumption structure, including social development level, economic system, industrial structure, demographic structure, prices, consumers' income level, and psychology. When the society is in a stable development stage, residents' propensity to consume and consumption structure are rigid and will not change easily. However, as the increase in income, residents' consumption behavior will change gradually, which leads to changes in residents' consumption structure.

According to studies, the only important factor which affects residents' consumption behavior in China is income at the present stage. Residents' consumption behavior basically conforms to the absolute income hypothesis of Keynes. China is a country with separate urban-rural structure. Urban and rural residents have a big gap in income level and consumption demand stage. Their consumption demands for various commodities vary greatly and so do consumption behaviors. Consumption structure of urban and rural residents is predicted as follows.

6.2.1.1 Estimation of urban and rural residents' marginal propensity to consume by commodity

1 Urban residents' marginal propensity to consume by commodity

   The per capita consumption expenditure of urban residents in China has grown rapidly. In 2011, the per capita consumption expenditure of urban residents in China was CNY 15,160.89, 3.68 times as high as that in 1993 after removing the factor of price changes. With the increase in consumption expenditures, the consumption structure of urban residents has also changed. Although the consumption expenditure on food continues to increase, the proportion of food in the total consumption has been declining year by year, and the Engel coefficient has dropped from 57.5% in 1978 to 36.3% in 2011. Correspondingly, residents' expenditures on transportation and communications, clothing, housing, and cultural and educational entertainment increased rapidly, accounting for 14.18%, 11.05%, 9.27%, and 12.21% of the total consumption expenditures per capita of urban residents, respectively, in 2011. It indicates that consumption of urban residents in China has been changing from subsistence consumption to living consumption.

Figure 6.2 shows the trend of consumption expenditure of urban residents over time calculated at the price of the current year. It can be seen from the figure that among the per capita consumption expenditure, food consumption is the largest, but with slow growth rate. Among the other consumption expenditures, transportation and communications expenditure grows most rapidly, followed by consumption expenditures in cultural and educational entertainment. The expenditure on clothing shows a downward trend before 2003 and an accelerated growth trend after 2003. The consumption expenditures on transportation and communications, cultural and educational entertainment, household equipment, and miscellaneous expenditures differ greatly around 2003. Changes in per capita consumption expenditure structure reflect diversified and enriched consumption of urban residents amid rising income.

For urban residents, set INC_t^U as the per capita disposable income of urban residents in the *t*th year, C_{it}^U as the per capita consumption expenditure of urban residents on *i*th category of commodity in the *t*th year, $i = 1, 2, \ldots, 8$, representing food, clothing, housing, household equipment and services, transportation and communications, cultural and educational entertainment, medical and healthcare, and others (miscellaneous), respectively. In order to remove the factor of price changes and make the income and consumption in different years comparable, this book converts both the income and consumption expenditures into constant prices in 2005, in which the income conversion is based on GDP index and the consumption expenditure conversion is based on consumer price index (CPI) by category. Since *China Statistical Yearbook* only provides CPI by category from 1994 to 2011, the sample period of the variables selected in this book is 1993–2011.

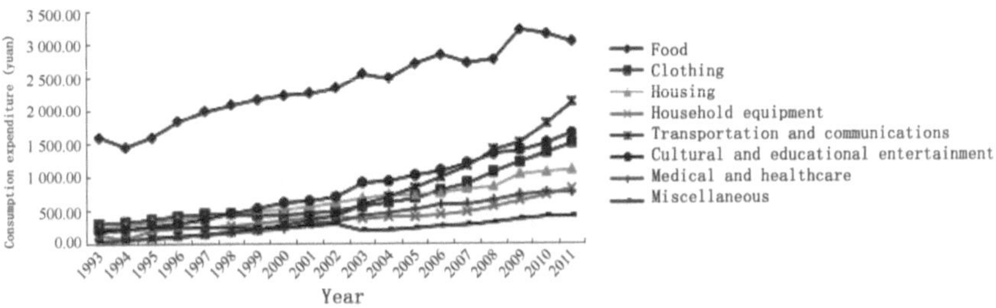

Figure 6.2 Trend of consumption by commodity of urban residents over time

According to the absolute income hypothesis of Keynes, a consumption function model is established:

$$C_{it}^{U} = \beta_{0i} + \beta_{1i}\text{INC}_{t}^{U} + \mu_{it}\,(i = 1,2,\ldots,\ 8) \tag{6.9}$$

It can be seen from Figure 6.2 that consumer behavior is inconsistent before and after 2003; therefore, a dummy variable is introduced as follows:

$$D_t = \begin{cases} 1, & t \geq 2003 \\ 0, & t < 2003 \end{cases} \tag{6.10}$$

It refers to changes in consumer behavior. The above model is revised as:

$$C_{it}^{U} = \beta_{0i} + \beta_{1i}\text{INC}_{t}^{U} + \beta_{2i}D_t + \beta_{3i}D_t \cdot \text{INC}_{t}^{U} + \mu_{it}\,(i = 1,2,\ldots,\ 8) \tag{6.11}$$

Model 6.11 is estimated with EViews6 software and the consumption function by category of urban residents can be obtained after deletion of insignificant variables. The results are shown in Table 6.2.

In terms of the estimated results, there are significant differences in urban residents' marginal propensity to consume commodities. The consumer behavior of urban residents has changed significantly before and after 2003. Before 2003, urban residents' marginal propensity to consume food is the highest, reaching CNY 0.2401, followed by expenditure on cultural and educational entertainment (CNY 0.1535), and transportation and communications (CNY 0.1096). The marginal propensity to consume housing is also high, reaching CNY 0.1013. The lowest marginal propensity to consume is other services (CNY 0.0128), followed by clothing (CNY 0.0425). After 2003, the marginal propensity to consume food, housing, household equipment and supplies, cultural and educational entertainment, and medical and healthcare has decreased to different degrees. Among them, the marginal propensity to consume food decreases the most, followed by cultural and educational entertainment and housing. In contrast, the marginal propensity to consume clothing, transportation and communications, and miscellaneous goods increases to different degrees. Among them, the marginal propensity to consume clothing increases the most, followed by transportation and communications.

According to the explanation of Household Survey Office for National Bureau of Statistics (NBS) in the residential survey, current per capita housing expenses of urban residents only include utility bills and fuel costs, house decorating costs, maintenance costs of building materials, rent, heating fees, property management fees, maintenance fees, and

Table 6.2 Estimation of the consumption function by commodity of urban residents

Dependent variable	*Explanatory variable*				*Statistics*				$\overline{R}^2$
	constant	*INC*	*D*	*D·INC*	*t (constant)*	*t (X)*	*t (D)*	*t (D·INC)*	
C_1^U	522.37	0.2401	1,385.58	−0.1718	2.228	5.787	4.218	−3.861	0.9361
C_2^U	166.5	0.0425	−562.9	0.0624	3.002	4.574	−7.662	6.276	0.9934
C_3^U	−163.76	0.1013	389.45	−0.0518	−2.563	9.474	4.602	−4.519	0.9834
C_4^U	−152.53	0.0725		−0.0195	−3.183	8.838		−3.832	0.9548
C_5^U	−447.8	0.1096	−384.86	0.0490	−6.341	9.277	−4.114	3.866	0.9965
C_6^U	−466.31	0.1535	651.52	−0.0731	−6.965	13.696	7.346	−6.088	0.9940
C_7^U	−304.41	0.0814	416.3	−0.0427	−8.048	12.857	8.308	−6.286	0.9935
C_8^U	178.74	0.0128	−195.85	0.0119	7.765	3.324	−6.423	2.875	0.9596

exclude expenditures on purchase and construction of a house or an imputed rent of self-owned houses. Therefore, the housing expenses of urban residents have been seriously underestimated. Since 2003, China's house prices have been growing increasingly. Housing expenses have surpassed expenditures on food, transportation and communications, and cultural and educational entertainment services, becoming major household expenses of urban residents. This is the reason why the consumer behavior of urban residents took a new turn in 2003. According to the consumption and income of urban residents calculated at constant prices in 2005, it can be estimated that the marginal propensity to consume of urban residents before 2003 was CNY 0.826, and it decreased to CNY 0.574 after 2003. The reason for such sharp decline is that the exorbitant housing prices have created excessive expenses on purchasing houses, and then the expenditure on food, education, and medical care has been cut down, which leads to a downward trend of the total consumption expenditure of residents.

Among the eight items of consumption expenditures, the marginal propensity to consume clothing and transportation and communications has increased significantly. On the one hand, the price index of these two categories of products is low, which has been under 100 for a long term, so its share calculated at constant prices has increased. On the other hand, with the gradual introduction of cars, mobile phones, and the Internet to ordinary households, urban residents' expenses on transportation and communication have increased rapidly, resulting in an increase in the share of clothing expenses and transportation and communications expenses.

Thus, with the rising income, the consumption of urban residents in China has experienced the third structural upgrade. The expenses on housing, automobiles, and communications of urban residents have grown rapidly, while the food expenses, as the subsistence consumption, have grown relatively slowly. Since 2003, the expenses on purchasing houses of urban residents have increased sharply, resulting in a great decline in the marginal propensity to consume food, cultural and educational entertainment, housing, medical and healthcare as well as significant changes in the consumption structure of urban residents.

2 Rural residents' marginal propensity to consume by commodity

Since the 1990s, rural residents' income has increased at a rate less than that of urban residents, resulting in weak consumption growth and slow changes in the consumption structure in rural areas. In 2011, the per capita net income of rural household in China was CNY 6,977.29, 2.97 times as high as that in 1993 after removing the factor of price changes. The Engel coefficient of rural residents decreased from 67.7% in 1978 to 40.4% in 2011, a decrease of 27.3 percentage points. However, after 2006, the Engel coefficient declined slowly, with a decline of only 2.64 percentage points in the next six years until 2011. Figure 6.3 shows the changes in the proportion of each commodity in the total consumption expenditure calculated at the price of the current year. It can be seen from the figure that the largest part of consumption of rural residents is still food, followed by housing expenditures, and the proportions of other commodity expenditures except miscellaneous items are relatively close, which are below 10%.

For rural residents, set INC_t^R as the per capita net income of rural residents in the tth year, C_{it}^R as the per capita consumption expenditure of rural residents on ith category of commodity in the tth year, $i = 1, 2, \ldots, 8$, representing food, clothing, housing, household equipment and services, transportation and communications, cultural and educational entertainment, medical and healthcare, and others, respectively. In order to remove the factor of price changes and make the income and consumption in different years comparable, this section converts both the income and consumption expenditures into constant prices in 2005, in which the income conversion is based on GDP index and the consumption expenditure conversion is based on CPI by category. Since *China Statistical Yearbook* only provides CPI by category from 1994 to 2011, the sample period of the variables selected in this section is 1993–2011.

According to the absolute income hypothesis of Keynes, a consumption function model is established:

$$C_{it}^R = \beta_{0i} + \beta_{1i}\text{INC}_t^R + \mu_{it}\,(i = 1,2,\ldots,8) \tag{6.12}$$

Since consumer behavior has been inconsistent during the whole sample period, dummy variables are introduced, respectively:

$$D_{it} = \begin{cases} 1, & t \geq 2000 \\ 0, & t < 2000 \end{cases} \quad (i = 2,4,5) \tag{6.13}$$

$$D_{it} = \begin{cases} 1, & t \geq 2005 \\ 0, & t < 2005 \end{cases} \quad (i = 1,3,6,7,8) \tag{6.14}$$

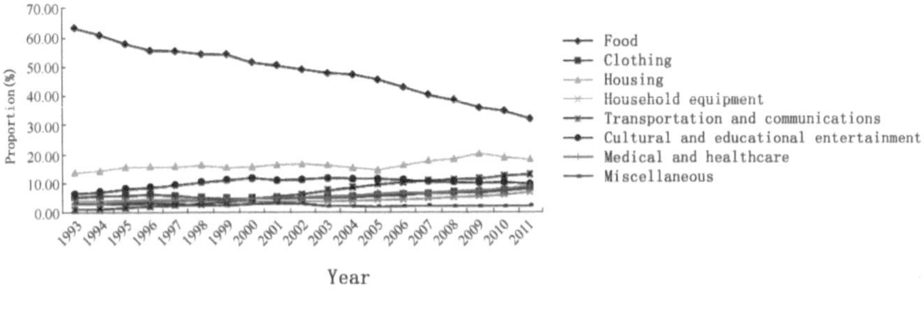

Figure 6.3 Changes in consumption structure of rural residents

It refers to changes in consumer behavior. The above model is revised as:

$$C_{it}^{R} = \beta_{0i} + \beta_{1i}\mathrm{INC}_{it}^{R} + \beta_{2i}D_{it} + \beta_{3i}D_{it} \cdot \mathrm{INC}_{it}^{R} + \mu_{it}\,(i = 1,2,\ldots,8) \quad (6.15)$$

Model 6.15 is estimated with EViews6 software and the consumption function by commodity of rural residents can be obtained after deletion of insignificant variables. The results are shown in Table 6.3.

In terms of the estimated results in Table 6.3, before the changes in consumer behavior of rural residents, among the consumption expenditures of rural residents calculated at constant prices, the marginal propensity to consume food is the highest, reaching CNY 0.1703, which decreases significantly to less than CNY 0.07 in 2005. The second largest marginal propensity to consume is housing expenses, reaching CNY 0.1612, free from significant changes during the whole sample period. The marginal propensity to consume cultural and educational entertainment is also high, reaching CNY 0.1453. After the changes in consumer behavior, the highest marginal propensity to consume falls in transportation and communications expenses, reaching CNY 0.0680 before 2005 and increasing by CNY 0.0780 to CNY 0.1460 in 2005, ranking only second to the marginal propensity to consume housing, which may be due to the gradual opening up of rural life and the transfer of rural surplus labor to urban areas. The marginal propensity to consume food and cultural and educational entertainment decreases by CNY 0.1067 and CNY 0.0998, respectively. In general, the marginal propensity to consume food and cultural and educational entertainment has been decreasing, while the marginal propensity to consume clothing, household equipment and services, and transportation and communications has increased to different degrees; the marginal propensity to consume other commodities remains unchanged, indicating that the consumption of rural residents has been upgrading as well.

6.2.1.2 *Prediction of consumption expenditure by commodity and total consumption of urban and rural residents*

1. Prediction of consumption expenditure by commodity of urban and rural residents. According to the consumption function by commodity of urban and rural residents, in order to predict the per capita consumption expenditure by commodity of residents in the future, it is necessary to know their income status in the future. According to relevant reports, the income of urban and rural residents is expected to maintain a growth rate of 7.3%–7.4% by 2020, doubling the income in 2020.[1] Based on the estimated average annual growth rate of 7.3%, with the income data of 2011 calculated at constant prices in 2005 as a benchmark, the

Table 6.3 Estimation of the consumption function by commodity of rural residents

Dependent variable	*Explanatory variable*				*Statistics*				$\overline{R}^2$
	constant	*INC*	D_i	$D_i{\cdot}INC$	*t (constant)*	*t (INC)*	$t\ (D_i)$	$t\ (D_i{\cdot}INC)$	
C_2^U	532.35	0.1703	423.71	−0.1067	22.74	17.698	11.879	−9.305	0.9945
C_3^U		0.0406	−124.83	0.0418		26.237	−12.252	13.374	0.9883
C_1^U	−109.15	0.1612			−5.417	26.022			0.9755
C_4^U		0.0319	−115.04	0.0376		24.245	−13.299	14.161	0.9877
C_5^U	−109.59	0.0680	−147.6	0.0780	−1.937	2.594	−2.48	2.921	0.9919
C_6^U	−170.05	0.1453	314.74	−0.0998	−10.298	21.397	12.51	−12.328	0.9926
C_7^U	−127.12	0.0871			−18.171	40.487			0.9897
C_8^U	20.158	0.0124			4.404	8.827			0.8209

per capita income of urban and rural residents from 2012 to 2020 can be estimated, as shown in Table 6.4.

According to the prediction, calculated at constant prices in 2005, the per capita disposable income of urban residents will reach CNY 34,079.06 in 2020 and the per capita net income of rural residents will reach CNY 10,447.35. Assuming that the marginal propensity to consume different commodities for urban and rural residents remains basically unchanged, substituting the income data into the consumption function model 6.11 and model 6.15, the per capita consumption expenditure by commodity of urban and rural residents in 2020 can be estimated and the corresponding consumption structure can be calculated, as shown in Table 6.5.

According to the prediction, the consumption expenditure of urban residents in 2020 will reach CNY 20,765.87, calculated at constant

Table 6.4 Estimated per capita income of urban and rural residents (yuan)

Year	*Per capita disposable income of urban residents*	*Per capita net income of rural residents*
2011	18,075.49	5,541.26
2012	19,395.00	5,945.77
2013	20,810.84	6,379.81
2014	22,330.03	6,845.54
2015	23,960.12	7,345.26
2016	25,709.21	7,881.47
2017	27,585.98	8,456.82
2018	29,599.76	9,074.16
2019	31,760.54	9,736.58
2020	34,079.06	10,447.35

Table 6.5 The per capita consumption expenditure by commodity and consumption structure of urban and rural residents in 2020

Category	*Urban residents*		*Rural residents*	
	Consumption expenditure (yuan)	*Consumption structure (%)*	*Consumption expenditure (yuan)*	*Consumption structure (%)*
Food	4,267.78	20.55	1,620.49	22.01
Clothing	3,178.41	15.31	736.59	10
Housing	1,912.39	9.21	1,574.47	21.38
Household equipment and services	1,655.18	7.97	610.77	8.3
Transportation and communications	4,573.23	22.02	1,268.19	17.22
Cultural and educational entertainment	2,922.99	14.08	620.13	8.42
Medical and healthcare	1,431.99	6.9	782.44	10.63
Miscellaneous	823.91	3.97	149.9	2.04
Total	20,765.87	100	7,362.98	100

prices in 2005. Transportation and communications will account for the largest amount of consumption expenditure, reaching CNY 4,573.23, accounting for 22.02% of total consumption expenditure, followed by food consumption expenditure (CNY 4,267.78, accounting for 20.55% of the total consumption expenditure), clothing expenses (accounting for 15.31% of the total consumption expenditure), and cultural and educational entertainment expenses (accounting for 14.08% of the total consumption expenditure). In terms of rural residents, the consumption expenditure calculated at constant prices in 2005 will reach CNY 7,362.98. Food and housing will be the two largest expenses, reaching CNY 1,620.49 and CNY 1,574.47, accounting for 22.01% and 21.38% of total consumption expenditure, respectively. The transportation and communications expenses will be CNY 1,268.19, making up the third largest consumption expenditure and accounting for 17.22% of total consumption expenditure. The proportion of medical and health expenses will rise to 10.63%. According to the standard put forward by the Food and Agriculture Organization of the United Nations, an Engle coefficient above 59% represents poverty, 50%–59% indicates barely meeting daily needs, 40%–50% represents a moderately well-off standard of living, 30%–40% represents a well-to-do standard of living, and below 30% represents a wealthy life. China's Engel coefficients of both urban and rural residents in 2020 have been below 30%, indicating that people have led quite a wealthy life. However, such calculation does not consider the factor of price changes. Food price index is usually the highest in the CPI, much higher than the composite price index. Therefore, when the consumption expenditure is calculated at constant prices, the proportion of food expenses will be underestimated, but so is the Engel coefficient.

2 Prediction of population and the ratio of urban to rural population in China. In order to obtain the structure of residents' total consumption, it is necessary to estimate the total consumption of urban and rural residents according to the urban and rural population in the future. Therefore, we need to project China's total population and the share of urban population in 2020. Figure 6.4 shows the demographic trend of China from 1980 to 2010. It can be seen from the figure that China's population growth rate has been declining slowly year by year and the population growth is declining. Therefore, this section forecasts China's population growth using Logistic models.

Given the Logistic model:

$$X_t = \frac{L}{1+ae^{-bt}} (t = 0,\ldots, 34) \tag{6.16}$$

Wherein L is the limit value of the total population.

In order to avoid estimating L, the model is transformed into a linear model:

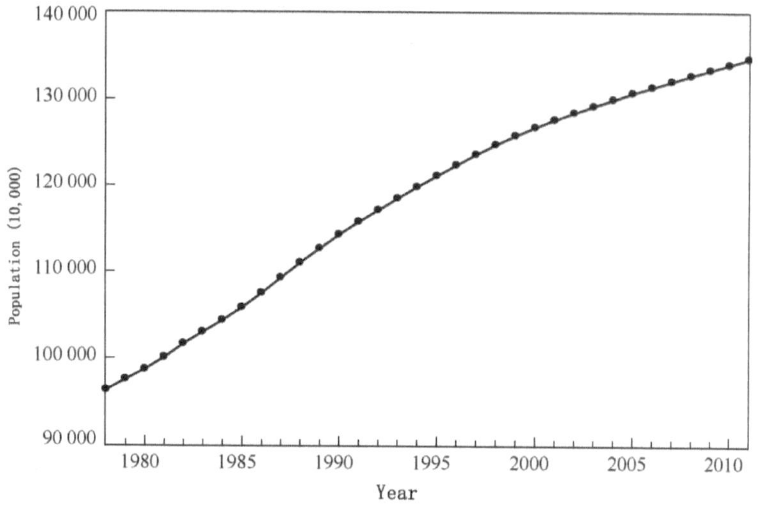

Figure 6.4 Timing diagram of the total population at the end of the year

$$\frac{1}{X_t} = \frac{1}{L}\left(1 - e^b\right) + e^b \frac{1}{X_{t-1}} + \mu_t \tag{6.17}$$

Model 6.17 is estimated using population data, then:

$$\frac{1}{X_t} = 2.68 \times 10^{-7} + 0.958246 \frac{1}{X_{t-1}} \tag{6.18}$$

$R^2 = 0.999\ 673$ $F = 94\ 914.98$

Figure 6.5 shows the changes in the share of urban population in China from 1978 to 2011. It can be seen from the figure that the share of urban population increases in a relatively slow manner before 1995 and increases rapidly after 1995 amid accelerated urbanization. Considering inconsistent speed of urbanization before and after 1995, the following variable is introduced:

$$D_t = \begin{cases} 1, & t \geq 1995 \\ 0, & t < 1995 \end{cases} \tag{6.19}$$

Assume that the share of urban population is a function of time t:

$$CT_t = \beta_0 + \beta_1 t + \beta_2 D_t + \beta_3 t D_t + \mu_t \ (t = 0, \ldots, 34) \tag{6.20}$$

Estimate the model with EViews6 software:

$$CT_t = 16.205 + 0.9979t - 8.589D_t + 0.2907t \cdot D_t \quad (6.21)$$

$$\overline{R^2} = 0.9806 F = 557.45 \text{D.W.} = 0.3096$$

According to the prediction model for both the total population and the proportion of urban population, the total population and the urban population proportion are predicted, respectively, and the total urban and rural population is calculated accordingly, as shown in Table 6.6. The prediction results show that China's total population will reach

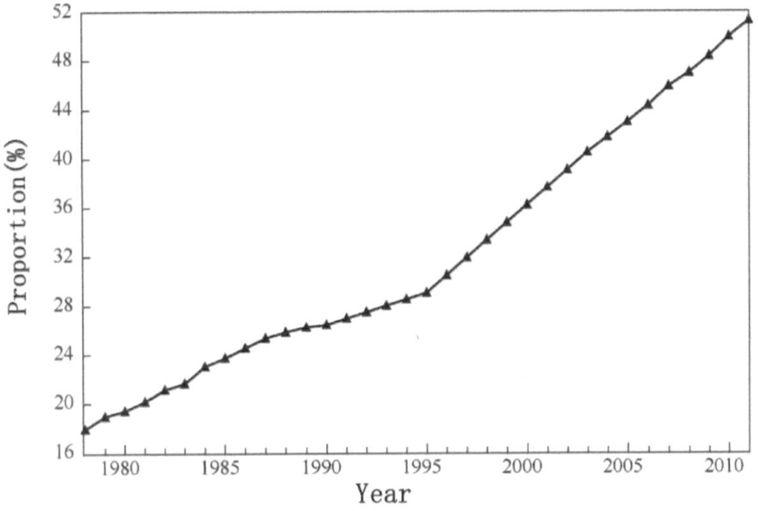

Figure 6.5 Timing diagram of changes in the proportion of urban population

Table 6.6 Prediction of the total population and urban and rural population by 2020

Year	*Population (10,000 people)*	*Share of urban population (%)*	*Urban population (10,000 people)*	*Rural population (10,000 people)*
2011	135,216.4	50.14059	67,798.30	67,418.1
2012	135,961.0	51.42923	69,923.70	66,037.30
2013	136,682.2	52.71787	72,055.94	64,626.26
2014	137,380.5	54.00651	74,194.41	63,186.09
2015	138,056.5	55.29515	76,338.55	61,717.95
2016	138,710.4	56.58379	78,487.60	60,222.80
2017	139,342.9	57.87243	80,641.12	58,701.78
2018	139,954.4	59.16107	82,798.52	57,155.88
2019	140,545.4	60.44971	84,959.29	55,586.11
2020	141,116.5	61.73835	87,123.00	53,993.50

1.411 billion in 2020 and the proportion of urban population will reach 61.74% by then.

3 Prediction of the total consumption of urban and rural residents by commodity. According to the urban and rural population and per capita consumption expenditure by commodity, the total consumption expenditure by commodity in the future can be obtained and the per capita consumption expenditure by commodity of urban and rural residents in 2020 can be estimated accordingly, as shown in Table 6.7.

6.2.2 Correspondence between residents' consumption structure and product structure

Since consumption structure is divided based on the importance of the means of consumption to people's lives and the way they are consumed, it is often difficult to tell which production department produces a specific type of goods. To optimize industrial pattern through adjusting the structure of final demand, it is necessary to obtain the correspondence relationship between consumer goods and product sectors. Due to statistical limitations, such correspondence is not available from the existing published statistics. This section transforms it into planning issues.

Table 6.7 Total consumption expenditure and total consumption structure of urban and rural residents by commodity in 2020

Category	*Urban residents*		*Rural residents*	
	Total consumption expenditure (CNY 100 million)	*Consumption structure (%)*	*Total consumption expenditure (CNY 100 million)*	*Consumption structure (%)*
Food	37,182.18	20.55	8,749.59	22.01
Clothing	27,691.26	15.31	3,977.11	10
Housing	16,661.32	9.21	8,501.11	21.38
Household equipment and services	14,420.42	7.97	3,297.76	8.3
Transportation and communications	39,843.35	22.02	6,847.40	17.22
Cultural and educational entertainment	25,465.97	14.08	3,348.30	8.42
Medical and healthcare	12,475.93	6.9	4,224.67	10.63
Miscellaneous	7,178.15	3.97	809.36	2.04
Total	180,918.49	100	39,755.31	100

6.2.2.1 The corresponding relationship between residents' consumption structure and product structure

According to the residents' consumption structure, the final products consumed by residents are classified into eight categories of commodities. Assume Y_{ij}^{C} as the jth category of commodity for household consumption $(j = 1,2,\ldots,8)$, which is the final product from the ith sector $(i = 1,2,\ldots,17)$. Obviously, the total amount of products in the ith sector for household spending Y_{i}^{C} is the sum of Y_{ij}^{C} $(j = 1,2,\ldots,8)$, i.e., $Y_{i}^{C} = \sum_{j=1}^{8} Y_{ij}^{C}$, while the jth category of commodity for household consumption is the sum of Y_{ij}^{C} $(i = 1,2,\ldots,17)$, i.e., $C_j = \sum_{i=1}^{17} Y_{ij}^{C}$. Denote $d_{ij} = Y_{ij}^{C} / C_j$, then d_{ij} represents the number of products in the ith sector contained in the per unit of jth category of commodities, which is called the distribution coefficient of consumer products. Thus:

$$\begin{bmatrix} Y_1^C \\ Y_2^C \\ \vdots \\ Y_m^C \end{bmatrix} = \begin{bmatrix} d_{11} & d_{12} & \cdots & d_{1n} \\ d_{21} & d_{22} & \cdots & d_{2n} \\ \vdots & \vdots & & \vdots \\ d_{m1} & d_{m2} & \cdots & d_{mn} \end{bmatrix} \begin{bmatrix} C_1 \\ C_2 \\ \vdots \\ C_n \end{bmatrix} m = 17, n = 8 \tag{6.22}$$

And:

$$\sum_{i=1}^{m} d_{ij} = 1 (j = 1,2,\ldots,8) \tag{6.23}$$

With $D = \left[d_{ij}\right]_{17\times 8}$ as the distribution coefficient matrix of consumer products, theoretically the total amount of household spending should equal the sum of final household spending. The following planning model is established:

$$\min \sum_{t} \sum_{i=1}^{17} \left[Y_i^C(t) - \sum_{j=1}^{8} d_{ij} C_j(t) \right]^2 (t = 1997, 2000, 2002, 2005, 2007) \tag{6.24}$$

$$s.t. \sum_{i=1}^{m} d_{ij} = 1 \; (j = 1,2,\cdots, 8) \tag{6.25}$$

$$d_{ij} \geq 0 (i = 1,2,\ldots, 17, j = 1,2,\ldots,8) \tag{6.26}$$

The above planning process is solved using Lingo 11.0 software. Considering a large bias for some coefficients close to zero in the solving process, a slight adjustment has been made in conjunction with the coefficient matrix compiled by Yanju Meng and Rongmei Xiang (2011), according to the statistical information from Beijing Municipal Bureau of Statistics. The results are shown in Tables 6.8 and 6.9.

6.2.2.2 Final product structure of household spending

According to the prediction on household consumption expenditure in the eight categories of goods in 2020 as well as the distribution coefficient matrix of consumer products of urban and rural residents, the product structure of the total household spending in 2020 can be obtained, as shown in Table 6.10 and Figure 6.6.

As shown in Table 6.10, the largest resident consumption demand lies in Sector 17, including education, medical care, public services, accounting for 15.65% of the total demand, followed by Sector 14 (retail, wholesale, catering, and accommodation sector), accounting for 12.39% of the total demand; the demand for Sector 3 (food, beverage, and tobacco products industry) and Sector 4 (textile and leather products industry) is also large, accounting for 10.99% and 11.7% of the total demand, respectively. Industries with smaller resident consumption demand mainly concentrate in the secondary industry, such as the mining industry (0.43%), the coking and petroleum processing industry (1.04%), the non-metallic mineral products industry (0.76%), and the metal products manufacturing industry (0.28%). The products are mainly used for investment in these emissions-intensive industries.

Comparison of the projected consumer product structure in 2020 with the consumer product structure in 2005 shows that based on the changes to the consumption structure of urban and rural residents, the proportion of products consumed in Sector 1 (agriculture), Sector 3 (food, beverage, and tobacco products industry), Sector 13 (transportation, warehousing, and post and telecommunication services), and Sector 16 (financial industry) will decrease to different degrees. Among them, the sharp drop in Sector 1 and Sector 3 is mainly due to the significant decrease of the share of food expenditure. Affected by the sharply increased expenditure on clothing, the proportion of products in Sector 4 (textile and leather product industry) will increase greatly. In addition, the proportion of products in the production and supply industries of electricity, heat, and water (Sector 6), the machinery and equipment manufacturing sector (Sector 11), the construction industry (Sector 12), the retail, wholesale, catering, and accommodation sector (Sector 14), the real estate and rental and leasing industry and commercial and service industries (Sector 15), and other service industries (Sector 17) will increase slightly.

Table 6.8 Distribution coefficient of consumer goods of urban residents

Sector	*Food*	*Clothing*	*Housing*	*Household equipment and services*	*Transportation and communications*	*Cultural and educational entertainment*	*Medical and healthcare*	*Miscellaneous*
1	0.1538	0.0000	0.0000	0.4993	0.0000	0.0000	0.0000	0.0000
2	0.0085	0.0000	0.0000	0.0000	0.0000	0.0000	0.0000	0.0000
3	0.3692	0.0000	0.0000	0.0007	0.0000	0.0000	0.0000	0.5000
4	0.1030	0.4903	0.0054	0.1407	0.0000	0.0524	0.0586	0.0379
5	0.0449	0.0000	0.0093	0.0203	0.0000	0.0000	0.0000	0.0693
6	0.0096	0.0000	0.3320	0.0000	0.0000	0.0000	0.0000	0.0000
7	0.0199	0.0000	0.0010	0.0000	0.0088	0.0000	0.0000	0.0000
8	0.0407	0.0000	0.0000	0.0419	0.0000	0.0017	0.3083	0.1942
9	0.0171	0.0000	0.0081	0.0327	0.0000	0.0000	0.0000	0.0000
10	0.0138	0.0000	0.0000	0.0000	0.0000	0.0000	0.0000	0.0000
11	0.0845	0.0000	0.0740	0.224	0.1654	0.0750	0.0068	0.0415
12	0.0000	0.0514	0.1660	0.0000	0.0000	0.0000	0.0000	0.0000
13	0.0000	0.0205	0.0000	0.0000	0.1677	0.0000	0.3491	0.0000
14	0.1217	0.2316	0.0409	0.0000	0.1777	0.1869	0.0000	0.0184
15	0.0137	0.0568	0.3634	0.0000	0.2345	0.0010	0.0000	0.0456
16	0.0000	0.1398	0.0000	0.0000	0.0326	0.0000	0.0910	0.0000
17	0.0000	0.0098	0.0000	0.0405	0.2135	0.6831	0.1863	0.0933

Table 6.9 Distribution coefficient of consumer goods of rural residents

Sector	*Food*	*Clothing*	*Housing*	*Household equipment and services*	*Transportation and communications*	*Cultural and educational entertainment*	*Medical and healthcare*	*Miscellaneous*
1	0.3193	0.0000	0.0001	0.0000	0.0000	0.0211	0.5000	0.0000
2	0.0044	0.0000	0.0699	0.0000	0.0000	0.0000	0.0000	0.0000
3	0.4214	0.2874	0.0543	0.5000	0.0000	0.0000	0.0000	0.0000
4	0.0272	0.7029	0.0180	0.1402	0.0000	0.0217	0.0570	0.0102
5	0.0200	0.0000	0.1033	0.0326	0.00000	0.0000	0.0000	0.0853
6	0.0000	0.0000	0.2243	0.0000	0.0000	0.0000	0.0000	0.0000
7	0.0027	0.0000	0.0038	0.0000	0.0186	0.0000	0.2358	0.0000
8	0.0262	0.0000	0.0029	0.0750	0.0000	0.0000	0.0000	0.2331
9	0.0075	0.0000	0.0430	0.0045	0.0000	0.0000	0.0000	0.0000
10	0.0069	0.0000	0.0050	0.0000	0.0000	0.0000	0.0000	0.0000
11	0.0344	0.0000	0.1042	0.2414	0.1927	0.0924	0.0005	0.0486
12	0.0000	0.0000	0.0453	0.0000	0.0000	0.0000	0.0000	0.0000
13	0.0075	0.0000	0.0612	0.0000	0.1689	0.0000	0.0000	0.0000
14	0.0820	0.0000	0.1271	0.0000	0.2826	0.0000	0.0000	0.0401
15	0.0292	0.0000	0.0734	0.0000	0.1414	0.2088	0.0000	0.2446
16	0.0070	0.0000	0.0647	0.0000	0.0000	0.0000	0.0000	0.0000
17	0.0047	0.0098	0.0000	0.0065	0.1959	0.6561	0.2068	0.3383

Table 6.10 Prediction on product structure of total household spending in 2020

Sector	*Per capita of urban residents (yuan)*	*Per capita of rural residents (yuan)*	*Total consumption of urban residents (CNY 100 million)*	*Total consumption of rural residents (CNY 100 million)*	*Total consumption of urban and rural residents (CNY 100 million)*	*Consumption structure (%)*
1	1,482.82	921.88	12,918.74	4,977.58	17,896.32	8.11
2	36.28	117.19	316.05	632.73	948.77	0.43
3	1,988.78	1,285.45	17,326.83	6,940.59	24,267.42	10.99
4	2,509.47	735.38	21,863.27	3,970.58	25,833.86	11.7
5	300.11	227.75	2,614.61	1,229.7	3,844.31	1.74
6	675.88	353.15	5,888.51	1,906.8	7,795.31	3.53
7	127.09	218.45	1,107.21	1,179.47	2,286.67	1.04
8	849.51	127.77	7,401.15	689.89	8,091.03	3.67
9	142.59	82.6	1,242.32	446.01	1,688.33	0.76
10	58.9	19.05	513.11	102.88	615.99	0.28
11	1,892.47	676.6	16,487.77	3,653.21	20,140.98	9.13
12	480.83	71.32	4,189.11	385.1	4,574.21	2.07
13	1,332	322.71	11,604.75	1,742.42	13,347.16	6.05
14	2,707.86	697.4	23,591.65	3,765.49	27,357.14	12.39
15	2,046.88	508.36	17,833.04	2,744.79	20,577.82	9.32
16	723.74	113.21	6,305.44	611.27	6,916.71	3.13
17	3,414.91	886.63	29,751.74	4,787.23	34,538.97	15.65
Total	20,770.09	7,364.91	180,955.29	39,765.72	220,721.01	100

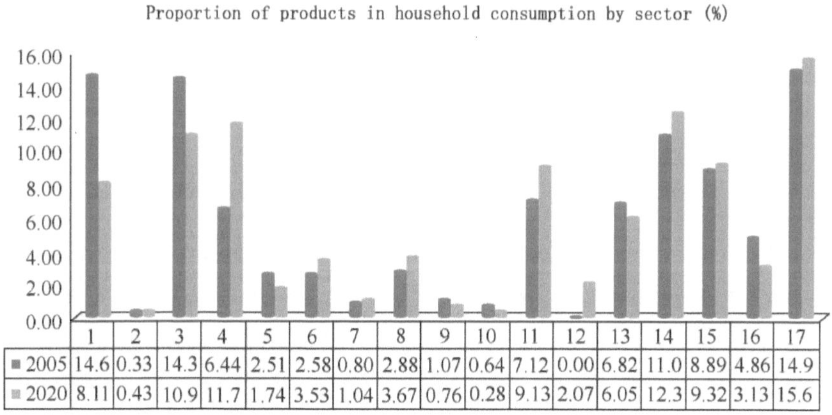

Figure 6.6 Comparison of residents' consumer product structure

1. Agriculture; 2. Mining industry; 3. Food, beverage, and tobacco products industry; 4. Textile and leather product industry; 5. Other manufacturing industries; 6. Production and supply industries of electricity, heat, and water; 7. Coking and petroleum processing industry; 8. Chemical industry; 9. Non-metallic mineral products industry; 10. Metal products manufacturing industry; 11. Machinery and equipment manufacturing sector; 12. Construction industry; 13. Transportation, warehousing, and post and telecommunication services; 14. Retail, wholesale, catering, and accommodation sector; 15. Real estate and rental and leasing industry and commercial and service industries; 16. Financial industry; 17. Other service industries.

6.2.3 Prediction on consumption and product structure of government departments

Government consumption refers to the expenditure on the consumption of the public service provided by the government to the whole society and the net expenditure on the goods and services provided by the government to the households at free charge or lower prices. Government expenditure mainly includes its expenditure on education, culture, science and technology, medical and healthcare, social security, as well as the administrative and operating costs of government departments. Government consumption and household consumption comprise the consumer demand of social final demand. Therefore, increasing government consumption can expand social demand to some extent, promote social output, and stimulate economic growth.

As shown in Figure 6.7, government consumption in China shows an upward trend year by year. In 2011, the total government consumption in China reached CNY 6.36161 trillion, accounting for 13.66% of the GDP. The proportion of government consumption in the total consumption also shows an upward trend in recent years, ranging from the lowest value of 20% in 1988, to more than 25% since 2000, till 27.8% in 2011. With a nationwide rollout of the universal healthcare and pension system, the proportion of government consumption in total consumption is expected to reach or even exceed 30% by 2020 and the proportion in GDP will increase to about 15%.

As shown in Table 6.11, government consumption is concentrated in certain sectors, most of which fall into other service industries, and a few of which are related to the real estate and rental and leasing industry and commercial and service industries before 2002. Since 2002, the agriculture and the transportation, warehousing, and post and telecommunication services

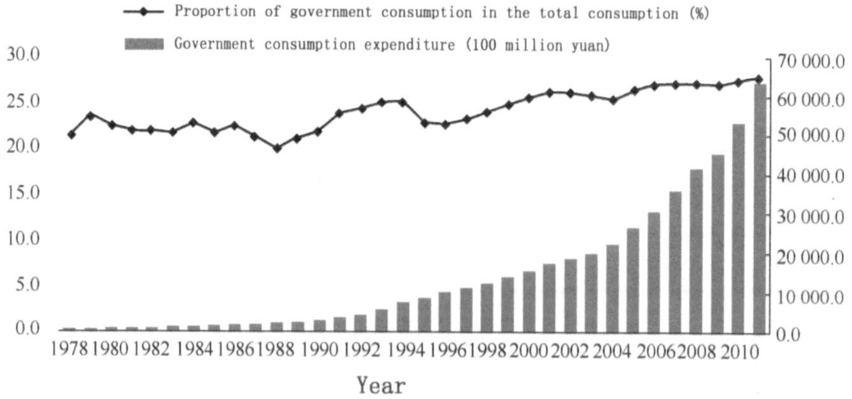

Figure 6.7 Government consumption and its proportion in the total consumption in China by year

have been included into the sectors of government consumption. In general, other service industries account for the majority of the government consumption, with a proportion of over 92% each year after 2002. Therefore, it can be estimated according to the product structure of government

Table 6.11 Product structure of government consumption in the compilation years (%)

Sector	*1997*	*2000*	*2002*	*2005*	*2007*
Agriculture	0.00	0.00	0.86	1.06	0.97
Mining industry	0.00	0.00	0.00	0.00	0.00
Food, beverage, and tobacco products industry	0.00	0.00	0.00	0.00	0.00
Textile and leather product industry	0.00	0.00	0.00	0.00	0.00
Other manufacturing industries	0.00	0.00	0.00	0.00	0.00
Production and supply industries of electricity, heat, and water	0.00	0.00	0.00	0.00	0.00
Coking and petroleum processing industry	0.00	0.00	0.00	0.00	0.00
Chemical industry	0.00	0.00	0.00	0.00	0.00
Non-metallic mineral products industry	0.00	0.00	0.00	0.00	0.00
Metal products manufacturing industry	0.00	0.00	0.00	0.00	0.00
Machinery and equipment manufacturing sector	0.00	0.00	0.00	0.00	0.00
Construction industry	0.00	0.00	0.00	0.00	0.00
Transportation, warehousing, and post and telecommunication services	0.00	0.00	1.6	2.24	4.61
Retail, wholesale, catering, and accommodation sector	0.00	0.00	0.00	0.00	0.00
Real estate and rental and leasing industry and commercial and service industries	7.19	10.29	0.53	0.4	1.62
Financial industry	0.00	0.00	0.00	0.00	0.77
Other service industries	92.81	89.71	97.01	96.3	92.03

consumption in 2007 that among the government consumption in 2020, agriculture will account for 1%, the transportation, warehousing, and post and telecommunication services will account for 5%, the real estate and rental and leasing industry and commercial and service industries will account for 2%, the financial industry will account for 1%, and other service industries will account for 91%.

6.2.4 Prediction on consumer product structure

Since some of the consumer products are directly imported, it will not have an impact on domestic production activities, nor stimulate economic growth. Therefore, the consumer products from direct imports must be deducted. Since the NBS does not provide a non-competitive input-output table, in this section, the product structure for the finally consumed domestic products is shown in Table 6.12, with the consumption of imported consumer products deducted against the 2005 input-output table for China's mainland provided by OECD. As for the consumption proportion, the household consumption accounts for 70% while the government consumption accounts for 30% of the final consumption.

As shown in Table 6.12, in the total consumption, the demand of other service industries is the largest, accounting for 38.39%, which is mainly due to the fact that over 90% of the government consumption is in this sector. Industrial sectors with larger consumption demand include the retail, wholesale, catering, and accommodation sector (8.78%), the real estate and rental and leasing industry and commercial and service industries (7.50%), the food, beverage, and tobacco products industry (7.76%), and the textile and leather product industry (7.85%). In general, the consumer demand for the tertiary industry is the largest, accounting for 63.06% of the total consumption; the consumer demand for the primary industry is the smallest, accounting for 6.03% of the total consumption. Therefore, expanding consumption will inevitably lead the industrial structure to a "tertiary-secondary-primary" model as well as the transformation into a low carbon economy.

6.2.5 Prediction on exported product structure

The growth of export demand has been one of the major drivers of China's economic growth. According to the input-output tables of China's mainland provided by OECD, among the three major final demands, export demand accounted for 19.5% in 1995. It rose to 20.78% in 2000 and then reached 28.95% in 2005. China's economy is heavily dependent on export, and the export product structure is more concentrated in a few categories after 2000. As shown in Table 6.13, the sector having the largest export share is the machinery and equipment manufacturing sector, followed by the textile and leather product industry, and the export shares of other manufacturing industries, the metal products manufacturing industry, and the chemical

Table 6.12 Prediction on consumption structure in 2020

Sector	*Total consumption structure*			*Consumption structure of the domestic products*		
	Household consumption	*Government consumption*	*Total consumption*	*Household consumption*	*Government consumption*	*Total consumption*
Agriculture	8.11	1.00	5.98	8.19	1.00	6.03
Mining industry	0.43	0.00	0.30	0.44	0.00	0.31
Food, beverage, and tobacco products industry	10.99	0.00	7.69	11.09	0.00	7.76
Textile and leather product industry	11.7	0.00	8.19	11.22	0.00	7.85
Other manufacturing industries	1.74	0.00	1.22	1.70	0.00	1.19
Production and supply industries of electricity, heat, and water	3.53	0.00	2.47	3.73	0.00	2.61
Coking and petroleum processing industry	1.04	0.00	0.73	1.03	0.00	0.72
Chemical industry	3.67	0.00	2.57	3.29	0.00	2.30
Non-metallic mineral products industry	0.76	0.00	0.53	0.79	0.00	0.55
Metal products manufacturing industry	0.28	0.00	0.20	0.27	0.00	0.19
Machinery and equipment manufacturing sector	9.13	0.00	6.39	8.42	0.00	5.89
Construction industry	2.07	0.00	1.45	2.19	0.00	1.53
Transportation, warehousing, and post and telecommunication services	6.05	5.00	5.74	6.22	5.00	5.85
Retail, wholesale, catering, and accommodation sector	12.39	0.00	8.67	12.54	0.00	8.78
Real estate and rental and leasing industry and commercial and service industries	9.32	2.00	7.12	9.85	2.00	7.50
Financial industry	3.13	1.00	2.49	3.21	1.00	2.55
Other service industries	15.65	91.00	38.26	15.84	91.00	38.39

industry are also large. Since 2000, the export share of the textile and leather product industry has decreased, while the share of the machinery and equipment manufacturing sector has increased significantly. Previous studies have shown that China's export product structure has undergone great changes: in terms of total exports, the proportion of primary products has decreased sharply and the proportion of manufactured products has far exceeded that of primary products; in terms of manufactured products, the proportion of capital-intensive products has exceeded that of labor-intensive products. However, China's export trade is still facing problems such as excessive proportion of labor-intensive products, relatively low grade of manufactured products, and excessively low proportion of high value-added and high-tech products.

For a country, the export product structure reflects not only its resource endowments, but also its social, economic, technological, and industrial development level to some extent. Therefore, it is very difficult to adjust export product structure significantly in a short period. As shown in Table 6.13, there are great changes in export product structure before and after 2002, and the export product structure has been relatively stable after 2002. Since 2000, due to the global dotcom bubble burst, the economic slowdown of developed countries, and the September 11 attacks, the international trade situation has deteriorated and the global international trade volume has shrunk sharply. As a result, China's foreign trade has also declined and trade products have become more concentrated in a few categories. In the following years, the global economy recovered gradually, but the economic outlook was not optimistic. The decline in the export share of China's textile and leather product industry after 2002 is a proof. Since then, the world economy has been hit hard by the 2008 financial crisis and its recovery has been hindered. With the global economic downturn, it is more difficult for China to significantly adjust its export product structure. Therefore, in this section, the average export share of each sector in 2002, 2005, and 2007 is used to predict the export product structure in 2020.

6.3 Estimation of the capital coefficient matrix *K*

In the end use column of the input-output model, the capital formation includes two parts: one is the fixed capital formation denoted by Y^{FI} and the other is the inventory formation denoted by Y^{SI}. Inventories are usually put into production in the next year as liquid assets. Therefore, the distribution of capital formation Y^{I} also includes two parts: the distribution of fixed capital formation and the distribution of inventory.

6.3.1 Distribution coefficient matrix of fixed capital formation

From the perspective of whole society, fixed capital is formed by investments in fixed assets of each sector. For any sector i, products for investment can be

Table 6.13 Estimation of export product structure in 2020 (%)

Sector	*1997*	*2000*	*2002*	*2005*	*2007*	*Prediction of 2020*
Agriculture	2.47	2.52	1.53	0.88	0.7	1.04
Mining industry	2.36	1.73	1.45	1.16	0.67	1.09
Food, beverage, and tobacco products industry	4.43	4.01	2.89	2.29	2.00	2.39
Textile and leather product industry	23.38	19.22	17.76	14.45	14.54	15.58
Other manufacturing industries	8.34	5.63	6.72	6.22	6.31	6.42
Production and supply industries of electricity, heat, and water	0.23	0.00	0.17	0.08	0.07	0.10
Coking and petroleum processing industry	1.08	0.97	0.85	1.03	0.80	0.89
Chemical industry	9.15	8.27	7.03	7.5	7.58	7.37
Non-metallic mineral products industry	1.81	1.70	1.35	1.32	1.55	1.41
Metal products manufacturing industry	6.86	6.25	4.93	7.00	9.12	7.02
Machinery and equipment manufacturing sector	23.43	35.16	33.75	42.16	42.35	39.42
Construction industry	0.15	0.11	0.34	0.31	0.43	0.36
Transportation, warehousing, and post and telecommunication services	3.54	3.28	4.69	4.62	4.69	4.66
Retail, wholesale, catering, and accommodation sector	7.79	6.46	9.33	7.28	4.97	7.19
Real estate and rental and leasing industry and commercial and service industries	4.56	4.33	3.24	0.93	3.36	2.51
Financial industry	0.10	0.07	0.07	0.08	0.09	0.08
Other service industries	0.31	0.29	3.89	2.71	0.78	2.46

provided to each sector of the national economy to compensate and increase the fixed asset investment of each sector.

Assume I_{ij} is the products of sector i used as an investment in sector j, and the matrix $I = \begin{bmatrix} I_{11} & I_{12} & \cdots & I_{1n} \\ I_{21} & I_{22} & \cdots & I_{2n} \\ \vdots & \vdots & & \vdots \\ I_{n1} & I_{n2} & \cdots & I_{nn} \end{bmatrix}$ denotes the transfer quantity of products used as an investment among sectors.

In the horizontal direction of matrix I, the sum of the total products for investment in sector i equals the fixed capital formation of sector i, that is:

$$\sum_{j=1}^{n} I_{ij} = Y_i^{FI} \; (i = 1, 2, \ldots, n) \tag{6.27}$$

In the vertical direction of the matrix I, the sum of the investment products of each sector in sector j should be equal to the fixed asset investment of sector j. Denote FI_j as the fixed asset investment of sector j, then:

$$\sum_{i=1}^{n} I_{ij} = FI_j \; (j = 1, 2, \ldots, n) \tag{6.28}$$

Assuming the investment cycle is one year, theoretically the total amount of fixed asset investment of the whole society in the tth year should equal the total amount of capital formation in the tth year, that is:

$$\sum_{i=1}^{n} Y_i^{I} = \sum_{j=1}^{n} FI_j \tag{6.29}$$

Let $g_{ij} = I_{ij} / Y_i^{FI}$, g_{ij} is the product quantity per unit of product of fixed capital formation in product sector i distributed to sector j as fixed capital investment. Obviously, $\sum_{i=1}^{n} g_{ij} = 1 \; (j = 1, 2, \ldots, n)$. The matrix $G = (g_{ij})_{n \times n}$ is called the distribution coefficient matrix of fixed capital formation. Since $I_{ij} = g_{ij} \cdot Y_i^{FI}$, then:

$$\begin{bmatrix} g_{11} & g_{21} & \cdots & g_{n1} \\ g_{12} & g_{22} & \cdots & g_{n2} \\ \vdots & \vdots & & \vdots \\ g_{1n} & g_{2n} & \cdots & g_{nn} \end{bmatrix} \begin{bmatrix} Y_1^{FI} \\ Y_2^{FI} \\ \vdots \\ Y_n^{FI} \end{bmatrix} = \begin{bmatrix} FI_1 \\ FI_2 \\ \vdots \\ FI_n \end{bmatrix} \tag{6.30}$$

However, in the statistics, the statistical calibers for the gross fixed capital formation and fixed asset investment are inconsistent. The gross fixed capital formation generally refers to the value of fixed assets purchased, transferred in, and produced for own use by resident units after deducting the fixed assets sold and transferred out. It can be classified into the gross fixed capital formation in tangible assets and the gross fixed capital formation in intangible assets. The gross fixed capital formation in tangible assets includes the value of construction projects, installation projects, and equipment and appliances purchase (or minus disposals) completed within a given period, as well as the value of land improvements, newly added livestock for draft, breeding, dairy, fur, recreation, and newly added cash trees. The gross fixed capital formation in intangible assets includes the value of exploration of mineral deposits, computer software, entertainment, and the original works of literature and art, etc. acquired (minus disposals). The investment in fixed assets in the whole society refers to the volume of activities in construction and purchases of fixed assets in monetary terms. The main differences between them are as follows: first, the fixed asset investment does not include fixed asset investment under CNY 50,000, while the gross fixed capital formation includes the corresponding investment statistics. Second, the gross fixed capital formation includes part of the net increase in intangible fixed assets, while the fixed asset investment does not include the corresponding part. Third, the gross fixed capital formation excludes the value of old fixed assets transferred out due to sales, barter transactions, and physical capital transfers, while the fixed asset investment does not exclude the corresponding value.[2]

However, for the whole society, due to a small proportion of the intangible fixed asset in the gross fixed capital formation as well as the old fixed assets transferred out for sales, barter transaction, and physical capital transfer in the investment in fixed assets in the whole society, the gross fixed capital formation almost equals the investment in fixed assets in the whole society in a certain period. Therefore:

$$\sum_{i=1}^{n} Y_i^I \approx \sum_{j=1}^{n} FI_j \tag{6.31}$$

It is difficult to obtain the distribution coefficient matrix G of fixed capital formation through surveys. Therefore, with reference to Decheng Fan and Xiaohui Wang(2011), it can be transformed into a planning issue. Due to the inconsistent economic behaviors before and after 2000, including the overheated investment demand and deteriorated economic structural imbalance after 2000, the investment coefficient may be different before and after 2000. Therefore, the years of 2002, 2005, and 2007 are selected as sample periods in this section. The data of fixed capital formation by sector comes from the input-output table of the corresponding year and the fixed asset investment by sector is compiled based on the data of the fixed asset investment from the *China Statistical Yearbook* of the corresponding year. The specific data are shown in Table 6.14.

An optimization model is established according to Equations (6.30) and (6.31):

$$\min = \sum_{t}\sum_{j=1}^{n}\left[FI_j(t)-\sum_{i=1}^{n}g_{ij}Y_i^{fI}(t)\right]^2 \quad (t=2002,2005,2007) \tag{6.32}$$

$$s.t.\sum_{i=1}^{n}g_{ij}=1(j=1,2,\ldots,n) \tag{6.33}$$

$$g_{ij}\geq 0\left(i=1,2,\ldots,n;\ j=1,2,\ldots,n\right) \tag{6.34}$$

The Lingo 11.0 software is used to obtain the distribution coefficient matrix *G* of fixed capital formation, as shown in Table 6.15.

6.3.2 Capital coefficient matrix K

1 Distribution coefficient of inventory. The increase in inventory in the gross capital formation usually enters the production link of the following year as liquid assets or consumables and the direct consumption coefficient matrix is used to decompose inventory vector to each operating sector. Therefore, the equation for the inventory of sector *i* in the *t*th year consumed by sector *j* in the *t* + 1th year is as follows:

$$\Delta S_{ij}^{CA}(t+1)=\frac{a_{ij}}{\sum_{j=1}^{n}a_{ij}}Y_i^{SI}(t)\left(i=1,2,\ldots,n;\ j=1,2,\ldots,n\right) \tag{6.35}$$

Wherein a_{ij} is the direct consumption coefficient.

Given that $\Delta x_j = X_j(t+1)-X_j(t)$, since *China Statistical Yearbook* only provides data of gross output by industry rather than data of gross output in the unlisted years of the book. The increase in gross output of non-industrial sector in the *t* + 1th year can be obtained from the input-output tables and sectoral added value. The input-output table of 17 sectors are merged into eight sectors, namely ten sectors under the industrial sector are merged into one sector. Given that the added value of the eight sectors in the *t* + 1th year is $v_j(t+1)$, according to the input-output model of the *t*th year:

$$X(t+1)=[E-\dot{\Phi}(t)]^{-1}V(t+1) \tag{6.36}$$

Table 6.14 Fixed asset investments and fixed capital formation CNY 100 million

Sector	*Fixed asset investment*			*Fixed capital formation*		
	2002	*2005*	*2007*	*2002*	*2005*	*2007*
Agriculture	849.65	2,323.66	3,403.50	772.73	1,411.94	1,067.17
Mining industry	1,636.36	3,587.35	5,878.80	0	0	0
Food, beverage, and tobacco products industry	644.37	2,450.49	4,309.78	0	0	0
Textile and leather product industry	535.57	2,143.96	3,281.40	0	0	0
Other manufacturing industries	468.64	2,160.61	3,091.01	259.51	621.36	1,963.21
Production and supply industries of electricity, heat, and water	4,843.86	7,554.42	9,467.60	0	0	0
Coking and petroleum processing industry	313.01	1,043.54	1,775.58	0	0	0
Chemical industry	1,179.84	3,909.99	5,841.88	0	0	0
Non-metallic mineral products industry	658.04	2,695.71	5,148.53	0	0	0
Metal products manufacturing industry	1,243.54	4,964.00	6,890.09	321.59	883.42	952.95
Machinery and equipment manufacturing sector	1996.69	7207.66	14166.87	12581.78	26636.07	35501.64
Construction industry	513.36	1,118.98	1,302.30	27,275.36	41,239.41	58,846.59
Transportation and post and telecommunication services	9,318.03	11,195.79	16,003.10	197.57	1,146.11	1,497.44
Retail, wholesale, catering, and accommodation sector	751.24	2,525.15	4,399.80	954.78	1,786.89	1,882.11
Real estate and rental and leasing industry and commercial and service industries	12,372.87	20,054.88	33,388.20	1,142.67	3,373.03	306.26
Financial industry	1,243.54	4,964.00	6,890.09	0.00	0.00	0.00
Other service industries	1,996.69	7,207.66	14,166.87	126.11	206.57	318.5
Total	40,565.30	87,107.86	139,405.39	45,634.10	79,309.80	10,742.87

The gross output of the eight sectors is calculated as $X_j(t+1)$. In the equation, $\dot{\Phi}(t)$ represents the diagonal matrix generated by the vector of intermediate input rates: $\left[\sum_{i=1}^{n} a_{i1} \quad \sum_{i=1}^{n} a_{i2} \quad \cdots \quad \sum_{i=1}^{n} a_{in} \right]'$.

Due to the great changes in sectors' inventory each year, the latest 2007 input-output table is used to calculate the inventory distribution coefficients in this section. Based on the added value of eight sectors in 2008 and the direct consumption coefficients matrix in 2007, the gross output value of the corresponding eight sectors in 2008 can be calculated according to the model (6.35). The gross output of the ten sub-sectors of the industrial sector is estimated based on the gross output value of the industrial sector and the gross output value of the major enterprise subsectors. Inventory distribution coefficient matrix is denoted as:

$$H = \left[h_{ij} \right] = \left[\Delta S_{ij}^{CA} / \Delta x_j \right] \tag{6.37}$$

2 Capital coefficient matrix. According to the distribution coefficient matrix G of the fixed capital formation as well as the fixed capital formation in 2007, the investment volume of products of the i sector in the j sector can be obtained. For new capital $\Delta S_{ij} = I_{ij} + \Delta S_{ij}^{CA}$, given that $k_{ij} = \dfrac{\Delta S_{ij}}{\Delta x_j}$, then the capital coefficient matrix K can be obtained. The results are shown in Table 6.16.

6.4 Balanced industrial structure and measurements of its potential in energy saving and emission reduction

6.4.1 Balanced industrial structure

6.4.1.1 Assumptions about the structure and composition of final demand

Investment and net exports have dominated China's economic growth in recent years. In terms of the final demand, the proportion of China's investment demand has remained around 30% and the proportion of the export demand has remained over 20%, while the consumer demand, especially household consumer demand, is seriously insufficient. Before 2000, the proportion of consumer demand in final demand was around 50%, but such figure was less than 40% in 2005. In terms of consumer demand, the proportion of government consumption demand has been increasing. However, the proportion of household consumer demand has been decreasing, and it dropped to 28.56% in 2005. This demand structure leads to a continuously

Table 6.15 Distribution coefficient matrix G of the fixed capital formation

Sector	*1*	*2*	*3*	*4*	*5*	*6*	*7*	*8*	*9*	*10*	*11*	*12*	*13*	*14*	*15*	*16*	*17*
1	0.0918	0.0000	0.0000	0.0249	0.0000	0.5981	0.2852	0.0000	0.0000	0.0000	0.0000	0.0000	0.0000	0.0000	0.0000	0.0000	0.0000
2	0.0000	0.0000	0.0000	0.0000	0.0000	0.0000	0.0000	0.0000	0.0000	0.0000	0.0000	0.0000	0.0000	0.0000	0.0000	0.0000	1.0000
3	0.0000	0.0000	0.0000	0.0000	0.0000	0.0000	0.0000	0.0000	0.0000	0.0000	0.0000	0.0000	0.0000	0.0000	0.0000	0.0000	1.0000
4	0.0000	0.0000	0.0000	0.0000	0.0000	0.0000	0.0000	0.0000	0.0000	0.0000	0.0000	0.0000	0.0000	0.0000	0.0000	0.0000	1.0000
5	0.0000	0.0000	0.0000	0.0000	0.0000	0.0000	0.0000	0.0000	0.0000	0.0000	0.0000	0.0000	0.0000	0.0000	0.0000	0.0000	0.0000
6	0.0000	0.0000	0.0000	0.0000	0.0000	0.0000	0.0000	0.0000	0.0000	0.0000	0.0000	0.0000	0.0000	0.0000	0.0000	0.0000	1.0000
7	0.0000	0.0000	0.0000	0.0000	0.0000	0.0000	0.0000	0.0000	0.0000	0.0000	0.0000	0.0000	0.0000	0.0000	0.0000	0.0000	1.0000
8	0.0000	0.0000	0.0000	0.0000	0.0000	0.0000	0.0000	0.0000	0.0000	0.0000	0.0000	0.0000	0.0000	0.0000	0.0000	0.0000	1.0000
9	0.0000	0.0000	0.0000	0.0000	0.0000	0.0000	0.0000	0.0000	0.0000	0.0000	0.0000	0.0000	0.0000	0.0000	0.0000	0.0000	1.0000
10	0.2193	0.0000	0.0000	0.2516	0.0000	0.2703	0.0000	0.0000	0.0000	0.2588	0.0000	0.0000	0.0000	0.0000	0.0000	0.0000	0.0000
11	0.0000	0.0000	0.0000	0.0000	0.0004	0.0991	0.0000	0.0334	0.0000	0.0875	0.0000	0.0000	0.2762	0.0000	0.0000	0.0000	0.5034
12	0.0000	0.0670	0.0401	0.0000	0.0317	0.0000	0.0000	0.0742	0.0260	0.0000	0.1823	0.0000	0.0727	0.0417	0.4643	0.0000	0.0000
13	0.1829	0.0000	0.0000	0.2619	0.0000	0.2776	0.0000	0.0000	0.0000	0.2776	0.0000	0.0000	0.0000	0.0000	0.0000	0.0000	0.0000
14	0.2237	0.000	0.0000	0.3071	0.0000	0.2473	0.0000	0.0000	0.0000	0.2219	0.0000	0.0000	0.0000	0.0000	0.0000	0.0000	0.0000
15	0.1506	0.0000	0.0000	0.0458	0.0000	0.5643	0.0000	0.0000	0.0000	0.2392	0.0000	0.0000	0.0000	0.0000	0.0000	0.0000	0.0000
16	0.0000	0.0000	0.0000	0.0000	0.0000	0.0000	0.0000	0.0000	0.0000	0.0000	0.0000	0.0000	0.0000	0.0000	0.0000	0.0000	0.0000
17	0.0000	0.0000	0.0000	0.0000	0.0000	0.0000	0.0000	0.0000	0.0000	0.0000	0.0000	0.0000	0.0000	0.0000	1.0000	0.0000	0.0000

Note: Sector numbers 1–17 represent as follows, respectively: 1. Agriculture; 2. Mining industry; 3. Food, beverage, and tobacco products industry; 4. Textile and leather product industry; 5. Other manufacturing industries; 6. Production and supply industries of electricity, heat, and water; 7. Coking and petroleum processing industry; 8. Chemical industry; 9. Non-metallic mineral products industry; 10. Metal products manufacturing industry; 11. Machinery and equipment manufacturing sector; 12. Construction industry; 13. Transportation, warehousing, and post and telecommunication services; 14. Retail, wholesale, catering, and accommodation sector; 15. Real estate and rental and leasing industry and commercial and service industries; 16. Financial industry; 17. Other service industries.

Table 6.16 Investment coefficient matrix *K*

Sector	*1*	*2*	*3*	*4*	*5*	*6*	*7*	*8*	*9*	*10*	*11*	*12*	*13*	*14*	*15*	*16*	*17*
1	0.0315	0.0004	0.0550	0.0433	0.0262	0.3493	0.0830	0.0035	0.0001	0.0000	0.0000	0.0003	0.0031	0.0042	0.0002	0.0000	0.0004
2	0.0000	0.0018	0.0001	0.0003	0.0004	0.0132	0.0360	0.0013	0.0064	0.0019	0.0000	0.0002	0.0002	0.0000	0.0000	0.0000	0.0000
3	0.0215	0.0005	0.0428	0.0137	0.0031	0.0032	0.0030	0.0030	0.0015	0.0004	0.0003	0.0005	0.0034	0.0169	0.0027	0.0030	0.0016
4	0.0000	0.0002	0.0001	0.0557	0.0051	0.0008	0.0001	0.0005	0.0005	0.0001	0.0001	0.0001	0.0008	0.0004	0.0013	0.0008	0.0004
5	0.0001	0.0005	0.0011	0.0018	0.0318	0.0007	0.0002	0.0008	0.0043	0.0011	0.0003	0.0006	0.0010	0.0006	0.4760	0.0077	0.0012
6	0.0000	0.0000	0.0000	0.0000	0.0000	0.0000	0.0000	0.0000	0.0000	0.0000	0.0000	0.0000	0.0000	0.0000	0.0000	0.0000	0.0000
7	−0.0001	−0.0004	0.0000	−0.0001	−0.0002	−0.0023	−0.0017	−0.0007	−0.0008	−0.0003	0.0000	−0.0001	−0.0041	−0.0000	−0.0005	−0.0005	−0.0001
8	0.0039	0.0019	0.0015	0.0118	0.0137	0.0012	0.0022	0.0195	0.0079	0.0006	0.0011	0.0012	0.0013	0.0004	0.0022	0.0009	0.0024
9	0.0000	0.0002	0.0001	0.0001	0.0003	0.0001	0.0001	0.0001	0.0046	0.0001	0.0001	0.0017	0.0000	0.0000	0.0000	0.0000	0.0000
10	0.0244	0.0049	0.0005	0.0686	0.0130	0.1437	0.0011	0.0015	0.0098	0.0359	0.0061	0.0103	0.0013	0.0001	0.0029	0.0004	0.0003
11	0.0015	0.0129	0.0010	0.0052	0.0149	1.9835	0.0075	0.1285	0.0114	0.2075	0.0211	0.0064	2.7891	0.0028	0.0273	0.0106	1.0368
12	0.0000	0.4522	0.2738	0.0000	0.5664	0.0000	0.0000	0.4606	0.3587	0.0000	0.4632	0.0000	1.2013	0.2040	6.5679	0.0000	0.0000
13	0.0317	0.0002	0.0001	0.1111	0.0003	0.2279	0.0000	0.0000	0.0004	0.0273	0.0000	0.0002	0.0008	0.0002	0.0002	0.0014	0.0001
14	0.0491	0.0006	0.0007	0.1646	0.0015	0.2559	0.0010	0.0005	0.0014	0.0277	0.0003	0.0005	0.0017	0.0006	0.0024	0.0067	0.0007
15	0.0593	0.0000	0.0000	0.0441	0.0000	1.0519	0.0000	0.0000	0.0000	0.0534	0.0000	0.0000	0.0000	0.0000	0.0000	0.0000	0.0000
16	0.0000	0.0000	0.0000	0.0000	0.0000	0.0000	0.0000	0.0000	0.0000	0.0000	0.0000	0.0000	0.0000	0.0000	0.0000	0.0000	0.0000
17	0.0000	0.0000	0.0000	0.0000	0.0000	0.0000	0.0000	0.0000	0.0000	0.0000	0.0000	0.0000	0.0000	0.0000	0.0766	0.0000	0.0000

Note: Sector numbers 1–17 represent as follows, respectively: 1. Agriculture; 2. Mining industry; 3. Food, beverage, and tobacco products industry; 4. Textile and leather product industry; 5. Other manufacturing industries; 6. Production and supply industries of electricity, heat, and water; 7. Coking and petroleum processing industry; 8. Chemical industry; 9. Non-metallic mineral products industry; 10. Metal products manufacturing industry; 11. Machinery and equipment manufacturing sector; 12. Construction industry; 13. Transportation, warehousing, and post and telecommunication services; 14. Retail, wholesale, catering, and accommodation sector; 15. Real estate and rental and leasing industry and commercial and service industries; 16. Financial industry; 17. Other service industries.

overheated investment in China, reduced efficiency of investment in driving economic growth, increasing dependence in export, expanding trade surplus, and deteriorated industrial overcapacity issues. If the economic structure keeps unchanged, the only way to maintain high GDP growth is to expand export and increase the proportion of investment in GDP, and then the proportion of consumption will decrease. In the end, the economic structure will be stuck in a vicious circle and the ultimate efficiency of economic growth will definitely decline.

In the 12th Five-Year plan period (2011–2015), the Chinese government has clearly started to gradually promote industrial restructuring and adjust distribution structure of national income, increase the proportion of wages in the primary distribution of income, raise people's incomes, and expand domestic demand. The purpose of promoting demand restructuring is to increase the contribution of consumption to economic growth, transform the economic growth from being driven by investment and exports to the one jointly driven by consumption, investment, and exports, so as to realize a long-term coordinated national economic growth.

Irrespective of the adjustment process, assuming that the national income distribution fits the consumption adjustments, then people's income increase can meet the requirements of the final consumption structure after continuous adjustments. For the demand structure in 2020, five scenarios are assumed according to the extent of adjustment. For Scenario 1, the final demand structure is assumed to return to that of 2000, in which the consumption accounts for 50%, investment accounts for 30%, and export accounts for 20%. With Scenario 1 as the benchmark, we assume the proportion of consumption increases by 5% gradually, and set investment and export rates accordingly. The details are shown in Table 6.17.

6.4.1.2 Equilibrium rate of growth

Given the consumption structure vector C, export structure vector E, and investment coefficient matrix K, Equation (6.8) is an equation with one unknown. For the direct consumption coefficient matrix A, it is obvious that the coefficient matrix in 2007 is closer in time. However, for the contribution to demand, imported products do not contribute to domestic production and the carbon emissions embodied in imported products will

Table 6.17 Equilibrium rate of growth under different scenarios

	Scenario 1	*Scenario 2*	*Scenario 3*	*Scenario 4*	*Scenario 5*
Consumption	50	55	60	65	70
Investment	30	30	25	25	20
Exports	20	15	15	10	10
Growth rate P	11.389	11.304	9.319	9.249	7.32

affect the estimate of carbon emission intensity, so the imported intermediate inputs must be deducted. The 2007 input-output table of China provided by the NBS does not distinguish between imported intermediate inputs and domestic intermediate inputs. Given that the direct consumption coefficient changes slightly in a short term, the 2005 domestic input-output table provided by OECD continues to be used in this section. For the purpose of distinguishing, the direct consumption coefficient matrix calculated by domestic intermediate input is denoted as *Ad*. Equation (6.8) becomes:

$$\mu'(E-A)(E-Ad-pEK)^{-1}(\alpha C+\beta E)=1 \tag{6.38}$$

Numerical methods can be used to obtain approximate solutions. The solutions to equilibrium rate of growth under different scenarios are shown in Table 6.17.

As shown in Table 6.17, various structures of final demand require different investments, which lead to different growth rates of the total output. Among the five scenarios, Scenario 1 requires the highest growth rate of the total output, which is 11.389%, while Scenario 5 requires the lowest growth rate of the total output, which is 7.320%. Among the five scenarios, the investment rate of the first two scenarios is 30% and the corresponding growth rate of the total output is above 11%, while such figures are 25% and around 9.2%, respectively, for Scenarios 3 and 4 and 20% and 7.320%, respectively, for Scenario 5. Therefore, the higher investment rate leads to the higher requirement on the growth rate of the total output. Under the same investment rate, the higher the consumption rate is, the higher the growth rate of the total output will be, in spite of small amplitude of change. This may be due to the increase in the proportion of products, including housing and transportation, in consumption structure and the proportion of light industrial products in exports.

6.1.4.3 Industrial structure with balanced growth

According to the dynamic input-output model, when the total output of each sector grows at rate *p*, the economic structure reaches a steady state. The industrial structure at this point is called a balanced industrial structure. Then:

$$V=\hat{A}_v X \tag{6.39}$$

Wherein V represents the vector of added value for each sector; $\hat{A}_v$ represents the diagonal matrix composed of the value-added coefficient for each sector, $\hat{A}_v = E-\hat{\Phi}(t)$.

According to Equations (6.5)–(6.7), given the total end use y, the added value for each sector is:

$$V=A_v(E-A-KP)^{-1}(\alpha C+\beta E)y \tag{6.40}$$

Theoretically, the total end use y and gross added value of GDP are equal. Therefore, the industrial structure T of the national economy (industrial structure calculated by value-added) is:

$$T = \hat{A}_v (E - A - pEK)^{-1} (\alpha C + \beta E) \tag{6.41}$$

Wherein $T = \begin{bmatrix} t_1 & t_2 & \cdots & t_n \end{bmatrix}^T$ and t_i represents the proportion of added value of sector i to GDP. According to Equation (6.41), the industrial structure under the five scenarios can be calculated, as shown in Table 6.18.

As shown in Table 6.18, compared with the industrial structure in 2005, under the five scenarios, the proportion of the primary industry has all decreased, the proportion of the secondary industry has decreased significantly, and the proportion of the tertiary industry has increased. In comparison, the structural adjustment in Scenario 1 is the smallest, while the

Table 6.18 Proportion of added value by sector in various scenarios

Industry	*Sector*	*2005*	*Scenario 1*	*Scenario 2*	*Scenario 3*	*Scenario 4*	*Scenario 5*
1	1	12.39	10.12	10.31	10.52	10.71	10.91
	Total	12.39	10.12	10.31	10.52	10.7	10.91
2	2	4.87	5.1	5	4.91	4.83	4.74
	3	3.95	3.08	3.19	3.36	3.46	3.63
	4	3.46	3.71	3.54	3.69	3.51	3.66
	5	3.43	3.42	3.29	3.25	3.12	3.08
	6	3.65	3.77	3.76	3.77	3.76	3.76
	7	1.4	1.46	1.44	1.43	1.41	1.4
	8	4.79	4.77	4.62	4.63	4.49	4.51
	9	2.31	2.02	1.99	1.8	1.77	1.6
	10	4.78	4.59	4.32	4.04	3.78	3.51
	11	10.09	9.61	9.06	8.55	8	7.47
	12	5.84	5.52	5.51	4.73	4.71	3.96
	Total	48.57	47.05	45.71	44.16	42.85	41.32
3	13	8.41	8.72	8.68	8.67	8.62	8.61
	14	9.01	9.61	9.59	9.73	9.71	9.86
	15	6.01	7.14	7.27	7.35	7.48	7.56
	16	3.39	3.49	3.57	3.66	3.74	3.82
	17	12.21	13.85	14.86	15.92	16.89	17.93
	Total	39.04	42.82	43.97	45.32	46.45	47.78

Note: Sector numbers 1–17 represent as follows, respectively: 1. Agriculture; 2. Mining industry; 3. Food, beverage, and tobacco products industry; 4. Textile and leather product industry; 5. Other manufacturing industries; 6. Production and supply industries of electricity, heat, and water; 7. Coking and petroleum processing industry; 8. Chemical industry; 9. Non-metallic mineral products industry; 10. Metal products manufacturing industry; 11. Machinery and equipment manufacturing sector; 12. Construction industry; 13. Transportation, warehousing, and post and telecommunication services; 14. Retail, wholesale, catering, and accommodation sector; 15. Real estate and rental and leasing industry and commercial and service industries; 16. Financial industry; 17. Other service industries.

proportion of the primary industry decreases the most, the proportion of the secondary industry decreases by 1.5%, and the proportion of the tertiary industry increases by 3.8%. However, the overall economic structure remains the "secondary-tertiary-primary" pattern. Under Scenarios 2 and 3, with moderate structural adjustment of the final demand, the proportions of the secondary and tertiary industries are similar after adjustment, both around 45%. Under Scenarios 4 and 5, with great structural adjustment of the final demand, the added value of the primary industry has increased slightly after the adjustment, and its proportion is near 11%. However, the proportion of the secondary industry has decreased to less than 43% and the proportion of the tertiary industry has exceeded 46%, which is significantly higher than that of the secondary industry. The economic structure has transformed from "secondary-tertiary-primary" to "tertiary-secondary-primary" pattern.

In terms of the subsectors, the proportion of added value in most sectors has not changed significantly. The proportion of the added value decreases more in agriculture, reaching about 2% drop. Among the secondary industry, the proportion of added value in most industries has decreased. The proportion changes slightly in the mining industries, the textile and leather product industry, and the production and supply industries of electricity, heat, and water, while the proportions of the machinery and equipment manufacturing sector and the construction industry decrease significantly. The proportion of the added value for each sector of the tertiary industry has increased. Among them, the largest increase is in the proportion of other service industries, followed by the real estate and rental and leasing industry and commercial and service industries. It indicates that the structural adjustment of the final demand and the increase in the proportion of consumption will surely promote consumption upgrading. The focus of household consumption will surely shift to education, culture, medical and health care, and services, which will, in turn, drive the development of the tertiary industry and promote the upgrading of the industrial structure.

6.4.2 Prediction on energy demand

6.4.2.1 Prediction on energy demand in the production sector

There are many factors that affect energy demand, but the most important factor is economic growth. Existing studies show that there is a long-term equilibrium relationship between energy consumption and GDP. Therefore, energy demand first depends on the GDP. To assess the impact of industrial restructuring on energy demand and to predict energy demand in 2020, the input-output relationship, the direct energy intensity of the total products calculated by energy end use for each sector, and the energy structure are assumed unchanged in this section, while the industrial structure is assumed changed in this section.

According to the direct energy consumption of each industrial sector and the input-output table in 2005 (former Sectors 15, 16, and 17 are merged into Sector 15), the direct energy intensity of each industrial sector can be calculated, as shown in Figure 6.8. Figure 6.8 shows that the highest direct energy intensity in 2005 lies in the non-metallic mineral products industry, reaching 3.395 tonnes/CNY 10,000, which is much higher than other industries, followed by the metal products manufacturing industry, reaching 1.120 tonnes/CNY 10,000, while the direct energy intensity of the other sectors are all less than 1 tonnes/CNY 10,000 .

Assuming that economy grows steadily, the GDP growth rate is 8.5% during high-speed growth, 7.5% during medium-speed growth, and 6.5% during low-speed growth. Based on the GDP in 2011 (calculated at constant prices in 2005), the GDP in 2020 is expected to be CNY 71,651.155 billion, CNY 65,922.206 billion, and CNY 60,606.102 billion at high, medium, and low economic growth rate, respectively. In addition, theoretically the final consumption is equal to the total value-added, according to Equation (6.5), then:

$$X(t) = (E - A - KP)^{-1}(\alpha C + \beta E) \cdot \text{GDP} \tag{6.42}$$

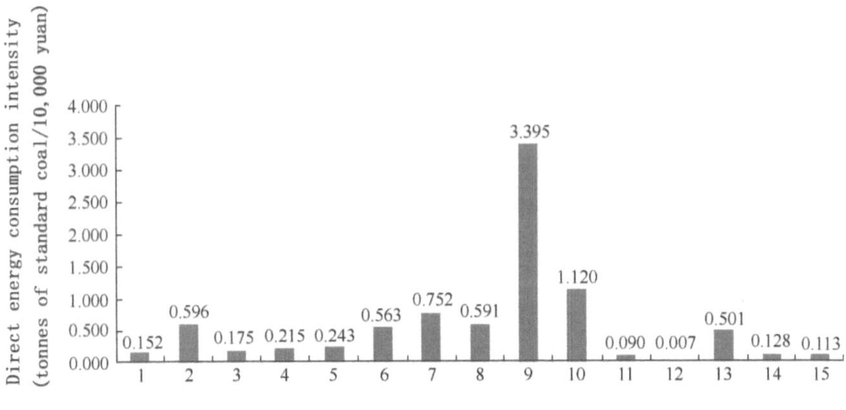

Figure 6.8 Direct energy intensity in 2005 by industrial sector

1. Agriculture; 2. Mining industry; 3. Food, beverage, and tobacco products industry; 4. Textile and leather product industry; 5. Other manufacturing industries; 6. Production and supply industries of electricity, heat, and water; 7. Coking and petroleum processing industry; 8. Chemical industry; 9. Non-metallic mineral products industry; 10. Metal products manufacturing industry; 11. Machinery and equipment manufacturing sector; 12. Construction industry; 13. Transportation, warehousing, and post and telecommunication services; 14. Retail, wholesale, catering, and accommodation sector; 15. Real estate and rental and leasing industry and commercial and service industries.

If the vector of the direct energy consumption coefficient of the total products for each sector is $L = \begin{bmatrix} l_1 & l_2 & \cdots & l_n \end{bmatrix}^T$, then the total energy consumption of each sector is:

$$E = L^T X \tag{6.43}$$

Assuming that the energy structure and energy efficiency remain unchanged, based on the energy consumption per unit of total products for each sector in 2005 (the data are shown in Figure 6.8), the energy consumption after industrial restructuring can be calculated according to the estimation of GDP at different growth rates.

6.4.2.2 Prediction on energy demand for household consumption

Since the production energy consumption and household energy consumption are separate in energy statistics, only the production energy consumption is calculated above. According to consumer theory, the unified form of consumption functions for household energy consumption is:

$$CS_t = \beta_0 + \beta_1 \mathrm{INC}_t + \beta_2 CS_{t-1} + \mu_t \tag{6.44}$$

Considering that the household energy consumption and the level of consumption increase simultaneously, the second-order Granger causality test for household energy consumption and total household consumption also shows that household consumption is the Granger cause of the total household consumption, but the total household consumption is not the Granger cause of household consumption, and income and consumption are highly linearly correlated. Therefore, the above model can be modified to:

$$\ln CS_t = \beta_0 + \beta_1 \ln CS_{t-1} + \beta_2 \ln \mathrm{ENE}_t + \mu_t \tag{6.45}$$

That is, the total household consumption depends on the total household consumption and household energy consumption of the previous year.

According to the total household consumption data from 1993 to 2010 (calculated at constant prices in 2005), the EViews 6 software is used to estimate the model (6.45), then:

$$\ln \hat{CS}_t = -0.1\,184 + 0.9\,565 \ln CS_{t-1} + 0.068\,1 \ln \mathrm{ENE}_t \tag{6.46}$$

$$R^2 = 0.9991 \quad \overline{R^2} = 0.\,9990 \quad F = 8633.\,2$$

Estimation results show good model fitting and significant energy variables, so the model can be used to predict the household energy consumption in 2020.

According to the structure of final demand where the proportion of consumption is α, assuming that the household consumption accounts for 70% of the consumer demand, then the household consumption should account for 0.7α of GDP. From this, the total household consumption in various scenarios and total household consumption of the previous year can be calculated and submitted into Equation (6.46) to obtain the total household energy consumption in 2020, as shown in Table 6.19.

6.4.3 Estimation of energy saving and emission reduction potential for industrial restructuring

To assess the energy saving and emission reduction capacity for industrial restructuring, the total energy consumption at high, medium, and low economic growth in 2020 are calculated in this section according to the 2005 model. The GDP in 2005 was CNY 18,493.74 billion, the total household consumption was CNY 7,090.60 billion, the total energy consumption was 2.360 billion tonnes of standard coal, and the household energy consumption was 253 million tonnes of standard coal. From this, it can be calculated that the energy consumption per unit of GDP is 1.1393 tonnes of standard coal/CNY 10,000 and the unit household energy consumption is 0.3569 tonnes of standard coal/CNY 10,000. With other conditions unchanged, according to the industrial structure in 2005, under the GDP growth rate of 6.5%, 7.5%, and 8.5%, respectively, the total energy consumption can be calculated to be 7.7339 billion, 8.4 122 billion and 9.1433 billion tonnes of standard coal, respectively.

As shown in Table 6.20, after industrial restructuring, the minimum energy consumption at low economic growth is 5.1951 billion tonnes of standard coal and the maximum energy consumption is 5.4881 billion tonnes of standard coal; the minimum energy consumption at medium economic growth is 5.7007 billion tonnes of standard coal and the maximum energy consumption is 6.0096 billion tonnes of standard coal; the minimum energy

Table 6.19 Prediction on the total household energy consumption in various scenarios (10,000 tonnes of standard coals)

GDP growth rate	*Scenario 1*	*Scenario 2*	*Scenario 3*	*Scenario 4*	*Scenario 5*
Low-speed growth	34,806.17	36,991.03	39,105.20	41,156.59	43,151.70
Medium-speed growth	41,878.37	44,507.17	47,050.92	49,519.12	51,919.61
High-speed growth	50,302.38	53,459.98	56,515.41	59,480.11	62,363.47

Table 6.20 Production, household, and total energy consumption in various scenarios (100 million tonnes of standard coals)

		2005 model	*Scenario 1*	*Scenario 2*	*Scenario 3*	*Scenario 4*	*Scenario 5*
Production energy consumption	Low-speed growth	69.046	51.4	50.431	49.513	48.546	47.636
	Medium-speed growth	75.102	55.908	54.855	53.856	52.804	51.815
	High-speed growth	81.629	60.767	59.622	58.536	57.393	56.318
Household energy consumption	Low-speed growth	8.293	3.481	3.699	3.911	4.116	4.315
	Medium-speed growth	9.02	4.188	4.451	4.705	4.952	5.192
	High-speed growth	9.804	5.03	5.346	5.652	5.948	6.236
Total energy consumption	Low-speed growth	77.339	54.881	54.13	53.424	52.662	51.951
	Medium-speed growth	84.122	60.096	59.306	58.561	57.756	57.007
	High-speed growth	91.433	65.797	64.968	64.188	63.341	62.554

consumption at high economic growth is 6.2554 billion tonnes of standard coal and the maximum energy consumption is 6.5797 billion tonnes of standard coal. These energy consumptions are much lower than those of the 2005 model. Among the various growth rates, Scenario 5 is the most energy efficient and Scenario 1 has the highest energy consumption, which indicates that the structure of final demand shifts toward low carbonization in consumption.

Under the premise that the energy structure remains unchanged, the energy saving potential and the emission reduction potential are the same. According to Table 6.20, the energy saving and the potential of energy saving and emission reduction in various scenarios are calculated. As shown in Table 6.21, in Scenario 1, where proportions of consumption, investment, and export in the final demand are 50%, 30%, and 20%, respectively, the production energy consumption is reduced by 1.7646–2.0862 billion tonnes, with 22.817% energy saving and emission reduction; in Scenario 2, where proportions of the consumption, investment, and export in the final demand are 55%, 30%, and 15%, respectively, the production energy consumption is reduced by 1.8615–2.2007 billion tonnes, with 24.069% energy saving and emission reduction; in Scenario 3, where proportions of the consumption, investment, and export in the final demand are 60%, 25%, and 15%, respectively, the energy consumption is reduced by 1.9533–2.3093 billion tonnes, with 25.257% energy saving and emission reduction; in Scenario 4, where proportions of the consumption, investment and export in the final demand are 65%, 25%, and 10%, respectively, the energy consumption is reduced by 2.0500–2.4236 billion tonnes, with 26.507% energy saving and emission reduction; and in Scenario 5, where proportions of the consumption, investment, and export in the final demand are 70%, 20%, and 10%, respectively, the energy consumption is reduced by 2.1410–2.5311 billion tonnes, with 27.683% energy saving and emission reduction.

In terms of household energy consumption, according to the relationship between total household consumption and household energy consumption from 1993 to 2010, calculation results show that the total household energy consumption is lower than that of the 2005 model, with significant effect in energy saving and emission reduction. In Scenario 1, the proportion of household consumption is 50% and the household energy consumption is reduced by about 480 million tonnes, which can save energy and reduce emissions by 5.221%–6.222%; in Scenario 2, the household energy consumption is reduced by about 450 million tonnes, which can save energy and reduce emissions by 4.876%–5.940%; in Scenario 3, the proportion of household consumption is 60% and the household energy consumption is reduced by about 430 million tonnes, which can save energy and reduce emissions by 4.541%–5.666%; in Scenario 4, the household energy consumption is reduced by about 400 million tonnes, which can save energy and reduce emissions by 4.217%–5.401%; and in Scenario 5, the proportion of household consumption rises to 70% and the household energy consumption is reduced

Table 6.21 Estimation of energy saving and emission reduction potential in various scenarios

	GDP growth rate	*Scenario 1*	*Scenario 2*	*Scenario 3*	*Scenario 4*	*Scenario 5*
Reduction in production energy consumption (100 million tonnes of standard coal)	Low-speed growth	17.646	18.615	19.533	20.5	21.41
	Medium-speed growth	19.194	20.247	21.246	22.298	23.287
	High-speed growth	20.862	22.007	23.093	24.236	25.311
Reduction in household energy consumption (100 million tonnes of standard coal)	Low-speed growth	4.812	4.594	4.382	4.177	3.978
	Medium-speed growth	4.832	4.569	4.315	4.068	3.828
	High-speed growth	4.774	4.458	4.152	3.856	3.568
Total reduction in energy consumption (100 million tonnes of standard coal)	Low-speed growth	22.458	23.209	23.915	24.677	25.388
	Medium-speed growth	24.026	24.816	25.561	26.366	27.115
	High-speed growth	25.636	26.465	27.245	28.092	28.879
Energy saving and emission reduction potential of production energy consumption (%)	Low-speed growth	22.817	24.069	25.257	26.507	27.683
	Medium-speed growth	22.817	24.069	25.257	26.507	27.683
	High-speed growth	22.817	24.069	25.257	26.507	27.683
Energy saving and emission reduction potential of household energy consumption (%)	Low-speed growth	6.222	5.94	5.666	5.401	5.144
	Medium-speed growth	5.744	5.431	5.129	4.836	4.551
	High-speed growth	5.221	4.876	4.541	4.217	3.902
Total energy saving and emission reduction potential (%)	Low-speed growth	29.039	30.009	30.923	31.908	32.826
	Medium-speed growth	28.561	29.5	30.386	31.342	32.233
	High-speed growth	28.038	28.944	29.798	30.724	31.585

by about 380 million tonnes, which can save energy and reduce emissions by 3.902%–5.144%. In the long run, savings of household energy consumption are due to technological progress, conscious energy-saving activities, and a low-carbon lifestyle of residents.

Overall, the potential of structural emission reductions is huge. Even a minor adjustment to the consumption rate and export rate in final demand to bring it back to the situation in 2000 (Scenario 1) would reduce emissions by about 28.5%. The greater the proportion of consumption in total demand, the greater the potential of energy saving and emission reduction will be. When the proportion of consumption reaches 65%, the total energy consumption can drop by more than 30%.

Notes

1 Data source: http://money.163.com/12/1113/19/8G7CMSDM00253B0H.html
2 Data source: http://baike.baidu.com/view/918374.htm

References

Chen Xikang, Yang Cuihong. *Input output technology*. Beijing: Science Press, 2011.
Fan Decheng, Wang Xiaohui. *Dynamic input-output model of china's industrial structure*. Beijing: Science Press, 2011.
Meng Yanju, Xiang Rongmei. Research on the joint model of input output and econometrics. *Journal of applied Statistics and Management*, 2011, 30(3): 531–540.
Zhu Jie. On the relationship between consumption structure and industrial structure. *Commercial Times*, 2007, 26(26): 90–91.

7 Energy restructuring and its potential in energy saving and emission reduction

7.1 Prediction on energy production and supply

7.1.1 Energy production

Energy supply refers to the quantity of energy that all energy sectors are willing and able to offer for sale at each possible price during a given period of time. Necessary energy supply is an important guarantee for economic sustainability and human well-being. Nowadays, fossil fuels dominate energy. The absolute scarcity of fossil fuel energy resources and its uneven distributions, coupled with the appropriately inelastic increase in energy demand, places energy supply on the short side of the market supply and demand. Therefore, increasing attention has been paid to energy supply in countries around the world.

A country's energy supply is determined by its domestic and foreign supply. Domestic supply is commonly referred to as energy production. Driven by energy demand, China's energy production has grown rapidly. China's total energy production was only 637 million tonnes of standard coal in 1980, and it had reached 2.969 billion tonnes of standard coal by 2010, a 3.66-fold increase in 30 years.

Since China's energy endowments are dominated by coal, China's energy production is also dominated by coal. Coal production has always accounted for more than 70% of China's total energy production, and it has exceeded 75% in the past two years. Although oil production in China has been increasing, the proportion of oil production in total energy production has been declining, from nearly 24% in 1980 to 9.8% in 2010. With the technological progress in natural gas exploration, China's natural gas production has grown significantly, and its share in the total energy production reached 4.2% in 2010. With the construction of a large number of hydropower stations and the rapid development of wind and nuclear power, China's clean power production grows rapidly. The proportion of clean power production in the total energy production exceeded 9% in 2010. In general, China has made great progress in energy production. Its energy output increases sharply and the structure is becoming increasingly diversified, as shown in Figure 7.1.

DOI: 10.4324/9781003388500-9

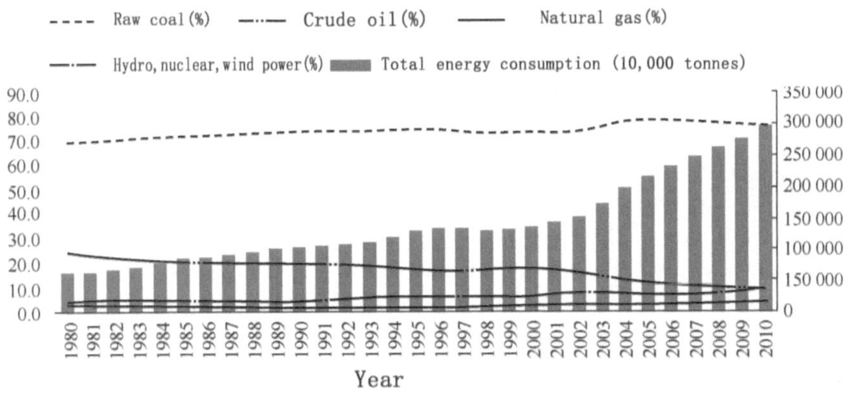

Figure 7.1 The total energy production and energy production structure in China

Even so, there is still a mismatch between energy production structure and its demand structure in China, and the contradiction between the structures of energy supply and demand is increasingly prominent. China has been completely energy self-sufficient, and even exported some energy by the 1980s. With the development of the economy, China's demand for energy has been increasing, especially for oil, which has led to the increasing volume of oil demand-supply gap. China started to import oil in 1993. Since then, oil imports have risen year by year, and its annual growth rate has reached 20% in recent years. China's import dependency rate for oil exceeded 50% in 2010, which has made oil supply the biggest threat to energy security.

7.1.2 Prediction on energy supply

There are many factors affecting energy supply, including energy endowments, energy prices, and energy investment. Among them, energy endowments have the largest impact on energy supply. Energy endowments refer to the quantity of energy resources a country or region possesses. The energy supply of a country or region is largely determined by the energy endowments. In general, the distribution of energy endowments is highly uneven on the planet, with significant regional differences in both quantity and quality.

Global proved reserves of coal stand at about 1.5980 trillion tonnes. The US, Russia, and China are the countries with the world's largest proven coal reserves. Among them, the US holds the biggest reserves of 246.64 billion tonnes, accounting for approximately 27.1% of the world's proven coal reserves. China is also a country rich in coal reserves; its proven coal reserve is 114.50 billion tonnes, accounting for 12.6% of the world's coal reserves. The distribution of oil resources is more concentrated than that of coal, with

75% of the world's proven oil reserves being concentrated in the Eastern Hemisphere. The top ten countries with biggest oil reserves hold 83% of the global oil reserves, with a half being found in the Middle East. China's oil reserves are relatively small and the proven reserves are only 2.2 billion tonnes. The distribution of natural gas resources is also uneven. According to the latest statistics, the remaining recoverable reserves of global proved natural gas were 191.05 trillion cubic meters in 2011. Russia holds the world's largest natural gas reserves at 47.57256 trillion cubic meters, accounting for nearly a quarter of the world's total proven gas reserves. China's natural gas reserves are small. It holds 3.02992 trillion cubic meters of proven gas reserves, accounting for only 1.59% of the world's total natural gas reserves.

Energy prices are also an important factor affecting energy supply. In general, other things being equal, the higher energy prices are the greater amounts of energy supply available. However, unlike other products, the short-term energy supply is hardly affected by prices since energy production requires high initial investment and physical capital investment, and there is too much lag time between investment and production. In addition, energy production is affected by technology. It is very difficult to increase production capacity in a short term when the technology remains unchanged.

In the long run, energy investment is the main factor affecting energy supply. The input of factors of production required in the early stage of energy production is large and the construction period is long. The investment in energy technology research and development is also large. According to existing experience, the increase in energy supply depends mostly on the increase in proved energy reserves and the improvement of exploitation technology. Therefore, a certain amount of guaranteed investment is the primary requirement to obtain a large amount of energy in the future.

As energy endowments, the main factor affecting energy supply, are uncertain and influenced by technology level, and different types of energy completely differ in energy endowments and market structures, it is more difficult to predict energy supply than to predict energy demand. The common methods for predicting energy supply include trend extrapolation, time series analysis, neural networks, grey system forecasting method and system dynamics method.

Existing studies on energy supply prediction are limited. There are a few short-term forecasts based on time series analysis, such as the forecast made by Yang Zhou et al. (2010), with the forecast period limited to about five years after the sample period. Yanming Li and Chuanping Zhang (2011) predicted the energy structure of 2020 using time series analysis and optimization models, estimating that the share of coal in the end use energy consumption will be about 60.85%, and such figure will be 32.89% for oil and 6.27% for natural gas. The systematic and long-term forecasts of energy supply are only mentioned in a few doctoral dissertations.

Lifeng Zhang (2006) made a forecast earlier. He predicted China's total energy production and primary energy production by type using trend extrapolation of time series analysis, GM (1, 1) model of grey system, and combined output forecast. According to his forecast, China's total energy production will be about 2.735 billion tonnes of standard coal by 2020, of which coal will contribute to about 2.010 billion tonnes of standard coal, oil will contribute to about 262 million tonnes of standard coal, natural gas will contribute to about 127 million tonnes of standard coal, and hydropower and nuclear power will contribute to about 336 million tonnes of standard coal.

Zhiru Deng (2011) used the GM (1, 1) model, the trend method, and the combined forecasting method to make a long-term forecast of China's total energy production and four primary energy productions, and the results of the three methods are relatively similar. According to the forecasts, the total energy production in 2020 will be 4.474–4.618 billion tonnes of standard coal, of which coal will contribute to 3.585–3.672 billion tonnes of standard coal, oil will contribute to 321–346 million tonnes of standard coal, natural gas will contribute to 191–456 million tonnes of standard coal, and clean power will contribute to 390–517 million tonnes of standard coal.

Both Lifeng Zhang's and Zhiru Deng's forecasting methods are based on time series data of energy production. Although the methods are almost the same, the results are quite different. The reason is that time series data reflects behavior patterns of economic phenomena within the sample period. If behavior patterns are consistent within and outside the sample period, future development trends can be better predicted. If behavior patterns are inconsistent within and outside the sample period or the time interval between the sample period and the forecast period is too long, then the forecast will be less accurate. Since Lifeng Zhang's prediction was made earlier and China's energy production has undergone a phase of rapid growth since then, the predicted result is seriously underestimated. In fact, China's energy production reached 2.969 billion tonnes of standard coal in 2010. Zhiru Deng's prediction is closer to the real situation.

Unlike the methods of the above two scholars, after considering factors such as energy resources, energy demand, energy transportation, energy investment, and ecological environment, Mingyu Li (2009) used a system dynamics model of the Hubbert curve to predict that China's coal and oil production will be 3.443 billion tonnes of standard coal and 199.25 million tonnes of standard coal by 2020, respectively.

In addition, Weidong Liu et al. (2010) predicted China's energy supply by type based on China's future energy supply scenarios. According to the prediction of the research group, in 2020, China's coal production will be about four billion tonnes (or 2.87 billion tonnes of standard coal). Domestic oil production will remain 180–200 million tonnes, exported crude oil will be 360–400 million tonnes, and oil available for consumption will be 520–600 million tonnes (or 743–857 million tonnes of standard coal). Domestic natural gas production will reach 200 billion cubic meters and natural gas imports will reach 85–100 billion cubic meters, so the total natural gas supply will be 285–300 billion cubic meters (or 379–399 million tonnes of standard coal). According to renewable energy targets, China's renewable energy will account for 15% of the total energy in 2020. It is predicted that the generation capacity of renewable energy (wind power, hydropower, nuclear power, and bioenergy) will be 1.6243–1.9393 trillion kWh (or 650–770 million tonnes of standard coal); the total energy supply will reach 4.6–5.5 billion tonnes of standard coal.

For the prediction results of the above scholars, in terms of energy production prediction, Lifeng Zhang's prediction was made earlier. This result is seriously underestimated; the predicted total energy production is less than China's actual situation in 2010, so Zhang's prediction is not used for reference. The predictions of coal production made by Yanming Li et al. and Weidong Liu et al. are also less than China's actual situation in 2010 (2.910 billion tonnes of standard coal), and therefore are not used for reference. Zhiru Deng and Mingyu Li's predictions of coal production are similar, reaching 3.585–3.672 billion tonnes of standard coal and 3.443 billion tonnes of standard coal, respectively. The prediction of Yunzhou Zhang et al. is also 3.44 billion tonnes of standard coal. Therefore, in this section, 3.443 billion tonnes of standard coal is used as the prediction of coal supply in 2020.

In terms of the prediction of oil production, Mingyu Li's prediction is the least, reaching 199.25 million tonnes of standard coal. The prediction of domestic oil production made by Weidong Liu et al. is moderate, reaching 257–286 million tonnes of standard coal, which is less than China's oil production in 2010 (291 million tonnes of standard coal). Zhiru Deng's prediction is 321–346 million tonnes of standard coal, which is reasonable and the median value of 333.5 million tonnes of standard coal is adopted as oil production in this section. For the oil imports, according to the prediction of Weidong Liu et al., it is 514–571 million tonnes of standard coal and the median value is 542.5 million tonnes of standard coal. Therefore, oil supply in 2020 is predicted to be 876 million tonnes of standard coal.

With the technological progress in natural gas exploration, China's natural gas reserves have increased significantly. Therefore, the deviation may be large if the predictions are entirely based on past production, such as Zhiru Deng's prediction. It is known that China's natural gas production was 124.7 million tonnes of standard coal in 2010, and the growth rate has remained nearly 7% in the past two years. Then it can be calculated that the natural gas production will be 267 million tonnes of standard coal in 2020, which is basically the same as the prediction of Weidong Liu et al. Weidong Liu et al. predicted that natural gas imports will be 113–133 million tonnes of standard coal in 2020. Therefore, China's natural gas supply is estimated to be 400 million tonnes of standard coal.

In terms of the prediction on primary power supply (hydropower, nuclear power, and wind power), according to Chinese government's commitment on the proportion of clean energy (15%), if the total energy supply is 5.5 billion tonnes of standard coal, the primary power supply should reach 825 million tonnes of standard coal, while China's primary power production was only 279 million tonnes of standard coal in 2010. According to the prediction of Weidong Liu et al., the maximum primary power supply may be 770 million tonnes of standard coal in 2020.

In conclusion, the possible total energy supply will be 5.489 billion tonnes of standard coal in 2020,of which, coal will be 3.443 billion tonnes of standard coal, accounting for 62.73% of total energy supply; oil will be 876 million tonnes of standard coal, accounting for 15.96% of total energy supply; natural gas will be 400 million tonnes of standard coal, accounting for 7.29% of total energy supply; hydropower, nuclear power and wind power will be 770 million tonnes of standard coal, accounting for 14.03% of total energy supply. The self-sufficient energy will be 4.8135 billion tonnes of standard coal and the energy self-sufficiency ratio will be 87.69%, which can basically ensure national energy security. Among them, the import dependency rate for oil is the largest, which is 61.9%. For domestic energy production, primary power faces the greatest pressure, with an annual growth of 10.7% required to meet the demand.

7.2 Internal substitution of energy and energy efficiency

7.2.1 Internal substitution of energy

7.2.1.1 Internal substitution of energy and energy saving and emission reduction

Energy substitution is very important in energy economics, and it has been a problem in economics. Energy substitution is divided into external substitution and internal substitution. The external substitution of energy mainly focuses on the substitution between energy and non-energy. If energy prices change or pressure of carbon emission reduction is great, the input proportion among raw materials, labor force, and energy sources may be adjusted to achieve maximum marginal production of energy, thereby saving energy and reducing emissions. The external substitution of energy focuses on the study of economic relations, such as the cost function in general. External substitution of energy is usually achieved through the reallocation of capital, labor, and energy elements, which can improve energy efficiency and save energy in the short term.

The internal substitution of energy, which mainly studies the mutual substitution between different types of energy, includes substitution of oil for coal, substitution of natural gas for oil or coal, and substitution of renewable energy for fossil fuels. It is actually the optimization of energy structure.

Since thermal efficiency and energy utilization of each energy resource are different, the economic output is also different. According to Quanbao Chen et al. (2005), among fossil fuels, natural gas has the highest efficiency, while coal has the lowest efficiency. The efficiency of natural gas is 30% higher than that of coal and the efficiency of oil is 23% higher than that of coal. In addition, for different energy sources, the carbon dioxide emissions from energy combustion per unit of calorific value vary greatly. In terms of energy combustion for 1 tonne of standard coal, coal emits the most carbon dioxide, followed by oil, and natural gas. Therefore, from the perspective of energy saving and emission reduction, the substitution of oil and natural gas for coal is an inevitable choice for optimization of energy structure. This is also confirmed by the empirical research about internal substitution of energy affecting energy efficiency (Han, 2007).

Chinese scholars focus more on the external substitution of energy. Zhongdong Yang (2007) used the transcendental logarithmic production function to study the energy substitution in manufacturing industries, and found a relatively strong substitution between capital and energy and between labor and energy. However, Chengjun Lu and Ruiming Zhou (2008) had a different view. After studying the energy substitution of China's subsector of manufacturing and energy substitution of China's industrial sector, they found more obvious substitution between labor and energy and not obvious substitution between capital and energy. Libo Wu (2011) reached the same conclusion as Chengjun Lu after studying the substitution among labor, capital, and energy in China's industrial production.Guangxiao Huang and Boqiang Lin (2011) analyzed models, data, and assumptions of many scholars and used meta-analysis to draw a conclusion: there is substitution relationship between capital and energy, so industrial energy consumption can be reduced through capital investment.

There have been only a few studies on internal substitution of energy in China, and only three relevant papers can be found at present. The earliest study on China's internal substitution of energy was conducted by Lei Huang and Yong Zhou in 2008, which showed that electricity has the highest output elasticity (0.497), followed by oil, coal, and natural gas (0.164). Energy factors have overall increasing returns to scale effect on economic output. The economic output rates of electricity and oil are higher than that of coal, and they can effectively substitute for coal. The technological progress rates of coal, oil, and natural gas decrease in sequence, but natural gas does not exhibit a feature of high-quality and high-efficiency energy. Hongliang Shi et al. (2010) drew a slightly different conclusion on the external substitution of energy in iron and steel industries: the output elasticity of electricity and coal is relatively stable, which is 0.9–1 for electricity and 0.3–0.4 for coal. The output elasticity of oil and natural gas is low, which may be related to the internal energy structure of iron and steel industries. Mingyi Wang (2012) introduced a time trend variable to reflect technological progress of the economic system and studied the internal substitution of energy in Shandong Province, and made the following conclusion: electricity has the highest output elasticity between 0.80 and 0.89; oil and coal have almost the same output elasticity, with oil between 0.60 and 0.69 and coal between 0.58 and 0.68; natural gas has relatively lower output elasticity between 0.11 and 0.19, with the output elasticity increasing over time.

Comparison of the above studies shows that although transcendental logarithmic production function models are used by all the studies, the characteristics of internal substitution of energy vary greatly due to different study objectives. In terms of output elasticity, the common conclusion is that electricity has the highest output elasticity, while natural gas has lower output elasticity. However, the measured quantities vary greatly. Specifically, in regards to the output elasticity of electricity, it is 0.9–1.0 in the iron and steel industries and 0.80–0.89 in Shandong province, while 0.497 at national average level, which indicates that the output elasticity of energy sources and the possibility of mutual substitution of energy sources vary greatly with regions, industries, and energy types; so it is necessary to conduct research separately. Moreover, the above studies are based on the primary energy and electricity only refers to clean power. In the final energy consumption, electricity consumption is far greater than clean power consumption, and the electricity mainly comes from coal-fired power generation. Therefore, substitution studies using data on primary energy may overestimate the substitution performance between electricity and coal.

7.2.1.2 Transcendental logarithmic production functions and energy substitution properties

Substitution is possible between different types of energy sources, and it is influenced by the current energy structure and technology level. Therefore, most studies on the internal substitution of energy prefer the production function that reflects technological relationship. The transcendental logarithmic production function model is a variable elasticity of substitution production function model, which is easy to estimate and highly inclusive. It belongs to quadratic response surface model in structure, so the interaction of inputs in production functions and differences in technological progress of all inputs can be better studied. In this section, a transcendental logarithmic production function model is established with capital, labor, and energy as input factors. Considering that the factors such as capital, labor, and technology level of the current year's economic production are largely determined by the economic aggregate of the previous year, in order to save variables, economic aggregate lagged by one period is used to replace explanatory variables such as capital and labor.

The energy input is calculated based on the final energy consumption of each industry. According to energy balance sheets and energy consumption data of industry by sector in the *China Energy Statistical Yearbook*, there are about 20 types of energy in the final consumption of each industry. By nature, energy can be divided into five categories. The first category is coal, which is mainly raw coal and products of coal, including coke and coking by-products. The second category is oil, including crude oil, gasoline, kerosene, and diesel, all of which derive from petroleum or petrochemical by-products. The third category is natural gas, which includes natural gas and liquefied natural gas (LNG). The fourth category is heat. The fifth category is electricity. The above five categories of energy are denoted by *C, O, G, H*, and *E*, respectively, in 10,000 tonnes of standard coal, and the output (GDP) is denoted by *Y*. All of them are converted into constant prices in CNY 100 million in 2005 based on GDP index.

Given the production function model of energy:

$$\begin{aligned}\ln Y_t = {} & \beta_0 + \beta_1 \ln Y_{t-1} + \beta_C \ln C_t + \beta_O \ln O_t + \beta_G \ln G_t + \beta_H \ln H_t + \beta_E \ln E_t + \\ & \beta_{CC} (\ln C_t)^2 + \beta_{CO} \ln C_t \ln O_t + \beta_{CG} \ln C_t \ln G_t + \beta_{CH} \ln C_t \ln H_t + \\ & \beta_{CE} \ln C_t \ln E_t + \beta_{OO} (\ln O_t)^2 + \beta_{OG} \ln O_t \ln G_t + \beta_{OH} \ln O_t \ln H_t + \\ & \beta_{OE} \ln O_t \ln E_t + \beta_{GG} (\ln G_t)^2 + \beta_{GH} \ln G_t \ln H_t + \beta_{GE} \ln G_t \ln E_t + \\ & \beta_{HH} (\ln H_t)^2 + \beta_{HE} \ln H_t \ln E_t + \beta_{EE} (\ln E_t)^2 + \mu_t\end{aligned} \tag{7.1}$$

Output elasticity refers to the proportionate change in output in response to a proportionate change in an input when other inputs remain constant. Output elasticity, which usually reflects the sensitivity of changes in the output to changes in input of production, may serve to evaluate transformative effects of resources input. According to Equation (7.1), the output elasticity of each energy source can be calculated.

Output elasticity of coal is:

$$\varepsilon_C = \beta_C + 2\beta_{CC} \ln C_t + \beta_{CO} \ln O_t + \beta_{CG} \ln G_t + \beta_{CH} \ln H_t + \beta_{CE} \ln E_t \tag{7.2}$$

Output elasticity of oil is:

$$\varepsilon_O = \beta_O + \beta_{CO} \ln C_t + 2\beta_{OO} \ln O_t + \beta_{OG} \ln G_t + \beta_{OH} \ln H_t + \beta_{OE} \ln E_t \tag{7.3}$$

Output elasticity of natural gas is:

$$\varepsilon_G = \beta_G + \beta_{CG} \ln C_t + \beta_{OG} \ln O_t + 2\beta_{GG} \ln G_t + \beta_{GH} \ln H_t + \beta_{GE} \ln E_t \tag{7.4}$$

Output elasticity of heat is:

$$\varepsilon_H = \beta_H + \beta_{CH} \ln C_t + \beta_{OH} \ln O_t + \beta_{GH} \ln G_t + 2\beta_{HH} \ln H_t + \beta_{HE} \ln E_t \tag{7.5}$$

Output elasticity of electricity is:

$$\varepsilon_E = \beta_E + \beta_{CE} \ln C_t + \beta_{OE} \ln O_t + \beta_{GE} \ln G_t + \beta_{HE} \ln H_t + 2\beta_{EE} \ln E_t \tag{7.6}$$

When two factors can be mutually substituted, then different combinations of factors can be used to produce the same amount of output. The marginal rate of substitution of a factor refers to the ratio of the increase of one factor to the decrease of another factor under constant production. The substitution capability between various energy sources can be expressed by the marginal rate of substitution, such as the substitution of oil for coal. $\mathbf{MRS}_{O\rightarrow C}$ denotes the marginal rate of substitution of oil for coal, i.e., the increase in oil use required in response to the decrease in per unit of coal use under constant production. Therefore:

$$\mathrm{MRS}_{O\rightarrow C} = \frac{\Delta O}{\Delta C} = \frac{dO}{dC}\ (\text{keep } Y \text{ constant}) \tag{7.7}$$

Given the ratio of output elasticity:

$$\frac{\varepsilon_C}{\varepsilon_0} = \frac{d\ln Y / d\ln C}{d\ln Y / d\ln O} = \frac{d\ln O}{d\ln C} = \frac{dO/O}{dC/C} \tag{7.8}$$

So:

$$\mathrm{MRS}_{O\rightarrow C} = \frac{dO}{dC} = \frac{\varepsilon_C}{\varepsilon_0}\frac{O}{C} \tag{7.9}$$

The substitution possibility between two factors can be expressed by the substitution elasticity, which refers to the proportionate change in two factor proportions to the proportionate change in the marginal rate of substitution, that is:

$$\begin{aligned}\sigma_{OC} &= \frac{d(O/C)}{O/C} / \frac{d(MRS_{O\rightarrow C})}{MRS_{O\rightarrow C}} = d\ln\left(\frac{O}{C}\right) / d\ln(MRS_{O\rightarrow C}) \\ &= d\ln\left(\frac{O}{C}\right) / \left[d\ln\left(\frac{\varepsilon_C}{\varepsilon_O}\right) + d\ln\left(\frac{O}{C}\right)\right] \\ &= \left(1 + \frac{d\varepsilon_C/\varepsilon_C - d\varepsilon_O/\varepsilon_O}{dO/O - dC/C}\right)^{-1} \\ &= \left(1 + \frac{2\alpha_{OO}\cdot\varepsilon_C/\varepsilon_O - \alpha_{CO}}{\varepsilon_O - \varepsilon_C}\right)^{-1}\end{aligned} \tag{7.10}$$

As expressed in Equation (7.9), the marginal rate of substitution between two factors is determined by the output elasticity of the two factors and the ratio of the two inputs, while the substitution elasticity between two factors is determined by the proportionate change of the output elasticity of the two factors and the ratio of the two inputs. The output elasticity is mainly limited by technology level. Therefore, the internal substitution of energy is also limited by technology level. Under the current technology level, energy sources with high economic output efficiency and low emissions per unit of calorific value can improve the efficiency of energy utilization, thereby saving energy and reducing emissions.

From the perspective of reducing carbon emissions, the lowest emissions per unit of calorific value fall into the clean energy, followed by natural gas and oil, while coal has the highest emissions per unit of calorific value. Therefore, the substitution of natural gas for coal, substitution of oil for coal, substitution of natural gas for oil, and substitution of clean power for coal, oil, and natural gas can effectively reduce carbon emissions with the same calorific value.

7.2.1.3 Partial least squares (PLS) estimation

The transcendental logarithmic production function is a parametric linear function and can be estimated by the least square method. However, due to the large number of variables in Model 6.1, severe multi-collinearity among the variables, and the existing statistical data's failure to provide sample data within a sufficient period of time, the ordinary least squares (OLS) estimation will enlarge the variance of the parameter estimator, which makes it difficult to interpret regression coefficients or even obtain the parameter estimates sometimes.

Stepwise regression, ridge regression, and principal component regression are all common solutions to multi-collinearity. The stepwise regression can reduce the collinearity by eliminating variables that cause collinearity, which may, on the one hand, reduce the estimate accuracy due to the loss of variable information and, on the other hand, deviate the study from its intended purpose due to removal of the explanatory variables. Since multi-collinearity causes singularity of matrix $X'X$ and reduces the accuracy of the OLS estimation, the ridge regression adds a positive constant matrix λI to matrix $X'X$ to reduce the singularity of matrix $X'X$. Although it can effectively solve the problem of estimate accuracy, the deviation of ridge regression parameter from the expectation will increase as the ridge parameter λ increases. Principal component regression combines the independent variables into several uncorrelated principal components through linear transformation by extracting the principal components of the variables and then applies regression on principal components with explained variables, thereby avoiding collinearity. However, since the principal components only cover the information of the independent variables, it is difficult to select principal components for regression, and it often lacks the ability to interpret the dependent variables.

Partial least squares (PLS) regression, also known as a second-generation regression analysis method, is a new type of method for multivariate statistical data analysis introduced and developed in recent years. It was first proposed by Wold et al. in 1983. PLS regression combines multiple linear regression, principal component analysis, and canonical correlation analysis method, which effectively solves the problem of regression modeling of multiple dependent variables to independent variables under inadequate sample size and multi-collinearity. PLS regression not only incorporates the idea of extracting information from explanatory variables in principal component regression, but also notices the interpretation of independent variables to dependent variables, which is neglected in principal component regression. It regards both dependent variables and independent variable as functions of some hidden variables and considers how to extract the most interpretable component that contains the largest amount of information on this basis. Meanwhile, PLS regression also allows regression modeling when sample size is less than the number of variables, with the original dependent variables included in the final model, so as to facilitate interpretation of the regression coefficient of each independent variable. In the past decade, PLS regression has developed rapidly in terms of theory, methods, and applications.

PLS regression usually assumes q dependent variables $\{y_1, \ldots, y_q\}$ and p independent variables $\{x_1, \ldots, x_p\}$. In order to study the statistical relationship between dependent variables and independent variables, we have observed n sample points, which construct the data tables $X = \{x_1, \ldots, x_p\}$ and $Y = \{y_1, \ldots, y_p\}$ of independent variables and dependent variables. PLS regression extracts components t_1 and u_1 from X and Y, respectively. That is, t_1 is the linear combination of $x_1, \ldots, x_p$, and u_1 is the linear combination of $y_1, \ldots, y_q$. When extracting these two components, the following two requirements are necessary for regression analysis: first, t_1 and u_1 should carry as much information about the variation in their respective data tables as possible, and second, the correlation between t_1 and u_1 should be the strongest. The two requirements indicate that t_1 and u_1 should best represent data tables X and Y, while the component of independent variables t_1 has the strongest ability to interpret the component of dependent variables u_1. After the first components t_1 and u_1 are extracted, the PLS regression applies regression of X on t_1 and Y on u_1, respectively. If the regression equation has achieved satisfactory accuracy, the algorithm will be terminated. Otherwise, a second round of component extraction will be performed using the residual information after X is interpreted by t_1 and Y is interpreted by u_1. This process loops until a satisfactory accuracy is reached. If a total of m components $t_1, \ldots, t_m$ are finally extracted from X, the PLS regression will apply the regression of y_k on $t_1, \ldots, t_m$ and then express it as a regression equation of y_k on the original variables $x_1, \ldots, x_p$, wherein $k = 1, 2, \ldots, q$.

7.2.2 Estimation of output elasticity of energy

7.2.2.1 Estimation of the transcendental logarithmic production function by sector

In order to study the internal substitution of energy of each industrial sector, final energy consumption data by sector is compiled according to *China Energy Statistical Yearbook* from 1993 to 2010 in this section. The final energy consumption data of each sector is combined into five categories: the first 15 sectors are production sectors and the last sector is household consumption sector. In terms of the output (GDP) data, the National Accounts section of *China Energy Statistical Yearbook 2011* provides GDP data of the industries, including agriculture, industry, construction, transport, storage and post, wholesale and retail trade, hotels and catering services, financial intermediation, real estate, and others over the years. *China Energy Statistical Yearbook* for each year provides the value added by sector, but the data for 2004, 2008, 2009, and 2010 are missing. In this section, interpolation and smoothing techniques are used to estimate the value-added ratio of 2003 and 2005–2007, and then the value added by sector is calculated according to the total output and value-added ratio by sector.

The PLS model is applied to each sector for estimation using a self-compiled MATLAB® program, and the results are shown in Tables 7.1 and 7.2.

From the estimation results of the 16 sectors, the goodness of fit of the models are all relatively high. Except for Sector 4, which is slightly lower, the goodness of fit of the models in other sectors all exceeds 0.9, indicating a good goodness of fit. In terms of the regression coefficients, except for Sectors 9 and 10, other sectors have negative cross effect terms and square effect terms, indicating that only these two sectors (the nonmetallic mineral products industry and the metal products manufacturing industry) have increasing returns to scale, while the other sectors have nonincreasing returns to scale overall.

7.2.2.2 Output elasticity of various energy sources

According to Equations (7.2)–(7.6), the output elasticity of coal, oil and natural gas, heat, and electricity for each sector can be calculated. The calculation results are listed in Table 7.2. Here, only the output elasticity for 2010 is given, as shown in Table 7.3. According to the calculation results, the sequence diagram of energy output elasticity by product of each sector is drawn, as shown in Figures 7.2–7.6.

1 Output elasticity of coal

   As shown in Figure 7.2, the output elasticity of coal in each sector shows a slight upward trend. The output elasticity of coal in each sector varies greatly. The largest output elasticity is in Sector 2 (Mining industry), reaching around 0.6. There are six sectors with output elasticity greater than zero, including the mining industry, production and supply industries of electricity, heat and water, the coking and petroleum processing industry, the nonmetallic mineral products industry, the metal products manufacturing industry, the retail, wholesale, and catering and accommodation sector. There is one sector with the output elasticity of coal approaching zero, which is agriculture. Output elasticity of coal in the remaining nine sectors are all significantly less than zero, and the

Table 7.1 The PLS estimation results for Sectors 1–8

Variables	*Sector 1*	*Sector 2*	*Sector 3*	*Sector 4*	*Sector 5*	*Sector 6*	*Sector 7*	*Sector 8*
1	0.1848	0.1090	0.1171	0.1820	0.1631	0.1723	0.1364	0.2671
2	−0.0308	0.1674	−0.2217	−0.350	−0.2301	0.0380	0.1426	−0.3354
3	0.0091	−0.0127	0.0622	0.0395	−0.0394	−0.1050	−0.0197	−0.0202
4	0.0005	0.0222	−0.0020	0.0014	−0.0456	−0.0051	0.1113	0.0573
5	0.0470	−0.0023	0.1276	0.0565	0.2011	0.0216	−0.1028	0.0585
6	0.1164	0.2748	0.1415	0.1579	0.2037	0.2815	0.0456	0.2580
7	−0.0023	0.0102	−0.0148	−0.0245	−0.0158	0.0026	0.0109	−0.0179
8	−0.0006	0.0102	0.0067	−0.0114	−0.0154	−0.0016	0.0026	−0.0098
9	0.0001	0.0076	−0.0003	−0.0007	−0.0063	0.0005	0.0120	−0.0009
10	0.0067	0.0053	0.0146	0.0023	0.0187	0.0023	0.0085	−0.0017
11	0.0021	0.0133	0.0153	0.0111	0.0175	0.0100	0.0084	0.0085
12	0.0007	−0.0007	0.0060	0.0043	−0.0033	−0.0098	−0.0008	0.0003
13	0.0001	0.0013	−0.0003	0.0004	−0.0066	−0.0014	0.0030	0.0041
14	0.0065	−0.0004	0.0133	0.0077	0.0155	−0.0033	−0.0019	0.0041
15	0.0029	0.0092	0.0092	0.0141	0.0120	0.0180	0.0004	0.0158
16	0.0000	0.0021	0.0004	−0.0045	−0.0047	−0.0115	0.0112	0.0028
17	0.0008	0.0007	−0.0002	0.0017	−0.0026	0.0007	0.0083	0.0034
18	0.0001	0.0072	−0.0002	0.0022	−0.0028	0.0014	0.0087	0.0078
19	0.0507	−0.0003	0.0118	0.0049	0.0179	0.0011	−0.0061	0.0040
20	0.0061	0.0032	0.0108	0.0073	0.0153	0.0091	0.0016	0.0092
21	0.0075	0.0164	0.0097	0.0098	0.0132	0.0165	0.0043	0.0133
C	6.6194	−1.0862	4.1547	6.6488	3.0875	1.7981	2.4300	3.6906
R^2	0.9766	0.9607	0.9621	0.8583	0.9056	0.9496	0.9678	0.9787

Note: Variables 1–21 represent the 1st–21st independent variables in the model, *C* represents a constant term, and R^2 is the goodness of fit of the model; Sectors 1–8 represent agriculture, mining industry, the food, beverage, and tobacco products industry, the textile and leather product industry, other manufacturing industries, production and supply industries of electricity, heat, and water, the coking and petroleum processing industry, and the chemical industry, respectively.

Table 7.2 The PLS estimation results for Sectors 9–16

Variables	*Sector 9*	*Sector 10*	*Sector 11*	*Sector 12*	*Sector 13*	*Sector 14*	*Sector 15*	*Sector 16*
1	0.1043	0.0418	0.1841	0.1548	0.0851	0.2449	0.1239	0.1011
2	0.1494	0.0680	−0.2459	−0.2405	−0.0851	−0.0195	−0.1452	−0.1569
3	0.0286	0.1171	−0.0134	0.0923	0.0407	0.1250	0.2739	0.0077
4	0.0221	0.0233	0.0910	0.0061	0.0259	−0.0274	−0.0011	0.0521
5	0.0362	0.1360	−0.2141	0.0267	−0.0047	−0.0054	0.0925	0.0198
6	0.0707	0.0811	0.1624	0.1672	0.0616	0.1417	0.0973	0.0399
7	0.0079	0.0033	−0.0168	−0.0196	−0.0061	−0.0006	−0.0104	−0.0084
8	0.0045	0.0083	−0.0070	0.0101	−0.0004	0.0076	0.0003	−0.0007
9	0.0022	0.0020	0.0103	0.0009	0.0043	−0.0024	−0.0002	0.0054
10	0.0098	0.0060	−0.0258	0.0036	−0.0024	0.0001	0.0053	0.0011
11	0.0056	0.0039	0.0143	0.0118	−0.0046	0.0108	0.0069	0.0030
12	0.0020	0.0081	−0.0007	0.0066	0.0025	0.0106	0.0172	0.0008
13	0.0025	0.0034	0.0082	0.0020	0.0025	−0.0026	−0.0001	0.0032
14	0.0060	0.0163	−0.0070	0.0053	0.0005	0.0009	0.0101	0.0012
15	0.0036	0.0098	0.0081	0.0095	0.0035	0.0144	0.0092	0.0015
16	0.0023	0.0023	0.0080	−0.0140	0.0033	0.0014	0.0002	0.0041
17	0.0079	0.0032	0.0102	0.0044	0.0044	0.0039	−0.0001	0.0034
18	0.0023	0.0023	0.0078	0.0015	0.0033	0.0006	−0.0001	0.0035
19	0.0050	0.0099	−0.0194	0.0071	0.0022	0.0048	0.0092	0.0016
20	0.0100	0.0066	0.0100	0.0051	0.0006	0.0026	0.0078	0.0019
21	0.0042	0.0042	0.0094	0.0124	0.0048	0.0099	0.0060	0.0024
C	1.3801	0.1977	8.4533	5.4599	7.1409	3.0435	3.8009	9.1494
R^2	0.9823	0.9870	0.9898	0.9936	0.9976	0.9849	0.9877	0.998

Note: Variables 1–21 represent the 1st–21st independent variables in the model, C represents a constant term, and R^2 is the goodness of fit of the model; Sectors 9–16 represent the nonmetallic mineral products industry, the metal products manufacturing industry, the machinery and equipment manufacturing sector, the construction industry, the transportation, storage, post and telecommunication services, the retail, wholesale, trade, and catering and accommodation sector, other service industries, and household consumption, respectively.

smallest value is in the chemical industry, which is approaching −0.7. In addition, output elasticities of coal in Sector 4 (textile and leather product industry) and Sector 11 (machinery and equipment manufacturing sector) are also much less than zero.

2 Output elasticity of oil

Figure 7.3 shows the trend of output elasticity of oil by sector. As shown in the figure, output elasticity of oil for each sector shows a slight upward trend. Sector 15 has the largest output elasticity, which is close to 0.7; Sector 6 (the production and supply industries of electricity, heat, and water) has the smallest output elasticity, which is −0.0666 in 2020. The output elasticity of oil in most sectors is greater than zero, while other manufacturing industries, production, and supply industries of electricity, heat, and water and the coking and petroleum processing industry have the output elasticity of oil less than zero. In general, there

Table 7.3 Output elasticity of energy by product for each sector in 2010

Sector	*Coal*	*Oil*	*Natural gas*	*Heat*	*Electricity*
1	−0.0429	0.0467	0.0028	0.3104	0.2823
2	0.6182	0.1523	0.1949	0.0703	0.8122
3	−0.2015	0.3346	−0.0054	0.5436	0.5288
4	−0.6718	0.1773	−0.0014	0.2502	0.5397
5	−0.3190	−0.0215	−0.2071	0.7771	0.7127
6	0.1770	−0.0666	−0.0471	0.1214	0.8069
7	0.5259	−0.0063	0.4895	−0.0771	0.2417
8	−0.6890	0.1099	0.2308	0.2558	0.8606
9	0.4400	0.1745	0.1423	0.3558	0.2806
10	0.2907	0.5541	0.1421	0.5410	0.3377
11	−0.5089	0.0067	0.4578	−0.5317	0.6076
12	−0.3021	0.3574	−0.0237	0.1878	0.5219
13	−0.1783	0.1353	0.1677	0.0391	0.1685
14	0.0968	0.4296	−0.0213	0.0924	0.4972
15	−0.2054	0.6974	−0.0019	0.3846	0.3732
16	−0.2312	0.0649	0.2536	0.1098	0.1683

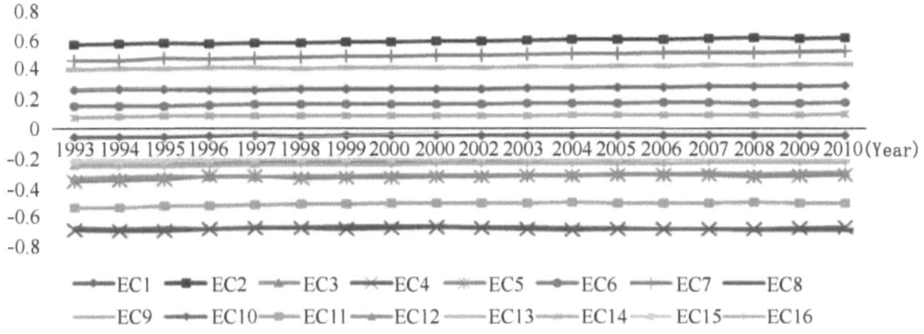

Figure 7.2 Output elasticity of coal by sector

are few sectors with high output elasticity of oil, and only five sectors with output elasticity greater than 0.3, including the food, beverage, and tobacco products industry, the metal products manufacturing industry, the construction industry, the retail, wholesale, catering and accommodation sector, and other industries. The output elasticity of oil in other sectors are all less than 0.2.

3 Output elasticity of natural gas

In comparison, the output elasticity of natural gas is lower. As shown in Figure 7.4, there are two sectors (the coking and petroleum processing industry and the machinery and equipment manufacturing sector) with the output elasticity of natural gas between 0.4 and 0.5, which is relatively high. The output elasticities of natural gas in the remaining sectors are less than 0.3. There are six sectors (the mining industry, the chemical industry, the nonmetallic mineral products industry, the metal products manufacturing industry, the transport, storage, and post services, and household service) with the output elasticity of natural gas greater than 0.1. There is only one sector (other manufacturing industries) with the output elasticity of natural gas less than zero, about −0.2, while the output elasticities of natural gas in other sectors are close to zero.

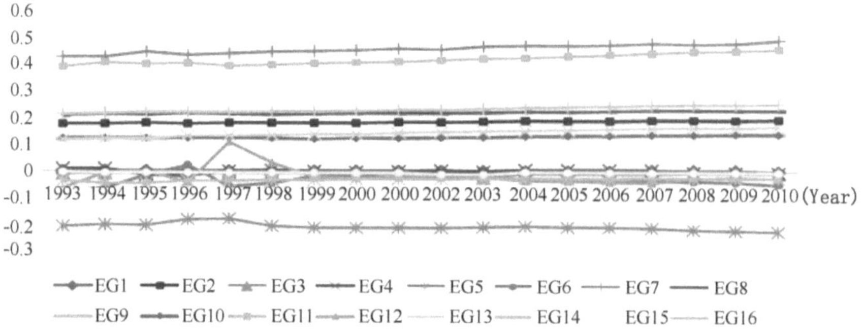

Figure 7.3 Output elasticity of oil by sector

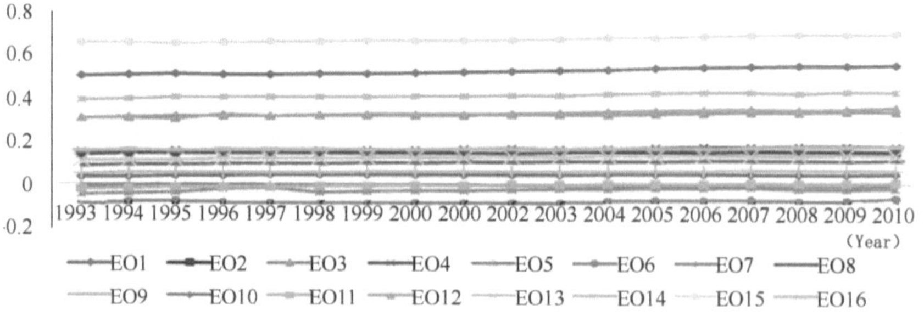

Figure 7.4 Output elasticity of natural gas by sector

4 Output elasticity of heat

As shown in Figure 7.5, the output elasticity of heat varies considerably among the sectors. Among them, other manufacturing industries have the largest output elasticity (close to 0.8), while the machinery and equipment manufacturing sector has the smallest output elasticity (around −0.5). The output elasticity of heat is generally greater than zero, and only two sectors (the coking and petroleum processing industry and the machinery and equipment manufacturing sector) have the output elasticity less than zero. The output elasticities of heat for the remaining sectors are distributed evenly among 0–0.6.

5 Output elasticity of electricity

As shown in Figure 7.6, output elasticity of electricity of each sector is greater than zero, and shows an upward trend. The chemical industry has the largest output elasticity of electricity, which reaches 0.8606 in 2010. The output elasticity of electricity of mining industry also exceeds 0.8. The household service has the smallest output elasticity of electricity, which is 0.1683. The output elasticity of electricity varies considerably among the sectors, and is distributed evenly among 0.1–0.9.

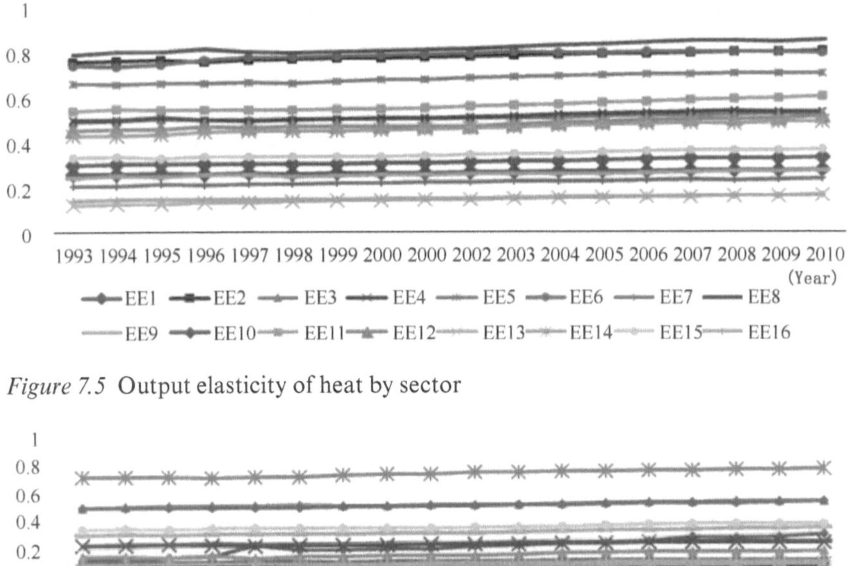

Figure 7.5 Output elasticity of heat by sector

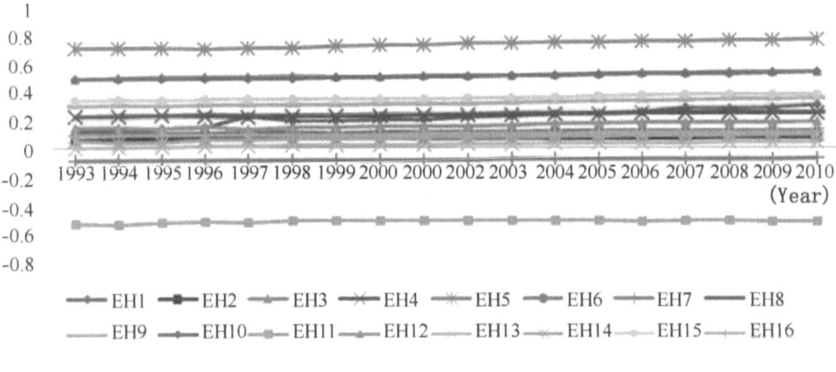

Figure 7.6 Output elasticity of electricity by sector

For the changing trends for the output elasticity of the five energy sources in each sector, except for natural gas, whose output elasticity showed relatively large fluctuations from 1996 to 1999, the output elasticities of the remaining energy sources are on the rise, indicating that the output elasticities of various energy resources are increasing due to technological progress. However, the rise rate is stable, indicating that the pace of technological progress is slow. Therefore, the output elasticities of the five energy sources from 1993 to 2010 in each sector changed very little.

7.2.3 Energy efficiency and internal substitution of energy

Energy efficiency involves the economic effect per unit of energy brings. It is a matter of energy utilization efficiency, as higher energy efficiency leads to higher economic effects. World Energy Council defines energy efficiency as "the practice of using less energy to provide the same amount of useful output from a service". In China, scholars also define energy efficiency. From the perspective of physics, "energy efficiency refers to the ratio of effective energy to the actual energy consumption in energy utilization". From an economic point of view, energy efficiency is the use of less energy to produce the same amount of services or useful output.

In general, the output elasticity of energy should be positive, which refers to the ratio of the growth rate of energy consumption to the growth rate of the output. And it is true in most scenarios in practice. Especially for the output elasticity of total energy consumption, the total output elasticity of energy must be positive before the inflection point of the environmental Kuznets curve (EKC). However, the output elasticity is not necessarily positive for a specific energy. Due to technological progress and optimization of internal energy structure in a sector, the consumption of certain energy may decrease as the output increases, in which case, the output elasticity of energy is not positive.

The higher the output elasticity of energy, the higher the economic efficiency of energy, which means the lower growth rate of energy input compared with economic growth rate; the output elasticity of energy is negative, which means that energy input grows negatively as the economy grows. If this effect is caused by technology progress, then this technological progress is energy saving. If this effect is caused by the internal adjustment of energy, then the energy structure is optimized. In terms of the current research methods, it is difficult to separate the impact of technology from the impact of energy structure. In conclusion, the output elasticity of energy is less than zero, which means that the energy intensity decreases and the energy efficiency increases.

According to Equation (7.7), under the premise that the output remains unchanged, if the increase in oil input is less than the decrease in coal input, that is, the marginal rate of substitution is less than one, then this internal substitution of energy is energy saving and highly efficient. The smaller the marginal rate of substitution, the greater the energy saving effect of the substitution. Then from Equation (7.9), it can be concluded that the marginal rate of substitution of two energy sources depends on the ratio of their output elasticity and the ratio of their inputs. In short, the marginal rate of substitution of two energy sources is directly proportional to the ratio of output elasticity and inversely proportional to the ratio of energy input. Taking the substitution of oil for coal as an example, the marginal rate of substitution of oil for coal is directly proportional to the $\varepsilon_C/\varepsilon_O$ and inversely proportional to the ratio of their input C/O. That is, the greater the output elasticity of coal, the smaller the input of coal; the greater the input of oil, the greater the marginal rate of substitution and the smaller energy-saving effect of the substitution of oil for coal. Conversely, the greater the output elasticity of oil, the smaller the input of oil; the greater the input of coal, the smaller the marginal rate of substitution and the greater energy-saving effect of the substitution of oil for coal. The internal substitution of energy is one of the major means to improve energy efficiency.

7.3 Energy restructuring under supply and substitution constraints

7.3.1 Optimization model of energy structure under supply and substitution constraints

In energy restructuring, the internal energy structure varies considerably among the sectors and the pace of technological progress varies among the sectors, which leads to different efficiencies and targets of internal substitution of energy among the sectors. Therefore, the energy restructuring must take into account the possibility of mutual substitution between different types of energy at current technology levels. The energy consumption structure is constrained by energy supply structure, especially in China, where substitution for coal in large quantities and an all-round way is impossible due to limited supply of oil and natural gas despite high economic efficiency and low carbon emission per unit of calorific value of oil and natural gas. Therefore, China's energy restructuring can only be carried out under the supply and substitution constraints.

C_i, O_i, G_i, H_i and E_i $(i = 1,2,\ldots, 16)$, respectively, denote the final consumption of coal, oil, natural gas, heat, and electricity in the i sector in 2020 according to the energy structure allocation by sector in 2010. Suppose the energy restructuring of coal, oil, natural gas, heat, and electricity in the ith sector are DC_i, DO_i, DG_i, DH_i and DE_i $(i = 1,2,\ldots, 16)$, respectively, the proportions of coal, oil, and natural gas in the total primary energy used for heating are x_1, x_2, and x_3, respectively, and for power generation are y_1, y_2, and y_3, respectively.

1 Supply constraints of energy restructuring

2 The use of coal can be divided into three parts. The first part is the direct use in each end use sector. According to the energy structure allocation by sector in 2010, C_i denotes the final consumption of coal in the ith sector and DC_i denotes the energy restructuring of coal in the ith sector. Therefore, the direct use of coal in the end use sector after restructuring is the sum of C_i and DC_i. The second part is coal for heating. Coal consumption is the total supply multiplied by the proportion of coal for heating x_1. The third part is coal for power generation. Coal consumption is the total supply multiplied by the proportion of coal for power generation y_1. The sum of these three should be less than the total supply of coal. According to the energy supply targets in 2020, including 3.443 billion tonnes of standard coal in coal supply, 876 million tonnes of standard coal in oil supply, and 400 million tonnes of standard coal in natural gas supply, then:

$$\sum_{i=1}^{16} C_i + \sum_{i=1}^{16} DC_i + 344300 \cdot x_1 + 344300 \cdot y_1 \leq 344300 \tag{7.11}$$

Supply constraints of oil and natural gas can also be obtained similarly, of which oil supply constraints can be expressed as:

$$\sum_{i=1}^{16} O_i + \sum_{i=1}^{16} DO_i + 87600 \cdot x_2 + 87600 \cdot y_2 \leq 87600 \tag{7.12}$$

Natural gas supply constraints can be expressed as:

$$\sum_{i=1}^{16} G_i + \sum_{i=1}^{16} DG_i + 40000 \cdot x_3 + 40000 \cdot y_3 \leq 40000 \tag{7.13}$$

Heat is secondary energy, which is converted from coal, oil, and natural gas. In the process of conversion, there is heat loss, that is, the difference between the energy consumption of heat production and end use heat. According to China's energy balance sheet in 2010, the heat loss rate for that year is calculated to be about 25.84%. Since the pace of progress in energy conversion technology is slow, it is assumed that the energy conversion efficiency in 2020 will remain the same as it was in 2010. The sum of the end use heat consumption of each sector is less than the total heat supply, and then the heat supply constraint is as follows:

$$\sum_{i=1}^{16} H_i + \sum_{i=1}^{16} DH_i \leq 0.7416 \cdot (344300 \cdot x_1 + 87600 \cdot x_2 + 40000 \cdot x_3) \tag{7.14}$$

The situation for electricity is more complicated than for heat. Electricity includes primary and secondary sources of electricity. Primary source of electricity, which mainly refers to hydropower, nuclear power, wind power, and also a very small amount of biomass power, does not produce emissions and serves as the cleanest energy source. Secondary source of electricity mainly refers to coal-fired power. Thermal energy is converted into electrical energy through coal combustion, which will produce a large amount of energy losses and pollution emissions. In China's energy statistics, there are two types of total energy statistics: the coal consumption method for power generation and the calorific value equivalent method. According to the calorific value equivalent, per kWh of electricity is equivalent to about 0.1229 kilogram of standard coal. However, according to coal consumption method for power generation, per kWh of electricity is converted into 0.4040 kilogram of standard coal, which means that the production of one kWh of electricity consumes about 0.4040 kilogram of standard coal. This huge difference is the energy loss in the process of converting coal into electricity. Since the calculation of electricity in this section is based on the coal consumption method for power generation, it is unnecessary to calculate the energy loss rate of power generation when calculating the electricity supply constraints. There are also losses in power transmission, namely transmission losses. Therefore, the power for the end use energy consumption is less than the total power production. According to China's energy balance sheet in 2010, the transmission loss rate is about 6.06%, which also serves as the transmission loss rate in 2020. Therefore, the total power supply in 2020 is 770 million tonnes of standard coal of primary source of electricity and coal-fired power, and the total consumption of end use power should not exceed the total supply of end use power. Then:

$$\sum_{i=1}^{16} E_i + \sum_{i=1}^{16} DE_i \leq 0.9394 \cdot \left(344300 \cdot y_1 + 87600 \cdot y_2 + 40000 \cdot y_3 + 77000\right) \tag{7.15}$$

3 Internal substitution constraints of energy in the sector

Taking the derivative of the energy production function Equation (7.1) of the sector, we have:

$$\frac{dY_t}{Y_t} = \beta_1 \frac{dY_{t-1}}{Y_{t-1}} + \varepsilon_C \frac{dC}{C} + \varepsilon_o \frac{dO}{O} + \varepsilon_G \frac{dG}{G} + \varepsilon_H \frac{dH}{H} + \varepsilon_E \frac{dE}{E} \tag{7.16}$$

In economics, the derivative $dy_t / y_t$of the logarithmic variable $\ln y_t$ represents the growth rate of the variable y_t. Therefore, Equation (7.16) indicates that the growth rate of the sectoral output is composed of six parts. The first part is $\beta_1 \frac{dY_{t-1}}{Y_{t-1}}$, which represents the impact of growth rate of total output (representing capital, labor, technology, etc.) in the previous year. Parts 2–6 represent the impact of different types of energy growth on the growth rate of sectoral output, respectively.

Obviously, the energy restructuring should at least not decrease the growth rate of sector output, so it is assumed that the growth rate of output in the tth year and the t − 1th year output growth rate are the same, both are η_Y, and the growth rate of sectoral output is at least greater than zero. It is required that:

$$\frac{\varepsilon_C}{C}dC+\frac{\varepsilon_O}{O}dO+\frac{\varepsilon_G}{G}dG+\frac{\varepsilon_H}{H}dH+\frac{\varepsilon_E}{E}dE=(1-\beta_1)\eta_Y\geq 0 \tag{7.17}$$

Wherein the differential of each type of energy such as dC and dO are the amounts of adjustment for each type of energy, and they are still denoted by *DC, DO, DG, DH*, and *DE* according to the above convention. It can be concluded from Equation (7.17) that the energy factor in the growth rate of sectoral output is only related to the output elasticity of energy and the energy use of each type of energy, while the internal substitution elasticity of energy is only determined by the output elasticity of each type of energy and the ratio of the use of two energy sources. Therefore, the constraint (Equation 7.17) to keep the growth rate of sectoral output from decreasing in the sectoral energy restructuring is actually the internal substitution constraints of energy.

4 Sectoral energy consumption constraints

After the energy restructuring, at least the total energy consumption of each sector should not increase. Therefore, the sum of energy adjustment of each sector should be less than zero, that is:

$$DC_i+DO_i+DG_i+DH_i+DE_i\leq 0(i=1,2,\cdots,16) \tag{7.18}$$

5 Constraints in adjustment range

6 Since the pace of technological progress is slow, the technology level is relatively stable over a period of time and the proportion of each energy source is relatively stable, the substitution property of energy will not change significantly. The energy restructuring can only be within a certain range; otherwise the law of substitution calculated according to the previous data will not be applicable to future predictions. The adjustment rage is assumed to be –30% to 30% in this section, considering the shortage of oil supply. Taking medium GDP growth rate as an example, under the sectoral energy structure in 2010, the total demand for oil will be 1.169–1.171 billion tonnes of standard coal, while the total oil supply is only 876 million tonnes of standard coal, and the energy gap must be filled by other energy sources. Therefore, at least 25.20% of the demand for oil should be met by internal substitution of energy. Hence:

$$-0.30\leq\frac{DC_i}{C_i}\leq 0.30(i=1,2,\ldots,16) \tag{7.19}$$

$$-0.30 \le \frac{DO_i}{O_i} \le 0.30(i = 1,2,\ldots,16) \tag{7.20}$$

$$-0.30 \le \frac{DG_i}{G_i} \le 0.30(i = 1,2,\ldots,16) \tag{7.21}$$

$$-0.30 \le \frac{DH_i}{H_i} \le 0.30(i = 1,2,\ldots,16) \tag{7.22}$$

$$-0.30 \le \frac{DE_i}{E_i} \le 0.30(i = 1,2,\ldots,16) \tag{7.23}$$

7 Energy structure for heat and power generation

In the energy conversion process, a combination of various energy by a certain proportion is required to convert primary energy into secondary energy. Since the conversion of thermal energy is easy, any of coal, oil, or natural gas can be used for the conversion, provided that $x_i \ge 0$ is required. However, a certain proportion of oil must be consumed in the conversion to electricity. So we assume $y_j \ge 0.03(j = 2)$, according to the proportion of oil for power generation in energy balance sheet in previous years. The maximum proportion of energy conversion is assumed to be no more than 60% of the energy. To sum up:

$$0 \le x_i,\ y_j \le 0.60(i = 1,2,3; j = 1,3) \tag{7.24}$$

$$0.03 \le y_j \le 0.60(j = 2) \tag{7.25}$$

8 Energy restructuring targets

9 After the energy supply constraints and internal substitution constraints of energy are met, the only goal of energy restructuring is to minimize carbon emissions. Carbon emissions from energy consumption can be calculated based on the coal, oil, and natural gas used in primary energy. According to the carbon emission coefficients of raw coal, crude oil, and natural gas and standard coal coefficients in Chapter 4, the emission coefficient is 2.6604 tonnes of carbon dioxide per tonne of standard coal for coal, 2.1141 tonnes of carbon dioxide per tonne of standard coal for crude oil, and 1.6257 tonnes of carbon dioxide per tonne of standard coal for natural gas. Therefore, the objective function to minimize carbon emissions can be expressed as:

$$\begin{aligned} \min 2.6604\left[\sum_{i=1}^{16}(C_i + DC_i) + 344300 \cdot x_1 + 344300 \cdot y_1\right] + \\ 2.1141\left[\sum_{i=1}^{16}(O_i + DO_i) + 87600 \cdot x_2 + 87600 \cdot y_2\right] + \\ 1.6257\left[\sum_{i=1}^{16}(G_i + DG_i) + 40000 \cdot x_3 + 40000 \cdot y_3\right] \end{aligned} \tag{7.26}$$

7.3.2 Results of energy restructuring

According to the results of industrial restructuring in Chapter 6, with energy consumption of each sector under the 15 scenarios with different economic growth rates and industrial restructuring as the benchmark, the consumption of coal, oil, natural gas, heat, and electricity in each sector are allocated on the basis of the energy structure in 2010, namely C_i, O_i, G_i, H_i, $E_i\,(i = 1,2,\ldots,16)$. The growth rate of the sectoral added value is calculated according to the total GDP growth rate. With the amount of sectoral energy adjustment DC_i, DO_i, DG_i, DH_i, $DE_i\,(i = 1,2,\ldots, 16)$ and the proportion of coal, oil, and natural gas in the total primary energy used for heating and power supply x_1, x_2, x_3, y_1, y_2, y_3 as unknown variables, the MATLAB program is used to solve the above planning models to obtain the adjusted energy consumption and energy structure for each sector. For the specific solution to the model, see Tables 7.3 and 7.4.

Table 7.4 Adjusted energy consumption by sector at low economic growth in 2020 (100 million tonnes of standard coal)

Sector	*Scenario 1*	*Scenario 2*	*Scenario 3*	*Scenario 4*	*Scenario 5*
Agriculture	1.005	1.03	1.056	1.081	1.107
Mining industry	3.423	3.374	3.335	3.287	3.249
Food, beverage, and tobacco products industry	0.740	0.771	0.815	0.845	0.889
Textile and leather product industry	1.271	1.218	1.278	1.225	1.285
Other manufacturing industries	1.193	1.156	1.146	1.109	1.098
Production and supply industries of electricity, heat, and water	3.035	3.047	3.062	3.074	3.09
Coking and petroleum processing industry	2.182	2.164	2.159	2.142	2.137
Chemical industry	5.754	5.606	5.653	5.505	5.551
Nonmetallic mineral products industry	4.112	4.055	3.712	3.657	3.32
Metal products manufacturing industry	8.772	8.298	7.804	7.33	6.837
Machinery and equipment manufacturing sector	1.469	1.392	1.32	1.243	1.168
Construction industry	0.654	0.657	0.566	0.569	0.48
Transportation, storage, and post and telecommunication services	3.659	3.66	3.674	3.676	3.69
Retail, wholesale, and catering and accommodation sector	1.15	1.154	1.178	1.182	1.206
Other sectors	2.163	2.289	2.416	2.541	0.636
Household services	2.652	2.818	2.98	3.136	3.288
Total	43.234	42.69	42.153	41.601	39.031

Tables 7.4 and 7.5 provide the total sectoral energy consumption at low and medium economic growth rates, respectively. Since energy demand exceeds energy supply at high economic growth rates, there is no feasible solution to the model under the given adjustment range, which means that the given energy supply and structure cannot meet the energy demand at high economic growth rates.

Meanwhile, according to the solutions of optimization model, the adjusted sectoral energy structures can be calculated under various scenarios. The sectoral energy structure under Scenario 5 at medium economic growth is shown in Table 7.6.

Comparison between the sectoral energy consumption structure of 2020 with that of 2010 is made, and the specific proportional changes are shown

Table 7.5 Adjusted energy consumption by sector at medium economic growth rate in 2020 (100 million tonnes of standard coal)

Sector	*Scenario 1*	*Scenario 2*	*Scenario 3*	*Scenario 4*	*Scenario 5*
Agriculture	1.113	1.14	1.169	1.197	1.226
Mining industry	3.74	3.687	3.644	3.592	3.55
Food, beverage, and tobacco products industry	0.804	0.836	0.885	0.917	0.965
Textile and leather product industry	1.388	1.331	1.396	1.339	1.404
Other manufacturing industries	1.299	1.259	1.248	1.208	1.196
Production and supply industries of electricity, heat, and water	3.329	3.342	3.359	3.372	3.389
Coking and petroleum processing industry	2.38	2.361	2.355	2.337	2.331
Chemical industry	6.275	6.114	6.165	6.003	6.053
Nonmetallic mineral products industry	4.725	4.694	4.295	4.267	3.877
Metal products manufacturing industry	9.566	9.049	8.51	7.993	7.455
Machinery and equipment manufacturing sector	1.599	1.516	1.437	1.353	1.271
Construction industry	0.715	0.718	0.619	0.622	0.524
Transportation, storage, and post and telecommunication services	4.007	4.008	4.023	4.025	4.041
Retail, wholesale, and catering and accommodation sector	1.264	1.269	1.295	1.3	1.326
Other sectors	2.363	2.5	2.639	2.776	2.916
Household services	3.214	3.415	3.611	3.8	3.984
Total	47.78	47.239	46.649	46.099	45.509

Table 7.6 Optimized sectoral energy structure at medium economic growth under Scenario 5 (%)

Sector	*Coal*	*Oil*	*Natural gas*	*Heating*	*Electricity*
Agriculture	18.13	27.56	0.16	0.08	54.06
Mining industry	26.21	7.8	12.04	1.45	52.51
Food, beverage, and tobacco products industry	34.77	7.84	1.31	13.83	42.24
Textile and leather product industry	18.31	6.55	0.34	12.06	62.74
Other manufacturing industries	27.98	3.89	0.62	11.94	55.57
Production and supply industries of electricity, heat, and water	22.29	0.71	0.06	2.24	74.71
Coking and petroleum processing industry	17.13	55.32	5.94	7.12	14.48
Chemical industry	27.53	12.77	11.56	11.67	36.48
Nonmetallic mineral products industry	48.74	7.55	2.92	0.23	40.56
Metal products manufacturing industry	56.54	2.16	1.08	2.97	37.25
Machinery and equipment manufacturing sector	17.01	7.71	4.27	2.25	68.75
Construction industry	7.58	58.98	0.22	0.6	32.63
Transportation, storage, and post and telecommunication services	1.63	77.7	8.6	0.38	11.68
Retail, wholesale, and catering and accommodation sector	17.58	15.94	4.31	2.94	59.23
Other sectors	9.57	34.59	2.23	3.08	50.53
Household services	19.59	14.35	14.79	8.03	43.24

in Table 7.7. It can be concluded that 14 out of the 16 sectors will reduce the proportion of coal use, among which the mining industry and the nonmetallic mineral products industry will cut the most, with a reduction rate of more than 11%. Two sectors could increase the proportion of coal use moderately, with 5.29% increase in the production and supply industries of electricity, heat, and water and 3.32% increase in the coking and petroleum processing industry. Eleven sectors should reduce the proportion of oil use, with the construction industry, the transportation, storage, post and telecommunication services, and the coking and petroleum processing industry as the top three having the oil reduced by 7.11%, 6.16%, and 4.19%, respectively. Five sectors could increase the proportion of oil consumption in energy: the proportion of oil use can be increased by 7.14% in other sectors, or by 5.36% in the retail, wholesale, and catering and accommodation sector, or by 2.82% in the textile and leather product industry, or by 1.82% in the food, beverage, and tobacco products industry, or by 0.75% in the metal products manufacturing industry. Since the proportion of natural gas in the energy structure of each sector is very small, the adjustment range for most sectors is not significant. Nine sectors need to increase the proportion of natural gas in the energy structure: the highest increase falls into the household service, which reaches 6.06%; followed by the chemical industry (4.60%); transportation, post, storage, and telecommunication services (3.60%); the proportion of natural gas in the energy structure of the mining industry and the coking and petroleum processing industry can also be increased moderately by 2.81% and 2.50%, respectively. The proportion of heat in the total energy consumption is the smallest, and heat is used mainly in the light industry sector. The proportion of heat use can be increased greatly in the food, beverage, and tobacco products industry, the textile and leather product industry, other manufacturing industries, and the chemical industry. Electricity is the most consumed energy in end use energy consumption. Among the 16 sectors, 11 sectors should reduce the proportion of electricity consumption. A reduction of more than 4% is required in other service industries, electricity, food, chemical industry, and household service; while five sectors

Table 7.7 Changes in sectoral energy structure compared to 2010 (%)

Sector	*Coal*	*Oil*	*Natural gas*	*Heating*	*Electricity*
Agriculture	−2.37	−3.6	0.06	0.03	5.87
Mining industry	−11.1	−3.3	2.81	0.34	11.27
Food, beverage, and tobacco products industry	−3.32	1.82	−0.13	5.67	−4.04
Textile and leather product industry	−1.04	2.82	−0.02	1.83	−3.58
Other manufacturing industries	−1.36	−0.19	−0.03	4.28	−2.7
Production and supply industries of electricity, heat, and water	5.29	−0.29	−0.02	0.53	−5.49
Coking and petroleum processing industry	3.32	−4.19	2.5	−0.54	−1.1
Chemical industry	−3.26	−1.51	4.6	4.5	−4.32
Nonmetallic mineral products industry	−11.01	−2.2	0.88	0.07	12.26
Metal products manufacturing industry	−1.54	0.75	0.48	1.33	−1.01
Machinery and equipment manufacturing sector	−0.13	−0.06	0.74	−0.02	−0.54
Construction industry	−0.91	−7.11	−0.03	0.24	7.82
Transportation, storage, and post and telecommunication services	−0.13	−6.16	3.6	0.16	2.51
Retail, wholesale, and catering and accommodation sector	−4.09	5.36	−1	0.99	−1.27
Other sectors	−1.28	7.14	−0.3	1.2	−6.76
Household services	−1.89	−1.38	6.06	1.38	−4.16

need to increase the proportion of electricity consumption, an increase of 12.26% is required for the nonmetallic mineral products industry, followed by the mining industry (11.27%), construction industry (7.82%), agriculture (5.87%), transportation, storage, and post and telecommunication services (2.51%).

In terms of internal substitution of energy by sector, the agriculture and the mining industry should substitute electricity and natural gas for coal and oil. The food, beverage, and tobacco products industry, the textile and leather product industry, and other manufacturing industries should substitute heat for coal and electricity. The production and supply industries of electricity, heat, and water and the coking and petroleum processing industry should substitute coal and natural gas for oil and electricity; the chemical industry should substitute natural gas and heat for other three energy sources. The nonmetallic mineral products industry should substitute electricity for coal. The metal products manufacturing industry and the machinery and equipment manufacturing sector have the smallest energy adjustment range, with little change in the proportion of each energy source. The construction industry should substitute electricity for oil. The transportation, storage, and post and telecommunication services should substitute natural gas and electricity for oil. The retail, wholesale, catering and accommodation sector, and other industries should substitute oil and natural gas for coal and electricity. The household services should substitute natural gas and heat for other energy sources.

7.3.3 The energy saving and emission reduction potential of energy restructuring

Taking the energy structure of each sector in 2010 as a benchmark, the energy saving and emission reduction potential of energy restructuring can be calculated. The specific results are shown in Table 7.8.

As shown in Table 7.8, energy restructuring can save 1.1061–1.2920 billion tonnes of standard coal at low economic growth rates and 1.1498–1.2316 billion tonnes of standard coal at medium economic growth rates. Based on the total energy consumption in the 2005 model where 7.734 billion tonnes of standard coal are required at low economic growth rates and 8.412 billion tonnes of standard coal are required at medium economic growth rates, the energy saving effect of energy restructuring contributes 21.17%–24.87% to energy consumption reduction.

According to the energy composition in 2010, the emission reduction effect of energy restructuring can be calculated. First, according to the energy balance sheet in 2010, the coal, oil, and natural gas consumed for heating and power generation can be calculated. The carbon emission is about 2.773 billion tonnes from power generation, and about 346 million tonnes from heating. The total thermal power generation is 1.059 billion tonnes of standard coal, and the total heat supply is 100 million tonnes of standard coal.

Table 7.8 Energy saving effect of energy restructuring

	GDP growth	*Scenario 1*	*Scenario 2*	*Scenario 3*	*Scenario 4*	*Scenario 5*
Energy consumption before adjustment (100 million tonnes of standard coal)	Low	54.881	54.13	53.424	52.662	51.951
	Medium	60.096	59.306	58.561	57.756	57.007
Energy consumption after adjustment (100 million tonnes of carbon dioxide)	Low	43.234	42.69	42.153	41.601	39.031
	Medium	47.78	47.239	46.649	46.099	45.509
Energy consumption reduction (100 million tonnes of carbon dioxide)	Low	11.647	11.44	11.271	11.061	12.92
	Medium	12.316	12.067	11.912	11.657	11.498
Energy saving contribution (%)	Low	21.22	21.13	21.1	21	24.87
	Medium	20.49	20.35	20.34	20.18	20.17

Table 7.9 Emission reduction effect of energy restructuring

	GDP growth	*Scenario 1*	*Scenario 2*	*Scenario 3*	*Scenario 4*	*Scenario 5*
Emissions before adjustment (100 million tonnes of carbon dioxide)	Low	129.323	127.435	125.64	123.725	116.167
	Medium	141.600	139.605	137.709	135.681	133.775
Emissions after adjustment (100 million tonnes of carbon dioxide)	Low	90.462	88.956	87.517	85.987	78.902
	Medium	103.204	101.704	100.12	98.593	97.007
Emissions reduction (100 million tonnes of carbon dioxide)	Low	38.861	38.479	38.123	37.738	37.265
	Medium	38.396	37.901	37.589	37.088	36.768
Emission reduction contribution (%)	Low	30.05	30.20	30.34	30.50	32.08
	Medium	27.12	27.15	27.3	27.33	27.48

In conjunction with the data of clean power as well as the transmission loss rate and heat loss rate, the electricity emission coefficient of final consumption is calculated to be 2.2036 tonnes of carbon dioxide per tonne of standard coal and the heat emission coefficient is 3.4561 tonnes of carbon dioxide per tonne of standard coal. According to the energy consumption structure of each sector, the total carbon dioxide emissions of each scenario can be calculated, as shown in Table 7.9.

As shown in Table 7.9, energy restructuring can reduce emissions by 3.7265–3.8861 billion tonnes of carbon dioxide at low economic growth rates and 3.6768–3.8396 billion tonnes of carbon dioxide at medium economic growth rates. Compared with the energy structure in 2010, the energy restructuring can reduce emissions by 30.05%–32.08% at low economic growth rates and 27.12%–27.48% at medium economic growth rates.

References

Chen Quanbao, Dai Xichao, Zhang Qingchun. Characteristics of China's primary energy consumption. *Statistics & Decision*, 2005, 14: 76–78.

Deng Zhiru. *Prediction of China's energy supply and demand.* Harbin: Harbin Engineering University, 2011.

Han Zhiyong, Fan Yu, Wei Yueming. Energy structure, marginal efficiency and substitution rate: an empirical study in China. *Energy*, 2007, 32: 935–942.

Huang Guangxiao, Lin Boqiang. Research on capital energy substitution in China's industrial sector-based on the perspective of meta-analysis. *Financial Research*, 2011, 54(6): 86–96.

Li Mingyu. *System dynamics model of energy supply and energy consumption.* Boston, MA: Northeastern University, 2009.

Li Yanming, Zhang Chuanping. Using time series and linear programming to analyze the energy structure of China in 2020. *Industrial Technology and Economy*, 2011, 30(05): 102–110.

Liu Weidong, Lu Dadao, Zhang lei, Wang Limao, Zhao Jian'an, Li Shenggong, Tang Zhipeng. *China's low-carbon economic development framework and scientific basis-path research to reduce carbon emissions per unit GDP by 40%–45% in 2020.* Beijing: The Commercial Press, 2010.

Lu Chengjun, Zhou Ruiming. Research on energy substitution in China's industrial sector-based on the revision of ALLEN's substitution elasticity model. *Quantitative and Technical Economic Research*, 2008, 25(5): 30–42.

Shi Hongliang, Chen Kai, Yan Bo. Analysis of substitution elasticity of energy in China iron and steel industry-based on transcendental logarithmic production function. *Technology Economics*, 2010, 29(9): 56–73.

Wang Mingyi. An empirical study on output elasticity and substitution elasticity of energy factors in Shandong Province-Ridge regression estimation based on transcendental logarithmic production function. *Technical Economy*, 2012, 31(4): 82–86.

Wold, S, Albano, C, Dunn, W.J, et al. Pattern recognition: finding and using regularities in multivariate data. *Food Research and Data Analysis*, 1983, 3: 183–185.

Wu Libo. Research on the substitution of labor, capital and energy in industrial production in China. *Electricity and Energy*, 2011, 32(6): 173–176.
Yang Zhongdong. Research on the energy substitution relationship of China's manufacturing industry. *Contemporary Economic Science*, 2007, 3: 1–6.
Zhang Lifeng. *China energy supply and demand forecast model and development countermeasures*. Beijing: Capital University of Economics and Business, 2006.
Zhou Yang, Wu Wenxiang, Hu Ying, Zhang Yushu. Forecast and analysis of energy supply and consumption in China. *Energy and Environment*, 2010, 03: 2–4.

8 Inter-industry allocation of carbon emission indices

8.1 Inter-industry allocation of carbon emission indices

8.1.1 Final consumption emissions and sectoral direct emissions

In carbon emission calculation of the *i*th sector based on final energy consumption, emissions from electricity and heat production in secondary energy are usually allocated to each sector according to the electricity and heat used. Therefore, the sectoral carbon emissions calculated are based on the principle of final consumption. In fact, emissions from electricity and heat production occur in Sector 6 (the production and supply industries of electricity, heat, and water) and no carbon emissions are produced when using electricity and heat in all sectors. Carbon emissions during the production process in all sectors are defined as direct carbon emissions. For sectors other than Sector 6, the direct emissions are the final consumption emissions minus emissions from heat and electricity, while the direct emissions of Sector 6 are the sum of its final consumption emissions and emissions from heat and electricity of other sectors. The carbon intensity calculated based on the final consumption emissions is defined as the final energy consumption intensity, while the carbon intensity calculated based on the sectoral direct emissions is defined as the sectoral direct carbon intensity.

Direct carbon intensity and final energy consumption intensity calculated based on energy data, GDP by sector, and total consumption data in 2005 are shown in Table 8.1.

As shown in Table 8.1, there is a big difference between direct emission intensity and final energy consumption intensity of the sector. For sectors other than Sector 6, among the energy consumed in the sectors, namely coal, oil, natural gas, heat, and electricity, only the first three have direct emissions. Therefore, these sectors should take full responsibility for emission reductions from these energy sources. Direct emissions of heat and electricity occur in Sector 6. The other sectors can only reduce emissions indirectly by reducing energy use, so they only have responsibility for indirect emission reductions. For Sector 6, it produces electricity and heat for other sectors and emits considerable carbon dioxide for other sectors. It has

DOI: 10.4324/9781003388500-10

Table 8.1 Carbon emissions and carbon intensity by sector in 2005

Sector	*Total emissions in 2005 (100 million tonnes of carbon dioxide)*	*Direct emission in 2005 (100 million tonnes of carbon dioxide)*	*GDP/total consumption (CNY 100 million)*	*Direct emission intensity (tonnes of carbon dioxide per CNY 10,000)*	*Final energy consumption intensity (tonnes of carbon dioxide per CNY 10,000)*
1	1.4178	0.7496	22420.0	0.3344	0.6324
2	2.9792	1.6263	9457.2	1.7196	3.1502
3	1.1201	0.6086	7637.9	0.7968	1.4665
4	1.5116	0.4977	5996.1	0.8301	2.521
5	1.5292	0.6043	3761.3	1.6065	4.0657
6	2.6674	23.3327	6399.4	31.6189	4.1682
7	1.4592	0.8236	2264.0	3.6379	6.4452
8	6.3143	3.0380	8852.6	3.4318	7.1327
9	4.9470	3.7191	3004.1	12.3800	16.4674
10	12.8211	8.6506	10056.8	8.6018	12.7487
11	2.0452	0.7244	19801.8	0.3658	1.0328
12	0.5059	0.2992	10367.1	0.2886	0.4880
13	3.8399	3.4573	10666.3	3.2413	3.6001
14	1.1519	0.4789	18161.9	0.2637	0.6343
15	2.1378	0.9357	46091.2	0.2030	0.4638
16	5.9234	2.8249	72652.5	0.3888	0.8153
Total	52.371	52.371		3.062	3.062

Note: Sectors 1–16 represent agriculture, the mining industry, the food, beverage, and tobacco products industry, the textile and leather product industry, other manufacturing industries, the production and supply industries of electricity, heat, and water, the coking and petroleum processing industry, the chemical industry, the nonmetallic mineral products industry, the metal products manufacturing industry, the machinery and equipment manufacturing sector, the construction industry, the transportation, storage, post and telecommunication services, the retail, wholesale, catering, and accommodation sector, other service industries, and household consumption, respectively.

direct responsibility for emissions other than final consumption rather than full responsibility for emission reductions. In view of the huge differences in carbon emissions and responsibility for emission reductions between the two calculation methods, the carbon emission indices for two calculation methods are listed below, respectively.

8.1.2 Inter-industry allocation of total carbon emissions

According to the calculated results in Chapters 6 and 7, the carbon emissions from final consumption of each sector in 2020 after industrial restructuring and energy restructuring can be obtained, and the direct carbon emissions of each sector can be obtained by adjusting the data for electricity and heat emissions accordingly. Tables 8.2 and 8.3 provide the sectoral emission reduction targets at low and medium economic growth rates, respectively.

Table 8.2 Indices of final consumption emissions and total direct emissions of each sector at low economic growth rate

Sectors	*Carbon dioxide emissions from final consumption (100 million tonnes of carbon dioxide)*					*Direct carbon emissions (100 million tonnes of carbon dioxide)*				
	Scenario 1	*Scenario 2*	*Scenario 3*	*Scenario 4*	*Scenario 5*	*Scenario 1*	*Scenario 2*	*Scenario 3*	*Scenario 4*	*Scenario 5*
1	1.963	2.003	2.047	2.085	2.071	1.093	1.12	1.148	1.175	1.204
2	6.698	6.576	6.48	6.356	6.092	3.64	3.589	3.547	3.496	3.456
3	1.637	1.7	1.795	1.857	1.904	0.86	0.895	0.946	0.981	1.032
4	2.572	2.455	2.568	2.452	2.47	0.806	0.773	0.811	0.777	0.816
5	2.52	2.435	2.407	2.322	2.221	1	0.97	0.961	0.93	0.921
6	5.75	5.737	5.74	5.722	5.494	36.943	36.276	35.913	35.229	31.282
7	4.753	4.713	4.7	4.66	4.602	3.752	3.722	3.713	3.683	3.675
8	12.35	12.009	12.096	11.756	11.575	6.872	6.695	6.751	6.574	6.629
9	9.103	8.956	8.184	8.04	7.183	6.937	6.841	6.262	6.169	5.601
10	19.88	18.759	17.61	16.496	15.089	13.806	13.06	12.282	11.536	10.76
11	2.75	2.592	2.447	2.289	2.061	1.006	0.953	0.904	0.851	0.8
12	1.31	1.311	1.127	1.13	0.936	0.955	0.959	0.826	0.83	0.7
13	7.426	7.422	7.445	7.441	7.425	6.727	6.729	6.754	6.757	6.784
14	2.222	2.219	2.257	2.253	2.218	1.018	1.021	1.042	1.046	1.067
15	4.193	4.418	4.651	4.871	1.182	2.202	2.329	2.459	2.586	0.648
16	5.334	5.652	5.963	6.256	6.381	2.847	3.025	3.198	3.366	3.529
Total	90.462	88.956	87.517	85.987	78.902	90.462	88.956	87.517	85.987	78.902

As shown in Table 8.2, the total carbon emissions range from 7.8902 billion to 9.0462 billion tonnes of carbon dioxide at low economic growth rates. In terms of direct carbon emissions, Sector 6 (production and supply industries of electricity, heat, and water) has the largest carbon emissions, reaching 3.1282–3.6943 billion tonnes of carbon dioxide, followed by the metal products manufacturing industry (Sector 10), with total emissions of 1.0760–1.3806 billion tonnes of carbon dioxide. The nonmetallic mineral products industry (Sector 9) also has large carbon emissions, reaching 560.1–693.7 million tonnes of carbon dioxide. By contrast, the metal products manufacturing industry contributes the most to the final consumption emissions, reaching 1.5089–1.9880 billion tonnes of carbon dioxide, followed by the chemical industry (Sector 8), with 1.1575–1.2350 billion tonnes of carbon dioxide, and the non-metallic mineral products industry, with 718.3–910.3 million tonnes of carbon dioxide. The final consumption emissions from the production and supply industries of electricity, heat, and water are not high, reaching 549.4–575.0 million tonnes of carbon dioxide.

The situations at medium economic growth and low economic growth are similar. As shown in Table 8.3, the total carbon emissions range from 9.701 billion to 13.020 billion tonnes of carbon dioxide at low economic growth rates. In terms of direct carbon emissions, Sector 6 (production and supply industries of electricity, heat, and water) has the largest emissions, reaching 4.2810–4.5195 billion tonnes of carbon dioxide, followed by the metal products manufacturing industry (Sector 10), with total emissions of 1.1702–1.5015 billion tonnes of carbon dioxide. By contrast, the metal products manufacturing industry contributes the most to the final consumption emissions, reaching 1.7225–2.2263 billion tonnes of carbon dioxide, followed by the chemical industry (Sector 8), with 1.3275–1.3961 billion tonnes of carbon dioxide, and the non-metallic mineral products industry (Sector 9), with 858.1–1.0487 billion tonnes of carbon dioxide. The final consumption emissions from the production and supply industries of electricity, heat, and water are not high, reaching less than 700 million tonnes of carbon dioxide.

In terms of the total carbon emissions target, under the low economic growth scenario, China's total carbon emissions will range from 7.890 billion to 9.046 billion tonnes of carbon dioxide; under the medium economic growth scenario, China's total carbon emissions will range from 9.701 billion to 10.320 billion tonnes of carbon dioxide; The carbon emissions under the low economic growth scenario are smaller than the carbon emission rights allocated, according to Zhongli Ding scheme (9.221 billion tonnes of carbon dioxide), Garnaut scheme (10.281 billion tonnes of carbon dioxide), the UNDP scheme (10.422 billion tonnes of carbon dioxide), and the Chinese Academy of Social Sciences scheme (11.194 billion tonnes of carbon dioxide). The carbon emissions under the medium economic growth scenario are higher than the carbon emission rights allocated according to Zhongli Ding scheme and comparable to Garnaut scheme, but lower than the carbon emission rights allocated by UNDP scheme and the Chinese Academy of

Table 8.3 Indices of final consumption emissions and total direct emissions of each sector at medium economic growth rate

Sectors	*Carbon dioxide emissions from final consumption (100 million tonnes of carbon dioxide)*					*Direct carbon emissions (100 million tonnes of carbon dioxide)*				
	Scenario 1	*Scenario 2*	*Scenario 3*	*Scenario 4*	*Scenario 5*	*Scenario 1*	*Scenario 2*	*Scenario 3*	*Scenario 4*	*Scenario 5*
1	2.259	2.308	2.361	2.408	2.46	1.189	1.218	1.249	1.278	1.31
2	7.624	7.493	7.389	7.258	7.154	3.959	3.903	3.858	3.803	3.759
3	1.865	1.937	2.045	2.115	2.222	0.895	0.931	0.985	1.021	1.075
4	2.979	2.845	2.977	2.842	2.973	0.877	0.841	0.882	0.846	0.887
5	2.883	2.787	2.754	2.657	2.624	1.088	1.055	1.045	1.012	1.002
6	6.693	6.69	6.7	6.694	6.701	45.195	44.491	44.028	43.285	42.81
7	5.271	5.225	5.209	5.162	5.147	4.1	4.068	4.057	4.025	4.016
8	13.961	13.574	13.665	13.275	13.366	7.475	7.282	7.343	7.151	7.211
9	10.487	10.419	9.515	9.461	8.581	7.011	7.002	6.404	6.419	5.837
10	22.263	21.02	19.737	18.5	17.225	15.015	14.204	13.358	12.547	11.702
11	3.169	2.991	2.827	2.649	2.48	1.096	1.039	0.985	0.928	0.872
12	1.467	1.47	1.264	1.268	1.068	1.039	1.043	0.898	0.903	0.761
13	8.196	8.193	8.219	8.217	8.244	7.317	7.319	7.346	7.35	7.379
14	2.56	2.56	2.605	2.605	2.649	1.107	1.111	1.134	1.138	1.161
15	4.779	5.04	5.308	5.565	5.829	2.416	2.556	2.699	2.839	2.981
16	6.747	7.152	7.545	7.919	8.285	3.425	3.64	3.848	4.05	4.246
Total	103.2	101.7	100.12	98.593	97.007	103.2	101.7	100.12	98.593	97.007

Social Sciences scheme. Therefore, even under the most favorable allocation scheme of carbon emission rights designed by Chinese scholars, China must spare no efforts in energy saving and emission reduction to control the emissions within quotas.

8.1.3 Inter-industry allocation of carbon intensity

Total carbon emissions are greatly affected by the sectoral value-added. In the process of industrial restructuring, the value-added of each sector changes greatly. Therefore, the carbon intensity indices after industrial restructuring and energy restructuring are also given in this sector. The carbon intensity index under low economic growth scenarios and the decrease compared to sectoral carbon intensity in 2005 are shown in Tables 8.4 and 8.5, respectively.

As shown in Tables 8.6 and 8.7, under medium economic growth scenarios, in terms of the carbon intensity, the total carbon intensity can be reduced to 1.472–1.565 tonnes of carbon dioxide per CNY 10,000 through industrial restructuring and energy restructuring. The emission reduction rate is slightly lower than that of the low economic growth scenarios, reaching 48.87%–51.94%. The carbon intensity targets and emission reduction rates by sector are similar to those of low economic growth scenarios.

8.2 Policy recommendations for achieving carbon intensity targets

8.2.1 Contributions of industrial restructuring and energy restructuring to carbon intensity targets

Table 8.8 shows the carbon emission reduction effects of industrial restructuring and energy restructuring.

Table 8.9 shows the contributions of industrial restructuring and energy restructuring to the reduction of the carbon intensity.

According to the target of a 40%–45% reduction in the carbon intensity per unit of GDP by 2020 set by the government and based on the carbon intensity per unit of GDP (3.062 tonnes of carbon dioxide per CNY 10,000) in 2005, it is estimated in this section that the emission reduction targets can be achieved simply through industrial restructuring and energy restructuring, regardless of the technological progress in energy saving and energy conversion. Under low economic growth scenarios, after industrial restructuring and energy restructuring, the carbon emissions per unit of GDP can be reduced to 1.302–1.493 tonnes of carbon dioxide per CNY 10,000, with a reduction rate of more than 51% in carbon intensity. Under medium economic growth scenarios, the carbon emissions per unit of GDP can be reduced to 1.472–1.565 tonnes of carbon dioxide per CNY 10,000, with a reduction rate of more than 48% in carbon intensity.

Table 8.4 Carbon intensity indices and reduction ratios for carbon emissions from final consumption at low economic growth rates

Sectors	*Carbon intensity per unit of value added (tonnes of carbon dioxide per CNY 10,000)*					*Carbon intensity reduction ratios (%)*				
	Scenario 1	*Scenario 2*	*Scenario 3*	*Scenario 4*	*Scenario 5*	*Scenario 1*	*Scenario 2*	*Scenario 3*	*Scenario 4*	*Scenario 5*
1	0.382	0.38	0.379	0.377	0.365	39.67	39.93	40.13	40.42	42.21
2	2.403	2.39	2.387	2.373	2.3	23.73	24.13	24.24	24.68	26.98
3	0.968	0.967	0.965	0.964	0.938	33.98	34.04	34.21	34.3	36.05
4	1.077	1.072	1.07	1.065	1.021	57.27	57.49	57.56	57.77	59.48
5	1.227	1.221	1.218	1.212	1.171	69.83	69.96	70.04	70.18	71.2
6	2.68	2.659	2.646	2.63	2.511	35.7	36.21	36.53	36.91	39.76
7	3.961	3.947	3.957	3.943	3.914	38.55	38.75	38.61	38.82	39.27
8	3.665	3.656	3.655	3.646	3.557	48.62	48.74	48.75	48.88	50.14
9	7.548	7.501	7.502	7.495	7.361	54.17	54.45	54.44	54.49	55.3
10	5.386	5.374	5.361	5.347	5.241	57.75	57.85	57.95	58.06	58.89
11	0.315	0.313	0.312	0.31	0.297	69.49	69.66	69.79	69.98	71.24
12	0.395	0.394	0.393	0.393	0.385	19.03	19.26	19.44	19.56	21.08
13	1.547	1.546	1.545	1.544	1.535	57.03	57.05	57.08	57.1	57.36
14	0.442	0.44	0.438	0.436	0.421	30.36	30.71	30.93	31.29	33.68
15	0.321	0.321	0.32	0.319	0.074	30.72	30.88	30.97	31.18	84.07
16	0.176	0.17	0.164	0.159	0.15	78.41	79.2	79.89	80.52	81.55
Total	1.493	1.468	1.444	1.419	1.302	51.25	52.06	52.84	53.66	57.48

Table 8.5 Carbon intensity indices and reduction ratios for direct carbon emissions at low economic growth rates

Sectors	*Carbon intensity per unit of value added (Tonnes of carbon dioxide per CNY 10,000)*					*Carbon intensity reduction ratios (%)*				
	Scenario 1	*Scenario 2*	*Scenario 3*	*Scenario 4*	*Scenario 5*	*Scenario 1*	*Scenario 2*	*Scenario 3*	*Scenario 4*	*Scenario 5*
1	0.212	0.212	0.212	0.212	0.212	36.48	36.48	36.5	36.5	36.46
2	1.306	1.304	1.306	1.305	1.305	24.07	24.15	24.03	24.11	24.12
3	0.509	0.509	0.508	0.509	0.508	36.17	36.09	36.19	36.12	36.21
4	0.338	0.337	0.338	0.337	0.337	59.34	59.35	59.29	59.36	59.35
5	0.487	0.486	0.486	0.486	0.486	69.7	69.72	69.72	69.77	69.78
6	17.219	16.813	16.552	16.192	14.298	45.54	46.83	47.65	48.79	54.78
7	3.127	3.117	3.126	3.116	3.126	14.05	14.31	14.08	14.34	14.08
8	2.039	2.038	2.04	2.039	2.037	40.57	40.61	40.55	40.59	40.65
9	5.752	5.73	5.74	5.751	5.74	53.54	53.72	53.63	53.55	53.63
10	3.741	3.741	3.739	3.74	3.738	56.51	56.51	56.53	56.53	56.55
11	0.115	0.115	0.115	0.115	0.115	68.49	68.51	68.49	68.48	68.48
12	0.288	0.288	0.288	0.288	0.288	0.18	0.13	0.16	0.1	0.2
13	1.401	1.402	1.402	1.402	1.403	56.76	56.75	56.75	56.73	56.72
14	0.202	0.202	0.202	0.202	0.202	23.26	23.31	23.3	23.27	23.26
15	0.169	0.169	0.169	0.169	0.04	16.87	16.75	16.62	16.52	80.05
16	0.094	0.091	0.088	0.085	0.083	75.84	76.66	77.38	78.02	78.61
Total	1.493	1.468	1.444	1.419	1.302	51.25	52.06	52.84	53.66	57.48

Table 8.6 Carbon intensity indices and reduction ratios for carbon emissions from final consumption at medium economic growth rates

Sectors	*Carbon intensity per unit of value added (tonnes of carbon dioxide per CNY 10,000)*					*Carbon intensity reduction ratios (%)*				
	Scenario 1	*Scenario 2*	*Scenario 3*	*Scenario 4*	*Scenario 5*	*Scenario 1*	*Scenario 2*	*Scenario 3*	*Scenario 4*	*Scenario 5*
1	0.404	0.402	0.402	0.4	0.399	36.18	36.37	36.51	36.74	36.89
2	2.514	2.504	2.502	2.491	2.483	20.19	20.53	20.58	20.93	21.17
3	1.014	1.013	1.01	1.009	1.006	30.85	30.91	31.1	31.2	31.39
4	1.147	1.142	1.14	1.135	1.13	54.5	54.71	54.76	55	55.16
5	1.29	1.285	1.281	1.275	1.272	68.27	68.39	68.48	68.63	68.72
6	2.868	2.851	2.839	2.829	2.816	31.19	31.61	31.89	32.14	32.45
7	4.038	4.023	4.031	4.016	4.025	37.34	37.58	37.45	37.7	37.56
8	3.809	3.799	3.797	3.785	3.776	46.6	46.74	46.77	46.93	47.07
9	7.994	8.023	8.019	8.108	8.085	51.46	51.28	51.31	50.76	50.9
10	5.545	5.536	5.524	5.513	5.501	56.5	56.58	56.67	56.75	56.85
11	0.334	0.332	0.331	0.33	0.329	67.68	67.82	67.91	68.06	68.19
12	0.407	0.406	0.405	0.405	0.404	16.63	16.77	16.93	17.02	17.21
13	1.57	1.569	1.568	1.568	1.567	56.4	56.41	56.44	56.45	56.47
14	0.468	0.466	0.465	0.463	0.462	26.24	26.5	26.71	26.96	27.18
15	0.337	0.336	0.336	0.335	0.335	27.4	27.51	27.57	27.72	27.78
16	0.205	0.197	0.191	0.185	0.18	74.89	75.81	76.6	77.33	77.98
Total	1.565	1.543	1.519	1.496	1.472	48.87	49.62	50.4	51.16	51.94

Table 8.7 Carbon intensity indices and reduction ratios for direct carbon emissions at medium economic growth rates

Sectors	*Carbon intensity per unit of value added (tonnes of carbon dioxide per CNY 10,000)*					*Carbon intensity reduction ratios (%)*				
	Scenario 1	*Scenario 2*	*Scenario 3*	*Scenario 4*	*Scenario 5*	*Scenario 1*	*Scenario 2*	*Scenario 3*	*Scenario 4*	*Scenario 5*
1	0.212	0.212	0.212	0.212	0.213	36.47	36.49	36.48	36.5	36.44
2	1.306	1.304	1.306	1.305	1.305	24.08	24.16	24.03	24.1	24.12
3	0.487	0.487	0.487	0.487	0.487	38.93	38.88	38.92	38.88	38.91
4	0.338	0.337	0.338	0.338	0.337	59.32	59.34	59.3	59.32	59.38
5	0.487	0.486	0.486	0.486	0.486	69.69	69.72	69.73	69.76	69.77
6	19.367	18.958	18.656	18.29	17.989	38.75	40.04	41	42.16	43.11
7	3.141	3.132	3.14	3.131	3.14	13.66	13.89	13.69	13.93	13.68
8	2.039	2.038	2.04	2.039	2.037	40.57	40.61	40.55	40.58	40.64
9	5.344	5.392	5.397	5.501	5.5	56.83	56.45	56.41	55.56	55.58
10	3.74	3.741	3.739	3.739	3.737	56.52	56.51	56.54	56.53	56.55
11	0.115	0.115	0.115	0.116	0.116	68.44	68.43	68.43	68.4	68.42
12	0.288	0.288	0.288	0.288	0.288	0.16	0.14	0.21	0.08	0.25
13	1.401	1.402	1.402	1.402	1.403	56.76	56.75	56.76	56.73	56.72
14	0.202	0.202	0.202	0.202	0.202	23.28	23.28	23.25	23.25	23.23
15	0.17	0.171	0.171	0.171	0.171	16.15	16.01	15.86	15.75	15.62
16	a	0.1	0.097	0.095	0.092	73.27	74.18	74.98	75.69	76.33
Total	1.565	1.543	1.519	1.496	1.472	48.87	49.62	50.4	51.16	51.94

Table 8.8 Carbon emission reduction effects of industrial restructuring and energy restructuring (tonnes of carbon dioxide per CNY 10,000)

	GDP growth	*Scenario 1*	*Scenario 2*	*Scenario 3*	*Scenario 4*	*Scenario 5*
Unit emissions	Low	1.493	1.468	1.444	1.419	1.302
	Medium	1.565	1.543	1.519	1.496	1.472
Intensity decrease	Low	1.569	1.594	1.618	1.643	1.76
	Medium	1.497	1.519	1.543	1.566	1.59
Industrial structure	Low	0.906	0.936	0.964	0.994	1.022
	Medium	0.892	0.92	0.947	0.976	1.003
Energy structure	Low	0.663	0.658	0.654	0.649	0.738
	Medium	0.605	0.599	0.596	0.59	0.587

Table 8.9 Contributions of industrial restructuring and energy restructuring to the reduction of the carbon intensity (%)

	GDP growth	*Scenario 1*	*Scenario 2*	*Scenario 3*	*Scenario 4*	*Scenario 5*
Reductions in the carbon intensity	Low	51.25	52.06	52.84	53.66	57.48
	Medium	48.87	49.62	50.4	51.16	51.94
The industrial structure reduces emission intensity	Low	29.6	30.57	31.47	32.45	33.36
	Medium	29.13	30.06	30.94	31.89	32.77
The energy structure reduces emission intensity	Low	21.65	21.49	21.37	21.21	24.12
	Medium	19.74	19.56	19.46	19.27	19.17
Contributions of the industrial structure to the reduction of the carbon intensity	Low	57.76	58.72	59.56	60.47	58.04
	Medium	59.61	60.58	61.39	62.33	63.09
Contributions of the energy structure to the reduction of the carbon intensity	Low	42.24	41.28	40.44	39.53	41.96
	Medium	40.39	39.42	38.61	37.67	36.91

Industrial restructuring has a great impact on energy saving and emission reduction. It can be seen from the simulation study in this section that at low economic growth rates, industrial restructuring (including technologies for energy saving in household services) can reduce the carbon intensity by 29.60%–33.36% and contributes 57.76%–60.47% to emission reductions. Under medium economic growth scenarios, industrial restructuring can reduce the carbon intensity by 29.13%–32.77% and contributes 59.61%–63.09% to emission reductions. If a 45% relative emissions reduction target is set, the contribution of industrial restructuring to the carbon emissions reduction target can reach more than 70%, which is close to the estimation of Lei Zhang et al. (2010). The potential for energy saving and emission reduction is huge, because energy restructuring includes the impact of technological progress. Under low economic growth scenarios, energy restructuring can reduce the carbon intensity by 21.21%–24.12% and contributes 39.53%–42.24% to emission reductions. Under medium economic growth scenarios, energy restructuring can reduce the carbon intensity by 19.17%–19.74% and contributes 36.91%–40.39% to emission reductions. The difference between the two is due to the fact that total demand for energy is small at low economic growth rates, so there is much room for energy restructuring. When the proportion of clean energy consumed at low economic growth rates is higher than that at medium economic growth rates, the energy structure is more optimized. The faster the economic growth, the greater the total demand for energy, the tighter the constraints on energy supply, the less the room for energy restructuring, and the smaller the emission reduction effect of energy restructuring.

8.2.2 Policy recommendations for achieving carbon intensity targets

Based on the above conclusions, the following recommendations for China's carbon reduction initiatives at current stage are proposed in this section:

1 In the international climate negotiations, only by adhering to the principle of convergence of per capita cumulative carbon dioxide emissions from final consumption, can China have more carbon emission rights? According to the allocation schemes of carbon emission rights proposed by the existing developed countries, the carbon emissions rights that China could obtain are far less than what China needs for its future development. Faced with this reality, China can only strive for more carbon emissions rights on the one hand and accelerate its transition to a low-carbon economy on the other hand.
2 Improve energy conversion efficiency and optimize energy structure. At current stage, China's demand for electricity is still strong. Since it is difficult to directly substitute fossil energy for electricity, improving energy conversion efficiency is still the most practical way. Through improving the efficiency of coal-based power generation, developing clean energy such as hydropower, nuclear power, and wind power, increasing the proportion of emissions-free energy, and reducing the transmission loss rate, carbon emissions from the power generation sector can be significantly reduced.
3 Strengthen the research and development of the energy saving technologies to improve the efficiency of energy use and reduce the direct energy consumption intensity of each sector. On the one hand, for energy use sectors, especially high energy consumption sectors, technological

innovation and technological progress should be enhanced to reduce energy consumption in the production process, so as to achieve more outputs with less input and pollution. On the other hand, enterprises could also substitute non-energy inputs for energy inputs through technological change in input, so as to save energy and reduce emissions indirectly.

4 Accelerate the optimization and upgrading of the industrial structure to improve the trade structure. China's energy supply is insufficient, the growth of resource-intensive products exports is unsustainable, and the export capacity is decreasing. Therefore, we must accelerate the optimization and upgrading of industrial structure, promote the expansion of traditional heavy chemical industries to low consumption, light pollution, and high-quality industries with optimized and upgraded structure. We must extend industrial chains, increase the value-added, and change the export pattern dominated by high-carbon products to reduce the carbon leakage in trade.

5 Reform the national income distribution system and increase resident incomes, so as to stimulate domestic demand for consumption, increase consumption rates, promote the shift from export-oriented, investment-driven economy to consumption-, investment-, and exports-driven economy, and make the consumption demand the most important driving factor.

6 Guide the transform of consumption models and directions. Since 2002, the consumption of urban and rural residents has gradually shifted to bulk commodities such as housing and automobiles. Although this is a natural process for consumption upgrading, the consumption upgrading of Chinese residents is inseparable from the investment boom and real estate boom in the current economic situation. In the process of adapting to industrial structure, resident consumption structure has also become one of the factors driving heavy industrialization. Such a trend is obviously not conducive to the upgrading of the industrial structure and the adjustment of the low-carbon industrial structure. Therefore, we must guide the consumption hotpots of urban and rural residents to education, culture, and services, so as to enhance the development of tertiary industries and promote the upgrading of the industrial structure.

7 Encourage scientific and technological innovation to promote the development and promotion of energy-saving technologies and products related to daily life. We should cultivate residents' awareness of environmental protection, and promote a "low-carbon" lifestyle. We should establish a new outlook on life and consumption among the residents and advocate a lifestyle of low energy, low consumption, and low expenses. We should reduce the use of fossil energy and thereby reduce carbon dioxide emissions in everyday life.

8 In terms of energy restructuring, we should encourage industrial sectors to study the energy substitutions suitable for their own development according to their energy consumption characters and the existing energy structure. We should actively encourage energy-saving technological progress and the substitution of gas for coal, gas for oil, and gas for electricity, so as to guide the energy structure advance toward a clean and optimized direction.

Reference

Zhang Lei, Li Yanmei, Huang Yuanxi, Wu Yingmei. Analysis of the potential of structural energy conservation and emission reduction in China. *China Soft Science*, 2011, 02: 42–51.

Part III

Inter-regional allocation of total carbon emissions and game analysis of carbon emission reductions for local government

Low-carbon development has become a long-term national development strategy under the current national conditions in China. Meanwhile, an efficient market mechanism has become an imperative for China's future low-carbon development. In terms of low-carbon policies, the Chinese government has released a specialized guideline to allocate the responsibilities for the carbon emission reduction targets during the 12th Five-year Plan period (2011–2015). However, some provinces, municipalities, and autonomous regions that are responsible for carbon emission reduction have been slow to take action, and they made little progress. In terms of market construction, breakthroughs have been made in the launch of pilot carbon markets, and all seven pilot carbon markets have been launched. However, since there is no effective quota allocation mechanism and the integration of the pilot carbon markets is weak, the construction of a unified carbon market is full of difficulties. Under this background, it is of great theoretical value and practical significance to study the carbon emission reduction maturity and quota allocation mechanisms in China.

In this part, we first divide the regions of China's carbon emissions through policy review and statistical analysis and analyze the regional characteristics to study the causes of regional differences in carbon emissions. Second, we have defined the concept of the carbon emission reduction maturity in China, applied the maturity measurement model to test the fairness and efficiency of inter-provincial quota allocations, and conducted an empirical analysis on the allocation of carbon emission reduction targets during the 12th Five-year Plan period (2011–2015). Finally, with local governments deemed as the players in this part, we establish a static game model, a signal game model, and an evolutionary game model for the dilemma of carbon emission reduction and provide the "static game—dynamic game—evolutionary game" model, a more systematic game analysis framework for carbon emission reduction dilemma in China. This not only complements the current research on the carbon emission reduction game among local governments, but also improves the research on the long-term interaction and evolution of carbon emission reduction initiatives among local governments.

DOI: 10.4324/9781003388500-11

9 Regional classification of carbon emissions and carbon emission indices

9.1 Basic analysis of carbon emissions in each region

9.1.1 Carbon emission accounting methods by region

The existing statistics in China do not directly provide data on carbon dioxide emissions at the regional and industrial levels and such data can only be calculated based on the energy consumption of regions and industries. *China Energy Statistical Yearbook* provides two types of energy consumption data by region: one is the data of total energy consumption by region, including the total consumption of coal, coke, crude oil, gasoline, kerosene, diesel, fuel oil, natural gas, and electricity; and the other is the energy balance sheet by region, which provides the final consumption of 28 kinds of primary energy in 30 regions.

There are two main methods to calculate regional carbon dioxide emissions in the existing literature. One method is to calculate carbon dioxide emissions according to the total consumption of coal, oil products, and natural gas for each region from the energy balance sheets by region, that is, multiply the total consumption of various energy sources by the carbon emissions coefficient of the corresponding energy source to obtain the carbon dioxide emissions of each region (Minglei Liu et al., 2011;Jinhe Jiang, 2011). This method is relatively general, because there are different types of subdivisions in coal and oil products and their carbon emission coefficients are different. Therefore, there will be a large inaccuracy in calculating carbon emissions with only one carbon emission coefficient. The other method is to calculate carbon dioxide emissions according to the final consumption of the 28 primary energy sources on the energy balance sheet by region. However, the selection of specific energy subdivisions may be different. For example, Yuan Yang et al. (2012) chose the final consumption of 16 kinds of energy to calculate carbon dioxide emissions, while Wenjing Yi et al. (2011) chose 18 kinds of energy for the calculation, and Guozhi Li and Zongzhi Li (2010) and Xianfeng Zhang et al. (2013) selected nine kinds of energy for the calculation.

In comparison, it is more reasonable to calculate carbon dioxide emissions using the final energy consumption by region. To be specific, carbon

DOI: 10.4324/9781003388500-12

dioxide emissions from the combustion of fossil energy in each region are calculated by the following equation:

$$E_{CO_2} = \sum_i A_i \times c_i \tag{9.1}$$

Wherein the consumption of the *i*th energy (unit: tonnes or cubic meters) is $Ai = F_i + T_i + H_i - N_i$, wherein F_i, T_i, H_i, and N_i are the final consumption of energy *i*, the energy consumption for power generation, the energy consumption for heating, and the energy consumption for industrial raw materials, respectively. The various energy data is from the *China Energy Statistical Yearbook* from previous years; c_i is the carbon dioxide emission coefficient of the *i*th energy (unit: kg-CO_2 / kg), and the details are shown in Table 9.1.

9.1.2 Carbon dioxide emission coefficients of energy

In terms of final energy consumption, primary energy consumption is categorized into 28 subdivisions, excluding eight energy types, namely other coke products from coking and other petroleum products from oil refining (including lubricating oil, grease, naphtha, paraffin, petroleum asphalt, petroleum coke, and other petroleum products). These energy sources are excluded because they are mainly used for non-fuel purposes and they do not produce carbon dioxide emissions. The proportions of coal gasification and coal gangue consumption in coal consumption are both small, and the emissions data is difficult to obtain, so they are negligible. The proportion of liquefied natural gas (LNG) and other energy consumption in the energy is extremely small, and the emission coefficients cannot be obtained, so they are negligible. The carbon dioxide emission coefficients of the other 16 energy sources are shown in Table 9.1.

9.1.3 Basic situation of carbon emissions by region

Equation (9.1) is used to calculate the carbon emission data of 30 provinces, municipalities, and autonomous regions (excluding Tibet) in Chinese mainland from 2003 to 2010. We observe their carbon emissions from the perspective of total carbon emissions, carbon intensity, and per capita carbon emissions (see Tables 9.1–9.3 for specific data). Among them, carbon intensity is the ratio of total carbon emissions to GDP, and the GDP of each province, municipality, and autonomous region is adjusted according to the constant price in 1996.

In terms of the carbon emissions data by region, the average carbon emissions of each province, municipality, and autonomous region have been increasing. As shown in Figure 9.1, the average value of the national total carbon emissions has been increasing from 2003 to 2010 with a slow upward trend. Among them, Shandong Province with the largest carbon emissions (Hebei was the largest emitter in 2003) has a relatively large increase in

Table 9.1 Carbon dioxide emission coefficients for 16 energy sources

(1) Type of energy sources	*(2) Average low calorific value (kJ/kg)*	*(3) Standard coal coefficient (kgce/kg)*	*(4) Carbon content per unit of calorific value (t-c/TJ)*	*(5) Carbon oxidation rate*	*(6) Carbon dioxide emission coefficient (kg-CO_2/kg)*
Raw coal	20,908	0.7143	26.37	0.94	1.9003
Cleaned coal	26,344	0.9000	25.41	0.93	2.2829
Other cleaned coal	8,363	0.2857	25.41	0.93	0.7247
Briquette	15,910	0.5429	33.56	0.9	1.7622
Coke	28,435	0.9714	29.42	0.93	2.8604
Coke oven gas	17,354	0.5929	13.58	0.98	0.8469
Blast furnace gas	3,763	0.1286	12.1	0.98	0.1636
Other coal gas	16,308	0.5571	12.1	0.98	0.7091
Crude oil	41,816	1.4286	20.08	0.98	3.0202
Gasoline	43,070	1.4714	18.9	0.98	2.9251
Kerosene	43,070	1.4714	19.6	0.98	3.0179
Diesel	42,652	1.4571	20.2	0.98	3.0959
Fuel oil	41,816	1.4286	21.1	0.98	3.1705
Liquefied petroleum gases	50,179	1.7143	17.2	0.98	3.1013
Refinery dry gases	46,055	1.5714	18.2	0.98	3.0119
Oilfield gas	38,931	1.3300	15.32	0.99	2.1622

Notes:

1 Columns (2) and (3) are from *The General Principles for Calculation of the Comprehensive Energy Consumption* (GB/T 2589-2008).

2 Columns (4) and (5) are from Tables 1.5 and 1.7 of the *Guidelines for Preparing Provincial Greenhouse Gas Inventories* (FGBQH [2011] No. 1041). Data on blast furnace gas is not available, so data for other gases is used as a substitute.

3 The calculation method of the last column: $(6) = (1) \times (4) \times (5) \times 10^{-6}$.

4 Except for natural gas and coal gas, which are measured in cubic meters, all other energy sources are measured in tons.

carbon emissions, while Hainan Province with the smallest carbon emissions has a relatively small increase.

The carbon emissions vary greatly in various provinces, municipalities, and autonomous regions nationwide. As shown in Figure 9.2, the country can be divided into five categories of regions according to the level of carbon emissions: The first category is the high-emissions regions with carbon emissions above 500 million tonnes of carbon dioxide, including the four neighboring provinces of Shandong, Hebei, Jiangsu, and Henan. The second category is the regions with higher carbon emissions of 300–500 million tonnes of carbon dioxide, including Inner Mongolia Autonomous Region, Guangdong Province, Liaoning Province, Shanxi Province, Zhejiang Province, and Hubei Province. The third category is the regions with medium carbon emissions of 200–300 million tonnes of carbon dioxide, including Sichuan Province, Hunan Province, Anhui Province, Heilongjiang Province, Shanxi Province, and Jilin Province. The fourth category is the regions with lower carbon emissions of 100–200 million tonnes of carbon dioxide, including Guizhou Province, Shanghai, Fujian Province, Yunnan Province, Xinjiang Uygur Autonomous Region, Guangxi Zhuang Autonomous Region, Jiangxi Province, Tianjin, Chongqing, Gansu Province, and Beijing. The last category is the lowest emission regions with carbon dioxide emissions less than 100 million tonnes, including Ningxia Hui Autonomous Region, Qinghai Province, and Hainan Province. Among all

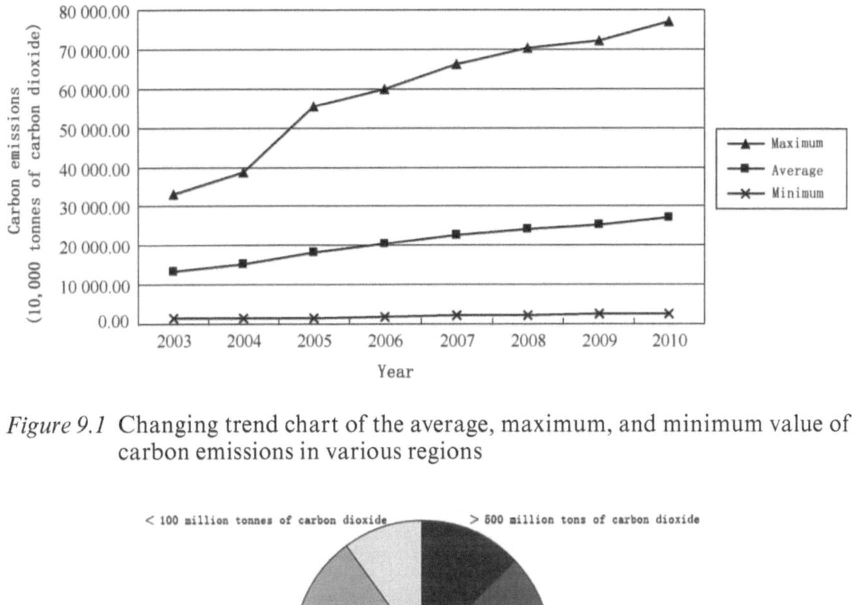

Figure 9.1 Changing trend chart of the average, maximum, and minimum value of carbon emissions in various regions

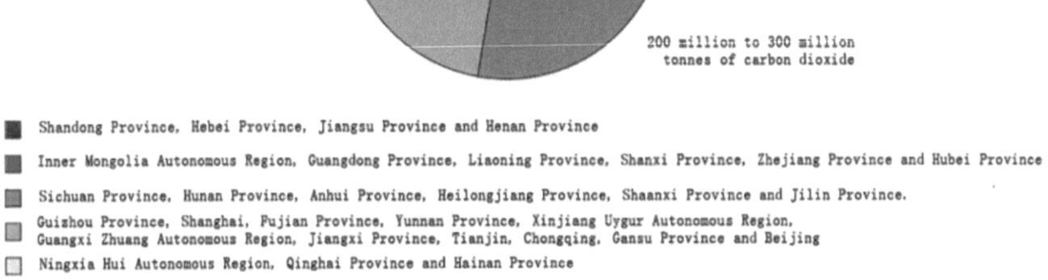

Figure 9.2 Differences in total carbon emissions nationwide in 2010

30 provinces, municipalities, and autonomous regions, Hainan Province has the lowest carbon emissions of 25.82 million tonnes of carbon dioxide, which accounts for 3.36% of that in Shandong Province, the largest carbon emitter nationwide.

Let's observe the changes and differences of two relative indices of carbon emissions, that is, carbon intensity (unit: tonnes of CO_2/CNY 10,000), and per capita carbon emissions (unit: tonnes of CO_2/person). As shown in Figures 9.3 and 9.4, the overall changing trend of carbon intensity and per capita carbon emissions are different. During the sample period, the carbon emissions per capita are increasing moderately, while the carbon intensity is stable with a slight drop. The changes for the average and minimum values of carbon intensity are the same, both of which are stable with a slight decline in 2005–2010. However, the maximum value of carbon intensity (in Ningxia Hui Autonomous Region from 2003 to 2010) increased slightly from 2004 to 2007 and also increased in 2010 compared with 2009. The carbon emissions per capita rise moderately and the maximum value of per capita carbon emissions, which occurred in Inner Mongolia Autonomous Region from 2004 to 2010, increased significantly.

Carbon intensity varies greatly among provinces in China. As shown in Figure 9.5, five provinces and autonomous regions had carbon intensity above five tonnes of carbon dioxide per CNY 10,000 in 2010, namely Ningxia Hui Autonomous Region, Shanxi Province, Inner Mongolia Autonomous Region, Guizhou Province, and Xinjiang Uygur Autonomous Region. Among them, the carbon intensity of Ningxia Hui Autonomous Region was as high as 11.47 tonnes of carbon dioxide per CNY 10,000. Seven provincial-level administrative units such as Gansu Province and Hebei Province had carbon intensity of three to five tonnes of carbon dioxide per CNY 10,000. Seven provincial-level administrative units such as Liaoning Province and Shandong Province had carbon intensity of two to three tonnes of carbon

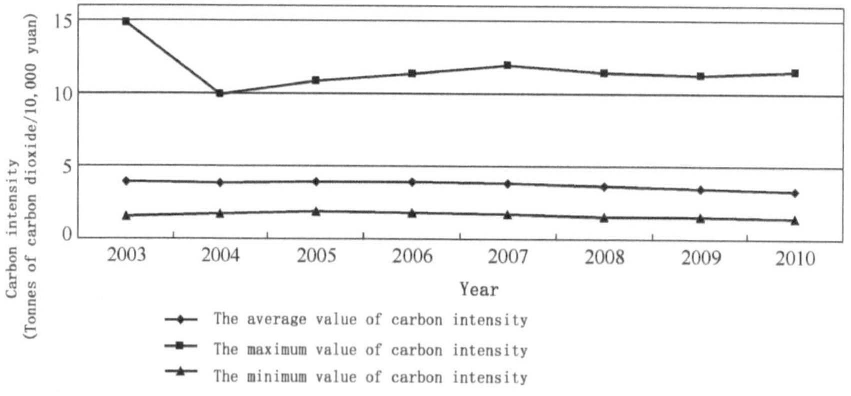

Figure 9.3 Evolution trend of the average, maximum, and minimum values of carbon intensity

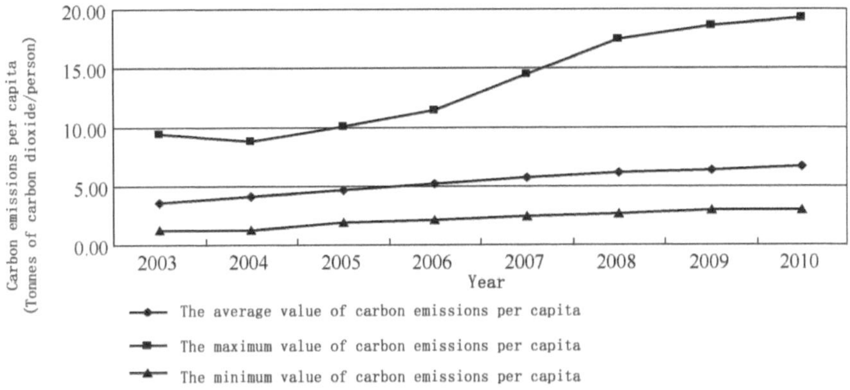

Figure 9.4 Evolution trend of the average, maximum, and minimum values of carbon emissions per capita

dioxide per CNY 10,000. Eleven provincial-level administrative units such as Jiangxi Province had carbon intensity of less than two tonnes of carbon dioxide per CNY 10,000, and Guangdong Province had the lowest carbon intensity of only 1.42 tonnes of carbon dioxide per CNY 10,000.

The per capita carbon emissions also vary significantly among provinces, municipalities, and autonomous regions. As shown in Figure 9.6, Inner Mongolia Autonomous Region, Ningxia Hui Autonomous Region, Shanxi Province, and Tianjin had carbon emissions per capita of more than 10 tonnes of carbon dioxide per person in 2010. Among them, the carbon emissions per capita of Inner Mongolia Autonomous Region were as high as 19.28 tonnes of carbon dioxide per person; The carbon emissions per capita of eight provincial-level administrative units, such as Liaoning Province, Hebei Province, and Shanghai, were six to ten tonnes of carbon dioxide per person. The carbon emissions per capita of 12 provincial-level administrative units such as Shanxi Province and Heilongjiang Province were four to six tonnes of carbon dioxide per person. The carbon emissions per capita of six provincial-level administrative units such as Yunnan Province and Hunan Province were less than 4 tonnes of carbon dioxide per person. Hainan had the smallest carbon emissions per capita of 2.97 tonnes of carbon dioxide per person, which accounted for only 15% of that of Inner Mongolia Autonomous Region.

In summary, we have observed the changing trends and regional differences of China's carbon emissions from the perspective of total carbon emissions, carbon intensity, and carbon emissions per capita. Carbon emissions in some provincial-level administrative units are similar, while in other provincial-level administrative units, they are quite different. Next, we will categorize the regions based on carbon emissions, focusing on the regional differences and changes in carbon emissions.

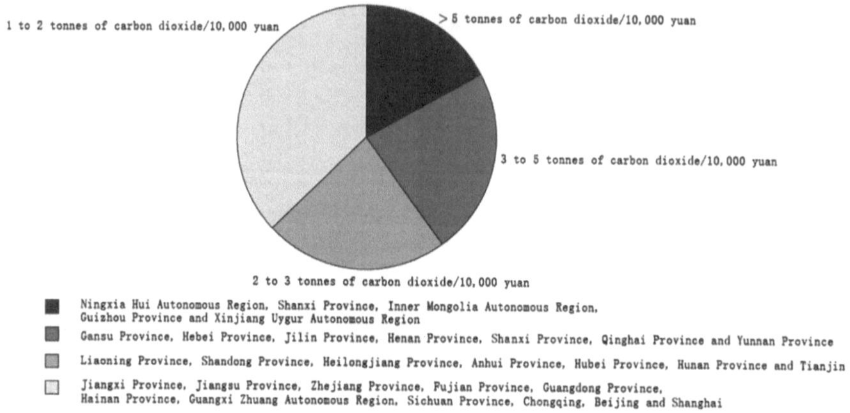

Figure 9.5 Differences in carbon intensity nationwide in 2010

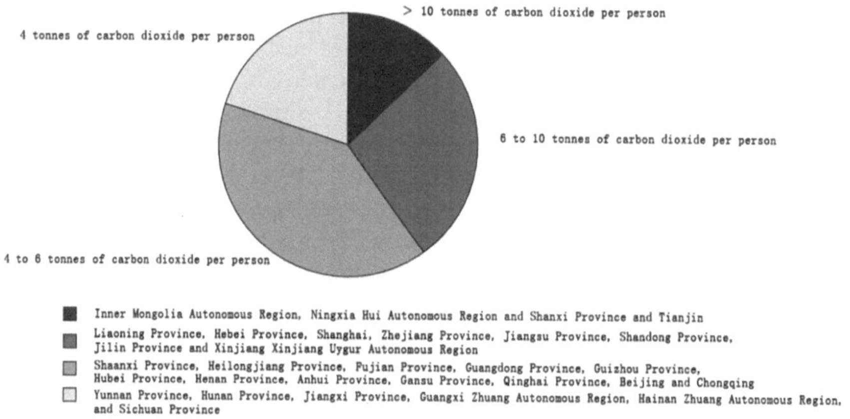

Figure 9.6 Differences in carbon emissions per capita nationwide in 2010

9.2 Regional classification of carbon emissions and analysis of regional characteristics

9.2.1 Clustering methods for multi-index panel data

As mentioned above, studies on panel data from a multivariate statistical perspective are few. Bonzo and Hermosilla (2002) introduced multivariate statistical methods to panel data analysis for the first time. Chinese scholarsJianping Zhu and Minken Chen (2007) studied cluster analysis of single-index panel data; Bingyun Zheng (2008) proposed clustering methods for multi-index panel data; and Juan Ren (2013) proposed a clustering method for multi-index panel data systems based on shape features. These three methods all use indices to measure distance, ignoring the correlation between indices, which leads to biased clustering results. Zelei Xiao et al. (2009) carried out dimension reduction of multi-index panel data to obtain one-dimensional indices using principal component analysis and then clustered the obtained single-index panel data. For this method, principal component analysis is used to analyze the cross-sectional data separately at each time, which cannot meet the requirement for uniformity in system analysis. Ruo'en Ren (2009) proposed global principal component analysis for time series solid data tables, but did not discuss factor analysis. Juan Ren (2013) proposed a new clustering method for multi-index panel data. The method first expands the original dataset according to the number of samples and then it reduces the dimensionality of the original dataset using factor analysis, which simplifies observation systems while preserving the data information. More importantly, it solves the problem of correlation between multiple indices by converting the dimensionality-reduced data into ordinary multi-index panel data and then cluster analysis is performed according to the Euclidean spatiotemporal distance. The empirical results show that this method can meet the requirements for uniformity in system analysis, ensuring that the indices are uncorrelated. The method can overcome biases caused by the mean processing in the time dimension, thus minimizing information loss. In this section, this method is used to classify regions of carbon dioxide emissions in China.

Multi-index panel data X should be expressed by a three-dimensional data table or a three-dimensional matrix, because it has three dimensions: samples, index, and time. Assuming that a sample X consists of q samples, each sample is characterized by p indices, the time length is T, X_{it}^{j} denotes the value of the jth index of the ith sample in the tth period, and the matrix of the sample X can be expressed as:

$$
\begin{array}{ccccccccccc}
X_{11}^{1} & \cdots & X_{11}^{j} & \cdots & X_{11}^{p} & \cdots & X_{1t}^{1} & \cdots & X_{1t}^{j} & \cdots \\
\vdots & \ddots & \vdots & \ddots & \vdots & \ddots & \vdots & \ddots & \vdots & \ddots \\
X_{i1}^{1} & \cdots & X_{i1}^{j} & \cdots & X_{i1}^{p} & \cdots & X_{it}^{1} & \cdots & X_{it}^{j} & \cdots \\
\vdots & \ddots & \vdots & \ddots & \vdots & \ddots & \vdots & \ddots & \vdots & \ddots \\
X_{q1}^{1} & \cdots & X_{q1}^{j} & \cdots & X_{q1}^{p} & \cdots & X_{qt}^{1} & \cdots & X_{qt}^{j} & \cdots
\end{array}
$$

$$
\begin{array}{ccccccc}
X_{1t}^{p} & \cdots & X_{1T}^{1} & \cdots & X_{1T}^{j} & \cdots & X_{1T}^{p} \\
\vdots & \ddots & \vdots & \ddots & \vdots & \ddots & \vdots \\
X_{it}^{p} & \cdots & X_{iT}^{1} & \cdots & X_{iT}^{j} & \cdots & X_{iT}^{p} \\
\vdots & \ddots & \vdots & \ddots & \vdots & \ddots & \vdots \\
X_{qt}^{p} & \cdots & X_{qT}^{1} & \cdots & X_{qT}^{j} & \cdots & X_{qT}^{p}
\end{array}
$$

9.2.1.1 Factor analysis of multi-index panel data

Before performing cluster analysis, we must first remove the correlation among the indices using factor analysis. In this way, we can obtain unified common factors and extract important information from multi-index panel data. To do so, we expand X into a two-dimensional table in order of the indices, which is denoted by $X^V = \left[X^1 \cdots X^j \cdots X^P\right]$. The matrix of one index X^j of sample X is expressed as:

$$X^j = \left[X_{11}^j \cdots X_{1t}^j \cdots X_{1T}^j \cdots X_{i1}^j \cdots X_{it}^j \cdots X_{iT}^j \cdots X_{q1}^j \cdots X_{qt}^j \cdots X_{qT}^j\right]^T$$

X^V is actually from the rewriting of the original X matrix into qT rows and p columns, and the original data is turned into a set of multi-index cross-sectional data. Factor analysis of multi-index panel data is a unified classical factor analysis of qT samples (Juan Ren, 2013). According to the definition of mean and variance, the mean and variance of this group of indices are:

The mean of the jth index:

$$\overline{X^j} = \frac{1}{Tq} \sum_{t=1}^{T} \sum_{i=1}^{q} X_{it}^j \tag{9.2}$$

The variance of the jth index:

$$\operatorname{var}\left(X^j\right) = \frac{1}{Tq-1} \sum_{t=1}^{T} \sum_{i=1}^{q} \left(X_{it}^j - \overline{X^j}\right)^2 \tag{9.3}$$

Normalize the data for X^V:

$$z_{it}^j = \frac{x_{it}^j - \overline{X^j}}{\operatorname{var}\left(X^j\right)} \tag{9.4}$$

Conduct factor analysis on the standardized data; the orthogonal factor model for R-type factor analysis is:

$$X_{p\times 1} = A_{p\times m} F_{m\times 1} + \varepsilon_{p\times 1}$$

And the following conditions are met:

1 $m \le p, E(F) = 0, E(\varepsilon) = 0$
2 $\operatorname{cov}(F, \varepsilon) = 0$
3 $\operatorname{var}(F) = I_m, \operatorname{var}(\varepsilon) = \operatorname{diag}(\sigma_1^2, \ldots, \sigma_j^2, \ldots, \sigma_p^2)$

Where in $F = (F_1, \ldots, F_m)$ is the common factor of X, which is an unobservable vector. Matrix $A = \left(a_{ij}\right)_{p\times m}$ is the factor loading matrix, a_{ij} is the factor loading of the ith variable X_i on the jth common factor F_j; $\varepsilon = (\varepsilon_1, \ldots, \varepsilon_m)$ is a special factor for X.

9.2.1.2 Cluster analysis of multi-index panel data

After dimension reduction by factor analysis of the multi-index panel data, the obtained factor scores are used as index values for cluster analysis. Corresponding to X_{it}^j, we denote the obtained factor score as f_{it}^j, and it forms matrix F:

$$\begin{matrix} F_{11}{}^1 & \cdots & F_{11}{}^j & \cdots & F_{11}{}^p & \cdots & F_{1t}{}^1 & \cdots & F_{1t}{}^j & \cdots & F_{1t}{}^p \\ \vdots & \ddots & \vdots & \ddots & \vdots & \ddots & \vdots & \ddots & \vdots & \ddots & \vdots \\ F_{i1}{}^1 & \cdots & F_{i1}{}^j & \cdots & F_{i1}{}^p & \cdots & F_{it}{}^1 & \cdots & F_{it}{}^j & \cdots & F_{it}{}^p \\ \vdots & \ddots & \vdots & \ddots & \vdots & \ddots & \vdots & \ddots & \vdots & \ddots & \vdots \\ F_{q1}{}^1 & \cdots & F_{q1}{}^j & \cdots & F_{q1}{}^p & \cdots & F_{qt}{}^1 & \cdots & F_{qt}{}^j & \cdots & F_{qt}{}^p \end{matrix}$$

$$\begin{matrix} \cdots & F_{1T}{}^1 & \cdots & F_{1T}{}^j & \cdots & F_{1T}{}^p \\ \ddots & \vdots & \ddots & \vdots & \ddots & \vdots \\ \cdots & F_{iT}{}^1 & \cdots & F_{iT}{}^j & \cdots & F_{iT}{}^p \\ \ddots & \vdots & \ddots & \vdots & \ddots & \vdots \\ \cdots & F_{qT}{}^1 & \cdots & F_{qT}{}^j & \cdots & F_{qT}{}^p \end{matrix}$$

Sample F can be expressed as a set of "spatial samples" in the spatial dimension, that is, F is expanded into a two-dimensional table in space, that is, $F^S = \left[F_1 \cdots F_i \cdots F_q \right]^T$. The matrix of a "spatial sample" F_i of sample F is expressed as:

$$F_i = \left[F_{i1}^1 \cdots F_{i1}^j \cdots F_{i1}^p \cdots F_{it}^1 \cdots F_{it}^j \cdots F_{it}^p \cdots F_{iT}^1 \cdots F_{iT}^j \cdots F_{iT}^p \right]$$

The statistics of F^S, a sample constituted by the above "spatial samples" are:

The mean of the jth index at time t:

$$\overline{F^j} = \frac{1}{Tq} \sum_{t=1}^{T} \sum_{i=1}^{q} F_{it}^j \tag{9.5}$$

The variance of the jth index at time t:

$$\operatorname{var}\left(F^j\right) = \frac{1}{T(q-1)} \sum_{t=1}^{T} \sum_{i=1}^{q} \left(F_{it}^j - \overline{F_t^j} \right)^2 \tag{9.6}$$

The mean of the jth index:

$$\overline{F^j} = \frac{1}{Tq} \sum_{t=1}^{T} \sum_{i=1}^{q} F_{it}^j \tag{9.7}$$

The variance of the jth index:

$$\operatorname{var}\left(F^j\right) = \frac{1}{T(q-1)} \sum_{t=1}^{T} \sum_{i=1}^{q} \left(F_{it}^j - \overline{F_t^j} \right)^2 \tag{9.8}$$

To address core issues in cluster analysis, we must figure out what statistics can be used to represent the degree of similarity between samples and what criteria can be used to determine the degree of similarity between classes. In the existing literature, without exception, Euclidean distance is used to describe the degree of similarity between samples. The Euclidean distance of multi-index panel data with time dimension is actually Euclidean spatiotemporal distance (Bingyun Zheng, 2008). The Euclidean spatiotemporal distance between the rth sample and the kth sample is denoted as d_{rk}, and its distance is:

$$d_{rk} = \left[\sum_{t=1}^{T} \sum_{j=1}^{p} \left(F_{rt}^{j} - F_{kt}^{j} \right)^2 \right]^{\frac{1}{2}} \tag{9.9}$$

After calculation of the distance between samples, the sum of the squared deviations (Wald's method) is used for clustering, and the sum of the squared deviations between samples of the gth class is denoted by S_g:

$$S_g = \sum_{t=1}^{T} \sum_{j=1}^{p} \sum_{i \in i^g} \left(F_{it}^{j} - \bar{F}_{gt}^{j} \right)^2 \tag{9.10}$$

Wherein i^g denotes the set of all sample numbers in the gth class, $\bar{F}_{gt}^{j}$ represents the mean of the jth index of all the samples in the gth class at time t.

The increase in the sum of the squared deviations when the rth class is merged with the kth class can be used to measure the distance between the rth class and the kth class, and the two classes with the smallest increase in the sum of the squared deviations are merged first. When the rth class and the kth class are merged, the distance function between them is:

$$D_{rk} = \Delta S_{rk} = \frac{n_r + n_p}{n_r + n_k} S_{rp} + \frac{n_r + n_q}{n_r + n_k} S_{rp} - \frac{n_r}{n_r + n_k} S_{pq} \tag{9.11}$$

Wherein n_r denotes the number of samples in the rth class, S_{rp} represents the sum of the squared deviations of the new class resulted from the merge of the rth class and the pth class; the rest of variables are similar.

9.2.2 Results and characteristics of regional classification

In classification of carbon emission regions, not only the differences in carbon emissions should be taken into account, but also economic factors, energy consumption factors, and population factors that affect the differences in carbon emissions should be considered. Therefore, it is necessary to select reasonable indices to reflect the carbon emissions, the economic development level, and the energy consumption level of each region. The existing literature differs in terms of the selection of indicators. Xin Sun (2010) proposed an index system evaluation method to reflect the efficiency of energy conservation and emission reduction in regions or enterprises. Sun suggested that the selected indices reflect energy efficiency and pollution emission efficiency, the energy conservation level and pollution emissions reduction level as well as the quality of economic development. Sun also, on the basis of the indices of saving energy and reducing emissions required in the Outline of the Eleventh Five-Year Plan for National Economic and Social Development, proposed a comprehensive evaluation index system for major pollutants such as chemical oxygen demand and sulfur dioxide, which mainly includes three indices: energy-saving systems, emission reduction systems, and development of economic system. In this book, Xin Sun's method is cited to choose the evaluation indices of carbon dioxide emissions. However, due to differences in data availability and research problems, some indices (such as the energy consumption per unit of value-added industrial output in each provincial-level administrative unit, which is hard to obtain and may produce biased results due to the difficulty in unifying statistical caliber during calculation of the enterprise scales and the total energy consumption) are removed and only the energy consumption per unit of GDP is used to represent the energy consumption. In addition, some of Sun's indices reflect the efficiency of energy conservation, such as the rate of energy consumption reduction per unit of GDP, the rate of carbon dioxide emission reduction, etc. Given that the carbon dioxide emission reduction is still in the initial stage, the existing efforts made by regions in energy conservation are ignored, and thus these indices are removed. As a result, only five indices are selected to reflect the carbon emissions of provincial-level administrative units in China. The detailed index and data sources are shown in Table 9.2.

According to the method in Section 9.2.1, a cluster analysis is performed on the data of five indices X_1, X_2, X_3, X_4, and X_5 of 30 provincial-level

Table 9.2 Evaluation indices of carbon emissions of each provincial-level administrative unit

Indices	*Calculation of indices*	*Data source*
Carbon emissions per unit of GDP (X_1)	Total carbon emissions/ GDP calculated at constant prices in 1996	Total carbon emissions are calculated by Section 2.1
Carbon emissions per capita (X_2)	Total carbon emissions/ Total population	Population data are from *China Statistical Yearbook*
Energy consumption per unit of GDP (X_3)	Total carbon emissions/ GDP calculated at constant prices in 1996	*China Energy Statistical Yearbook* and *China Statistical Yearbook*
Per capita GDP (X_4)	Calculated at constant prices in 1996	*China Statistical Yearbook*
The proportion of the tertiary industry in GDP (X_5)	From *China Statistical Yearbook*, no calculations are required	*China Statistical Yearbook*

administrative units from 2003 to 2010. First, according to the method in Section 9.2.1.1, the data is expanded into a two-dimensional table in order of the indices and a factor analysis on the five indices is carried out. Two factors are extracted, with one reflecting energy consumption and the other reflecting economic conditions. These two factors in 2010 are used to make a diagram (Figure 9.7), where the horizontal axis is the energy consumption factor and the vertical axis is the economic development factor. All analyses in this chapter are performed with the software R.

As shown in Figure 9.7, the carbon emissions of some provincial-level administrative units are very similar, such as the carbon emissions among Beijing, Zhejiang Province, Jiangsu Province, and Fujian Province; the carbon emissions between Heilongjiang Province and Hubei Province; and the carbon emissions among Hainan Province, Jiangxi Province, Anhui Province, and Chongqing. However, Figure 9.7 only reflects the situation in 2010. According to the data from 2003 to 2010, further cluster analysis is conducted using factor 1 and factor 2 as instructed in Section 9.2.1.2. The results show that China can be classified into five categories of regions, and these regions are ranked by the average carbon intensity from low to high, as shown in Table 9.3.

As shown in Figure 9.8, the regional classification results of carbon emissions in China using cluster analysis are quite different from China's administrative divisions. The economic indices of these five categories of regions are calculated, as shown in Table 9.4.

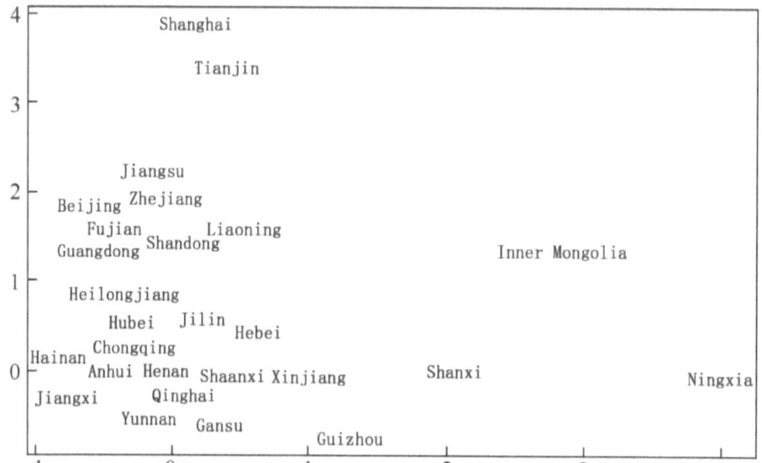

Figure 9.7 Matrix diagram of energy consumption factors and economic development factors of provincial-level administrative units in the Chinese mainland in 2010

Table 9.3 Regional classification of carbon emissions in China based on cluster analysis of multi-index panel data

Category	*Provinces, autonomous regions, and municipalities directly under the central government*	*Average carbon intensity (tonnes of carbon dioxide/CNY 10,000)*							
		2010	*2009*	*2008*	*2007*	*2006*	*2005*	*2004*	*2003*
1	Tianjin and Shanghai	1.72	1.89	2.01	2.18	2.35	2.54	2.58	2.62
2	Jiangsu Province, Zhejiang Province, Guangdong Province, Fujian Province, Liaoning Province, Shandong Province, Hubei Province, Beijing, and Heilongjiang Province	1.98	2.11	2.24	2.44	2.53	2.51	2.47	2.43
3	Guangxi Zhuang Autonomous Region, Sichuan Province, Anhui Province, Chongqing, Hunan Province, Hainan Province, Shanxi Province, Henan Province, Yunnan Province, and Jiangxi Province	2.44	2.64	2.75	2.86	2.86	2.9	2.63	2.75
4	Hebei Province, Jilin Province, Gansu Province, Qinghai Province, and Xinjiang Uygur Autonomous Region	4.08	4.28	4.53	4.68	4.9	4.97	4.85	4.48
5	Shanxi Province, Guizhou Province, Ningxia Hui Autonomous Region, and Inner Mongolia Autonomous Region	8.02	8.48	8.75	9.07	9.15	9.08	9.1	9.93

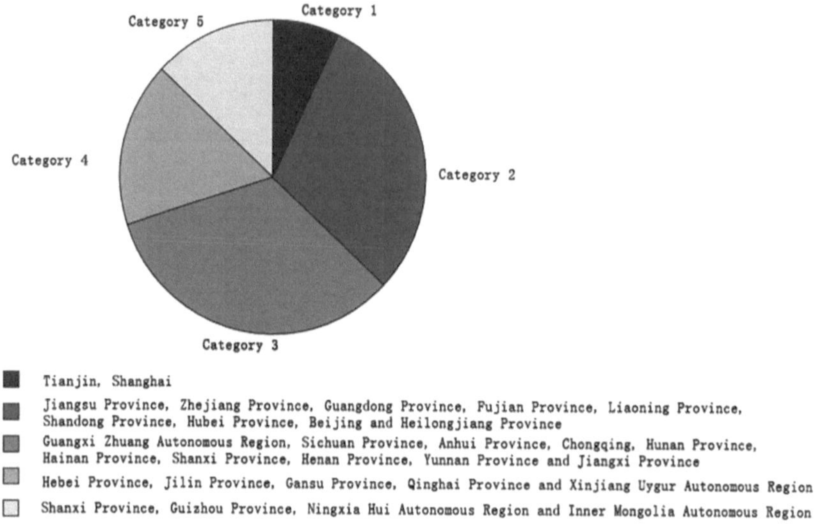

Figure 9.8 Regional classification of carbon emissions based on cluster analysis

Taking 2010 as an example, as shown in Table 9.4, there are significant differences in economic development, carbon dioxide emissions, and energy consumption among the five categories of regions.

The first category of regions is characterized by a high level of development, high emissions, and low energy consumption. High level of development means that the economy is the most developed and the GDP per capita is the highest in these regions. High emissions mean that the carbon emissions per capita are higher in the regions and low energy consumption means that the carbon intensity and energy consumption per unit of GDP are the lowest in these regions. Taking 2010 as an example, the per capita GDP of the first category of regions was the highest, reaching CNY 54,145 per person, of which Shanghai (CNY 56,800 per person) ranked first in China. At the same time, the carbon emissions per capita in the first category of regions are also higher, second only to the fifth category of regions, among which, carbon emissions per capita was 10.10 tonnes of carbon dioxide in Tianjin and 8.39 tonnes of carbon dioxide in Shanghai. From a national perspective, Tianjin's per capita carbon emissions ranked fourth, just behind Inner Mongolia Autonomous Region, Ningxia Hui Autonomous Region, and Shanxi Province.

The second category of regions is characterized by a high level of development, moderate emissions, and low energy consumption. These regions are also relatively developed, but the carbon emissions per capita are moderate and slightly lower than the national average. Among these regions, except

Table 9.4 Comparison of indices among the five categories of regions in 2010

Category	*Provinces, autonomous regions, and municipalities directly under the central government*	*Carbon intensity (tonnes of carbon dioxide per CNY 10,000)*	*Carbon emissions per capita (tonnes of carbon dioxide per person)*	*Energy consumption per unit of GDP (tonnes of standard coal per CNY 10,000)*	*Per capita GDP (CNY 10,000 per person)*
China		3.2713	6.6844	1.552	2.3947
1	Tianjin and Shanghai	1.7191	9.2428	0.9379	5.4145
2	Jiangsu Province, Zhejiang Province, Guangdong Province, Fujian Province, Liaoning Province, Shandong Province, Hubei Province, and Beijing	1.9838	6.3341	1.0117	3.2484
3	Guangxi Zhuang Autonomous Region, Sichuan Province, Anhui Province, Chongqing, Hunan Province, Hainan Province, Shanxi Province, Henan Province, Yunnan Province, and Jiangxi Province	2.4361	3.9951	1.2152	1.6734
4	Hebei Province, Jilin Province, Gansu Province, Qinghai Province, and Xinjiang Uygur Autonomous Region	4.0796	6.811 2	2.1524	1.7035
5	Shanxi Province, Guizhou Province, Ningxia Hui Autonomous Region, and Inner Mongolia Autonomous Region	8.0214	12.7580	3.1659	1.6311

Note: The data in the table are the mean for each index category.

for Liaoning Province and Shandong Province, where carbon emissions per capita are higher than the national level, carbon emissions per capita in the rest of the regions are lower than the national level. The carbon intensity and energy consumption per unit of GDP in the regions are low.

The regions in the third, fourth, and fifth categories are relatively less developed, with the per capita GDP lower than the national level. However, there are great differences in per capita carbon emissions and energy consumption.

The regions in the third category are characterized by low level of development, low emissions, and low energy consumption. The economic development of the regions is lower than the national average. The per capita carbon emissions, which reach only 3.9951 tonnes of carbon dioxide per person, are also the lowest among all the regions and less than half of that of the regions in the first category. The energy consumption per unit of GDP is 1.2152 tonnes of standard coal per CNY 10,000, which is lower than the national average.

The regions in the fourth category are characterized by a low level of development, moderate emissions, and high energy consumption. The per capita GDP of the regions is slightly higher than that of regions in the third and fifth categories, but lower than the national average. The carbon emissions per capita of the regions are relatively close to the national average. The energy consumption per unit of GDP and carbon intensity is high, which are 39% and 25% higher than the national average, respectively.

The regions in the fifth category are characterized by a low level of development, high emissions, and high energy consumption. The regions are the most underdeveloped. Except for Inner Mongolia Autonomous Region, where the per capita GDP is higher than the national average, the per capita GDP in the rest of the provincial-level administrative units is lower than the national average. The per capita GDP in Guizhou Province and Ningxia Hui Autonomous Region ranked the third lowest and fourth lowest in China, respectively. At the same time, the per capita carbon emissions of the regions are the highest, about 3.2 times of the regions of the third category. The carbon intensity and energy consumption per unit of GDP are the highest, which are 4.67 times and 3.38 times of the regions having the lowest value, respectively.

The changing trends of carbon intensity and carbon emissions per capita in the five categories of regions are different (Figures 9.9 and 9.10). As shown in Figure 9.11, the carbon intensity of the five categories of regions all showed a downward trend from 2003 to 2010. The carbon intensity of the first category of regions decreased year by year; it had never increased in eight years. The carbon intensity of the fifth category of regions only increased in 2006, while the carbon intensity of the third category of regions only increased in 2005; both of the increases were small. The carbon intensity in the remaining years all showed a downward trend. The changing trends of carbon intensity of the second and fourth categories of regions are the most

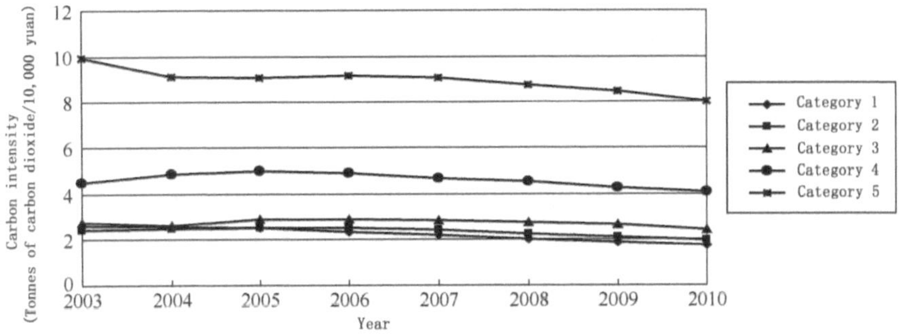

Figure 9.9 Changing trends of carbon intensity in five categories of regions

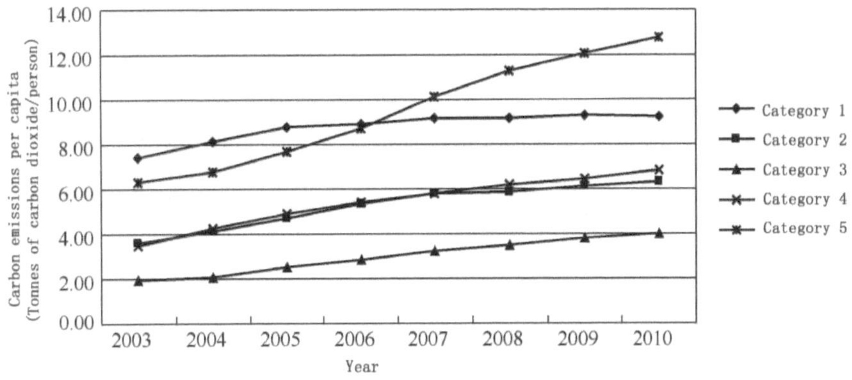

Figure 9.10 Changing trends in carbon emissions per capita in five categories of regions

similar; both showed a slight upward trend at first and then a decreased trend year by year. Among them, the carbon intensity of the second category of regions increased slightly from 2003 to 2006, and decreased year by year after 2006. The carbon intensity of the fourth category of regions increased slightly from 2003 to 2005, and decreased year by year after 2005.

The five categories of regions differ greatly in carbon intensity. Carbon intensity of the fifth and fourth categories of regions is relatively large, while the carbon intensity of the first, second, and third categories of regions are relatively small. In addition, the differences among the annual carbon intensity of the first, second, and third categories of regions from 2003 to 2005 are very small, and the gap among the three has been gradually larger after 2005. The most economically developed regions of the first and second categories have a smaller increase in carbon emissions per capita; especially for regions of the first category in 2008 and 2010, the increase in carbon emissions per capita were negative. For the economically underdeveloped regions of the third, fourth, and fifth categories, the increase in carbon emissions per capita is relatively large, with an average annual growth rate of around 10%. Especially in regions of the fifth category from 2005 to 2008, the increase in carbon emissions per capita was the largest, reaching 13.30%, 13.82%, 16.24%, and 11.55%, respectively.

9.3 Analysis of the causes of regional differences in carbon emissions

9.3.1 Econometric model of national panel data

In this section, we analyze the causes for the differences in carbon emissions among five categories of regions through examining the carbon intensity and factors affecting carbon emissions per capita in different regions. The STIRPAT model is used for analyzing the factors affecting carbon emissions.

The STIRPAT model is developed on the basis of the IPAT model. The traditional Kuznets curve focuses on the impact of economic growth on environment. In order to explain the impact of economic growth on carbon emissions in the context of multiple factors of influence, Ehrlich et al. proposed the IPAT model, arguing that environment is affected by three factors: population, affluence, and technology. Waggoner et al. further divided the technological factors into two factors—energy use intensity and energy efficiency—and proposed the ImPACT model. York et al. proposed the STIRPAT model to address the shortcomings that the IPAT and ImPACT models could not reflect the asymmetry of impacts of driving factors.

According to the IPAT model, environmental degradation (I, usually measured by pollutant emissions) is related to economic growth (A, usually expressed by per capita GDP), population size (P), and technology level (T, usually measured by pollutant emissions per unit of GDP):

$$I = PAT \tag{9.12}$$

York et al. pointed out that the IPAT model could not perform hypothesis testing on the driving factors of environmental degradation. In addition, the model assumes that the driving factors of environmental degradation in different periods are in the same proportion. In order to overcome the shortcomings, York et al. proposed the STIRPAT model:

$$I_t = aP_t^b A_t^c T_t^d e_t \tag{9.13}$$

Wherein a, b, c, and d are the model parameters to be estimated, e_t is the random error term.

In practice, the above equation is generally estimated in a logarithmic form:

$$\ln(I_t) = \ln(a) + b\ln(P_t) + c\ln(A_t) + d\ln(T_t) + \varepsilon_t \tag{9.14}$$

Based on the above STIRPAT model, carbon emissions per capita and carbon intensity are used as the explained variables, and economic development level, industrial structure, energy structure, and urbanization level are used as the driving factors. The specific model is as follows:

$$\ln(\text{CEI}_{it}) = \beta_0 + \beta_1 ln(\text{PGDP}_{it}) + \beta_2 \left[ln(\text{PGDP}_{it}) \right]^2 + \beta_3 \text{INDU}_{it} \cdot + \beta_4 \text{COAL}_{it} + \beta_5 ln(\text{EC}_{it}) + \beta_6 \text{NONA}_{it} + u_{it} \tag{9.15}$$

$$\ln(\text{PEC}_{it}) = \beta_0 + \beta_1 ln(\text{PGDP}_{it}) + \beta_2 \left[ln(\text{PGDP}_{it}) \right]^2 + \beta_3 \text{INDU}_{it} + \beta_4 \text{COAL}_{it} + \beta_5 ln(\text{EC}_{it}) + \beta_6 \text{NONA}_{it} + u_{it} \tag{9.16}$$

Wherein, CEI denotes carbon intensity, PEC represents carbon emissions per capita.

The selected explanatory variables are as follows:

1 Economic development level

A number of literatures have demonstrated that the relationship between carbon dioxide emissions and per capita income is nonlinear. The environmental Kuznets curve shows that the relationship between environmental pollution and economic growth conforms to an inverted U-shaped curve for a long time. Based on this theory, in this section, per capita GDP is used as an index of economic development. Both linear and quadratic terms are included in the model and the logarithm of per capita GDP is used. The data processing of per capita GDP is the same as that in Section 9.1.

2 Industrial structure

The changes in industrial structure have a great impact on carbon emissions. First, the carbon intensity of different industries varies significantly. The secondary industry, especially industrial sector, consumes more energy. Therefore, if the proportion of secondary industry, especially the industrial sector and heavy industries, is larger, the carbon dioxide emissions will be relatively larger, provided that other factors remain the same. Moreover, changes in the industrial structure affect energy efficiency, and ultimately the total carbon emissions and carbon intensity. In this section, the share of the added value of secondary industry in GDP is used to represent the industrial structure and the data is directly from the *China Statistical Yearbook* from the previous years. Since the data itself is a ratio, no log transformation is used in the model.

3 Energy structure and energy intensity

Carbon dioxide emissions are mainly from the combustion of fossil fuels and the carbon emission coefficients vary greatly in energy sources. The carbon dioxide emissions from combustion of coal arc 1.6 times those from natural gas and 1.2 times those from oil. The share of coal consumption in the primary energy (coal, oil, and natural gas) consumption is called energy consumption structure. The consumption of coal, crude oil, and natural gas by region in the calculation are from the *China Energy Statistical Yearbook* over the years. In addition to the energy consumption structure, energy intensity, that is, the ratio of energy consumption to GDP, is incorporated into the energy structure. The higher the energy intensity, the greater the carbon emissions, provided that other conditions remain the same. In the model, the energy intensity is transformed into logarithm and the share of coal consumption in primary energy does not require logarithmic transformation, since it is already a ratio.

4 Level of urbanization

The process of urbanization must be accompanied by large-scale infrastructure construction, which will lead to a large increase in the consumption of production materials, such as cement and steel, and thus increase carbon dioxide emissions greatly. Of course, urbanization will change people's living habits, and the energy consumption of the urban population is also much higher than that of the rural population, and the significant increase in energy consumption is the main reason for the increase in carbon dioxide emissions (Limin Du, 2010). Being consistent with the existing literature, the proportion of non-agricultural population in the total population is used as the index of urbanization level, and the data can be found in *Chinese Population and Employment Statistics Yearbook*.

The names, meanings, and sources of all explanatory variables are shown in Table 9.5. The sample data in this section includes data from 30 provincial-level administrative units from 2003 to 2010. There are 240 observed values for each variable, and the descriptive statistics of the explanatory variables and explained variables are shown in Table 9.6.

9.3.2 Causes of regional differences

Panel data is used to analyze the driving factors of carbon emissions. Before panel data analysis, the setup of panel data model should be tested first. There are three types of panel data, namely constant coefficient models without individual effects, varying intercept models, and varying coefficient models (Tiemei Gao, 2009).

The panel data model can be simplified to the following form:

$$y_i = \alpha_i e + x_i \beta_i + u_i e = (1,1,\ldots,1)' \, i = (1,2,\ldots,N) \tag{9.17}$$

The constant coefficient models without individual effects can be expressed as the following form:

$$y_i = \alpha e + x_i \beta + u_i \left(i = 1,2,\ldots,N\right) \tag{9.18}$$

Table 9.5 Indices of factors affecting carbon emissions

Explanatory variables	*Indices*	*Variables*	*Data calculation and source*
Economic development	Per capita GDP (Units: CNY 10,000 per person)	PGDP	GDP is calculated at constant prices in 1996
Industrial structure	The proportion of the secondary industry in GDP (%)	INDU	From *China Statistical Yearbook*
Energy structure	The share of coal consumption in primary energy (%)	COAL	The consumption of coal, crude oil, and natural gas are calculated after being converted into standard coal according to the coefficients of 0.7143, 1.4286, and 12.143
	The ratio of energy consumption to GDP (tonnes of standard coal/ CNY 10,000)	EC	GDP is calculated at constant prices in 1996
Level of urbanization	The proportion of non-agricultural population in the total population (%)	NONA	From *China Population and Employment Statistics Yearbook*

Table 9.6 Descriptive statistics of variables

Variables	*Average value*	*Standard deviation*	*Minimum value*	*Maximum value*	*Sample size*
CEI	3.7193	2.3787	1.4201	14.7977	240
PEC	5.3161	2.9866	1.2716	19.2837	240
PGDP	1.6951	1.0243	0.3358	5.6830	240
INDU	0.4781	0.0749	0.2258	0.6148	240
COAL	0.7672	0.1698	0.1735	0.9979	240
EC	1.7909	1.0249	0.7755	5.6626	240
NONA	0.3677	0.1635	0.1558	0.8856	240

The varying intercept models can be expressed as the following form:

$$y_i = \alpha_i e + x_i \beta + u_i \left(i = 1,2,\dots,N\right) \tag{9.19}$$

The varying coefficient models can be expressed as the following form:

$$y_i = \alpha_i e + x_i \beta_i + u_i \left(i = 1,2,\dots,N\right) \tag{9.20}$$

$$\mathrm{H}_1 : \beta_1 = \beta_2 = \dots = \beta_N$$

$$H_2 : \alpha_1 = \alpha_2 = \cdots = \alpha_N$$
$$\beta_1 = \beta_2 = \cdots = \beta_N$$

If the hypothesis H_2 is not rejected, it is considered that the sample data conforms to the constant coefficient model and no further test is required. If hypothesis H_2 is rejected, hypothesis H_1 needs to be tested. If the hypothesis H_1 is not rejected, the sample data is considered to conform to the varying intercept model. Otherwise, it conforms to the varying coefficient models.

The *F* statistic for testing H_2 is:

$$F_2 = \frac{(S_3 - S_1)/[(N-1)(K+1)]}{S_1/[NT - N(K+1)]} \sim F[(N-1)(K+1), NT - N(K+1)] \quad (9.21)$$

The *F* statistic for testing H_1 is:

$$F_1 = \frac{(S_2 - S_1)/[(N-1)K]}{S_1/[NT - N(K+1)]} \sim F[(N-1)K, NT - N(K+1)] \quad (9.22)$$

Wherein S_1, S_2, and S_3 are the residual sum of squares estimated from the varying coefficients models, varying intercept models, and constant coefficient models, respectively. *N* is the number of cross-sections, *T* is the number of time periods, and *K* is the number of explanatory variables.

The model setup is tested by the national data and regional data of the five categories of regions, and the results are shown in Table 9.7.

As shown in Table 9.7, the varying intercept models should be used in the whole country and the constant parameter model is used in three out of the five categories of regions, which also reflects the reasonableness of the regional classification to a certain extent.

Next, the national data are used for estimation. Table 9.7 shows that the national data should be subject to varying intercept models. The varying intercept models can be categorized into two types: fixed effects models and random effects models. Generally, a Hausman test is run to decide between the two effects models, but here the Hausman test fails. Therefore, both fixed effects and random effects models are used for estimation, and AR (1) is introduced to eliminate serial correlation. In addition, to eliminate heteroscedasticity, the generalized least squares (GLS) method with cross-section heteroscedasticity is used for estimation. The results are shown in Table 9.8.

As shown in Table 9.8, there is no big difference in the estimation results between the fixed effects and random effects models. The fixed effects model with AR (1) can better control the autocorrelation of the model and improve the overall goodness of fit of the model, thus the fixed effects model is used for the explanation. The driving factors of carbon emissions per capita and carbon intensity are examined through Table 9.8.

1 Among the factors affecting carbon emissions per capita, the shares of per capita GDP, energy intensity, and coal in primary energy are among

Table 9.7 Tests for the setup of Models 9.21 and 9.22

	Statistics	*Statistical value (Model 9.21)*	*Statistical value (Model 9.22)*	*Critical value*	*Conclusions (Model 9.21)*	*Conclusions (Model 9.22)*
China	F_2	3.51	3.51	1.66	Varying intercept	Varying intercept
	F_1	1.01	1.01	1.67		
First category of regions	F_2	4.57	6.44	19.35	Constant coefficient	Constant coefficient
	F_1	5.22	7.20	19.33		
Second category of regions	F_2	17.25	17.23	2.79	Varying coefficient	Varying coefficient
	F_1	11.90	11.89	2.81		
Third category of regions	F_2	1.38	1.38	2.62	Constant coefficient	Constant coefficient
	F_1	0.47	0.47	2.63		
Fourth category of regions	F_2	16.10	16.10	4.50	Varying coefficient	Varying coefficient
	F_1	11.72	11.71	4.53		
Fifth category of regions	F_2	0.44	0.44	5.79	Constant coefficient	Constant coefficient
	F_1	0.47	0.47	5.82		

the top three, respectively. Among the factors affecting carbon intensity, the shares of energy intensity, coal, and per capita GDP in primary energy are among the top three, respectively. Comparing Columns 1, 3, 2, and 4 in the table, we can see that among the factors affecting carbon emissions per capita and carbon intensity, the distinct difference is only in the per capita GDP and the effects of other factors are almost the same. The coefficient of per capita GDP for the linear term of carbon emissions per capita is 1.2023, but the coefficient for the linear term of carbon intensity is 0.2024. Therefore, the impact of per capita GDP on carbon emissions per capita is far greater than its impact on carbon intensity. This explains why the carbon intensity of each region has been decreasing, while the carbon emission per capita has been increasing. During the sample period, the per capita GDP in each region has been increasing and the increased GDP leads to an increase in carbon emissions per capita. Although the increased GDP also increases carbon intensity, the sharp decrease of energy intensity, another important factor in the sample period, results in a downward trend in carbon intensity.

2 Among the factors affecting carbon emissions per capita, per capita GDP has the greatest positive effect, and the impact of per capita GDP

Table 9.8 Estimation results of factors affecting carbon emissions across the country

Explained variables: In (PCE)			*Explained variables: In (CEI)*	
Explanatory variables	*Column 1*	*Column 2*	*Column 3*	*Column 4*
In (PGDP)	1.2023[b]	1.1321[a]	0.2024[c]	0.1321[b]
In (PGDP)^2	−0.0880[b]	−0.0486[a]	−0.0880[b]	−0.0486[b]
INDU	−0.0207	0.1005	−0.0207	0.1004
COAL	0.3844[b]	0.3573[b]	0.3845[a]	0.3573[a]
In (EC)	1.1747[c]	1.0397[b]	1.1748[c]	1.0397[a]
NONA	−0.5633[c]	−0.1643	−0.5637[c]	−0.1643
AR (1)	0.2573[c]		0.2574[c]	
Model	Fixed effects model with varying intercept	Random effects model with varying intercept	Fixed effects model with varying intercept	Random effects model with varying intercept
Adjusted R^2	0.9920	0.8874	0.9949	0.6872
DW	2.0189	1.3583	2.0188	1.3582

Note: [a] means significant at 10%; [b] means significant at 5%; [c] means significant at 1%.

on carbon emissions per capita conforms to the Kuznets curve, that is, the relationship between economic growth and carbon emissions per capita shows an inverted U-shaped curve. Energy intensity is also an important factor. If energy intensity is reduced by 1%, carbon emissions per capita will be reduced by 1.1747%. The proportion of coal in primary energy has a significant impact on carbon emissions per capita. If the proportion of coal in primary energy decreases by 1%, carbon emissions per capita will decrease by 0.3844%. The *Action Plan* for *Prevention and Control of Air Pollution* released by the Chinese government in 2013 plans to reduce the proportion of coal consumption in energy consumption to below 65% by 2017. If this target can be successfully achieved, it will have a significant effect on reducing carbon emissions per capita and energy intensity.

3 Among the factors affecting carbon intensity, energy intensity is the most important one. A 1% reduction in energy intensity will lead to a 1.1748% reduction in carbon intensity. The proportion of coal in primary energy has the second largest impact on carbon intensity. If the proportion of coal in primary energy decreases by 1%, the carbon intensity will decrease by 0.3845%. The impact of per capita GDP on carbon intensity also follows the Kuznets curve, but the impact is much less than the impact on carbon emissions per capita.
4 Changes in industrial structure show no significant impact on carbon emissions per capita or carbon intensity. In terms of carbon intensity, during the sample period, the carbon intensity of all regions shows a

downward trend, but changes in the share of the added value of secondary industry in the GDP vary among provincial-level administrative units. The proportion of the added value of secondary industry in GDP for each region is shown in Figures 9.11–9.13.

As shown in Figure 9.11, from 2003 to 2010, in the first and second categories of regions, the proportion of the added value of secondary industry in GDP decreased in Beijing, Shanghai, Heilongjiang Province, Guangdong Province, Jiangsu Province, and Zhejiang Province. Among which, Beijing had the sharpest decrease, while the proportion of the remaining five provincial-level administrative units increased.

As shown in Figure 9.12, during the sample period, the proportion of the added value of secondary industry in GDP increased in all 15 provincial-level administrative units in the third and fourth categories of regions. Among them, Guangxi Zhuang Autonomous Region, Chongqing, and Jiangxi Province recorded the largest increase.

As shown in Figure 9.13, in the fifth category of regions, the proportion of the added value of secondary industry in GDP in Inner Mongolia Autonomous Region has risen significantly; Shanxi has no significant changes, while Guizhou Province and Ningxia Hui Autonomous Region have even decreased in this regard.

Most of the provincial-level administrative units in the third, fourth, and fifth categories of regions as well as some provincial-level administrative units in the first and second categories of regions have shown an upward trend in the proportion of added value of secondary industry in GDP, which demonstrates that the process of industrialization in these regions is still improving and the industrialization trend is prevailing.

In summary, from the perspective of the proportion of the added value of secondary industry in GDP, the industrial structure varies greatly among the different regions in China. During the sample period,

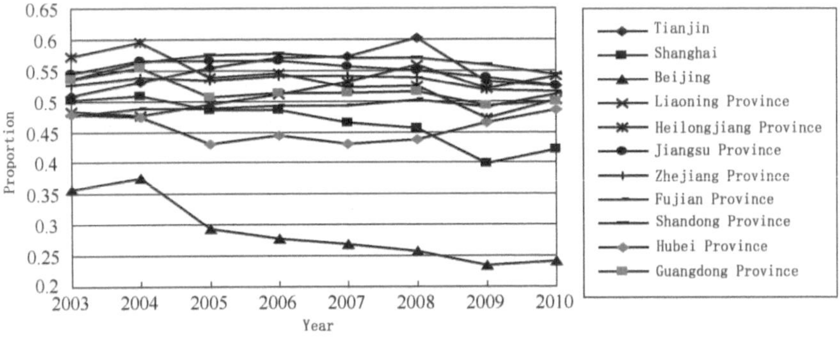

Figure 9.11 Changes in the proportion of the added value of secondary industry in GDP of the first and second categories of regions

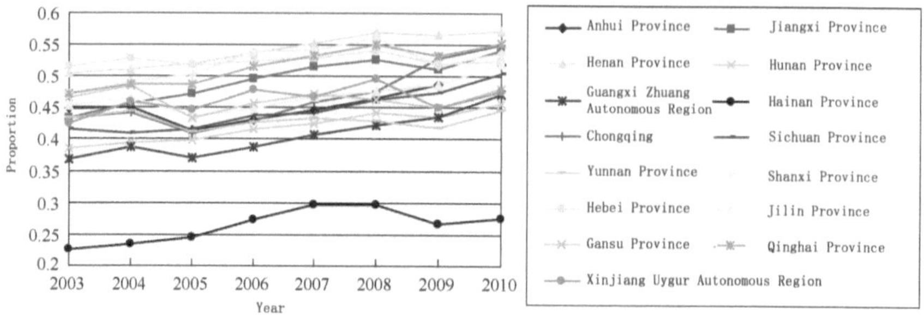

Figure 9.12 Changes in the proportion of the added value of secondary industry in GDP of the third and fourth categories of regions

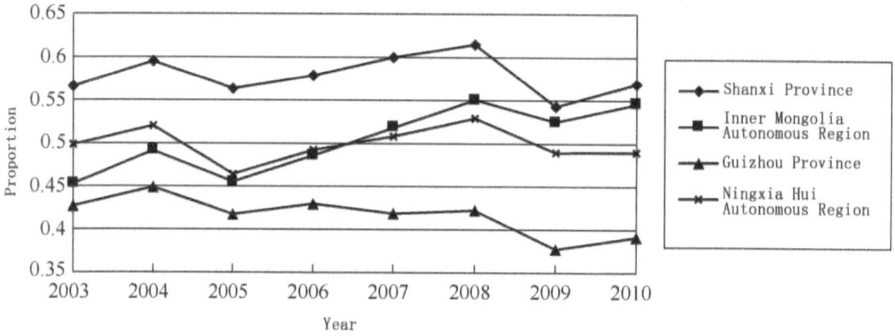

Figure 9.13 Changes in the proportion of the added value of secondary industry in GDP of the fifth category of regions

the proportion of the added value of secondary industry in GDP has decreased in 13 provincial-level administrative units[1] and increased in the other 17 provincial-level administrative units. Changes in industrial structure have no significant impact on carbon emissions per capita and carbon intensity.

5 The increase in the proportion of non-agricultural population does not lead to an increase in carbon intensity and carbon emissions per capita. However, it has the opposite effect. During the sample period, the proportion of non-agricultural population showed an upward trend in all provincial-level administrative units, especially in Hainan Province, Shanxi Province, and Chongqing, which had the largest increase of 40.7%, 39.4%, and 39.1%, respectively. The proportion of non-agricultural population is an important index of the urbanization, which should accompany changes in residents' consumption habits and urban expansion of infrastructure, thus leading to an increase in total carbon emissions. However, at present, the increase in the non-agricultural

population in some cities may be limited to the level of household registration reform and has no real impact on carbon emissions yet.

Next, we take carbon intensity as an example to explore the differences in factors affecting carbon intensity among different regions. As shown in Table 9.5, the factors affecting carbon intensity in a descending order include energy intensity, the proportion of coal in primary energy, and economic development. First, energy intensity is the most important factor affecting carbon intensity. As shown in Figure 9.14, energy intensity of different regions varies greatly. Energy intensities in the first, second, and third categories of regions are relatively low and their gaps are small, while the energy intensities in the fourth and fifth regions are relatively large, especially in the fifth category of regions. In 2010, for example, energy intensities in the five categories of regions were 0.9379, 1.0117, 1.2152, 2.1523, and 3.1659, respectively. The fifth category of regions has the highest energy intensity, which is 3.4 times that of the first category of regions with the lowest energy intensity. The top six provinces and autonomous regions in order of energy intensity from high to low are Ningxia Hui Autonomous Region, Qinghai Province, Shanxi Province, Guizhou Province, Xinjiang Uygur Autonomous Region, and Inner Mongolia Autonomous Region. Among them, Ningxia Hui Autonomous Region has the highest energy intensity of 4.46 tonnes of standard coal per CNY 10,000, which is 5.7 times that of Fujian Province with the lowest energy intensity. Energy intensity is the leading cause of the large differences in carbon intensity among different regions.

Second, in terms of the proportion of coal in primary energy, as shown in Figure 9.15, the proportion of coal in primary energy varies greatly among the five categories of regions. In 2010, for example, coal accounted for 96% of primary energy in the fifth category of regions, and this figure was 99.35%, 98.38%, and 96. 25%, respectively, for Guizhou Province, Shanxi Province, and Inner Mongolia Autonomous Region. The proportion of coal in primary energy was relatively low in the first and second categories of regions, reaching around 65%. The proportion was the lowest in Beijing, reaching only 42.92%, less than half of that in the fifth category of regions.

Finally, in terms of the economic development of each region, as shown in Figure 9.16, the per capita GDP of the first and second categories of regions are much higher than that of the third, fourth, and fifth categories of regions. In 2010, for example, Shanghai with the highest per capita GDP of CNY 56,800 per person was 6.76 times that of Guizhou Province with the lowest per capita GDP of CNY 8,400 per person. Therefore, China's economic development and carbon intensity conform to the Kuznets curve. The first and second categories of regions with higher level of economic development are likely to fall on the descending section of the Kuznets curve earlier, leading to a win-win

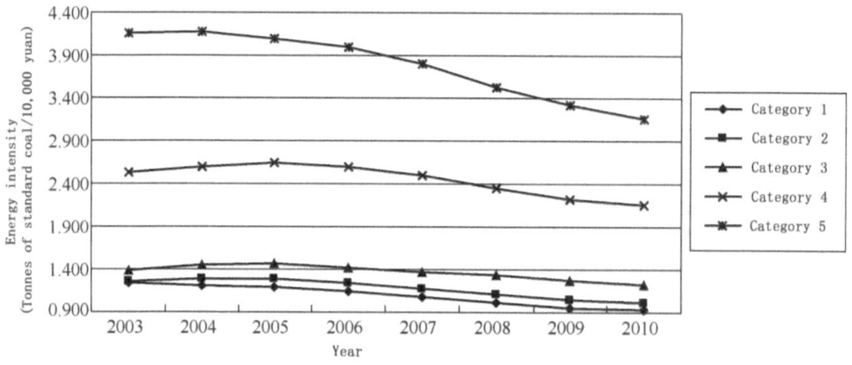

Figure 9.14 Changing trends of energy intensity in five categories of regions

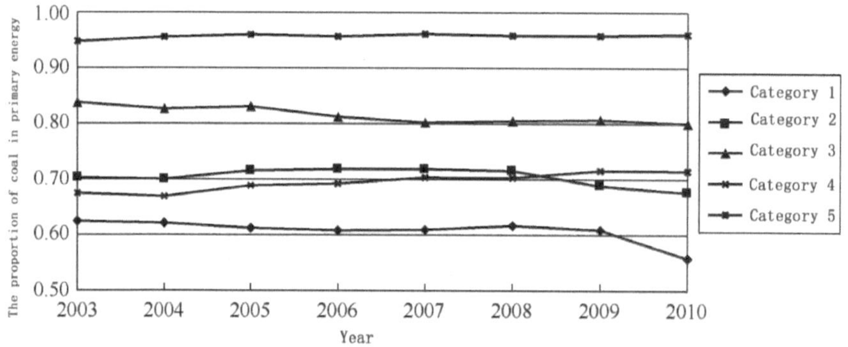

Figure 9.15 The proportion of coal in primary energy in the five categories of regions

situation of economic growth and environmental improvement. However, the third, fourth, and fifth categories of regions with lower levels of economic development will face the dilemma of economic growth and carbon emission reduction.

In summary, the large regional differences in energy intensity, the proportion of coal in primary energy, and the level of economic development lead to differences in carbon emissions among different regions.

Note

1 The 13 provincial-level administrative units are Beijing, Guangdong Province, Jiangsu Province, Zhejiang Province, Shandong Province, Shanghai, Hainan Province, Guizhou Province, Shanxi Province, Inner Mongolia Autonomous Region, Xinjiang Uygur Autonomous Region, Ningxia Hui Autonomous Region, and Gansu Province.

References

Bonzo, D.C., Hermosilla, A.Y. Clustering panel data via perturbed adaptive simulated annealing and genetic algorithms. *Advances in Complex Systems*, 2002, 4: 339–360.

Du Limin. Impact factors of China's carbon dioxide emissions: provincial panel data analysis. *South China Journal of Economics*, 2010 (11): 20–33.

Gao Tiemei. Econometric analysis methods and modeling: EViews application and examples. Beijing: Tsinghua University Press, 2009.

Jiang Jinhe. An evaluation and decomposition analysis of carbon emissions in China. *Resources Science*, 2011, 33 (4): 597–604.

Li Guozhi, Li Zongzhi. Regional difference and influence factors of China's carbon dioxide emissions. *Chinese Journal of Population, Resources and Environment*, 2010, 5: 22–27.

Liu Minglei, Zhu Lei, Fan Ying. Evaluation of carbon emission performance and estimation of marginal CO_2 abatement costs for provinces of China: a non-parametric distance function approach. *China Soft Science*, 2011, 3: 106–114.

Ren Juan. Fusion clustering analysis of multivariate panel data. *Journal of Applied Statistics and Management*, 2013, 1: 57–67.

Sun Xin. Research on fluctuations and convergency of efficiency in energy conservation and emission reduction in China. *Journal of Statistics and Information*, 2010, 6: 101–107.

Xiao Zelei, Li Bangyi, Liu Sifeng. Analysis and empirical research on clustering method based on multidimensional panel data. *Mathematical Statistics and Management*, 2009, 28(05): 831–838. doi: 10.13860/j.cnki.sltj.2009.05.

Yang Yuan, Cai Wenjia, Wang Can, et al. Regional allocation of CO_2 intensity reduction targets based on cluster analysis. *Climate Change Research*, 2012, 3 (4): 220–228.

Yi Wenjing, Zou Lele, Guo Jie, et al. How can China reach its CO_2 intensity reduction targets by 2020? A regional allocation based on equity and development. *Energy Policy*, 2011, 39(5): 2407–2415.

Zhang Xianfeng, Han Xue, Zhang Qingcai. Regional difference and influence factors of carbon emissions: empirical analysis based on partial least squares method. *Journal of Industrial Technological Economics*, 2013, 7: 100–109.

Zheng Bingyun. The clustering analysis of multivariable panel data and its application. *Journal of Applied Statistics and Management*, 2008, 27 (2): 265–270.

Zhu Jianping, Chen Minken. Cluster analysis of panel data and its application. *Statistical Research*, 2007, 04: 11–14. doi: 10.19343/j.cnki.11-1302/C.2007.04.003.

10 Equity and efficiency test for regional allocation of carbon emission index

10.1 Quota allocation theory

10.1.1 Basis of quota allocation

Since the UN Standing Committee ratified the negotiations on the Climate Change Convention in December 1990, scholars at home and abroad have discussed the design of quota allocation schemes for international carbon emission reduction. The discussion focuses on the criteria on which quota allocation schemes are constructed and fairness measurement of the constructed quota allocation scheme. According to the study of Wenju Wang and Feng Li (Table 10.1), the current international accounting criteria of the quota allocation scheme include carbon emissions from the current year, carbon emissions per unit of GDP, cumulative carbon emissions, per capita carbon emissions, per capita cumulative carbon emissions, and cumulative carbon emissions per unit of GDP. The principles of fairness for each accounting standard are:

(1) The principle of fairness considering current responsibilities

(2) The principle of fairness considering economic development

(3) The principle of fairness considering historical responsibilities

(4) The principle of fairness considering human rights equality

(5) The principle of fairness considering human rights equality, historical responsibility, and future demands

(6) The principle of fairness considering population size, economic capacity, and historical responsibility, respectively

Since the adoption of the *Kyoto Protocol* in 1997 and the Conference of the Parties serving as the meeting of the Parties to the Kyoto Protocol on its first session, domestic scholars have focused on how to construct a relatively fair quota allocation scheme[1] of global carbon emissions for China under the global carbon trading mechanism. Wenying Chen and Zongxin Wu (1998a) estimated the cumulative carbon emissions of major countries in the world and conducted a comparative study on four types of quota allocation schemes for per capita emissions based on whether or not historical responsibility was considered. They found that historical responsibility

DOI: 10.4324/9781003388500-13

Table 10.1 Carbon emission accounting standards embodied in various international emission reduction schemes and their principles of fairness

Number	*Scheme*	*Designer*	*Time*	*Accounting standards*	*The principle of fairness*
1	United Nations Framework Convention on Climate Change and the Kyoto Protocol	United Nations Climate Change Conference	1992/1997	Carbon emissions of the current year	Consider current responsibilities
2	Clear Skies and Global Climate Change Action	The US government	2001	Carbon emissions per unit of GDP	Consider economic development
3	Brazil's Climate Pledge	Brazilian government	2002	Cumulative carbon emissions	Consider historical responsibilities
4	Contraction and Convergence and Stern Review	Global Commons Institute and Nicholas Stern	2004/2008	Carbon emissions per capita	Consider human rights equality
5	China's carbon budget plan	Chinese Academy of Social Sciences	2007	Cumulative carbon emissions per capita	Consider human rights equality, historical responsibility, and future needs
6	Greenhouse Gas Development Rights Program	Stockholm Environment Institute, Sweden	2008	Cumulative carbon emissions per unit of GDP	Consider population size, economic capacity, and historical responsibility

significantly affected the results of carbon emission quota allocation and the principle of per capita cumulative carbon emissions based on population and considering historical responsibility is fairer and more favorable to China. Wenying Chen and Zongxin Wu (1998b) conducted a simulation study on the global carbon trading of two quota allocation schemes, namely the quota allocation scheme of carbon emissions under the principle of fairness with per capita carbon emissions as the accounting standard and the quota allocation scheme of carbon emissions under the principle of efficiency with carbon intensity of GDP as the accounting standard. The results show that quota allocation scheme of carbon emissions with carbon intensity of GDP as the accounting standard will make developed countries and regions the sellers in the global carbon trading market, while developing countries and regions the buyers of the global carbon trading market, contradicting with the fact that developed countries and regions should bear the majority of the historical responsibility for carbon emissions. However, the quota allocation scheme of carbon emissions with per capita carbon emissions as the accounting standard is more practical. The research group of the Development Research Center of the State Council (2009) has constructed a quota allocation scheme of global greenhouse gas emission reduction based on the principle of "not to impose uncompensated external harm to other countries", and concluded that a reasonable quota allocation scheme of future carbon emissions rights must take into account the cumulative carbon emissions of all countries and uphold the principle of equal per capita emissions, so that all countries can achieve no uncompensated external harm to other countries. Jiahua Pan and Ying Chen (2009) conducted a comprehensive analysis of the quota allocation scheme of global carbon emission under the conditions that the total global carbon budget was rigidly constrained to ensure climate security. Pan and Chen concluded that a fair and sustainable global carbon budget scheme required basic carbon emission demand based on human development. This scheme also takes the cumulative per capita carbon emissions index as the fundamental standard. Zhongli Ding et al. (2009) set the global atmospheric carbon concentration target for the year 2050 and took the year 1900 as the starting point to calculate the carbon emission allowances that should be allocated to countries in the world from 1900 to 2050. Ding concluded that the quota allocation scheme of carbon emissions which can best reflect the principle of fairness and the principle of "common but differentiated responsibilities" is also a quota allocation scheme based on cumulative per capita emission index.

In addition to the study on the selection of accounting standards for quota allocation and the interpretation of fairness principles, another important research field of quota allocation theory is to measure the fairness of carbon emission quota allocation under established accounting standards. The Gini coefficient method and the Theil index method have been used in relevant studies to measure the fairness of the quota allocation of international carbon emission. Those who use the Gini coefficient method include Heil and Wodon (1997), Padilla and Serrano (2006), and Junyong Qiu et al. (2011), while those who use the Theil index method include Duro and Padilla (2006). In terms of the domestic fairness measurement of the quota allocation of carbon emissions, the Gini coefficient method and the Theil index method are mainly used in relevant studies. Those who use Gini coefficient method include Lishan Xiao et al. (2011) and Huajun Liu and Hao Zhao (2012), while those who use the Theil index method include Jian Zhou and Diandian Yi (2012). Although both the Gini coefficient method and the Theil index method provide a medium quantitative method for the fairness measurement of carbon emissions quota allocation, the Gini coefficient method fails to fully decompose the fairness of the subsamples in the overall sample, while the Theil index method cannot reflect the distribution characteristics of subsamples within the group despite its capability to completely decompose sample subgroups. Moreover, neither the Gini coefficient method nor the Theil index method can solve the dilemma of cross-period comparison, since the ranking and distribution of sample subgroups vary greatly in different periods. On this basis, Wenju Wang and Feng Li used relative deprivation coefficients to conduct a comprehensive comparison of quota allocation schemes of global carbon emission based on various principles of fairness. The calculation principle is shown in Section 4.3.

10.1.2 Review of quota allocation theory

The current research on quota allocation theory of carbon emissions mainly focuses on the reference and fairness measurement of quota allocation schemes at the international level. However, since the National Development and Reform Commission issued the *Notice on Carrying out Pilot Programs on Carbon Emissions Trading* in 2011 and agreed to carry out the pilot carbon emission trading in seven regions, including Beijing, Tianjin, Shanghai, Chongqing, Hubei Province, Guangdong Province, and Shenzhen, some domestic scholars have begun to conduct studies on quota allocation methods for participants in the carbon trading market. On the one hand, the study focuses on the summary of experience in and introduction to the quota allocation methods of overseas carbon trading markets, especially the summary and analysis of quota allocation methods for trading entities in the EU's carbon trading system. For example, Xiaowei Xuan and Hao Zhang (2013) conducted comprehensive comparisons and analysis on the quota allocation methods of carbon emissions assigned to enterprises with carbon emission reduction targets in greenhouse gas emissions trading market of four countries and regions, including grandfathering for European greenhouse gas emissions trading market, auction for US greenhouse gas emission reduction system, the fixed price purchase method for Australian carbon trading market, and hybrid method for New Zealand carbon trading market. Maorong Zhou and Xiujie Tan (2013) conducted a comprehensive evaluation of the reform of the third phase of European carbon trading system in terms of the coverage, total amount setting, and allocation methods of quota allocation, based on a comprehensive review of the problems in the implementation of the first and second phases of the European carbon trading system. In addition, Kaijie Li and Ruxiao Qu (2012) also conducted a comprehensive review of domestic and foreign literatures on the quota allocation of initial carbon emissions in carbon trading markets. On the other hand, after nearly two years of preparation, Shenzhen carbon emissions trading market was officially opened on June 18, 2013, becoming the first pilot carbon market in China. By June 19, 2014, when Chongqing carbon emission trading market was opened, all the pilot carbon markets in seven provinces and municipalities have been launched. Some scholars have conducted a comprehensive comparison and study on the quota allocation methods of initial carbon emissions in China's pilot carbon market. Feng Li and Wenju Wang conducted a comprehensive comparison of the quota allocation methods of initial carbon emissions used in the other six pilot carbon markets in China, except for Chongqing, which adopted enterprise self-declaration allocation method. The study showed that the six pilot carbon markets have common features in their quota allocation methods, but each pilot market has its own characteristics, and no unified quota allocation method has been found yet. Furthermore, Maosheng Duan and Tao Pang (2014) conducted an exploratory study on regional quota allocation schemes under the unified carbon market in China. The study focused on advantages and disadvantages of the top-down and bottom-up quota allocation schemes with assumed entities at central authorities, local authorities, and enterprise level, and proposed a brand-new quota allocation scheme based on the localized hierarchical management system.

From the above studies, it can be seen that the current theoretical studies on quota allocation of carbon emissions mainly focus on the discussion of the fairness principle of the quota allocation scheme at international level. The design of quota allocation schemes in China's pilot carbon market and unified carbon market is almost neglected. Although some exploratory studies are on the quota allocation scheme in China's unified carbon market, they mainly focus on the determination of quota allocation scales among different entities and neglect the accumulated discussion on fairness principles at the international level, making it difficult to reach a consensus on fairness, which is the foundation and core of consensus on quota allocation schemes. At present, all seven pilot carbon trading markets in China have been launched. The establishment of a unified national carbon market has entered a critical phase. However, the vast territory and complex terrain make the fair allocation of inter-provincial quota allocation of carbon emissions a necessary prerequisite for the successful launch of the unified national carbon market. In the future, it is still necessary to study the design of the inter-provincial initial quota allocation scheme in the unified national carbon market according to the major quota allocation schemes of global carbon emission and their fairness principles, so as to provide suggestions for the selection of inter-provincial quota allocation schemes in the unified carbon market. Moreover, the current indices for measuring the fairness of quota allocation schemes of international carbon emissions mainly include carbon emissions of the current year, cumulative carbon emissions, carbon emissions per capita, cumulative carbon emissions per capita, carbon emissions per unit of GDP, and cumulative carbon emissions per unit of GDP. In the future, the fairness measurement for quota allocation schemes of carbon emission reduction based on the maturity index will be a new perspective. What's more, the current study, which is on the quota allocation of international carbon emissions based on the above six basic indices, mainly focuses on the fairness measurement of the quota allocation of carbon emissions rather than measurement of the quota allocation efficiency of carbon emissions. In the future, the maturity measurement model can also be used to measure and compare the carbon emission reduction efficiency of different quota allocation schemes of carbon emissions, which can better improve the theory of quota allocation of carbon emissions.

The quota allocation of carbon emissions is the key to the design of the carbon emission reduction market mechanism and the principle of fairness is the basis for consensus on the quota allocation scheme of carbon emissions. According to Weizhong Wang et al. (2002), although the *Kyoto Protocol* adopted in December 1997 specified that the greenhouse gas emissions of industrialized countries should be reduced by at least 5% compared with 1990 by 2012, it does not specify the specific carbon emissions quota of each country. As a result, the carbon emission reduction actions of various countries still depend on the consciousness of each country to a large extent, making it difficult to reverse the continuous upward trend of greenhouse gas emissions. According to Yi Wang and Yu Huang (2011), two factors make for an acceptable international quota allocation scheme of carbon emissions among countries: the difference in the understanding of the principle of fairness and the uncertainty about ecological and economic impacts of carbon emissions. Among them, fairness is the focus of research on quota allocation of carbon emissions, which is the basis for the construction of the global climate market mechanism. According to Yan Zheng and Fan Liang (2011), an international quota allocation scheme of carbon emissions accepted by all countries in the world as a practical scheme for the international climate regime depends on two factors: whether the scheme is based on a solid principle of fairness and whether the scheme is highly operable and feasible. According to Wenju Wang and Guiyang Zhuang, in the Kyoto Protocol agenda, international climate negotiations mainly focus on the quota allocation of greenhouse gas emission reduction among countries. That is, under the global greenhouse gas reduction target, countries commit to their own carbon emission reduction obligations and obtain carbon emission quotas through negotiation. They actively construct market mechanisms or take administrative measures to fulfill their own emission reduction obligations. Finally, global carbon market will be constructed and improved to facilitate the trading of carbon emission quotas among countries so as to achieve the global carbon reduction targets. Therefore, the fairness of quota allocation plays a significant role in the agreement of the quota allocation scheme of carbon emission reduction and the successful implementation of the carbon market mechanism construction.

10.2 Design of a unified carbon market quota allocation mechanism

10.2.1 Comparison of the principle of fairness of major international quota allocation schemes

Most of the aforementioned schemes include three core contents:

(1) Quantifying greenhouse gas concentrations and future global emission space based on global climate goals

(2) Formulating international quota allocation schemes of carbon emission based on specific fairness principles

(3) Designing market mechanisms for countries to fulfill their carbon reduction obligations.

Among them, the ultimate goal and key point of various quota schemes of international carbon emissions are still the determination of the principle of fairness. Similar to any other rights allocation schemes, different allocation standards will directly lead to different allocation results. Therefore, the fairness of the allocation standards has become the contentious issue in negotiations of various international quota allocations of carbon emissions. Due to their different positions, countries will adopt various self-interested ways to interpret and apply different fairness principles and propose corresponding international quota allocation schemes of carbon emissions. Table 10.1 shows several major global quota allocations of carbon emissions and their fairness principles since the adoption of the *United Nations Framework Convention on Climate Change* compiled by Wenju Wang and Feng Li.

As shown in Table 10.1, the *United Nations Framework Convention on Climate Change* (UNFCCC) and the *Kyoto Protocol* share the responsibilities of carbon emission reduction and allocate carbon emission quotas according to the carbon emission levels of countries and their proportions in global carbon emissions on the basis of global greenhouse gas emissions in 1990. The principle of "common but differentiated responsibilities" specified by UNFCCC in 1992, although taking into account the differences in carbon emission reduction capabilities between developed and developing countries at different stages of development to a certain extent, still takes "current responsibility" as the principle to evaluate the fairness in the quota allocation of carbon emissions, which obviously "neglects the individual fairness and the development rights and interests of developing countries" (Jiahua Pan and Yan Zheng, 2009). Later, the US announced its withdrawal from the *Kyoto Protocol* in 2001, and at the same time announced the *Clear Skies and Global Climate Change Action* and hoped that *Clear Skies and Global*

Climate Change Action could replace the *Kyoto Protocol.* The core idea of *Clear Skies and Global Climate Change Action* is to gradually reduce the intensity of greenhouse gas emissions per unit of GDP while maintaining sustainable economic growth, thus combining the quota allocation of carbon emissions with economic development. Obviously, despite the efforts to minimize its responsibility for carbon emission reduction, the US proposal is of positive significance for developing countries to implement large-scale carbon emission reduction plan by taking "economic development" as a fairness principle to evaluate the quota allocation of carbon emissions. The first quantified emission reduction target of China announced in 2009 also took carbon emissions per unit of GDP as an index. In 2002, the Brazilian government submitted the *Brazil's Climate Pledge* to the United Nations Climate Conference, proposing that greenhouse gases have cumulative effects in the atmosphere and the greenhouse gas emissions of developed countries since the industrial revolution are the leading cause of current global climate change. Therefore, when formulating an international carbon emission reduction quota allocation plan, various countries should not only take into account the current carbon emission responsibilities of each country, but also trace the historical carbon emission responsibilities of each country, so as to better reflect the fairness of the quota allocation of carbon emissions among countries. It can be seen that the *Brazil's Climate Pledge* reflects the principle of "historical responsibility" in favor of developing countries. However, it is still biased due to its overemphasizing the retrospect of responsibility in the past and failure to consider the current and future development needs of countries in different development stages. The Contraction and Convergence plan proposed by the Global Commons Institute in 2004 and the research report *Breaking the Climate Change Deadlock: A Global Agreement for a Low-Carbon Future*, written by former World Bank chief economist Stern in 2008, propose to take the per capita carbon emission as a metric and reach convergence of global per capita carbon emission at a certain point in the future with the joint efforts of developed and developing countries. Although these two schemes imply the principle of carbon emission allowance allocation based on "interpersonal equality", they pay more attention to the fairness in the convergence of the end point while ignoring the fairness of the same starting point, that is, the two schemes ignore the cumulative effect of carbon emissions and the different development stages and needs of different countries, ignore the historical responsibilities of developed countries, and limit the future development space of developing countries.

The above schemes are all based on a single principle of fairness, and cannot fully reflect the multifaceted differences in carbon emissions among countries. In 2007, two scholars from the Chinese Academy of Social Sciences, Pan Jiahua and Chen Ying, submitted the carbon budget plan to the 14th Conference of the Parties to the UNFCCC, which began to comprehensively consider a variety of fairness principles with cumulative carbon emission per capita as a measurement index for the allocation of carbon emission allowances. On the one hand, it continues the retrospect of the historical emission responsibilities of developed countries in the *Brazil's Climate Pledge* and on the other hand, it starts from interpersonal fairness in consistent with the basic starting point of the principle of interpersonal equality, so that the various fairness principles such as interpersonal equality and historical responsibility are well combined, which better reflects the differences in carbon emission reduction responsibilities, capabilities, and development needs of different countries and groups. The *Greenhouse Gas Development Right Program* proposed by the Stockholm Environment Institute of Sweden in 2008 also takes into account various principles of fairness such as population size, economic capacity, and historical responsibility. It advocates that only rich people have the responsibility and ability to reduce carbon emissions and different carbon emission quotas should be granted to the rich and the poor. These ideas are of positive significance. Its scheme of carbon emission reduction, which fully considers the multidimensional principle of fairness, is designed to share the responsibility of global carbon emission reduction with historical cumulative carbon emission and GDP as the core indicators. Taking into account various principles of fairness and integrating the multiple goals of carbon emission reduction and sustainable development, the carbon budget plan and the Swedish plan have achieved great repercussions in the international community.

On the whole, the design of the inter-provincial allowance allocation scheme in the national unified carbon market needs to fully learn from the latest progress in the fairness principle of global allowance allocation, learn from the advantages of each scheme as much as possible, and take into account various principles of fairness.

10.2.2 Unified carbon market allowance allocation scheme with different fairness principles

The principle of fairness is the basis for the formulation of the carbon emission allowance allocation plan and the selection of carbon emission measurement indicators is the key to the fairness principle. Different fairness principles often correspond to different carbon emission measurement indicators, and the measurement results of different carbon emission measurement indicators will in turn lead to different judgments and interpretations of the fairness of the allocation of carbon emission allowances. As shown in Table 10.1, the principle of current responsibility corresponds to the carbon emissions of the current year, the principle of economic development corresponds to the carbon emissions per unit of GDP, the principle of historical responsibility corresponds to the cumulative carbon emissions, and the principle of interpersonal equality corresponds to the per capita carbon emissions, the principle of interpersonal equality and historical responsibility corresponds to the cumulative carbon emissions per capita, and the principle of economic development and historical responsibility corresponds to the cumulative carbon emissions per unit of GDP. Based on different fairness principles and carbon emission measurement indicators, different provincial allowance allocation schemes are often formulated. The following is a quantitative design of the inter-provincial allowance allocation based on the above-mentioned fairness principles and carbon emission measurement indicators, taking a single region as an example.

10.2.2.1 Situations based on the current responsibility principle

Suppose there are $i = 1, 2,..., n$ regions and $t = 1,2, \ldots, m$ periods, with 1 as the starting period, j as the reference period, m as the ending period, and k as the any target period between j and m. According to the current responsibility principle, the actual carbon emissions in the jth period and the target carbon emissions in the mth period should be fully considered when the allowances of the ith region for the mth period is allocated in the jth period. Usually, in consideration of the quantitative relationship between the actual carbon emissions in the jth period and the target carbon emissions in the mth period, the target carbon emissions in the mth period will be set as a specific percentage of the actual carbon emissions in the jth period, and the target carbon emissions will be assigned as its quota allocation. Under this principle, assuming that the target carbon emissions in the kth period of the ith region is a linear function of the actual carbon emissions in the jth period, the allowances allocated for the ith region in the kth period are:

$$E_{ik}^{*} = \delta_{ik} E_{ij} \tag{10.1}$$

Where in δ_{ik} is the linear function relationship coefficient between the target carbon emissions in the kth period in the ith region and the actual carbon emissions in the jth period.

According to the current responsibility principle, compared with other regions, the larger the actual carbon emission E_{ij} in the jth period in the ith region, the smaller its δ_{ik} should be. According to the principle of convergence, an ideal situation in the ending period would be all regions with equal carbon emissions, that is:

$$E_{1m} = E_{2m} = \cdots = E_{nm} \tag{10.2}$$

10.2.2.2 Situations based on the historical responsibility principle

According to the principle of historical responsibility, to allocate the allowances of the ith region for the mth period in the jth period, the actual accumulated carbon emissions in the *1-j* period and the target accumulated carbon emission in the *j-m* period should be fully considered. Under this principle, assuming that the target carbon emissions in the kth period of the

ith region is a linear function of the expected cumulative carbon emissions from the first to the kth period, the quota allocation of the ith region in the kth period is:

$$E_{ik}^{*} = \gamma_{ik} \sum_{t=1}^{k} E_{it} \tag{10.3}$$

Wherein γ_{ik} is the linear function relationship coefficient between the target carbon emissions in the kth period in the ith region and its expected cumulative carbon emissions from the first to the kth period.

According to the principle of historical responsibility, the larger the actual cumulative carbon emission $\sum_{t=1}^{j} E_{it}$ of the ith region in the jth period, the smaller its γ_{ik} should be. According to the principle of convergence, an ideal situation in the ending period would be all regions with equal cumulative carbon emissions, that is:

$$\sum_{t=1}^{m} E_{1t} = \sum_{t=1}^{m} E_{2t} = \cdots = \sum_{t=1}^{m} E_{nt} \tag{10.4}$$

10.2.2.3 Situations based on the principle of interpersonal equality

According to the principle of interpersonal equality, to allocate the allowances of the ith region for the mth period in the jth period, the actual per capita carbon emissions in the jth period and the target per capita carbon emissions in the mth period should be fully considered. Under this principle, assuming that the target per capita carbon emissions of the ith region in the kth period is a linear function of the actual per-capita carbon emissions in the jth period, the quota allocation of the ith region in the kth period is:

$$E_{ik}^{*} = P_{ik} \left[\lambda_{ik} \left(\frac{E_{ij}}{P_{ij}} \right) \right] \tag{10.5}$$

Wherein P_{ij} is the population size of the ith region in the jth period, P_{ij} is the expected population size of the ith region in the kth period, λ_{ik} is the linear function relationship coefficient between the target per capita carbon emissions of the ith region in the kth period, and its actual per capita carbon emissions in the jth period.

According to the principle of interpersonal equality, compared with other regions, the larger the actual per capita carbon emissions $\frac{E_{ij}}{P_{ij}}$ in the jth period of the ith region, the smaller its λ_{ik} should be. According to the principle of convergence, an ideal situation in the ending period would be all regions with equal per capita carbon emissions, that is:

$$\frac{E_{1m}}{P_{1m}} = \frac{E_{2m}}{P_{2m}} = \cdots = \frac{E_{nm}}{P_{nm}10} \quad (10.6)$$

10.2.2.4 Situations based on the principle of interpersonal equality and historical responsibility

According to the principle of interpersonal equality and historical responsibility, to allocate the allowances of the ith region for the mth period in the jth period, the actual per capita cumulative carbon emissions in the jth period and the target per capita cumulative carbon emissions in the mth period should be fully considered. Under this principle, assuming that the target per capita cumulative carbon emissions of the ith region in the kth period is a linear function of its actual per-capita cumulative carbon emissions in the jth period, the quota allocation for the ith region in the kth period is:

$$E_{ik}^{*} = P_{ik}\left\{\beta_{ik}\left[\left(\sum_{t=1}^{j} E_{it}\right) / P_{ij}\right]\right\} \quad (10.7)$$

Wherein $\sum_{t=1}^{j} E_{it}$ is the actual cumulative carbon emission from the first to the jth period, β_{ik} is the linear function relationship coefficient between the target per capita cumulative carbon emissions in the kth period of the ith region and the actual per capita cumulative carbon emissions in the jth period.

According to the principle of interpersonal equality and historical responsibility, compared with other regions, the larger the actual per capita cumulative carbon emissions $\frac{\sum_{t=1}^{j} E_{it}}{P_{ij}}$ in the jth period of the ith region, the smaller its β_{ik} should be. According to the principle of convergence, an ideal situation in the ending period would be all regions with equal per capita cumulative carbon emissions, namely:

$$\frac{\sum_{t=1}^{m} E_{1t}}{P_{1m}} = \frac{\sum_{t=1}^{m} E_{2t}}{P_{2m}} = \cdots = \frac{\sum_{t=1}^{m} E_{nt}}{P_{nm}} \quad (10.8)$$

10.2.2.5 Situations based on the principle of economic development

According to the principle of economic development, the allocation of quotas of the ith region for the mth period in the jth period should fully consider its actual carbon emissions per unit of GDP in the jth period and the target carbon emissions per unit of GDP in the mth period. Under this principle, assuming that the target carbon emissions per unit of GDP in the kth period of the ith region is a linear function of its actual carbon emissions per unit of GDP in the jth period, the allowance allocation in the kth period of the ith region is:

$$E_{ik}^{*} = \mathrm{GDP}_{ik}\left[\alpha_{ik}\left(\frac{E_{ij}}{\mathrm{GDP}_{ij}}\right)\right] \tag{10.9}$$

Wherein $\mathrm{GDP}_{ik}$is the expected economic scale in the kth period of the ith region, GDP_{ij} is the economic scale of the ith region in the jth period; α_{ik} is the linear function relationship between the target carbon emission per unit of GDP of the ith region in the kth period and its actual carbon emission per unit of GDP in the jth period.

According to the principle of economic development, compared with other regions, the larger the actual carbon emission per unit of GDP $\frac{E_{1j}}{\mathrm{GDP}_{1j}}$ of the ith region in the jth period, the smaller its α_{ik} should be. According to the principle of convergence, an ideal situation in the ending period would be all regions with equal carbon emissions per unit of GDP, that is:

$$\frac{E_{1j}}{\mathrm{GDP}_{1j}} = \frac{E_{2j}}{\mathrm{GDP}_{2j}} = \cdots = \frac{E_{nj}}{\mathrm{GDP}_{nj}} \tag{10.10}$$

10.2.2.6 Situations based on the principles of economic development and historical responsibility

According to the principle of economic development and historical responsibility, the allocation of quotas for the mth period of the ith region in the jth period should fully consider its actual cumulative carbon emissions per unit of GDP in the jth period and the target cumulative carbon emissions per unit of GDP in the mth period. Under this principle, assuming that the target cumulative carbon emissions per unit of GDP in the kth period of the ith region is a linear function of the actual cumulative carbon emissions per unit of GDP in the jth period, then the allowance allocation of the ith region in the kth period is:

$$E_{ik}^{*} = \mathrm{GDP}_{ik}\left\{\chi_{ik}\left[\frac{\sum_{t=1}^{j} E_{it}}{\mathrm{GDP}_{ij}}\right]\right\} \tag{10.11}$$

Wherein χ_{ik} is the linear function relationship coefficient between the actual cumulative carbon emissions per unit of GDP in the kth period of the ith region and the target cumulative carbon emissions per unit of GDP in the jth period.

According to the principles of economic development and historical responsibility, compared with other regions, the larger the actual cumulative carbon emissions per unit of GDP $\frac{\sum_{t=1}^{j} E_{it}}{\text{GDP}_{ij}}$ of the ith region in the jth period, the smaller its χ_{ik} should be. According to the principle of convergence, an ideal situation in the ending period would be all regions with equal cumulative carbon emissions per unit of GDP, that is:

$$\left(\sum_{t=1}^{m} E_{1t}\right) / \text{GDP}_{1j} = \left(\sum_{t=1}^{m} E_{2t}\right) / \text{GDP}_{2j} = \cdots = \left(\sum_{t=1}^{m} E_{nt}\right) / \text{GDP}_{nj} \qquad (10.12)$$

10.2.2.7 Comprehensive comparative analysis of different quota allocation schemes

As shown in the above analysis, different carbon emission allowance allocation schemes are based on different principles of fairness and their results are also different. From the perspective of the consideration of the principle of fairness in each plan, the plan based on the principle of historical responsibility considers not only the allocation of current responsibility, but also the retrospect of historical responsibility, so it is better than the plan based on the principle of current responsibility. The scheme based on interpersonal equality and historical responsibility takes into account the principles of fairness in many aspects such as interpersonal equality, historical responsibility, and realistic development, so it is better than the scheme based on the principle of interpersonal equality or historical responsibility. The scheme based on the principle of economic development and historical responsibility, as a combination and extension of the above two schemes, is naturally superior to any of the two scheme. It can be seen that the scheme based on the principles of interpersonal equality and historical responsibility and the scheme based on the principles of economic development and historical responsibility can comprehensively reflect the core themes of the above four schemes based on different principles of fairness. The former focuses on the fairness that reflects the basic needs of human existence, while the latter focuses on the fairness of social and economic development. These two schemes have little overlap in the connotation of fairness and can be used for reference and comprehensively applied in the inter-provincial allowance allocation scheme in the unified national carbon market.

For example, in the stage of rapid economic development, the weight of the principles of interpersonal equality and historical responsibility can be appropriately reduced, while after the economy has developed to a certain extent, the weight of the principles of economic development and historical responsibility can be appropriately reduced. Qianting Zhu et al. (2015) used two modeling methods, bottom-up and top-down, to simulate and analyze the carbon emission-level control scheme, the single-principle scheme, and the weighted principle scheme, and held the view that the weighted principle scheme is more fair and feasible, as the single-principle scheme may lead to extreme distribution results under certain principles due to the large uncertainty of the scheme. Therefore, Zhu supports comprehensive application of different fairness principles.

Although it takes time to build a unified national carbon market, there is no substantive plan for the allocation of inter-provincial carbon emission quotas, nor relevant research. However, *Notice of the State Council on Printing and Issuing the Work Plan for Greenhouse Gas Emission Control in the 12th Five-Year Plan period* has decomposed the task of reducing carbon dioxide emissions per unit of GDP in 2015 to various provinces, municipalities directly under the Central Government, and autonomous regions. With the continuous advancement of the construction of a unified carbon market in China, in the future, the Chinese government will implement quota allocation control plan management for carbon emissions in various provinces, municipalities, and autonomous regions based on specific quota allocation plans and scientifically allocate restrictive quota to all provinces, municipalities, and autonomous regions under the condition of total amount control. As mentioned above, the allocation of carbon emission allowances is a very complex issue, which involves not only the fairness principle and the selection of carbon emission accounting indicators, but also the overall fairness of the allocation of carbon emission allowances and the measurement of emission reduction effects. Among them, the latter is more critical and important in building a national unified carbon market quota allocation mechanism. As pointed out by Deyong Song and Xiping Liu (2013), it is a fundamental work to realize the relative fairness of carbon emission space under the condition of total amount control. To this end, Jun Yang et al. (2012) estimated carbon dioxide emissions through the physical energy consumption of China's provinces, municipalities, and autonomous regions from 1997 to 2009, and used a measure of income inequality—the Lorenz curve and Gini coefficient—to study the differences in carbon dioxide emissions among provinces, the equalization of carbon dioxide emissions across provinces, and the realization of China's emission reduction targets. They found that different from the unbalanced economic development in China, the inter-provincial carbon dioxide emissions in China showed a convergence feature. Deyong Song and Xiping Liu (2013) redefined the carbon Lorentz curve and carbon Gini coefficient in carbon emission equality on the basis of the carbon emission data of various regions in China from 1978 to 2010 from the perspective of historical cumulative carbon emissions per capita, calculated carbon Gini coefficient (0.24), and considered that China's inter-provincial carbon emissions are relatively fair. Besides, they conducted spatial distribution of carbon emissions in 2020 in various regions of China from the perspective of historical cumulative carbon emissions per capita. Wenju Wang and Feng Li used the relative deprivation coefficient to analyze the fairness of various international carbon emission accounting standards based on the idea of the Gini coefficient and calculated the relative deprivation coefficient of carbon emissions among G8 countries, B4 countries and N7 countries from 1992 to 2011. It is found that there are large differences in the fairness measurement results under different accounting standards, and the accounting standards for per capita cumulative carbon emissions based on the adjustment of carbon emissions embedded in international trade can better reflect the principle of "common but differentiated responsibilities". Therefore, the carbon emission reduction scheme formulated in this manner will be more equitable.

In the above analysis, it is often difficult to achieve the ideal state of the termination period based on the principle of convergence. In fact, the difference in carbon emissions in each region based on different carbon emission measurement indicators in the termination period is smaller than that in the reference period. Regarding the measurement of the difference in carbon emissions in different regions, the above-mentioned Gini coefficient method or a more matured relative deprivation coefficient method can be used. The maturity index used in this chapter can also provide a fairness test for the impact of different allowance allocation methods on the carbon emission reduction process in each region and the difference in carbon emissions in each region. At the same time, the above analyses are all carried out under the assumption of total amount control and all take into account the overall carbon emission reduction efficiency brought about by different allowance allocation schemes. The maturity index used in this chapter can also provide an efficient test for the impact of different allowance allocation methods on China's overall carbon emission reduction process so as to well integrate the carbon emission reduction maturity measurement and the design of the allowance allocation mechanism. The design of the allowance allocation mechanism can also contribute to the improvement of the maturity index.

In view of the absence of a specific plan for the allocation of inter-provincial carbon emission quotas in China as well as the country's external commitments aimed at GDP carbon emission intensity, the following part of this chapter will take the decomposition of carbon emission reduction targets among provinces, municipalities, and autonomous regions, as specified in the *Notice of the State Council on Printing and Issuing the Work Plan for Greenhouse Gas Emission Control in the 12th Five-Year Plan period* as an example, and test the fairness and efficiency of carbon emission allowance allocation based on maturity index.

10.3 Regional quota allocation fairness and efficiency test

10.3.1 Analysis of carbon emission reduction target decomposition in the 12th Five-Year Plan period

In order to better implement China's carbon emission reduction targets in 2015 in the 12th Five-Year Plan, the National Development and Reform Commission issued the *Notice of the State Council on Printing and Issuing the Work Plan for Greenhouse Gas Emission Control in the 12th Five-Year Plan period* (hereinafter referred to as the *Notice*), decomposing the goal of reducing the carbon emission intensity of the national GDP by 17% in 2015 compared with 2010 to provinces, municipalities directly under the Central Government, and autonomous regions. Table 10.2 shows the breakdown of the targets for the reduction of GDP carbon emission intensity and GDP energy consumption intensity in China's provinces, municipalities, and autonomous regions during the 12th Five-Year Plan period according to the *Notice*. As can be seen from Table 10.2, the decomposition of national carbon emission reduction targets in 2015 among provinces, municipalities, and autonomous regions as per the *Notice* has an obvious one-size-fits-all feature. Except for Xinjiang, Qinghai, Tibet, and Hainan, the GDP carbon emission intensity of other regions decreases by 16%–20%. The GDP carbon emission intensity of the eastern region has a relatively sharp decline,

Table 10.2 Reduction of carbon emission intensity and energy consumption intensity of GDP nationwide during the 12th Five-Year Plan period (%)

Region	*Carbon intensity reduction target of GDP*	*Reduction target of energy consumption intensity of GDP*	*Region*	*Carbon intensity reduction target of GDP*	*Reduction target of energy consumption intensity of GDP*
Beijing	18.00	17.00	Hubei	17.00	16.00
Tianjin	19.00	18.00	Hunan	17.00	16.00
Hebei	18.00	17.00	Guangdong	19.50	18.00
Shanxi	17.00	16.00	Guangxi	16.00	15.00
Inner Mongolia	16.00	15.00	Hainan	11.00	10.00
Liaoning	18.00	17.00	Chongqing	17.00	16.00
Jilin	17.00	16.00	Sichuan	17.50	16.00
Heilongjiang	16.00	16.00	Guizhou	16.00	15.00
Shanghai	19.00	18.00	Yunnan	16.50	15.00
Jiangsu	19.00	18.00	Tibet	10.00	10.00
Zhejiang	19.00	18.00	Shanxi	17.00	16.00
Anhui	17.00	16.00	Gansu	16.00	15.00
Fujian	17.50	16.00	Qinghai	10.00	10.00
Jiangxi	17.00	16.00	Ningxia	16.00	15.00
Shandong	18.00	17.00	Xinjiang	11.00	10.00
Henan	17.00	16.00			

followed by the northeastern region, the central region, and the western region. Compared with the socioeconomic development level of each region, there is no obvious difference in the reduction of GDP carbon emission intensity among regions.

It can be seen from Table 10.2 that the reduction targets of GDP energy consumption intensity in each region is consistent with the reduction targets of GDP carbon emission intensity. According to the aforementioned improved Kaya identity, the reduction in carbon emission intensity of energy consumption can be calculated, as shown in Table 10.3.

It can be seen from Table 10.3 that the carbon emission intensity of energy consumption in the 30 provinces, municipalities directly under the Central Government, and autonomous regions during the 12th Five-Year Plan period decreased by 1.2% in most of the regions and by 1.8% and 1.1% in a few regions, except for Heilongjiang and Qinghai, which remained unchanged in this regard. This is mainly due to the fact that the *Notice* has basically the same targets for the reduction of GDP carbon emission intensity and GDP energy consumption intensity in all provinces, municipalities, and autonomous regions. This also reflects the reality that China's carbon emission reduction is currently more concentrated on strengthening the reduction of GDP energy consumption intensity. In addition, as mentioned above, the *Notice* has obvious one-size-fits-all features for the reduction targets of GDP carbon emission intensity and GDP energy consumption intensity of provinces, municipalities, and autonomous regions, which also leads to a one-size-fits-all reduction targets in carbon emission intensity of energy consumption.

10.3.2 Carbon emission reduction maturity measurement model

The construction of China's carbon emission reduction maturity measurement model in this chapter can be described in the following four levels. It is worth noting that, considering that the current carbon emission reduction targets announced by China are mainly GDP carbon emission intensity indicators, the selection of the basic indicators of China's carbon emission reduction maturity measurement model will be based on the converted Kaya identity, that is, $\frac{\mathrm{CO}_{2i}}{\mathrm{GDP}_i} = \left(\frac{E_i}{\mathrm{GDP}_i}\right)\left(\frac{\mathrm{CO}_{2i}}{E_i}\right)$. As shown in the converted Kaya identity, the carbon emission intensity of GDP is jointly determined by the energy consumption intensity of GDP and the carbon emission intensity of energy consumption. Taking GDP carbon emission intensity as the basic indicator can reflect the final effect of carbon emission reduction of economic growth in each region, and using GDP energy consumption intensity and energy consumption carbon emission intensity as basic indicators can reflect the driving factors of carbon emission reduction in each region. The values of these three basic indicators are inversely related to the level of carbon emission reduction.

Table 10.3 Three basic indicators by region in 2010 and 2015 (%)

Region	*2010*			*2015*			*Reduction in energy consumption intensity of GDP*
	Energy consumption intensity of GDP	*Carbon intensity of energy consumption*	*Carbon intensity of GDP*	*Energy consumption intensity of GDP*	*Carbon intensity of energy consumption*	*Carbon intensity of GDP*	
Beijing	43.27	81.94	35.45	42.75	68.01	29.07	1.2
Tianjin	61.74	94.34	58.25	60.99	77.36	47.18	1.2
Hebei	115.12	104.6	120.42	113.74	86.82	98.75	1.2
Shanxi	141.29	95.35	134.71	139.61	80.09	111.81	1.2
Inner Mongolia	121.4	101.35	123.04	119.97	86.15	103.35	1.2
Liaoning	98.55	99.17	97.73	97.36	82.31	80.14	1.2
Jilin	84.96	90.07	76.52	83.95	75.66	63.51	1.2
Heilongjiang	73.54	90.75	66.74	73.54	76.23	56.06	0
Shanghai	49.46	88.84	43.94	48.86	72.85	35.59	1.2
Jiangsu	49.7	100.73	50.07	49.1	82.6	40.55	1.2
Zhejiang	47.36	91.44	43.3	46.78	74.98	35.08	1.2
Anhui	67.45	91.63	61.8	66.65	76.97	51.29	1.2
Fujian	55.63	79.65	44.31	54.64	66.9	36.55	1.8
Jiangxi	61.78	88.63	54.76	61.05	74.45	45.45	1.2
Shandong	72.45	95.05	68.87	71.58	78.9	56.47	1.2
Henan	72.7	101.92	74.1	71.84	85.61	61.5	1.2
Hubei	94.78	75.95	71.99	93.66	63.8	59.75	1.2
Hunan	80.21	74.78	59.99	79.26	62.82	49.79	1.2
Guangdong	44.02	84.58	37.23	43.22	69.35	29.97	1.8
Guangxi	71.94	79.31	57.06	71.1	67.41	47.93	1.2
Hainan	58.86	77.67	45.71	58.21	69.9	40.69	1.1
Chongqing	93.34	72.99	68.12	92.23	61.31	56.54	1.2
Sichuan	83.32	68.37	56.96	81.83	57.43	46.99	1.8
Guizhou	138.55	87.94	121.84	136.92	74.75	102.35	1.2
Yunnan	96.29	80.49	77.5	94.59	68.41	64.71	1.8
Shanxi	75.95	88.35	67.09	75.04	74.21	55.69	1.2
Gansu	112.86	89.93	101.49	111.53	76.44	85.25	1.2
Qinghai	135.09	57.33	77.44	135.09	51.6	69.7	0
Ningxia	183.8	112.15	206.13	181.64	95.32	173.15	1.2
Xinjiang	124.86	82.62	103.16	123.47	74.36	91.81	1.1

1 Measurement model of relative development degree of inter-provincial carbon emission reduction.

The basic idea of Dunn's grey correlation analysis is to measure the similarity of the change trend of system factors based on the distance between corresponding points in the sequence. In practical applications, it is necessary to first determine the reference sequence and several comparison sequences and then use the correlation model to figure out the correlation coefficient between each comparison sequence and the reference sequence. Larger coefficient indicates greater correlation between the comparison sequence and the reference sequence and closer sequence curves. If the reference sequence is the optimal development sequence, greater correlation coefficient between the comparison sequence and the reference sequence indicates closer distance between the development path of the comparison sequence and the optimal development path and the higher relative development level. Assuming that the evaluation object is area m, the comparison period is n years, x is the basic indicator such as the carbon emission intensity of output value, the energy consumption intensity of output value, or the carbon emission intensity of energy consumption, the set composed of the comparison sequence x_i in the ith area is: $x_i = \{x_i(1), x_i(2), \ldots, x_i(n)\}$

The set composed of the reference sequence x_0 is: $x_0 = \{x_0(1), x_0(2), \ldots, x_0(n)\}$

Since the basic index is negatively correlated with the regional carbon emission reduction level, the reference series select the lowest value of the basic index in each region, $x_0(k) = \min_{1 \le i \le m} \{x_i^k\} k = 1, 2, \ldots, n$. The formula for calculating the gray correlation coefficient of the ith region in the kth year is

$$\xi_i(k) = \frac{\Delta_{\min} + \rho \Delta_{\max}}{\Delta_{ik} + \rho \Delta_{\max}} \tag{10.13}$$

wherein p is the resolution coefficient.

As usual, the value of p is 0.5. Regarding the value of the resolution coefficient p, Lv Feng (1997) conducted a special study: $\Delta_{\min} = \min_i \min_k |x_0(k) - x_i(k)|$ is the minimum value of the absolute difference between all comparison sequences and the reference sequence in the whole period, $\Delta_{\max} = \max_i \max_k |x_0(k) - x_i(k)|$ is the maximum value of the absolute difference between all comparison sequences and the reference sequence in the whole period, and $\Delta_{ik} = |x_0(k) - x_i(k)|$ is the absolute difference between the comparison sequence and the reference sequence in the ith region in the kth year. It can be seen that $\xi_i(k)$ is the relative development index of carbon emission reduction in the ith region in the kth year. The larger the value, the higher the relative development level. The formula for calculating the relative development index of the average carbon emission reduction in the ith region during the whole period is as follows:

$$D_i = \frac{1}{n}\sum_{k=1}^{n}\xi_i(k) \tag{10.14}$$

2 The measurement model of the relative development degree of overall carbon emission reduction.

Similar to formula (10.14), the formula for calculating the overall average development index of each region in the kth year is as follows:

$$D_k = \frac{1}{m}\sum_{i=1}^{m}\xi_i(k) \tag{10.15}$$

Since the simple arithmetic average method cannot reflect the impact of regional pattern changes on the overall process of carbon emission reduction in China, this section constructs the formula for calculating the overall average development index of each region in the kth year considering the regional pattern changes:

$$D_k^{\dagger} = \sum_{i=1}^{m}\omega_i\xi_i(k) \tag{10.16}$$

Wherein ω_i is the proportion of the GDP of the ith region in the whole, $D_k^{\dagger} - D_k$ is the impact of the regional pattern change on the overall development index of China's carbon emission reduction. The larger the value is, the greater the impact will be.

3 The measurement model for the coordination degree of the overall carbon emission reduction.

The essence of the distance coordination degree model is to measure the coordination level of the economic system by measuring the ratio between the Euclidean distance and the Chebyshev distance between the actual state and the ideal state of the economic system. Based on the aforementioned assumptions, the Euclidean distance measurement formula between the actual value and the optimal value of the basic indicators of each region or industry in the kth year is:

$$o_k = \sqrt{\sum_{i=1}^{m}\left[x_0(k) - x_i(k)\right]^2} \tag{10.17}$$

The Chebyshev distance measure between the actual value and the optimal value of the basic indicator in the ith region during the whole period is as follows:

$$q_i = \max_{1 \le k \le n} \left\{ \left| x_0(k) - x_i(k) \right| \right\} \tag{10.18}$$

Based on Equations (10.17) and (10.18), the formula for measuring the overall coordination index of carbon emission reduction in each region in the kth year is:

$$C_k = 1 - \sqrt{\frac{(o_k)^2}{\sum_{i=1}^{m} (q_i)^2}} \tag{10.19}$$

Obviously, $0 \le C_k \le 1$, the larger the C_k value, the smaller the deviation of the actual state of each region from the ideal state, and the higher the overall coordination of carbon emission reduction in each region or industry.

4 Coordinated development measure of overall carbon emission reduction.

Although the distance coordination degree model has strong rationality, the calculation results may also have the low-level coordination problem mentioned by Bonai Fan and Xiaolong Bian (2013), that is, the economic system may achieve a high degree of coordination at a lower level of development, so that the coordination degree coefficient cannot effectively reflect the overall picture of the coordinated development of the economic system. On this basis, the overall coordinated development index measurement formula constructed by the overall average development index and the overall coordination index is as follows:

$$H_k = \sqrt{D_k C_k} \tag{10.20}$$

It can be seen that the value of H_k is also between 0 and 1. The larger the value of H_k, the better the overall coordinated development of carbon emission reduction in China.

10.3.3 Fairness test of inter-provincial quota allocation based on maturity

Table 10.4 shows the development index of the three basic indicators in each region in 2010 and 2015, calculated according to the above-mentioned inter-provincial carbon emission reduction development degree formula.

As shown in Table 10.4:

1 Compared with 2010, the development index based on energy consumption intensity of GDP in 2015 is unchanged in Beijing, decreased slightly in Heilongjiang and Qinghai, and increased slightly in other areas
2 Compared with 2010, the development index based on the carbon intensity of energy consumption in 2015 increased by 15%–20% in the eastern region except for Hainan, increased by about 15% in the northeast and central regions, and increased by 10%–15% in the west region except for Qinghai and Tibet

Table 10.4 The development index of the three basic indicators by region in 2010 and 2015

Region	*Area*	*Energy consumption intensity of GDP*		*Carbon intensity of energy consumption*		*Carbon intensity of GDP*	
		2010	*2015*	*2010*	*2015*	*2010*	*2015*
East	Beijing	100	100	56.58	66.15	100	100
	Tianjin	92.89	92.97	46.43	55.46	89.03	91.08
	Hebei	77.05	77.26	40.42	47.66	68.53	72.64
	Shanghai	97.5	97.53	50.45	60.15	95.61	96.6
	Jiangsu	97.4	97.43	42.5	50.85	92.68	94.16
	Zhejiang	98.33	98.35	48.47	57.84	95.93	96.86
	Fujian	95.12	95.3	58.97	67.7	95.43	96.11
	Shandong	89.21	89.32	45.95	54.02	84.7	87.1
	Guangdong	99.69	99.81	54.07	64.37	99.05	99.52
	Hainan	93.93	93.98	61.2	63.67	94.75	94.09
Northeast	Liaoning	81.35	81.54	43.39	51.08	74.81	78.37
	Jilin	85.26	85.41	49.49	57.14	81.83	84.31
	Heilongjiang	88.85	88.68	48.98	56.56	85.54	87.27
Central	Shanxi	71.1	71.35	45.76	52.96	65.08	69.1
	Anhui	90.89	90.98	48.33	55.84	87.53	89.28
	Jiangxi	92.87	92.95	50.61	58.39	90.55	91.87
	Henan	89.12	89.24	41.84	48.53	82.72	85.09
	Hubei	82.4	82.57	63.27	72.44	83.51	85.78
	Hunan	86.72	86.85	64.76	74.09	88.29	89.93
West	Inner Mongolia	75.53	75.75	42.15	48.15	67.87	71.35
	Guangxi	89.37	89.48	59.34	66.98	89.54	90.75
	Chongqing	82.81	82.98	67.2	76.76	84.99	87.07
	Sichuan	85.76	86.06	74.4	84.61	89.59	91.17
	Guizhou	71.68	71.92	51.17	58.08	68.17	71.63
	Yunnan	81.98	82.31	58.08	65.61	81.48	83.85
	Shanxi	88.07	88.19	50.84	58.65	85.4	87.42
	Gansu	77.61	77.81	49.6	56.36	73.69	76.71
	Qinghai	72.43	72.31	100	100	81.5	81.99
	Ningxia	63.18	63.46	36.92	42.32	52.01	56.22
	Xinjiang	74.72	74.92	55.92	58.5	73.21	74.68

3 Compared with 2010, the development index based on the carbon intensity of GDP in 2015 increased by 0%–6% in the eastern region except for Hainan, increased by about 3% in the northeast region, increased by 2%–6% in the central region, and increased by 1%–8% in the west region

It can be seen that although the carbon emission intensity of energy consumption in 2015 decreased slightly compared with that in 2010, the development index of carbon emission reduction based on the carbon emission intensity of energy consumption in all regions increased by more than 10%. Although the energy consumption intensity of GDP in 2015 increased by more than 15% compared with 2010, the development index of carbon emission reduction based on energy consumption intensity of GDP in all regions only showed a slight increase of less than 1%.

Table 10.5 shows the changes in the ranking of the development index of the three basic indicators in each region in 2010 and 2015.

As shown in Table 10.5:

(1) The ranking of each region in the development index based on energy consumption intensity of GDP did not change between 2010 and 2015

(2) Compared with 2010, ranking of the development index based on carbon intensity of energy consumption increased in a certain degree in the eastern region in 2015 except for Hainan, unchanged in the central and northeastern regions, increased in Shanxi, and decreased in the rest of the western regions

(3) Compared with 2010, the development index based on carbon intensity of GDP decreased in Hainan, increased in Tianjin, Shandong, and Jiangsu, and unchanged in the rest of the eastern region in 2015; decreased in Heilongjiang and unchanged in the rest of the central and northeastern regions; increased in Yunnan and Shanxi, decreased in Qinghai, Guangxi, and Chongqing, and unchanged in the rest of the western region

It can be concluded that compared with 2010, the energy consumption intensity of GDP and carbon intensity of GDP in 2015 decreased significantly, while the development index ranking of carbon emission reduction based on energy consumption intensity of GDP and carbon intensity of GDP in each region did not change significantly. However, compared with 2010, the carbon intensity of energy consumption in 2015 increased slightly, while the development index ranking of carbon emission reduction based on carbon intensity of energy consumption in each region changed significantly.

Table 10.6 shows the development index of the three basic indices in the four regions in 2010 and 2015. The coefficient of variation is used as the dispersion of the development index of each area within each region.

Table 10.5 Changes in the ranking of the development index of the three basic indicators by region in 2010 and 2015

Province/ Region	*Province*	*Energy consumption development of GDP*		*Development of energy consumption and carbon emissions*		*Carbon emission development of GDP*	
		Rank change	*Increase (%)*	*Rank change*	*Increase (%)*	*Rank change*	*Increase (%)*
East	Beijing	0	0.00	2	16.90	0	0.00
	Tianjin	0	0.09	0	19.45	1	2.31
	Hebei	0	0.28	0	17.90	0	6.01
	Shanghai	0	0.03	4	19.24	0	1.03
	Jiangsu	0	0.03	0	19.65	1	1.59
	Zhejiang	0	0.02	3	19.34	0	0.97
	Fujian	0	0.19	2	14.79	0	0.71
	Shandong	0	0.13	0	17.56	1	2.83
	Guangdong	0	0.12	2	19.04	0	0.47
	Hainan	0	0.05	−5	4.04	−1	−0.69
Northeast	Liaoning	0	0.23	0	17.72	0	4.75
	Jilin	0	0.17	0	15.46	0	3.02
	Heilongjiang	0	−0.19	0	15.49	−1	2.03
Central	Shanxi	0	0.34	0	15.72	0	6.17
	Anhui	0	0.11	0	15.54	0	1.99
	Jiangxi	0	0.08	0	15.38	0	1.45
	Henan	0	0.13	1	16.00	0	2.86
	Hubei	0	0.21	0	14.50	0	2.72
	Hunan	0	0.16	0	14.39	0	1.85
West	Inner Mongolia	0	0.28	−1	14.21	0	5.13
	Guangxi	0	0.12	0	12.87	−1	1.35
	Chongqing	0	0.20	0	14.23	−1	2.45
	Sichuan	0	0.34	0	13.73	0	1.77
	Guizhou	0	0.33	−3	13.50	0	5.08
	Yunnan	0	0.40	0	12.97	1	2.90
	Shanxi	0	0.14	1	15.36	1	2.37
	Gansu	0	0.26	−3	3.63	0	4.09
	Qinghai	0	−0.16	0	0.00	−1	0.60
	Ningxia	0	0.43	0	14.63	0	8.08
	Xinjiang	0	0.27	−3	4.61	0	2.00

As shown in Table 10.6:

(1) Based on the development index of energy consumption intensity of GDP, the coefficient of variation decreased by only 0.06% in the eastern region, 0.20% in the northeastern region, 0.09% in the central region, and 0.03% in the western region. Therefore, the decrease in energy consumption intensity of GDP has led to a decrease in the coefficient of variation of the development index for each area within the four major regions, which indicates that the decline in carbon intensity of GDP of the provinces,

Table 10.6 Development index of the three basic indices by region in 2010 and 2015

Province/ Region	*Statistical indices*	*Development of energy consumption of GDP*		*Development of carbon emissions of energy consumption*		*Development of carbon emission of GDP*	
		2010	*2015*	*2010*	*2015*	*2010*	*2015*
East	Mean	94.11	94.19	50.5	58.79	91.57	92.82
	Variance	6.86	6.81	7.02	6.76	9.27	8.06
	Coefficient of variation	7.29	7.23	13.89	11.51	10.12	8.68
Northeast	Mean	85.15	85.21	47.29	54.93	80.73	83.31
	Variance	3.75	3.57	3.38	3.34	5.45	4.53
	Coefficient of variation	4.4	4.2	7.15	6.08	6.75	5.44
Central	Mean	85.52	85.66	52.43	60.37	82.95	85.17
	Variance	7.94	7.87	9.45	10.52	9.24	8.28
	Coefficient of variation	9.28	9.19	18.02	17.42	11.14	9.73
West	Mean	78.47	78.65	58.69	65.09	77.04	79.35
	Variance	7.97	7.97	17.27	16.6	11.41	10.53
	Coefficient of variation	10.16	10.13	29.43	25.51	14.81	13.27

municipalities, and autonomous regions during the 12th Five-Year Plan is conducive to the convergence of the development index of each region. Among them, the greatest convergence effect on the development index lies in the northeastern region, followed by the central region, then the eastern region, and finally the western region.

(2) Based on the development index of carbon intensity of energy consumption, the coefficient of variation decreased by only 2.38% in the eastern region, 1.07% in the northeast region, 0.60% in the central region, and 3.92% in the western region. Therefore, the decrease in carbon intensity of energy consumption has led to a decrease in the coefficient of variation of the development index of each area within the four major regions, which indicates that the decline in carbon intensity of GDP of the provinces, municipalities, and autonomous regions during the 12th Five-Year Plan is conducive to the convergence of the development index of each region. Among them, the greatest convergence effect on the development index lies in the western region, followed by the eastern region, then the northeastern region, and finally the central region.

(3) Based on the development index of carbon intensity of GDP, the coefficient of variation decreased by only 1.54% in the western region, 1.44% in the eastern region, 1.41% in the central region, and 1.31% in the northeastern region. Therefore, due to the combined effect of energy consumption intensity of GDP and carbon intensity of energy consumption, the decline in the

carbon intensity of GDP has led to a decrease in the coefficient of variation of the development index of each area within the four regions, which indicates that the decline in carbon intensity of GDP of the provinces, municipalities and autonomous regions during the 12th Five-Year Plan is conducive to the convergence of the development index of each region. Among them, the greatest convergence effect on the development index lies in the western region, followed by the eastern region, then the central region, and finally the northeastern region. Therefore, the decline in the carbon dioxide emission index per unit of GDP in each region during the 12th Five-Year Plan is conducive to the convergence of the development index of carbon emission reduction based on the three basic index measures within the four regions, and the most favorable one is the convergence of development index based on carbon intensity of energy consumption within each region.

On the whole, in both the development index ranking changes and the development index changes, the decline in the CO_2 emissions per unit of GDP in each region during the 12th Five-Year Plan has the greatest impact on the development index based on the carbon intensity of energy consumption, followed by the changes in the development index based on carbon intensity of GDP, and finally the changes in development index based on energy consumption intensity of GDP. Therefore, compared with 2010, the energy consumption intensity of GDP and carbon intensity of GDP in 2015 have decreased significantly, but the development index ranking of carbon emission reduction based on energy consumption intensity of GDP and carbon intensity of GDP in each region has not changed significantly. However, compared with 2010, the carbon intensity of energy consumption in 2015 only increased slightly, while the development index ranking of carbon emission reduction based on carbon intensity of energy consumption of each region changed significantly. Therefore, future policies should be more inclined to adjust the carbon intensity of energy consumption. In addition, from the perspective of the impact of regional convergence, the decline in carbon dioxide emissions per unit of GDP in each region during the 12th Five-Year Plan has the greatest impact on the convergence of energy consumption intensity of GDP among areas in the northeast region and has the greatest impact on the convergence of carbon intensity of energy consumption among areas in the western region. The combined impact leads to the greatest effect on the convergence of carbon intensity of GDP among areas in the western region.

10.3.4 Maturity-based test of overall quota allocation efficiency

10.3.4.1 Efficiency test based on the overall carbon emission reduction development index

Table 10.7 shows the overall development index of the three basic indices from 2003 to 2015, calculated according to the aforementioned formula.

Table 10.7 Overall development index of the three basic indices from 2003 to 2015 (%)

Year	*Energy intensity of GDP*	*Emission intensity of energy consumption*	*Carbon intensity of GDP*
2003	79.17	60.33	77.23
2004	79.89	51.37	78.22
2005	79.15	61.53	77.51
2006	80.61	59.96	78.88
2007	80.64	67.99	79.25
2008	81.46	66.66	80.29
2009	83.35	62.23	81.93
2010	85.76	53.57	83.43
2011	83.89	54.20	81.01
2012	86.35	55.21	83.26
2013	85.89	61.03	85.4

As shown in Table 10.7:

(1) Compared with 2010, in 2015, China's overall development index of carbon emission reduction based on energy consumption intensity of GDP increased slightly by 0.2%

(2) China's overall development index of carbon emission reduction based on carbon intensity of energy consumption increased significantly by 13.93%

(3) Due to the combined effect of energy consumption intensity of GDP and carbon intensity of energy consumption, China's overall development index of carbon emission reduction based on carbon intensity of GDP also increased by 2.36%

Table 10.7 also shows that with energy consumption intensity of GDP as a basic index, the overall development index in 2015 decreased to a certain extent compared with 2012, while with carbon intensity of energy consumption as a basic index, the overall development index in 2015 increased significantly compared with 2012. It can be concluded that the analysis of carbon emission reduction target in a relatively uniform manner has significantly increased the development of overall carbon intensity of energy consumption at the expense of the development of the overall energy consumption intensity of GDP, while the energy consumption intensity of GDP is the main driver of carbon emission reduction in China under the current situation. Therefore, the future policy formulation requires differentiated policies for provinces, municipalities, and autonomous regions.

10.3.4.2 Test based on the overall carbon emission reduction coordination index

Table 10.8 shows the overall coordination index of the three basic indices from 2003 to 2015, calculated according to the aforementioned formula.

Table 10.8 Overall coordination index of the three basic indices from 2003 to 2015 (%)

Year	*Energy intensity of GDP*	*Emission intensity of energy consumption*	*Carbon intensity of GDP*
2003	6.72	28.21	6.31
2004	27.74	6.09	20.47
2005	32.05	34.48	24.39
2006	38.12	30.49	30.15
2007	39.89	47.88	31.88
2008	44.38	41.77	37.37
2009	50.82	35.51	45.05
2010	59.04	13.41	50.26
2011	54.7	12.6	44.52
2012	62.26	16.59	53.35
2013	59.46	35.86	57.84

As shown in Table 10.8:

(1) Compared with 2010, in 2015, China's overall coordination index of carbon emission reduction based on energy consumption intensity of GDP increased slightly by less than 0.1%

(2) China's overall development index of carbon emission reduction based on carbon intensity of energy consumption increased significantly by 167.4%

(3) Due to the combined effect of energy consumption intensity of GDP and carbon intensity of energy consumption, China's overall development index of carbon emission reduction based on carbon intensity of GDP also increased to a certain extent, with an increase of 15.1%

Table 10.8 also shows that with energy consumption intensity of GDP as a basic index, the overall coordination index in 2015 also decreased to a certain extent compared with 2012, while with carbon intensity of energy consumption as a basic index, the overall development index in 2015 increased significantly compared with 2012. It can be concluded that similar to the characteristics of changes in the overall development index of carbon emission reduction, the analysis of carbon emission reduction target in a relatively uniform manner has greatly increased the overall coordination of carbon intensity of energy consumption at the expense of the overall coordination of energy consumption intensity of GDP, while energy consumption intensity of GDP is the main driver of carbon emission reduction in China under the current situation. Therefore, it is necessary to formulate differentiated policies for provinces, municipalities, and autonomous regions.

10.3.4.3 Test based on the overall coordinated development index of carbon emission reduction

Table 10.9 shows the overall coordinated development index of the three basic indices from 2003 to 2015, calculated according to the aforementioned overall development index and coordination index of carbon emission reduction.

Table 10.9 Overall coordinated development index of the three basic indices from 2003 to 2015 (%)

Year	*Energy intensity of GDP*	*Carbon intensity of energy consumption*	*Carbon intensity of GDP*
2003	23.06	41.25	22.08
2004	47.07	17.69	40.02
2005	50.37	46.06	43.47
2006	55.43	42.75	48.77
2007	56.72	57.06	50.27
2008	60.13	52.77	54.77
2009	65.09	47.01	60.75
2010	71.16	26.81	64.76
2011	67.74	26.13	60.05
2012	73.32	30.27	66.65
2013	71.46	46.78	70.28

As shown in Table 10.9:

(1) Compared with 2010, in 2015, the overall coordinated development index of China's carbon emission reduction based on energy consumption intensity of GDP increased slightly, with an increase of less than 0.42%

(2) The overall development index of China's carbon emission reduction based on carbon intensity of energy consumption increased significantly by 74%

(3) Due to the combined effect of energy consumption intensity of GDP and carbon intensity of energy consumption, China's overall development index of carbon emission reduction based on carbon intensity of GDP also increased by 8.5%

Table 10.9 also shows that with energy consumption intensity of GDP as a basic index, the overall coordinated development index in 2015 decreased to a certain extent compared with 2012, while with carbon intensity of energy consumption as a basic index, the overall development index in 2015 increased significantly compared with 2012. It can be concluded that the joint convergence of the overall development index and the coordination index of carbon emission reduction has intensified the decline in the overall coordinated development index based on the energy consumption intensity of GDP as well as the increase in the overall coordinated development index based on the carbon intensity of energy consumption.

Note

1 Without detailed description, the carbon emission quota allocation and carbon emission reduction quota allocation mentioned in this section have the same meaning. In the case of the total carbon emission limit, the carbon emission reduction quota allocation and carbon emission quota allocation are only a problem.

References

Chen Wenying, Wu Zongxin. Historical responsibility for climate change and carbon emission right allocation. *China Environmental Science*, 1998a (06): 481–485.

Chen Wenying, Wu Zongxin. Carbon emission permit allocation and trading. *Journal of Tsinghua University (Science and Technology)*, 1998b (12): 15–18.

Ding Zhongli, Duan Xiaonan, Ge Quansheng, et al. Control of atmospheric carbon dioxide concentration in 2050: calculation of carbon emission rights in each country. *Scientia Sinica (Terrae)*, 2009 (8): 1009–1027.

Duan Maosheng, Pang Tao. Key issues in allowance allocation in China's future unified national emissions trading scheme. *Wuhan University Journal: Philosophy and Social Science*, 2014 (5): 5–12.

Emilio, P., Alfredo, S. Inequality in CO_2 emissions across countries and its relationship with income inequality: A distributive approach. *Energy Policy*, 2006, 34: 1762–1772.

Fan Bonai, Bian Xiaolong. Research on the actual measurement and spatial distribution of China's provincial economic and social development coordination. *Administration and Law*, 2013 (12): 31–38.

Heil, M.T., Wodon, Q.T. Inequality in CO_2 emissions between poor and rich countries. *The Journal of Environment & Development*, 1997, 6 (4): 426–452.

Li Kaijie, Qu Ruxiao. Economic effect and insights of initial allocation of carbon emission allowances. *Journal of International Economic Cooperation*, 2012 (03): 21–24.

Liu Huajun, Zhao Hao. Empirical analysis of the regional differences of China's carbon dioxide emissions intensity. *Statistical Research*, 2012, 29 (6): 46–50.

Lv Feng. Research on the resolution coefficient of grey system correlation degree. *System Engineering Theory and Practice*, 1997(6): 50–55.

Pan Jiahua, Chen Ying. The carbon budget scheme: an institutional framework for a fair and sustainable world climate regime. *Social Sciences in China Press*, 2009 (5): 83–100.

Pan Jiahua, Zheng Yan. Responsibility and individual equity for carbon emissions rights. *World Economics and Politics*, 2009 (10): 6–17.

Qiu Junyong, Zhong Dingsheng, Yu Qiaocui, et al. Equity analysis of global CO_2 emissions based on Gini coefficient. *China Soft Science*, 2011 (4): 14–21.

Song Deyong, Liu Xiping. Spatial distribution of provincial carbon emissions. *Chinese Journal of Population, Resources and Environment*, 2013 (5): 7–13.

Wang Weizhong, Chen Bin, Lu Chuanyi, et al. The Koyto protocol and allocation of carbon emission permits. *Journal of Tsinghua University (Philosophy and Social Sciences)*, 2002 (10): 18–21.

Wang Yi, Huang Yu. Equity and uncertainty: the key problems for the allocation of world carbon emissions. *Chinese Journal of Population, Resources and Environment*, 2011, 136 (S2): 271–275.

Xiao Lishan, Wang Run, Liu Jian, et al. Energy-related carbon emission and low carbon energy development in Fujian Province. *Environmental Science and Technology*, 2011, 34 (11): 199–204.

Xuan Xiaowei, Zhang Hao. International experiences and lessons of carbon emission permit allocation method. *Chinese Journal of Population, Resources and Environment*, 2013 (12): 10–15.

Yang Jun, Wang Jia, Zhang Zongyi. Inter-provincial discrepancy and abatement target achievement in carbon emissions: a study on carbon Lorenz curve. *Acta Scientiae Circumstantiae*, 2012 (08): 2016–2023.

Zheng Yan, Liang Fan. Principles of climate justice and the construction of international climate regime. *World Economics and Politics*, 2011 (6): 69–90.

Zhou Jian, Yi Diandian. Studies on provincial differences, influential factors and reduction mechanisms of China's carbon dioxide emission. *Shanghai Journal of Economics*, 2012 (11): 65–80.

Zhou Maorong, Tan Xiujie. The reform of EU emissions trading scheme phase. *Journal of International Trade*, 2013 (05): 94–103.

Zhu Qianting, Wu Jing, Hong Haidi, Wang Zheng. Simulation on carbon permits allocation in the Post-Kyoto era. *Acta Scientiae Circumstantiae*, 2015, 35 (1): 329–336.

11 The dilemma and game analysis of carbon emission reduction for local government

11.1 Situation of China's carbon market

11.1.1 The policy to promote China's carbon market construction

There is a general consensus that the construction of carbon market is an important way to promote China's overall carbon emission reduction. The *Outline of the 12th Five-Year Plan (2011–2015) for National Economic and Social Development of the People's Republic of China* sets a target of "reducing carbon dioxide emissions per unit of GDP by 17%" in the next five years. In order to achieve this development goal, a variety of means will be comprehensively utilized, such as saving energy and improving energy efficiency, adjusting industrial structure and energy structure, and increasing forest carbon sinks. In addition, it is also necessary to "explore establishing standard, labeling and certification system for low-carbon products, establish and improve the statistical and accounting system for greenhouse gas emissions, and gradually establish a carbon emissions trading market". On November 8, 2012, Hu Jintao delivered a keynote report at the 18th National Congress of the Communist Party of China (CPC) entitled "Firmly March on the Path of Socialism with Chinese Characteristics and Strive to Complete the Building of a Moderately Prosperous Society in All Respects". According to the report, major progress should be made in building a resource-conserving and environmentally friendly society; energy consumption and carbon dioxide emissions per unit of GDP should decrease sharply. In addition, we should carry out trials for trading energy savings, carbon emission rights, pollution discharge rights, and water rights. On November 12, 2013, the Third Plenary Session of the 18th CPC Central Committee adopted the *Decision of the CPC Central Committee on Major Issues Concerning Comprehensively Deepening Reforms*. The decision states that "to build an ecological civilization, we must establish a comprehensive ecological civilization system" and also "develop a market for environment protection and push ahead with a trading system for energy savings, carbon emissions rights, pollution discharge rights, and water rights". On August 31, 2011, the State Council issued a *Notice on Printing and Distributing the*

DOI: 10.4324/9781003388500-14

Comprehensive Work Plan for Energy Conservation and Emission Reduction in the 12th Five-Year Plan Period (2011–2015), proposing to "advance trials of trading pollution discharge rights and carbon emission rights", improve the trials of paying for the use and trading of pollution discharge rights of major pollutants, establish and improve the carbon emissions trading market, carry out studies and formulate guidelines to launch a pilot project for paying for the use and trading of pollution emission rights, and actively carry out trade in pollution rights on a trial basis. In addition, a voluntary emission reduction mechanism is required to promote the construction of the carbon emissions trading market.

In order to fulfill the requirements of the above-mentioned major documents for the development of the carbon trading market, the National Development and Reform Commission (NDRC) and other ministries and commissions have issued a series of policies to promote the construction of China's carbon market. Some provinces, municipalities, and autonomous regions have also issued a series of pilot policies for the carbon market development.

11.1.1.1 Policies at the national level

To gradually establish a national carbon emissions trading market in the 12th Five-Year Plan (2011–2015) and achieve China's target for controlling greenhouse gas emissions at a lower cost by 2020 using market mechanisms, the NDRC approved Beijing, Tianjin, Shanghai, Chongqing, Hubei Province, Guangdong Province, and Shenzhen to carry out pilot programs on carbon emissions trading. The NDRC also issued the *Notice on Carrying out Pilot Programs on Carbon Emissions Trading* (F.G.B.Q.H. [2011] No.2601) on October 29, 2011, which has made explicit requirements for the pilot programs on carbon emissions trading in Beijing, Tianjin, Shanghai, Chongqing, Guangdong Province, Hubei Province, and Shenzhen. To carry out voluntary emissions reduction program in a well-regulated way, encourage the whole society to participate in emissions reduction activities, and accumulate experience and lay a technological and normative foundation for the gradual establishment of a carbon emission trading market under cap rules, the State Council issued the *Notice on Printing and Distributing the Work Plan for Controlling Greenhouse Gas Emissions in the 12th Five-Year Period* (2011–2015) on December 1, 2011, proposing to "explore establishing a carbon emissions trading market" through a step-by-step implementation plan. In terms of the implementation plan, the first step is to establish a voluntary emission reduction trading mechanism. We should actively carry out the voluntary emission reduction trading activities by establishing the basic management framework, trading process, and supervision methods of the voluntary emission reduction trading mechanism, and establishing a trading registration system and an information release system. The second step is to carry out the pilot programs on carbon emission trading. We should further implement the allocation plan for greenhouse gas emission rights and formulate corresponding regulations and administrative measures to ensure the launch and operation of the pilot carbon market, so as to gradually form a regional carbon emissions trading system. The third step is to strengthen the support system of trading carbon emissions. We will formulate work specifications and certification rules, carry out studies and formulate accounting methods for emission reduction, carry out strict approval conditions and procedures, and strengthen supervision and capacity building. The fourth step is to strengthen the qualification examination and verification of carbon emission trading bodies and third-party verification and certification bodies, enrich governing bodies, cultivate professionals, and gradually establish a unified registration and supervision system. On June 13, 2012, the NDRC issued the *Notice on the Interim Measures for the Administration of Voluntary Greenhouse Gas Emission Reduction Program*, which standardized six kinds of voluntary greenhouse gas emission reduction programs, including carbon dioxide (CO_2), methane (CH_4), nitrous oxide (N_2O), hydrofluorocarbons (HFCs), perfluorocarbons (PFCs), and sulfur hexafluoride (SF_6). According to the Notice, the "certified voluntary emission reduction" recorded by the national authorities and certified by the certification bodies is measured in "tonnes of carbon dioxide equivalent", registered in the National Register and traded within registered trading institutions, or used to offset carbon emission reductions. Such reduction must be cancelled from the National Register after the trading is completed.

In addition, on December 31, 2012, the Ministry of Industry and Information Technology, the NDRC, the Ministry of Science and Technology, and the Ministry of Finance jointly formulated and released the *Action Plan for Coping with Climate Change in the Industrial Sector*, which proposed to "establish and improve market mechanisms for low-carbon development in the industrial sector" under the guidance of the government and participation of enterprises by giving full play to the market signals and incentives of carbon prices, so as to improve the market mechanism for the industrial sector to respond to climate change and reduce the cost of controlled greenhouse gas emissions. At the same time, we should encourage industrial enterprises to participate in voluntary emissions reduction trading, and support key enterprises in petrochemical, chemical, steel and iron, and cement industries to engage in pilot programs on carbon emissions trading, so as to lay a solid foundation for the launch of the national carbon emissions trading market. On September 19, 2014, the NDRC released *China's National Plan on Climate Change (2014–2020)*, which clearly stated the five-step requirements for "establishing a carbon trading system": First, promote voluntary emission reduction programs, explore an offset mechanism between the project-based voluntary emission reduction trading and carbon emissions trading; Second, further carry out pilot programs on carbon emissions trading in seven provinces and municipalities—Beijing, Tianjin, Shanghai, Chongqing, Hubei Province, Guangdong Province, Shenzhen, and formulate corresponding support policies; Third, accelerate the establishment of the national carbon emissions trading market. Based on the review of the trials of voluntary greenhouse gas emission reduction trading and pilot programs on carbon emissions trading, we should study and formulate a general plan for carbon emissions trading, and outline strategic goals, targeted approaches, action steps and support measures for the construction of the national carbon emissions trading market; Fourth, improve the support system for carbon emissions trading. We should formulate methods to certify emission reductions for carbon emission reduction projects in different industries, establish a registration system and information release system for carbon emissions trading, strengthen qualification review and supervision, and accelerate the professionals training in carbon emissions trading; Fifth, align studies with global carbon emissions trading markets. We should make an overall plan for the layout of trading platforms for carbon emissions, actively participate in the formulation of multilateral carbon emissions trading rules and systems on global and industrial scales, keep an eye on the development of carbon trading markets in other countries (regions), and explore cooperation mechanisms between China and other countries (regions) in bilateral and multilateral carbon emissions trading activities.

11.1.1.2 Implementation policies of local governments

1 Implementation policies for the construction of pilot carbon markets in Beijing. In October 2011, the NDRC declared Beijing as one of the pioneers in piloting carbon emissions trading. In October 2012, the NDRC approved the pilot implementation plan of Beijing. On November 22, 2013, Beijing Municipal Commission of Development and Reform (MCDR) issued the *Notice on Carrying out Pilot Programs on Carbon Emissions Trading* (J.F.G.G. [2013] No. 5).On November 22, 2013, Beijing Municipal Commission of Development and Reform (MCDR) and Beijing Financial Work Bureau jointly promulgated the *Notice on Printing and Distributing the Implementation Rules for the Over-the-Counter Trading of Carbon Emission Allowances in Beijing (for Trial Implementation)* (J.F.G.G. [2013] No. 7) to ensure the well-regulated development of the over-the-counter trading of carbon emission allowances. On December 27, 2013, the 8th Session of the Standing Committee of the 14th Beijing Municipal People's Congress adopted the *Decision of the Standing Committee of Beijing Municipal People's Congress on Carrying out Pilot Programs on Carbon Emissions Trading In Beijing Under Strict Control Over Total Carbon Emissions* to further ensure the smooth implementation of the pilot program. On May 6, 2014, Beijing Municipal Commission of Development and Reform issued the *Notice on Printing and Distributing Provisions of Regulating Discretionary Power in Imposing Administrative Penalty of Carbon Emissions Trading* to promote the institutionalization and standardization while imposing the administrative penalties

according to law, strictly regulate the discretionary power in imposing administrative penalties of carbon emission trading, and safeguard the legitimate rights and interests of relevant legal entities. In June 2014, Beijing Municipal Commission of Development and Reform and Beijing Financial Work Bureau jointly issued the *Notice on Printing and Distributing Measures for the Operation and Management of the Open Market of Carbon Emissions Trading in Beijing (for Trial Implementation).* On September 2, 2014, Beijing Municipal Development and Reform Commission and Beijing Municipal Forestry and Parks Bureau jointly issued the *Notice on Printing and Distributing Measures for the Administration of Carbon Emission Offsets in Beijing (for Trial Implementation)* (J.F.G.G. [2014] No. 6).

2 Implementation policies for the construction of pilot carbon markets in Shanghai. Guided by the *Notice of the General Office of the NDRC on Carrying out the Pilot Programs on Carbon Emission Trading*, Shanghai Municipal People's Government issued the *Implementation Opinions on the Pilot Programs on Carbon Emission Trading in Shanghai* on July 3, 2012 (H.F.F. [2012] No. 64). To promote enterprises to fulfill their responsibilities for controlling carbon emissions, achieve carbon emission control targets in Shanghai, standardize the relevant management of carbon emission activities, and promote the healthy development of the carbon emissions trading market, on November 6, 2013, the 29th Executive Meeting of Shanghai Municipal People's Government adopted the *Trial Measures for the Administration of Carbon Emissions in Shanghai* (Shanghai Government Order No.10), which was promulgated by Shanghai Municipal People's Government on November 18, 2013. On November 22, 2013, guided by the *Trial Measures for the Administration of Carbon Emissions in Shanghai* and the *Implementation Opinions on the Pilot Programs on Carbon Emission Trading in Shanghai*, Shanghai Municipal Development and Reform Commission (MDRC) issued the *Notice on Printing and Distributing Allocation and Management Plan of Carbon Emission Allowance from 2013 to 2015 in Shanghai* (H.F.G.H.Z. [2013] No.168). On November 22, 2013, under the above-mentioned three regulations, Shanghai Municipal Development and Reform Commission issued the *Notice on Printing and Distributing the Interim Regulations on the Registration Administration of Carbon Emission Allowances in Shanghai* (H.F.G.H.Z. [2013] No. 170).On January 10, 2014, guided by the *Trial Measures for the Administration of Carbon Emissions in Shanghai*, Shanghai Municipal Development and Reform Commission released the *Notice on Printing and Distributing the Interim Measures for the Administration of Third-Party Institutions for Carbon Emissions Verification in Shanghai* (H.F.G.H.Z.[2014] No.5). On March 12, 2014, Shanghai Municipal Development and Reform Commission issued the *Notice on Printing and Distributing the Rules for Carbon Emissions Verification in Shanghai (for Trial Implementation)* (H.F.G.H.Z. [2014] No.35)

to further implement the aforementioned regulations and promote the effective operation of the pilot carbon markets.

3 Implementation policies for the construction of pilot carbon markets in Shenzhen. On October 30, 2012, in accordance with the basic principles of laws and administrative regulations and the *Work Plan for Controlling Greenhouse Gas Emissions in the 12th Five-Year Plan Period* released by the State Council, the 18th Session of the Standing Committee of the Fifth Shenzhen Municipal People's Congress approved the *Certain Regulations for Administration of Carbon Emissions in Shenzhen Special Economic Zone* to accelerate the transformation of the economic growth model, optimize the allocation of environmental resources, appropriately control the total energy consumption, and promote the continuous reduction of carbon intensity. To build an environment-friendly and resource-conserving society, accelerate the transformation of the economic growth model, promote energy conservation, emission reduction, green and low-carbon development, establish and standardize the carbon emissions trading market, and achieve the greenhouse gas emission targets, the 105th Session of the Standing Committee of the Fifth People's Congress of Shenzhen Municipal reviewed and adopted *the Interim Measures for the Administration of Carbon Emissions Trading in Shenzhen*(Government Order No.262 in 2014)according to the *Certain Regulations for Administration of Carbon Emissions in Shenzhen Special Economic Zone* on March 19, 2014.

4 Implementation policies for the construction of pilot carbon markets in Tianjin. On February 5, 2013, according to the *Notice of* the *NDRC on Approving the Implementation Plan for the Pilot Programs of Low-Carbon Cities in Tianjin* and the *Notice of the General Office of the NDRC on Carrying out Pilot Programs on Carbon Emissions Trading*, Tianjin Municipal People's Government issued the *Notice on Printing and Distributing the Implementation Plan for the Pilot Programs on Carbon Emissions Trading in Tianjin*. On December 18, 2013, Tianjin Development and Reform Commission (Tianjin DRC) released the *Notice on the List of Enterprises Included in the Pilot Programs on Carbon Emissions Trading in Tianjin*. The list of included enterprises was determined based on the carbon emission caps in Tianjin, carbon emissions of relevant industries and results of initial carbon verification and accounting. In addition, in order to implement the *Notice of the State Council on Printing and Distributing the Work Plan for Controlling Greenhouse Gas Emissions in the 12th Five-Year Plan Period*, Tianjin Municipal People's Government issued the *Notice on Printing and Distributing the Interim Measures for the Administration of Carbon Emissions Trading in Tianjin* (J.Z.B.F. [2013] No.112) on December 20, 2013. On December 24, 2013, Tianjin Development and Reform Commission issued the *Notice on Carrying out Pilot Programs on Carbon Emissions Trading* (J.F.G.H.Z. [2013] No.1345) according to the relevant provisions of the *Interim Measures for the Administration of*

Carbon Emissions Trading in Tianjin and the *Implementation Plan for the Pilot Programs on Carbon Emissions Trading in Tianjin*, as well as the progress in the pilot programs on carbon emissions trading.

5 Implementation policies for the construction of pilot carbon markets in Chongqing. On April 26, 2014, Chongqing Municipal People's Government issued the *Notice on Printing and Distributing the Interim Measures for the Administration of Carbon Emissions Trading in Chongqing* (Y.F.F. [2014] No.17) according to the *Notice of the General Office of the NDRC on Carrying out the Pilot Programs on Carbon Emission Trading*. On May 28, 2014, guided by the *Interim Measures for the Administration of Carbon Emissions Trading in Chongqing*, Chongqing Development and Reform Commission (Chongqing DRC) issued the *Notice on Printing and Distributing the Detailed Regulations for the Administration of Carbon Emission Allowances in Chongqing (for Trial Implementation)* (Y.F.G.H. [2014] 538). At the same time, it also issued the *Notice on Printing and Distributing the Detailed Regulations for Carbon Emissions Accounting, Reporting and Verification of Industrial Enterprises in Chongqing(for Trial Implementation*) (Y.F.G.H. [2014] No.542), the *Notice on Printing and Distributing the Guidelines for Carbon Emissions Accounting and Verification of Industrial Enterprises in Chongqing* (*for* Trial *Implementation*) (Y.F.G.H. [2014] No.544), the *Notice on Printing and Distributing the Norms for the Carbon Emissions Verification of Enterprises in Chongqing (for Trial Implementation)* (Y.F.G.H. [2014] No.547) and the *Notice on Issuing the Carbon Emission Allowances in Chongqing in 2013* (Y.F.G.H. [2014] No.548).

6 Implementation policies for the construction of pilot carbon markets in Guangdong Province. On September 7, 2012, guided by the *Notice of the General Office of the NDRC on Carrying out the Pilot Programs on Carbon Emission Trading*, People's Government of Guangdong Province issued the *Notice on Printing and Distributing the Implementation Plan for the Pilot Programs on Carbon Emissions Trading in Guangdong Province* (Y.F.H. [2012] No.264). On November 25, 2013, Guangdong Provincial Development and Reform Commission (Guangdong PDRC) issued the *Notice on Printing and Distributing the Initial Allocation and Work Plan for Carbon Emission Allowances in Guangdong Province (for Trial Implementation)* (Y.F.G.Z.H.H. [2013] No.3537) according to the requirements of the *Notice on Printing and Distributing the Implementation Plan for the Pilot Programs on Carbon Emissions Trading in Guangdong Province*. On December 17, 2013, the 17th Session of the Standing Committee of the 12th Guangdong Provincial People's Congress adopted the *Trial Measures for the Administration of Carbon Emissions in Guangdong Province* (Guangdong Government Order No.197) to achieve the target of greenhouse gas emissions reduction, give full play to the role of market mechanisms, and regulate the administration of carbon emissions. In order to better regulate pilot

programs on carbon emissions trading, under the *Trial Measures for the Administration of Carbon Emissions in Guangdong Province*, Guangdong Provincial Development and Reform Commission issued the *Notice on the Detailed Regulations for Carbon Emissions Information Reporting and Verification of Enterprises in Guangdong Province* (for Trial Implementation) (Y.F.G.Z.H. [2014] No.145) on March 18, 2014, the *Notice on Printing and Distributing the Detailed Measures for the Administration of Carbon Emission Allowances in Guangdong Province (for Trial Implementation)* (Y.F.G.Z.H. [2014] No.149) on March 20, 2014,and the *Notice on Printing and Distributing the Implementation Plan for the Allocation of Carbon Emission Allowances in Guangdong Province in 2014* (Y.F.G.Q.H. [2014] No.495) on August 18, 2014.

7 Implementation policies for the construction of pilot carbon markets in Hubei Province. On February 18, 2013, guided by the *Notice of the General Office of the NDRC on Carrying out the Pilot Programs on Carbon Emission Trading*, People's Government of Hubei Province issued the *Notice on Printing and Distributing the Implementation Plan for the Pilot Programs on Carbon Emissions Trading in Hubei Province* (E.Z.B.F. [2013] No.9). On March 17, 2014, the executive meeting of People's Government of Hubei Province reviewed and adopted *the Interim Measures for the Administration of Carbon Emissions Trading in Hubei Province* (Hubei Government Order No.371) to strengthen the construction of carbon emissions trading market, regulate the administration of carbon emissions, effectively control greenhouse gas emissions, and promote the construction of a resource-saving and environment-friendly society.

The NDRC approved Beijing, Tianjin, Shanghai, Chongqing, Hubei Province, Guangdong Province and Shenzhen to carry out pilot programs on carbon emissions trading and issued the *Notice on Carrying out Pilot Programs on Carbon Emissions Trading* (F.G.B.Q.H. [2011] No.2601) on October 29, 2011. Since then, a series of implementation policies for the construction of pilot carbon markets in Shenzhen, Shanghai, Beijing, Guangdong, Tianjin, Chongqing and Hubei have made explicit requirements for the pilot programs on carbon emissions trading, which provided a strong guarantee for the launch and operation of the pilot carbon market in the seven provinces and cities.

11.1.2 Operation of China's pilot carbon markets

At the end of October 2011, the NDRC issued the *Notice on Carrying out Pilot Programs on Carbon Emissions Trading*, an official approval to the pilot programs on carbon emissions trading in Beijing, Tianjin, Shanghai, Chongqing, Hubei Province, Guangdong Province and Shenzhen. After nearly two years of preparation, the Shenzhen carbon emissions trading market officially opened on June 18, 2013 as the first pilot carbon market launched in China. Subsequently, the Shanghai carbon emissions trading market opened on November 26, 2013, the Beijing carbon emissions trading market opened on November 28, 2013, the Guangdong carbon emissions trading market opened on December 19, 2013, the Tianjin carbon emissions trading market opened on December 26, 2013, the Hubei carbon emissions trading market opened on April 2, 2014, and Chongqing carbon emissions trading market opened on June 19, 2014. Since then, all the seven local-level pilot carbon markets have been launched. The operation of the seven pilot carbon markets since their opening is as follows.[1]

1 The operation of the pilot carbon emissions trading market in Shenzhen
2 Figure 11.1 shows the carbon emissions trading in the pilot carbon market in Shenzhen. As shown in Figure 11.1, since the Shenzhen carbon emissions trading market was officially launched on June 18, 2013, there have been transactions every month except in July 2013. In terms of the change in transaction volume, the largest transaction volume was in June 2014, reaching more than 1 million tonnes; followed by December 2014, reaching more than 500,000 tonnes. There is an obvious period effect on the transaction volume, which is related to the market operation rules and the rules for corporate carbon emission rights settlement. Among them, the transaction volume of the highest peak is more than twice that of the second peak. In terms of the change in transaction price, from September 2013 to June 2014, the market transaction price has been relatively high, CNY 70–80/tonne. In the second half of 2014, the market transaction price showed a continuous downward trend. As of December 2014, the market transaction price had dropped to CNY 13/tonne, a decrease of 84% compared with the peak price of CNY 83/tonne in March 2014. On the one hand, it was affected by market supply, and on the other hand, it was affected by market expectations. It can be concluded that the correlation between market transaction volume and transaction price is weak. Overall, from the official launch of the Shenzhen carbon emissions trading market to the end of 2014, a total of 2.2596 million tonnes of carbon had been traded in the Shenzhen carbon trading market, with a transaction amount of CNY 123 million and a transaction unit price of CNY 55/tonne.
3 The operation of the pilot carbon emissions trading market in Shanghai
4 Figure 11.2 shows the carbon emissions trading in the pilot carbon market in Shanghai. As shown in Figure 11.2, since the Shanghai carbon emissions trading market was officially launched on November 26, 2013, there have been transactions every month, except in July and August 2014. In terms of the change in transaction volume, the largest transaction volume was in June 2014, reaching 816,500 tonnes, followed by December 2014 (333,200 tonnes). There is an obvious period effect on the transaction volume, which is related to the market operation rules and the rules for corporate carbon emission rights settlement. Among them, the transaction volume of the highest peak is more than twice that of the second peak. In terms of the change in transaction price, the transaction price remained at

around CNY 30/tonne in December 2013 and January 2014, around CNY 40/tonne from February 2014 to June 2014, and around CNY 35/tonne from September 2014 to December 2014. There is no obvious period effect in the transaction price. It can be concluded that the correlation between market volume and transaction price is also weak. Overall, from the official launch of the Shanghai carbon emissions trading market to the end of 2014, a total of 1.714 million tonnes of carbon had been traded in the Shanghai carbon trading market, with a transaction amount of CNY 651 million and a transaction unit price of CNY 38/tonne.

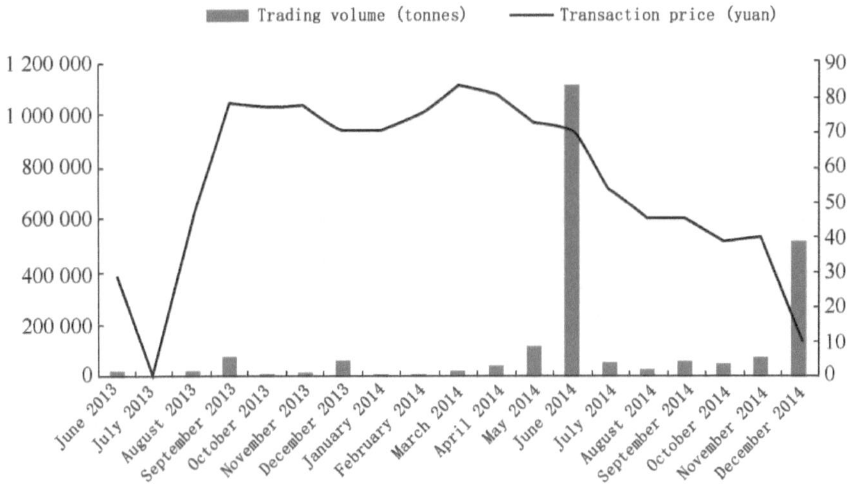

Figure 11.1 Carbon emissions trading in the pilot carbon market in Shenzhen

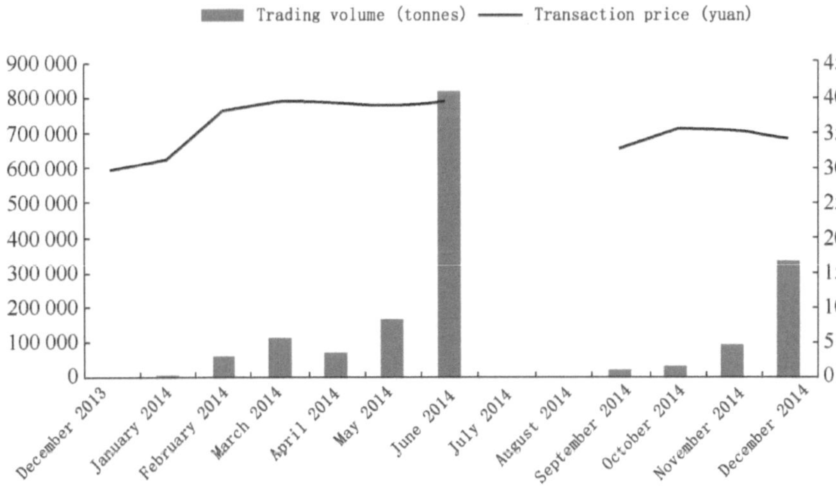

Figure 11.2 Carbon emissions trading in the pilot carbon market in Shanghai

5 The operation of the pilot carbon emissions trading market in Beijing

6 Figure 11.3 shows the carbon emissions trading in the pilot carbon market in Beijing. As shown in Figure 11.3, since the Beijing carbon emissions trading market was officially launched on November 28, 2013, there have been transactions every month. In terms of the change in transaction volume, the largest transaction volume was in June 2014, reaching 438,200 tonnes, followed by July 2014 (364,800 tonnes). There is an obvious period effect on the transaction volume, which is related to the market operation rules and the rules for corporate carbon emission rights settlement. Among them, the transaction volume of the highest peak is 1.2 times that of the second peak. In terms of the change in transaction price, except for July 2014, when the market transaction price reached CNY 70/tonne, the market transaction prices were CNY 50–55/tonne in other months, and there is no obvious period effect. It can be concluded that the correlation between market volume and transaction price is weak. Overall, from the official launch of the Beijing carbon emissions trading market to the end of 2014, a total of 1.0588 million tonnes of carbon had been traded in the Beijing carbon trading market, with a transaction amount of CNY 631 million and a transaction unit price of CNY 60/tonne.

7 The operation of the pilot carbon emissions trading market in Guangdong Province

8 Figure 11.4 shows the carbon emissions trading in the pilot carbon market in Guangdong Province. As shown in Figure 11.4, since the Guangdong carbon emissions trading market was officially launched on December 19, 2013, there have been transactions every month, except

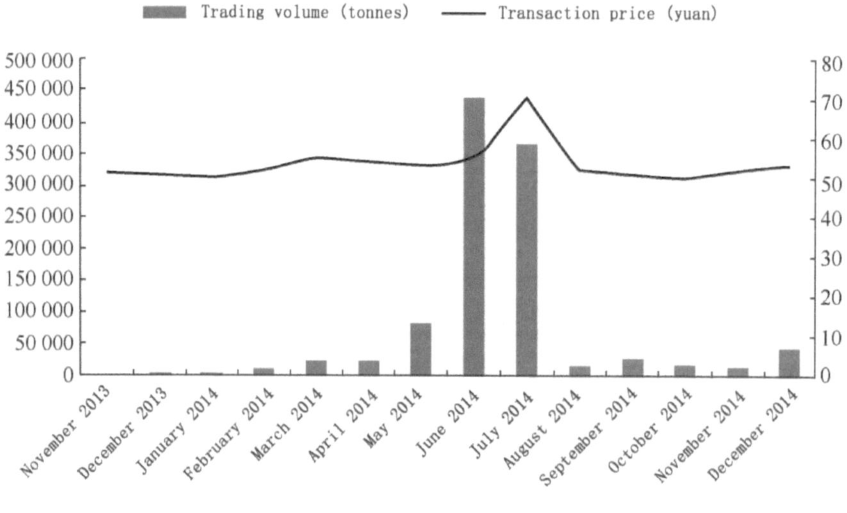

Figure 11.3 Carbon emissions trading in the pilot carbon market in Beijing

in January and February 2014. In terms of the change in transaction volume, the largest transaction volume was in June 2014, reaching 451,800 tonnes, followed by July 2014 (410,600 tonnes). There is an obvious period effect on the transaction volume, which is related to the market operation rules and the rules for corporate carbon emission rights settlement. Among them, the transaction volume of the highest peak is 1.1 times that of the second peak. In terms of the change in transaction price, the peak of market transaction price was in May 2014, reaching CNY 68/tonne. The previous market transaction price was more than CNY 60/tonne. Since May 2014, the market transaction price has maintained a continuous downward trend. As of December 2014, the market transaction price has dropped to CNY 21/tonne, a 69% decrease compared to the peak price. There is no obvious period effect in the transaction price. It can be concluded that the correlation between market volume and transaction price is also weak. Overall, from the official launch of the Guangdong carbon emissions trading market to the end of 2014, a total of 1.1757 million tonnes of carbon had been traded in the Guangdong carbon trading market, with a transaction amount of CNY 635 million and a transaction unit price of CNY 54/tonne.

9 The operation of the pilot carbon emissions trading market in Tianjin

10 Figure 11.5 shows the carbon emissions trading in the pilot carbon market in Tianjin. As shown in Figure 11.5, since the Tianjin carbon emissions trading market was officially launched on December 26, 2013, there have been transactions every month. In terms of the change in

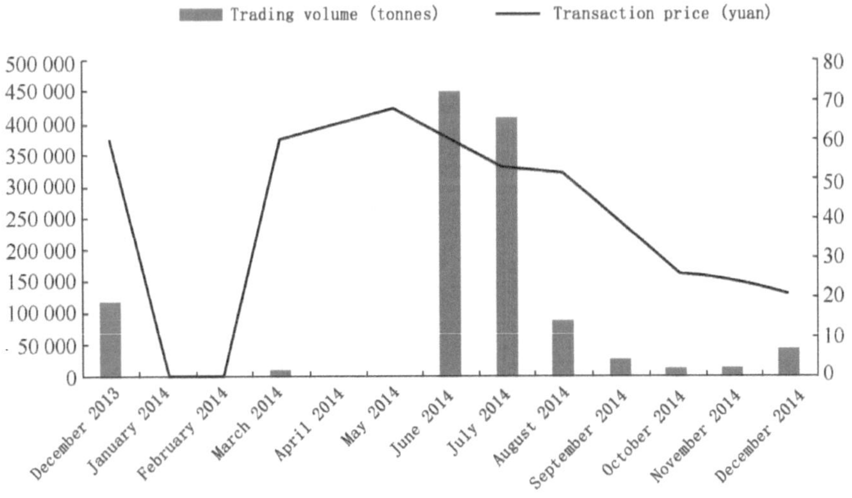

Figure 11.4 Carbon emissions trading in the pilot carbon market in Guangdong Province

transaction volume, the largest transaction volume was in July 2014, reaching 836,800 tonnes, followed by January 2014, reaching only 43,000 tonnes. There is an obvious period effect on the transaction volume, which is related to the market operation rules and the rules for corporate carbon emission rights settlement. Among them, the transaction volume of the highest peak is nearly 20 times that of the second peak. In terms of the change in transaction price, the transaction price remained at CNY 25–30/tonne in December 2013 and February 2014, remained at CNY 30–40/tonne from March 2014 to June 2014, dropped to below CNY 20/tonne in July 2014, and remained at CNY 25–30/tonne from August 2014 to December 2014. There is no obvious period effect in the transaction price. It can be concluded that the correlation between market volume and transaction price is also weak. Overall, from the official launch of the Tianjin carbon emissions trading market to the end of 2014, a total of 1.0071 million tonnes of carbon had been traded in the Tianjin carbon trading market, with a transaction amount of CNY 206 million and a transaction unit price of CNY 20/tonne.

11 The operation of the pilot carbon emissions trading market in Hubei Province

12 Figure 11.6 shows the carbon emissions trading in the pilot carbon market in Hubei Province. As shown in Figure 11.6, since the official launch of the Hubei carbon emissions trading market on April 2, 2014, there have been transactions every month. In terms of the change in transaction volume, the largest transaction volume was in April 2014 when

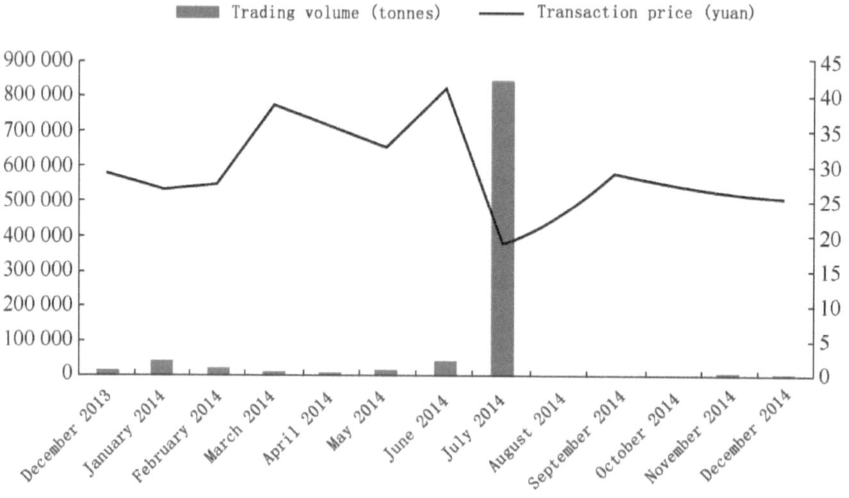

Figure 11.5 Carbon emissions trading in the pilot carbon market in Tianjin

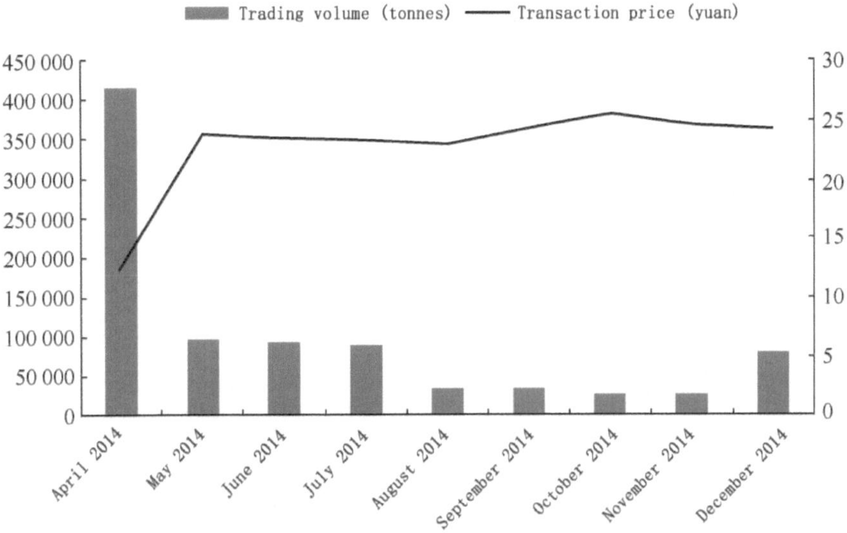

Figure 11.6 Carbon emissions trading in the pilot carbon market in Hubei Province

the market was officially launched, reaching 4.1496 million tonnes, followed by May 2014, the month after the official launch of the market, reaching 975,000 tonnes. There is an obvious period effect on the transaction volume, which is related to the market operation rules and the rules for corporate carbon emission rights settlement. Among them, the transaction volume of the highest peak is more than four times that of the second peak. In terms of the change in transaction price, except for the month of April 2014 when the market was officially launched with a market transaction price of CNY 12/tonne, the market transaction prices in other periods remained at CNY 20–25/tonne, and there was no obvious period effect. It can be concluded that the correlation between market volume and transaction price is also weak. Overall, from the official launch of the Hubei carbon emissions trading market to the end of 2014, a total of 8.9814 million tonnes of carbon had been traded in the Hubei carbon trading market, with a transaction amount of CNY 166 million and a transaction unit price of CNY 18/tonne.

13 The operation of the pilot carbon emissions trading market in Chongqing

14 Figure 11.7 shows the carbon emissions trading in the pilot carbon market in Chongqing. Since the Chongqing carbon emission trading market was officially launched on June 19, 2014, there have been no transactions, except for the month when the market was officially launched. The transaction volume was 145,000 tonnes in the month when the market was officially launched and the market transaction price was CNY 31/tonne.

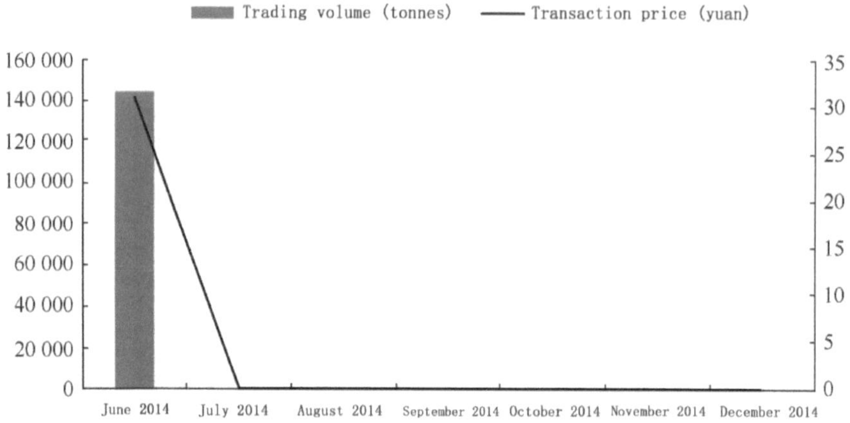

Figure 11.7 Carbon emissions trading in the pilot carbon market in Chongqing

11.1.3 Development dilemmas of China's pilot carbon market

The trading volume of the pilot carbon markets is quite different in terms of scale and change trend, and there are obvious discontinuities in the trading of some pilot carbon markets. Table 11.1 shows the changes in the trading volume of the seven pilot carbon markets in China since the launch of trading. Except for the three pilot markets in Beijing, Tianjin, and Hubei Province, all the other four pilot carbon markets have no trading volume in some months. Especially in Chongqing, except for the month when the market was launched, there had been no transactions until the end of 2014.

As shown in Table 11.1, there are obvious mid-year effects, end-of-year effects, and market start-up effects in the changes in the trading volume of each pilot carbon market. The mid-year effect is shown by the transaction peak of Shenzhen, Beijing, Guangdong Province, and Shanghai in June 2014 and a transaction peak of Tianjin in July 2014. The end-of-year effect is shown by the second peak of transaction in Shenzhen and Shanghai at the end of 2014 and a significantly increased transaction volume in Hubei in December 2014. The market start-up effect is shown by the transaction peak in both Hubei and Chongqing in the launch month of the current year. Comparing the peak transaction volume of each pilot market, the peak transaction volume of Hubei is the largest at 4.1496 million tonnes; followed by Shenzhen at 1.1114 million tonnes; then Tianjin and Shanghai at 836,800 tonnes and 816,500 tonnes, respectively; Beijing and Guangdong at 438,200 tonnes and 451,800 tonnes, respectively; and Chongqing at 145,000 tonnes. It can be calculated that the peak transaction volume of the first-ranked Hubei market is nearly 30 times that of the last ranked Chongqing market. There are huge differences in the change and scale of the trading volume in different pilot carbon markets.

Table 11.1 Changes in trading volume in the seven pilot carbon markets in China (10,000 tonnes)

	Shenzhen	*Beijing*	*Guangdong*	*Shanghai*	*Tianjin*	*Hubei*	*Chongqing*
June 13, 2013	2.11						
July 13, 2013	0.00						
August 13, 2013	2.30						
September 13, 2013	7.29						
October 13, 2013	0.94						
November 13, 2013	1.08	0.08					
December 13, 2013	6.01	0.18	12.01	0.33	1.72		
January 14, 2014	0.84	0.31	0.00	0.57	4.30		
February 14, 2014	0.81	0.93	0.00	6.10	1.89		
March 14, 2014	2.03	2.15	0.59	11.33	1.22		
April 14, 2014	3.75	2.26	0.01	6.97	0.77	414.96	
May 14, 2014	11.53	8.10	0.01	16.48	1.56	97.50	
June 14, 2014	111.14	43.82	45.18	81.65	4.12	91.98	14.5
July 14, 2014	4.98	36.48	41.06	0.00	83.68	89.01	0.00
August 14, 2014	2.36	1.46	8.98	0.00	0.16	33.86	0.00
September 14, 2014	5.32	2.76	2.52	2.24	0.14	34.95	0.00
October 14, 2014	4.57	1.72	1.44	3.11	0.06	27.37	0.00
November 14, 2014	7.35	1.32	1.54	9.31	0.63	28.90	0.00
December 14, 2014	51.54	4.32	4.23	33.32	0.45	79.61	0.00

There are also significant differences in the level and change of transaction price in different pilot carbon markets and obvious jumps in the transaction prices in some pilot carbon markets. Table 11.2 shows the changes in transaction prices in the seven pilot carbon markets in China since the launch of trading. The transaction price in the Beijing carbon trading market is the most stable. It was kept at CNY 50–55/tonne, except for July 2014 when there was an abnormal fluctuation in the transaction price. In Hubei carbon trading market, the transaction price is kept at CNY 22–26/tonne, except for the month when the market was launched, where the transaction price was CNY 12.35/tonne. The transaction price in the Shanghai carbon trading market is relatively stable. It was kept at CNY 29–40/tonne, except in July and August 2014 when there was no transaction. The transaction price of the Shenzhen carbon market and the Guangdong carbon market both decreased significantly. The transaction price in the Shenzhen carbon market had decreased since March 2014 and dropped to CNY 12.53/tonne by December 2014, a decrease of 85% compared with the peak price in March 2014.The transaction price of the carbon market in Guangdong Province had been declining since May 2014. As of December 2014, the market transaction price had dropped to CNY 20.82/tonne, a decrease of 69% compared with the peak price in May 2014. The transaction price in the Tianjin carbon market was characterized by periodic fluctuations. The market transaction price was basically stable at around CNY 25/tonne from September 2014 to December 2014.

As shown in Table 11.2, as of December 2014, the transaction prices in each pilot carbon market were: CNY 12.53/tonne in Shenzhen, CNY 52.85/tonne in Beijing, CNY 20.82/tonne in Guangdong Province, CNY 34.18/tonne in Shanghai, CNY 25.27/tonne in Tianjin, CNY 24.17/tonne in Hubei Province, and no transaction in Chongqing. Among them, the transaction price in Beijing is the highest, which is more than four times higher than that of Shenzhen, where the transaction price is the lowest. Therefore, there are huge differences in the level and change of transaction price in different carbon markets.

Under the combined influence of transaction volume and transaction price, the transaction amount and its changes also vary greatly among pilot markets, and there is no obvious correlation between transaction volume and transaction price. Table 11.3 shows the changes in the transaction amount in the seven pilot carbon markets in China since the launch of trading.

As shown in Table 11.3, due to the relatively stable transaction price in the Beijing carbon trading market, the changes in transaction amount are consistent with those of transaction volume. The transaction amount reached the peak in June and July of 2014, namely CNY 24.12 million and CNY 25.49 million, respectively. The transaction price in the Shanghai carbon trading market is also relatively stable, so the changes in transaction amount are consistent with those of transaction volume. The price reached the first peak in June 2014 (CNY 32.43 million) and a second peak in December 2014

Table 11.2 Changes in transaction prices in the seven pilot carbon markets in China (CNY/ton)

	Shenzhen	*Beijing*	*Guangdong*	*Shanghai*	*Tianjin*	*Hubei*	*Hubei*
June 13, 2013	29.00						
July 13, 2013	0.00						
August 13, 2013	43.61						
September 13, 2013	78.46						
October 13, 2013	76.76						
November 13, 2013	77.62	51.25					
December 13, 2013	70.58	51.22	60.17	29.58	28.55		
January 14, 2014	70.52	50.46	0.00	31.14	26.31		
February 14, 2014	75.35	51.91	0.00	38.29	26.98		
March 14, 2014	83.5	55.00	60.35	39.25	38.59		
April 14, 2014	80.8	54.12	63.88	39.25	35.64	12.35	
May 14, 2014	72.46	53.08	67.90	38.78	32.42	23.86	
June 14, 2014	70.75	55.05	60.00	39.72	40.91	23.26	30.74
July 14, 2014	53.80	69.87	52.32	0.00	18.09	23.25	0.00
August 14, 2014	45.15	51.81	51.90	0.00	22.52	22.95	0.00
September 14, 2014	45.42	51.31	38.82	32.79	28.84	24.34	0.00
October 14, 2014	38.74	50.13	26.15	35.61	27.25	25.37	0.00
November 14, 2014	40.41	52.13	24.44	35.21	25.87	24.41	0.00
December 14, 2014	12.53	52.85	20.82	34.18	25.27	24.17	0.00

Table 11.3 Changes in transaction amount in the seven pilot carbon markets in China (CNY 100 million)

	Shenzhen	*Beijing*	*Guangdong*	*Shanghai*	*Tianjin*	*Hubei*	*Chongqing*
June 13, 2013	61						
July 13, 2013	0						
August 13, 2013	100						
September 13, 2013	572						
October 13, 2013	72						
November 13, 2013	84	4					
December 13, 2013	424	9	723	10	49		
January 14, 2014	59	16	0	18	113		
February 14, 2014	61	48	0	234	51		
March 14, 2014	169	118	35	445	47		
April 14, 2014	303	122	0	274	28	5,124	
May 14, 2014	835	430	1	639	51	2,327	
June 14, 2014	7,863	2,412	2,711	3,243	169	2,140	446
July 14, 2014	268	2,549	2,148	0	1,513	2,069	0
August 14, 2014	107	76	466	0	4	777	0
September 14, 2014	242	142	98	73	4	851	0
October 14, 2014	177	86	38	111	2	694	0
November 14, 2014	297	69	38	328	16	706	0
December 14, 2014	646	228	88	1,139	11	1,924	0

(CNY 11.39 million). Although the transaction price of the Hubei carbon trading market in the launch month was only half of that in other months, the transaction volume in the launch month was several times higher than that in other months and the transaction amount in the launch month was also the highest for the whole year, reaching CNY 51.24 million. Despite an obvious downward trend in the transaction prices of carbon trading in Shenzhen and Guangdong, since there is no complete negative correlation between transaction volume and transaction price, the changes in the transaction amount show no clear trends under the combined effect of the two factors. Among them, the peak transaction amount is mainly affected by transaction volume. Although the transaction price of carbon trading in Tianjin is characterized by periodic changes, the peak value of its transaction is also mainly affected by transaction volume.

In general, the peak value of carbon trading in Shenzhen is the largest among the seven pilot carbon markets, nearly 18 times that of Chongqing, where the transaction amount is the lowest. It can be concluded that there are also huge differences in the level and change of transaction amount in different pilot carbon markets. At the same time, there is no consistent correlation between the transaction volume and transaction amount of the above seven pilot carbon markets. Therefore, the price discovery of the above seven pilot carbon markets has not been significantly reflected, and the operation of each pilot carbon market still needs to be improved.

The scale of each pilot carbon market varies greatly, and there is no obvious correspondence between the market scale and the carbon emissions in the region of the pilot carbon markets. Overall, as shown in Table 11.4, since official launch of the seven pilot carbon markets in China, the total transaction volume has reached 16.34 million tonnes, the transaction amount has reached CNY 506.23 million, and the average transaction price has reached CNY 31/tonne. Among them, since official launch of the Shenzhen carbon trading market, its transaction volume has reached 2.26 million tonnes, accounting for 13.83% of the total transaction volume of the seven pilot carbon markets; its transaction amount has reached CNY 124.41 million, accounting for 24.38% of the total transaction amount of the seven pilot carbon markets; and its average transaction price has reached CNY 55/tonne, 1.8 times that of the overall average price. Since official launch of the Beijing carbon trading market, its transaction volume has reached 1.06 million tonnes, accounting for 6.48% of the total transaction volume of the seven pilot carbon markets; its transaction amount has reached CNY 63.09 million, accounting for 12.46% of the total transaction amount of the seven pilot carbon markets; and its average transaction price has reached CNY 60/tonne, 1.9 times that of the overall average price. Since official launch of the Guangdong carbon trading market, its transaction volume has reached 1.18 million tonnes, accounting for 7.19% of the total transaction volume of the seven pilot carbon markets; its transaction amount has reached CNY 63.46 million, accounting for 12.54% of the total transaction amount of the seven pilot carbon markets; its average transaction price has reached CNY 54/tonne, 1.7 times that of the overall average price. Since official launch of the Shanghai carbon trading market, its transaction volume has reached 1.71 million tonnes, accounting for 10.49% of the total transaction volume of the seven pilot carbon markets; its transaction value has reached CNY 65.12 million, accounting for 12.86% of the total transaction amount of the seven pilot carbon markets; its average transaction price has reached CNY 38/tonne, 1.3 times that of the overall average price. Since official launch of the Tianjin carbon trading market, its transaction volume has reached 1.01 million tonnes, accounting for 6.16% of the total transaction volume of the seven pilot carbon markets; its transaction amount has reached CNY 20.58 million, accounting for 4.06% of the total transaction amount of the seven pilot carbon markets; its average transaction price has reached CNY 20/tonne, 0.7 times that of the overall average price. Since official launch of the Hubei carbon trading market, its transaction volume has reached 8.98 million tonnes, accounting for 54.96% of the total transaction volume of the seven pilot carbon markets; its transaction amount has reached CNY 166.11 million, accounting for 32.81% of the total transaction amount of the seven pilot carbon markets; its average transaction price has reached CNY 18/tonne, 0.6 times that of the overall average price. Since official launch of the Chongqing carbon trading market, its transaction volume has reached 150,000 tonnes, accounting for 0.89% of the total transaction volume of the seven pilot carbon markets; its transaction amount has reached CNY 4.46 million, accounting for 0.99% of the total transaction amount of the seven pilot carbon markets; its average transaction price has reached CNY 30/tonne, basically the same as the overall average price.

As shown in Table 11.4, in the economically developed regions such as Shenzhen, Beijing, Guangdong Province, and Shanghai, the proportions of the transaction amount of the four carbon markets in the total transaction amount are significantly higher than their proportions of the transaction volume in the total transaction volume, that is, their average

Table 11.4 Comprehensive comparison of the transaction in the seven pilot carbon markets in China as of December 2014

	Transaction volume (10,000 tonnes)	*Proportion (%)*	*Transaction amount (CNY 10,000)*	*Proportion (%)*
Shenzhen	226	13.83	12,341	24.38
Beijing	106	6.48	6,309	12.46
Guangdong	118	7.19	6,346	12.54
Shanghai	171	10.49	6,512	12.86
Tianjin	101	6.16	2,058	4.06
Hubei	898	54.96	16,611	32.81
Chongqing	15	0.89	446	0.88
Total	1,634		50,623	

transaction prices are higher than the overall average transaction price. While in Tianjin, Hubei, and Chongqing, the proportions of the carbon market transaction amount in the total transaction amount are significantly lower than their proportions of the transaction volume in the total transaction volume, that is, their average transaction prices are lower than the overall average transaction price. On the whole, there are significant differences in the transaction volume, transaction amount, and average transaction price of different pilot carbon markets in China, and there is no obvious correspondence between the transaction volume of each pilot carbon market and the carbon emission scale in the region. This is not only the development dilemma of the current pilot carbon market, but also the biggest dilemma for the construction of a unified national carbon market in the future.

11.2 Static game analysis on the carbon emission reduction dilemma and technological cooperation dilemma for local governments

According to the *Comprehensive Work Plan for Energy Conservation and Emission Reduction in the 12th Five-Year Plan Period* and the *Work Plan for Controlling Greenhouse Gas Emissions in the 12th Five-Year Plan Period*, provinces, municipalities, and autonomous regions shoulder the primary responsibility for carbon emissions reduction in China. The conflict of interests in carbon emissions reduction among provinces, municipalities, and autonomous regions is often manifested in two aspects. On the one hand, under the dual pressures of economic development and carbon emission reduction, as the interest body, provinces, municipalities, and autonomous regions will make different choice to reduce carbon emissions based on the demand of economic development, which poses a dilemma for carbon emissions reduction in provinces, municipalities, and autonomous regions. On the other hand, under the policy of coordinated regional development and cross-regional promotion of low-carbon technologies, provinces, municipalities, and autonomous regions may choose to perform independent technological innovation for carbon emissions reduction or introduce advanced technology of carbon emissions reduction from other regions, which pose a dilemma for inter-provincial technological cooperation on carbon emissions reduction. In this section, three classical static game models are developed for corresponding researches.

11.2.1 Static game analysis on the carbon emission reduction dilemma for local governments

Game theory is the study of how rational players (participants) choose their own strategies and the equilibrium of such strategies in order to maximize their own interests in a situation where interests interact with each other (Wenju Wang , 2010). In the game of inter-provincial carbon emission reduction, various provinces, municipalities, and autonomous regions play the game to maximize their own interests. According to the research and analysis of the aforementioned literature under the static game framework with complete information, different distribution of interests between the two parties leads to different game equilibrium results. Among them, the complete information static game about the inter-provincial carbon emission reduction dilemma can be analyzed by constructing three most classical game models, namely the prisoner's dilemma, the boxed pigs game, and the chicken game.

11.2.1.1 Prisoner's dilemma game analysis on local governments' carbon emission reduction dilemma

The famous prisoner's dilemma game analysis is the most common method to study the cooperation difficulties between two game players due to conflict of interests. Suppose there are two local governments (A and B) with similar levels of economic development and atmospheric pollution, the carbon emission reduction game between the two local governments is described as follows:

1 If both local governments adopt the carbon emission reduction strategy, then both sides can obtain eight units of benefit from the improvement of the atmosphere environment, but at the same time pay five units of benefit due to losses of economic growth and costs of carbon emission reduction. Therefore, the net benefit of both local governments is three units of benefit.
2 If neither local government adopts the carbon emission reduction strategy, both sides can obtain six units of benefit from economic development, but at the same time pay five units of benefit due to the further deterioration of atmospheric pollution. Therefore, the net benefit of both local governments is one unit of benefit.
3 If one local government adopts the carbon emission reduction strategy and the other does not adopt the carbon emission reduction strategy, then the local government that adopts the carbon emission reduction strategy will obtain four units of benefit from improvement of the atmospheric environment, but at the same time pay five units of benefit due to losses of economic growth and costs of carbon emission reduction. The local government that does not adopt the carbon emission reduction strategy also obtains four units of benefit from improvement of the atmospheric environment as well as six units of benefits for economic growth. Therefore, the net benefit is −1 unit for the local government that adopts the carbon emission reduction strategy and ten units for the local government that does not adopt the carbon emission reduction strategy.

Table 11.5 Prisoner's dilemma game of local governments' carbon emission reduction dilemma

B	*A*	
	Emission reduction	*No emission reduction*
Emission reduction	3, 3	−1, 10
No emission reduction	10, −1	1, 1

Payments for both sides are shown in Table 11.5.

As shown in Table 11.5, the result of the Nash equilibrium is that both local government A and local government B choose not to reduce carbon emissions. The prisoner's dilemma reflects a profound issue that individual rationality and collective rationality often conflict with each other. Although the overall social welfare will benefit from both local governments' carbon emission deduction, if local government A chooses to reduce carbon emissions and local government B chooses not to reduce carbon emissions, then local government A will lose more than it gains, while government B will sit back and enjoy the benefit. This would end up with both local governments' rejection to reduce carbon emissions, and all local government welfares cannot be improved due to the Nash equilibrium in this situation.

11.2.1.2 The chicken game analysis on the local governments' carbon emission reduction dilemma

In the chicken game analysis, we also assume two local governments A and B with the same level of economic development and air pollution; the same situation as the prisoner's dilemma game includes:

1 If both local governments adopt the carbon emission reduction strategy, then both sides can obtain eight units of benefit from the improvement of the atmosphere environment, but at the same time pay five units of benefit due to losses of economic growth and costs of carbon emission reduction. Therefore, the net benefit of both local governments is three units of benefit.
2 If neither local government adopts the carbon emission reduction strategy, both sides can obtain six units of economic development, but at the same time pay five units of benefit due to the further deterioration of atmospheric pollution. Therefore, the net benefit of both local governments is one unit of benefit.

However, if one local government adopts the carbon emission reduction strategy and the other local government does not adopt the carbon emission reduction strategy, then the local government that adopts the carbon

Table 11.6 The chicken game of the local governments' carbon emission reduction dilemma

B	A	
	Emission reduction	*No emission reduction*
Emission reduction	3,3	2, 10
No emission reduction	10, 2	1,1

emission reduction strategy will obtain seven units of benefit from improvement of the atmospheric environment, but at the same time pay five units of benefit due to losses of economic growth and costs of carbon emission reduction. The local government that does not adopt the carbon emission reduction strategy also obtains four units of benefits from improvement of the atmospheric environment as well as six units of benefits for economic growth. Therefore, the net benefit is two units for the local government that adopts the carbon emission reduction strategy and ten units for the local government that does not adopt the carbon emission reduction strategy.

Payments for both sides are shown in Table 11.6.

As shown in Table 11.6, under the Nash equilibrium, if local government A chooses to reduce carbon emissions, local government B will choose not to reduce carbon emissions. On the contrary, if local government B chooses to reduce carbon emissions, local government A will choose not to reduce carbon emissions. There are two Nash equilibriums in the chicken game: the overall social welfare is not improved due to both local governments' carbon emission reduction, and the overall social welfare is not the worst due to both local governments' rejection to reduce carbon emissions.

11.2.1.3 Boxed pigs game analysis on local governments' carbon emission reduction dilemma

In the boxed pigs game analysis, we assume a local government A and a local government B, with the economic development level of local government A much higher than that of local government B. The carbon emission reduction game between the two local governments is described as follows:

1 If both local governments adopt the carbon emission reduction strategy, then local government A with a higher level of economic development will obtain 12 units of benefit from the improvement of the atmospheric environment (a good environment will produce greater benefits for those with higher incomes), but at the same time pay five units of benefit due to losses of economic growth and costs of carbon emission reduction. Therefore, the net benefit of carbon emission reduction for local government A with a higher level of economic development is seven units of benefit. Local government B, which is less economically developed,

obtains seven units of benefit from the improvement of the atmospheric environment, but at the same time pays five units of benefit due to losses of economic growth and costs of carbon emission reduction. Therefore, the net benefit of carbon emission reduction for underdeveloped local government B is two units of benefit.

2 If neither local government adopts the carbon emission reduction strategy, both sides can obtain six units of benefit from economic development, but at the same time pay five units of benefit due to further deterioration of atmospheric pollution. Therefore, the net benefit of both local governments is one unit of benefit.
3 Local government A with higher economic development level adopts the carbon emission reduction policy, while local government B which is less economically developed does not adopt the carbon emission reduction policy. Local government A with higher level of economic development obtains ten units of benefit from improvement of the atmospheric environment, but at the same time pays five units of benefit due to losses of economic growth and costs of carbon emission reduction. Therefore, the net benefit of carbon emission reduction for local government A with higher level of economic development is five units, while the local government B, which is less economically developed, obtains four units of benefit from improvement of the atmospheric environment.
4 Local government B, which is less economically developed, adopts the carbon emission reduction policy, while local government A with higher level of economic development does not adopt the carbon emission reduction policy. Local government B obtains four units of benefit from improvement of the atmospheric environment, but at the same time pays five units of benefit due to losses of economic growth and costs of carbon emission reduction. Therefore, the net benefit of carbon emission reduction for local government B is −1 unit of benefit and local government A obtains ten units of benefit from improvement of the atmospheric environment.

Payments for both sides are shown in Table 11.7.

As shown in Table 11.7, in this case, under the Nash equilibrium, the optimal strategy of underdeveloped local government B is not to reduce carbon emissions regardless of the act of the local government A with a higher level

Table 11.7 Boxed pigs game of local governments' carbon emission reduction dilemma

B	*A*	
	Emission reduction	*No emission reduction*
Emission reduction	2, 7	−1, <u>10</u>
No emission reduction	<u>4</u>, <u>5</u>	<u>1</u>, 1

of economic development. The Nash equilibrium can be obtained through the iterated dominance. That is, local government A with a higher level of economic development reduces carbon emissions, while local government B, which is less economically developed, sits back and enjoys the benefit. Therefore, both local governments in economically developed regions and local governments in the economically backward regions are morally obliged to reduce carbon emissions. In fact, economically developed regions are often required to consciously undertake the responsibility for carbon emission reduction.

11.2.2 Static game analysis on the technological cooperation dilemma for local governments' carbon emission reduction

11.2.2.1 Prisoner's dilemma game analysis on the technological cooperation dilemma for local governments' carbon emission reduction

In non-repetitive games, the payoff structure—the payoff of cooperation-cooperation (CC) versus defection-defection (DD) and the payoff of defection-cooperation (DC) versus cooperation-defection (CD)—is the basis for analyzing cooperation. Here, a more general formulation of the aforementioned prisoner's dilemma game is made. Suppose there are two local governments A and B, and each local government has two strategies available for technological innovation of carbon emission reduction: cooperation and defection (abbreviated as C and D). If R represents the benefit from CC, T represents the benefit from DC, S represents the benefit from CD, and P represents the benefit from DD, then the benefit matrix of the two players is shown in Table 11.8.

Among them, the first benefit value in the benefit sequence represents B's benefit, and the second benefit value represents A's benefit. Suppose that:

1 $T > R$, that is, when one local government chooses to cooperate, the other local government will gain more benefits if it chooses defection rather than cooperation
2 $P > S$, that is, when one local government chooses to defect, the other local government will gain more benefits if it chooses defection rather than cooperation

Table 11.8 Prisoner's dilemma game of the technological cooperation dilemma for local governments' carbon emission reduction

B	*A*	
	Cooperation	*No cooperation*
Cooperation	R, R	S, T
No cooperation	T, S	P, P

3 $2R > 2P$, that is, the scenario where both local governments choose to cooperate is better than the scenario where both choose to defect
4 $2R > T + S$, that is, the scenario where both local governments choose to cooperate is better than the scenario where they alternately choose defection and cooperation

When the above conditions are satisfied, as shown by the underline in Table 11.8, finally the strategic choice (defection-defection) of the two local governments becomes the Nash equilibrium of the game. In this dilemma, if both players choose to cooperate, their situation will be improved, because not only $2R > 2P$, but also $2R > T + S$ (cooperation-cooperation) is the optimal strategic choice for both players. Different from the research focus of the aforementioned prisoner's dilemma, the prisoner's dilemma described here is that in the process of carbon emission reduction, two local governments are required to work together to produce huge benefits from carbon emission reduction in some fields, such as major innovations in carbon emission reduction technologies. If the two local governments can work together, it is possible to make major innovations in some carbon emission reduction technologies. However, due to the lack of a good contract or agreement, governments can copy and learn from the other side who has made major innovations, which naturally poses the prisoner's dilemma in the cooperation on carbon emission reduction technology.

11.2.2.2 Stag hunt game analysis on the technological cooperation dilemma for local governments' carbon emission reduction

It is worth noting that in a series of non-repetitive games between two local governments regarding the cooperation on major technological innovations in carbon emission reduction, there is also a classic game model that is corresponding to the prisoner's dilemma game model and facilitates the cooperation, namely the stag hunt game (Fudenberg and Tirole, 1991). As shown in Table 11.9, unlike the prisoner's dilemma game, in this game, two local governments jointly carry out a major innovation in carbon emission reduction technology. They will obtain high cooperation benefits (R) if they make it through cooperation. However, if one local government defects and pursues a short-term trivial innovation in carbon emission reduction technology, the major innovation in carbon emission reduction technology will fail. The defector will obtain less benefit from the defection (T), while the other local government will obtain nothing (S). If both players pursue the short-term trivial technological innovations in carbon emission reduction halfway, they will gain benefit less than the benefit (P) resulted from only one defector. Therefore, the payoff structure of this game is: $R > T > P > S$. Under this payoff structure, the cooperation stability can be ensured only when each local government believes that the other will cooperate. However, in a single round of the stag hunt game, the benefit from major technological innovations can significantly reduce the temptation of defection to local governments.

Table 11.9 Stag hunt game of the technological cooperation dilemma for local governments' carbon emission reduction

B	*A*	
	Cooperation	*No cooperation*
Cooperation	*R*, *R*	*S*, *T*
No cooperation	*T*, *S*	*P*, *P*

11.3 Signal game analysis on local governments' carbon emission reduction dilemma

The five-year plan and various special plans are important ways for local governments to release their development goals. Faced with the dilemma of economic growth and carbon emission reduction, in terms of economic planning, local governments with different growth expectations may either make different demands for carbon emission reduction or the same demand for carbon emission reduction. In the planning and implementation stage, local governments with different economic growth rates may adopt different carbon emission reduction policies or the same carbon emission reduction policies. Comparing the two processes, we find that the economic growth expectations and the demands for carbon emission reduction of a large number of local governments are inconsistent with the actual implementation. That is, some local governments have reduced the demand for carbon emission reduction in order to ensure economic growth, some have reduced the demand for economic growth to ensure carbon emission reduction, and some have reduced both the demand for economic growth and the demand for carbon emission reduction. It can be concluded that facing the dilemma of economic growth and carbon emission reduction, local governments' actions conform to the characteristics of signal senders in the obvious signal game. These characteristics make the signal game model a good tool for analyzing the classification of relevant local governments and their carbon emission reduction policy.

11.3.1 Game hypothesis analysis

The signal game developed by Spence as a dynamic game with incomplete information has been widely used in the economics literature. For example, according to the aforementioned literature analysis, the carbon emission reduction regulation game between local governments and enterprises has obvious signaling game characteristics, where local governments are the senders (denoted by *S*) and enterprises are the receivers (denoted by *R*). The sequence and relevant assumptions of signaling game are as follows:

1 According to the principle of Harsanyi transformation, the type of local governments is chosen naturally according to a specific probability

distribution $p(t)$, where $\sum p(t)=1$. $T=\{(t_1,t_2)\}$ is the type space of a local government, t_1 denotes that the local government is an environment-preferred type, and t_2 denotes that the local government is a growth-preferred type. If r represents the probability to choose an environment-preferred government naturally, then *1-r* represents the probability to choose a growth-preferred government naturally. $T=\{(t_1,t_2)\}$ is the private information of the local government. That is, the local government knows its type, while the enterprises do not know the type of the local government.

2 Set the signal space that a local government can choose as $m(t)\in M$, where $M=\{m_1, m_2\}$. m_1 denotes that the local government has declared to carry out strict carbon emission reduction and m_2 denotes that the local government has declared to ensure economic growth. According to the signal $m(t)\in M$ sent by the local government, an enterprise can make an inference about the probability distribution (a prior probability) of the type of local government. Assuming that p is the probability to infer an environmentally preferred government from the signal m_1, then *1-p* is the probability to infer a growth-preferred government. Similarly, if q is the probability to infer an environmentally preferred government from the signal m_2, then *1-q* is the probability to infer a growth-preferred government. After inferring the type of the local government, enterprises choose the action$a(m)\in A$, where $A=\{a_1, a_2\}$ denotes the action space of the enterprise. a_1 denotes that the enterprise inputs more in carbon emission reduction, while a_2 denotes that the enterprise inputs less in carbon emission reduction.

3 The information sets of local governments as information senders are $I_S(x_1)$ and $I_S(x_2)$, which correspond to observed natural choices of t_1 and t_2, and actions of m_1 and m_2, respectively. Corresponding to the information set, there are four pure strategies for the signaling of the local government, namely: Strategy 1 (m_1, m_1), that is, the local government sends the signal m_1 regardless of the natural type (t_1 or t_2) of the local government. Strategy 2 (m_1, m_2), that is, if nature assigns the local government type t_1, then the local government sends the signal m_1, and if nature assigns the local government type t_2, then the local government sends the signal m_2. Strategy 3 (m_2, m_1), that is, if nature assigns the local government type t_2, then the local government sends the signal m_1, and if nature assigns the local government type t_1, then the local government sends the signal m_2. Strategy 4 (m_2, m_2), that is, the local government sends the signal m_2, regardless of the natural type (t_1 or t_2) of the local government.

4 The information sets of enterprises as information receivers are $I_R(x_3,x_4)$ and $I_R(x_5,x_6)$, which correspond to the observed signals m_1 and m_2, and actions a_1 and a_2, respectively. Corresponding to the information set, there are also four pure strategies for the actions of

enterprises, namely: Strategy 1 (a_1, a_1), that is, the enterprise chooses the action a_1 regardless of the signal sent by the local government (m_1 or m_2). Strategy 2 (a_1, a_2), that is, if the local government sends the signal m_1, then the enterprise chooses the action a_1, and if the local government sends the signal m_2, then the enterprise chooses the action a_2. Strategy 3 (a_2, a_1), that is, if the local government sends the signal m_1, then the enterprise chooses the action a_2, and if the local government sends the signal m_2, then the enterprise chooses the action a_1. Strategy 4 (a_2, a_2), that is, the enterprise chooses the action a_2, regardless of the signal sent by the local government (m_1 or m_2).

5. Given the type of the local government $T = \{(t_1, t_2)\}$, the signal space of the local government $m(t) \in M$, the action space of the enterprise $a(m) \in A$, and the strategy space of the local government and the enterprise $S(m_i, m_j)$ and $S(a_i, a_j)$, where i, j = (1,2), the payoff functions $U_S(t_i, m_i, a_i)$ and $U_R(t_j, m_j, a_j)$ of local governments and enterprises can be denoted as:

   1 $U_S(t_1, m_1, a_1) = W_1 - G_1, U_R(t_1, m_1, a_1) = -C$, which means that the environmentally preferred government releases a signal to strictly reduce carbon emissions, and enterprises act according to the signal by strictly reducing carbon emissions. The social welfare improved due to the government's carbon emission reduction is W_1, but the loss caused by the decline in economic growth is G_1 and cost of enterprises to strictly reduce carbon emissions is C.

   2 $U_S(t_1, m_1, a_2) = G_1' - W_1', U_R(t_1, m_1, a_2) = B - F$, which means that the environmentally preferred government releases a signal to strictly reduce carbon emissions, and enterprises do not act according to the signal by not further reducing carbon emissions. The benefit government obtains from economic growth is G_1', but the loss in social welfare due to atmospheric pollution is W_1'. The benefit of production obtained by the enterprise is B and the penalty for excessive carbon emissions is F.

   3 $U_S(t_1, m_2, a_1) = W_1 - G_1 - A, U_R(t_1, m_2, a_1) = -C$, denoting that the environmentally preferred government releases a signal to pursue economic growth, and enterprises do not act according to the signal, but strictly control the carbon emissions. The social welfare benefit government obtains from improvement of the environment governance is W_1 and the loss caused by the decline in the economic growth is G_1. At the same time, the loss of government image and reputation is A and the investment cost for enterprises to strictly control carbon emission reduction is also C.

   4 $U_S(t_1, m_2, a_2) = G_1' - W_1' - A, U_R(t_1, m_2, a_2) = B - F$, denoting that the environmentally preferred government releases a signal to pursue economic growth, and enterprises act according to the signal and decrease carbon emission reduction. The benefit government obtains

from the economic growth is G_1' and the loss in social welfare due to atmospheric pollution[2] is W_1'. At the same time, the loss of government image and reputation is A, the benefit of production for enterprises is B, and the penalty for excessive carbon emissions is F.

5 $U_S(t_2, m_1, a_1) = W_2 - G_2 + D, U_R(t_2, m_1, a_1) = -C$, indicating that the growth-preferred government releases a signal to strictly reduce carbon emissions, and enterprises act according to the signal by strictly reducing carbon emissions. The social welfare benefit government obtains from atmospheric governance is W_2. At the same time, the loss caused by the decline in the economic growth is G_2, the environmental reputation value is D, and the investment cost for enterprises to strictly reduce carbon emissions is C.

6 $U_S(t_2, m_1, a_2) = G_2' - W_2' + D, U_R(t_2, m_1, a_2) = B$, indicating that the growth-preferred government releases a signal to strictly reduce carbon emissions, and enterprises do not act according to the signal by not further reducing carbon emissions. The benefit government obtains from economic growth is G_2' and the loss in social welfare due to atmospheric pollution is W_2'. The environmental reputation value gained for the government is D and the benefit of production for enterprises is B.

7 $U_S(t_2, m_2, a_1) = W_2 - G_2, U_R(t_2, m_2, a_1) = -C$, which means that the growth-preferred government releases a signal to pursue economic growth, and enterprises do not act according to the signal, but strictly control the carbon emissions. The social welfare benefit government obtains from atmospheric governance is W_2, the loss caused by the decline in the economic growth is G_2, and the investment cost for enterprises to strictly reduce carbon emissions is C.

8 $U_S(t_2, m_2, a_2) = G_2' - W_2', U_R(t_2, m_2, a_2) = B$, which means that the growth-preferred government releases a signal to pursue economic growth, and enterprises act according to the signal and decrease carbon emission reduction. The benefit government obtains from economic growth is G_2', the loss in social welfare due to atmospheric pollution is W_2', and the benefit of production for enterprises is B.

Regarding the payoff function, different types of governments have different judgments on the improvement of the social welfare brought by the atmospheric governance and the economic growth brought by atmospheric pollution. For an environmentally preferred government, the improvement of the social welfare brought by the atmospheric governance is less than the economic growth brought by atmospheric pollution, that is, $W - G > 0$. For a growth-preferred government, the improvement of the social welfare brought by atmospheric governance is less than the economic growth brought by atmospheric pollution, namely $W - G < 0$. On this basis, the signal game model between local governments and enterprises can be represented by the game tree shown in Figure 11.8.

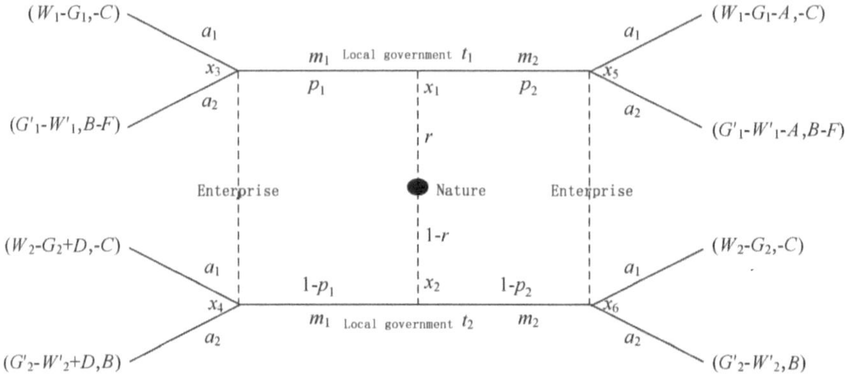

Figure 11.8 Signal game tree of carbon emission reduction regulation between local governments and enterprises

11.3.2 Game equilibrium analysis

Regarding the solution of the signal game equilibrium of local governments' environmental regulation, first, it is necessary to satisfy three conditions for the perfect Bayesian Nash equilibrium:

1 The local government knows its own type and its choice occurs in single decision-making node information set, while the enterprise does not know the type of local government and needs to observe the signal of the local government before taking action. That is, the choice of the enterprise occurs in non-single decision-making node information set. Therefore, after observing signal m_i released by the local government, the enterprise must make an inference about which type of local government would release m_i. This inference can be expressed with a probability distribution $p(t_i \mid m_i)$, wherein $\sum p(t_i \mid m_i) = 1$.
2 For each m_i released by the local government, given the inferred posterior probability $p(t_i \mid m_i)$, the action $a^*(m_i)$ taken by the enterprise must satisfy the expectation-maximization of the enterprise, that is, $a^*(m_i) \in \arg\max U_R(m_i, a_i)$. Similarly, for any government type t_i by nature, given the corporate action $a^*(m_i)$, the signal $m^*(t_i)$ released by the local government must satisfy its expectation-maximization, that is, $m^*(t_i) \in \arg\max U_S\{t_i, m_i, a^*(m_i)\}$.
3. For each m_i released by the local government, if a t_i in the type space of the local government leads to $m^*(t_i) = m_i$, then the posterior probability inferred by the enterprise through m_i to t_i must depend on a

Bayesian rule and the local government's choice of signaling strategies, namely:

$$p(t_i \mid m_j) = \frac{p(m_i \mid t_i) \cdot p(t_i)}{\sum_{t_i \in T_j} p(m_i \mid t_i) \cdot p(t_i)} \tag{11.1}$$

Under the condition that the above three signal game equilibriums are satisfied, there may be three sub-classes of equilibriums in the signal game: separating, pooling, and semi-separating. Among them, the semi-separating equilibrium is only a state between the separating equilibrium and the pooling equilibrium. In the semi-separating equilibrium, the benefit of the local government will be less than that of the separating equilibrium. Therefore, the discussion of the semi-separating equilibrium can be ignored when comparing the advantages and disadvantages of the equilibrium from the perspective of local governments. Here, only the separating equilibrium and the pooling equilibrium are analyzed. The conditions for the realization and meanings of the two equilibriums are as follows.

11.3.2.1 Conditions for the realization of the separating equilibrium and its meaning

In the separating equilibrium, a local government sends signals according to its own situation: if it is the growth-preferred type, it sends signals to accelerate economic growth; if it is the environmentally preferred type, it sends signals to strictly reduce carbon emissions. Enterprises take corresponding actions according to the signals sent by the government: if the signal is to accelerate economic growth, they will not reduce carbon emissions; if the signal is to strictly control carbon emissions, they will strictly reduce carbon emissions. On the basis of the above signal game, three conditions are required to satisfy the perfect Bayesian Nash equilibrium:

1 The posterior probability condition, that is, the enterprise must make a posterior probability inference according to the Bayes' rule on specific signals sent by the specific type of government. According to the meaning of the separating equilibrium, we know that the separating equilibrium requires the local government to have no incentive to cheat. That is, the government will not send the signal of strict carbon emission reduction as a growth-preferred government, nor will it send the signal of accelerating economic growth as an environmentally preferred government. In this case, the posterior probability conditions when the enterprise infers the type of local government based on the signal should

satisfy $p(t_1 \mid m_1)=1$, $p(t_1 \mid m_2)=0$ and also $p(t_2 \mid m_2)=1$, $p(t_2 \mid m_1)=0$. According to the Bayes' rule:

$$p(t_1 \mid m_1)=\frac{p(m_1 \mid t_1)\cdot p(t_1)}{\sum_{t_i \in T_j} p(m_1 \mid t_i)\cdot p(t_i)}=\frac{rp_1}{rp_1+(1-r)(1-p_1)}=1 \tag{11.2}$$

Thus, $p_1 = 1$. Similarly, $p_2 = 0$.

2 After the posterior probability is obtained, the enterprise will choose the expectation-maximization strategy. According to the meaning of the separating equilibrium and the game tree in Figure 11.8, enterprises will take strict carbon emission reduction actions when they receive the signal m_1 and they will not further reduce carbon emissions when they receive signal m_2. In order to achieve the expectation-maximization of the enterprise, it is required that: $-C > B - F$, $B > -C$.

3 When the enterprise's action strategy is given, the local government will adopt a signaling strategy that can achieve its expectation-maximization. According to the meaning of the separating equilibrium and the game tree in Figure 11.8, if the local government is an environmentally preferred type, it will send the signal to strictly reduce carbon emissions, while if it is a growth-preferred type, it will send the signal to accelerate economic growth. In order to achieve the expectation-maximization of the local government, the following conditions need to be satisfied:

$$\left.\begin{aligned} W_1 - G_1 &> G_1' - W_1' - A \\ W_2 - G_2 + D &< G_2' - W_2' \end{aligned}\right\} \tag{11.3}$$

That is, $W_1 + W_1' > G_1 + G_1' - A$, $G_2 + G_2' > W_2 + W_2' + D$.

To sum up, the condition for the separating equilibrium of the signal game for local government's environmental regulation is:

$$\left.\begin{aligned} F - C &> B \\ B &> -C \\ W_1 + W_1' &> G_1 + G_1' - A \\ G_2 + G_2' &> W_2 + W_2' + D \end{aligned}\right\} \tag{11.4}$$

Wherein $B > -C$ is obvious. Meanings of the other inequalities are:

$F - C > B$ shows that to achieve the separating equilibrium, first of all, the environmentally preferred local government must set up a penalty mechanism for enterprises not reducing carbon emissions, and enterprises must bear the risk of loss F from being investigated and punished for excessive carbon emissions, and F must be greater than the sum of the investment cost C for strict carbon emission reduction and the economic benefit B brought by the enterprise's laissez-faire carbon emissions strategy.

$W_1 + W_1' > G_1 + G_1' - A$ shows that to achieve the separating equilibrium, it also requires that the sum of W_1 and W_1' must be higher than the difference between $G_1 + G_1'$ and A. Where W_1 denotes the value evaluation of environmentally preferred local governments on improvement of social welfare brought by a certain degree of carbon emission reduction, W_1' denotes the value evaluation of growth-preferred local governments on improvement of social welfare brought by a certain degree of atmospheric governance; $G_1 + G_1'$ denotes the benefit of both types of local governments from increase in the economic growth brought by the same carbon emissions; A denotes the disguise cost and loss of reputation of environmentally preferred local governments due to release of false signals.

$G_2 + G_2' > W_2 + W_2' + D$ shows that to achieve the separating equilibrium, it also requires that the sum of G_2 and G_2' must be higher than the sum of $W_2 + W_2'$ and D. Where G_2 denotes the benefit of environmentally preferred local governments from increase in the economic growth brought by the same carbon emissions, G_2' denotes the benefit of growth-preferred local governments from increase in the economic growth brought by a certain degree of carbon emissions; $W_2 + W_2'$ denotes the benefit of growth-preferred local governments from improvement of social welfare brought by a certain degree of carbon emission reduction; D denotes the reputation value of growth-preferred local governments due to release of false signals.

Overall, the conditions for achieving separating equilibrium depend on four factors:

1 The magnitude of the risk of loss (F) of the enterprise from being investigated and punished for environmental pollution. The larger the F, the greater the probability of achieving the separating equilibrium.
2 Preferences of local governments for atmospheric governance and economic growth. The greater the preference, the greater the probability of achieving the separating equilibrium.
3 The amount of the disguise cost and loss of reputation A of environmentally preferred local governments due to release of false signals. Similarly, greater value of A indicates greater probability of achieving the separating equilibrium.
4 The amount of the reputation value D of growth-preferred local governments due to release of false signals. Smaller value of D indicates greater probability of achieving the separating equilibrium.

11.3.2.2 Conditions and meanings of pooling equilibrium

In a pooling equilibrium, both a growth-preferred local government and an environmentally preferred local government release the signals to strengthen or weaken carbon emission reduction regulations. In this case, enterprises will think that the signals released by the local governments have no useful information, so it will not correct the prior probability, that is, $p(t_1 \mid m_1) = r$, $p(t_2 \mid m_1) = 1 - r$. Similarly, $p(t_1 \mid m_2) = r$, $p(t_2 \mid m_2) = 1 - r$. According to Bayes' rule:

$$p(t_1 \mid m_1) = \frac{p(m_1 \mid t_1) \cdot p(t_1)}{\sum_{t_i \in T_j} p(m_1 \mid t_i) \cdot p(t_i)} = \frac{rp_1}{rp_1 + (1-r)(1-p_1)} = r \tag{11.5}$$

$$p(t_2 \mid m_1) = \frac{p(m_1 \mid t_2) \cdot p(t_2)}{\sum_{t_i \in T_j} p(m_1 \mid t_i) \cdot p(t_i)} = \frac{(1-r)(1-p_1)}{rp_1 + (1-r)(1-p_1)} = 1 - r \tag{11.6}$$

Thus, $p_1 = 0.5$. Similarly, $p_2 = 0.5$.

After obtaining the above-mentioned posterior probabilities, in response to the different signals released by the local governments, the enterprise will enhance or undermine air pollution control accordingly. These two actions will lead to the following two different pooling equilibrium scenarios:

Scenario 1: If both the growth-preferred local government and the environmentally preferred local government are pooled in a signal of strict atmospheric governance and enterprises enhance carbon emission reduction, then two conditions need to be satisfied.

1 According to the above posterior probability, enterprises will benefit more from enhanced carbon emission reduction than undermined carbon emission reduction, namely:

$$-rC + (1-r)(-C) > r(B - F) + B(1-r) \tag{11.7}$$

That is: $r > B + \frac{C}{F}$.

2 After a given enterprise adopts a strict carbon emission reduction strategy, for both a growth-preferred government and an environmentally preferred government, the expected utility resulted from the release of a signal to enhance carbon emission reduction should be greater than that from the release of a signal to pursue economic growth:

$$\left.\begin{array}{l} W_1 - G_1 > W_1 - G_1 - A \\ W_2 - G_2 + D > W_2 - G_2 \end{array}\right\} \tag{11.8}$$

That is: $A > 0$, $D > 0$.

To sum up, in the first scenario, the conditions for the pooling equilibrium in the signal game for a local government to conduct environmental regulation are:

$$\left.\begin{aligned} & r > \frac{B+C}{F} \\ & A > 0 \\ & D > 0 \end{aligned}\right\} \tag{11.9}$$

It is obvious that $A > 0$ and $D > 0$. Enterprises will not revise the prior probability. When enterprises infer that the probability of environmentally preferred local governments is greater than $(B + C)/F$, they will adopt strict carbon emission reduction. A local government, environmentally preferred or growth-preferred, will release a strict carbon emission reduction signal, thus resulting in a pooling equilibrium.

Scenario 2: If both the growth-preferred local government and the environmentally preferred local government are pooled in a signal of undermined carbon emission reduction and enterprises undermine carbon emission reduction, then two conditions need to be satisfied.

1 According to the above-mentioned posterior probability, enterprises will benefit more from undermined carbon emission reduction than enhanced carbon emission reduction, namely:

$$-rC+(1-r)(-C)<r(B-F)+B(1-r) \tag{11.10}$$

That is: $r < B + C/F$.

2. After a given enterprise adopts a relaxed environment governance strategy, for both a growth-preferred government and an environmentally preferred government, the expected utility resulting from the release of a signal to undermine carbon emission reduction should be greater than that from the release of a signal to enhance carbon emission reduction:

$$\left.\begin{aligned} & G_1' - W_1' < G_1' - W_1' - A \\ & G_2' - W_2' + D < G_2' - W_2' \end{aligned}\right\} \tag{11.11}$$

That is: $A < 0$, $D < 0$.

To sum up, in the second case, the conditions for the pooling equilibrium in the signal game for a local government to conduct carbon emission reduction regulation are:

$$\left.\begin{aligned} & r < (B+C)/F \\ & A < 0 \\ & D < 0 \end{aligned}\right\} \tag{11.12}$$

Wherein, $A < 0$ indicates that under the social background of pursuing economic growth, a signal for relaxed carbon emission reduction released by an environmentally preferred local government will not damage the reputation. Instead, it is conducive to establishing the image of pursuing economic growth and attracting investment, and thus making a positive contribution. The loss of reputation is negative, that is, A is less than zero. $D < 0$ indicates that under the social background of pursuing economic growth, a signal for strict carbon emission reduction released by a growth-preferred local government will not improve reputation or contribute to the image of pursuing economic growth and attracting investment. Instead, it will make a negative contribution. The value of reputation improvement is negative, that is, D is less than zero. Enterprises will not revise the prior probability. When enterprises infer that the probability of growth-preferred local governments is less than $B + C)/F$, it will undermine carbon emission reduction. A local government, environmentally preferred or growth-preferred, will release a relaxed carbon emission reduction signal, thus resulting in a pooling equilibrium.

11.3.3 Main conclusions

It can be concluded from the above analysis that there are two equilibriums in the signal game of carbon emission reduction regulation between local governments and enterprises, but each equilibrium requires certain conditions:

1 In a separating equilibrium, the signals truly reflect the private information of the governments: a growth-preferred government sends a signal to accelerate economic growth, while an environmentally preferred government sends a signal to strictly reduce carbon emissions. To achieve good carbon emission reduction control, the environmentally friendly government needs more incentives for carbon emission reduction control, while the growth-friendly government needs a weakened evaluation mechanism of economic performance.
2 In a pooling equilibrium, both types of local governments release the signals to strengthen or weaken carbon emission reduction regulations, and enterprises will think that the signals released by the local governments have no useful information. In this case, to achieve good carbon emission reduction control, it is very important for enterprises to have past experience with local governments. That is, local governments need to have strict carbon emission reduction constraints for local enterprises.
3 Regardless of the type of government, for enterprises, first it is necessary to establish a comprehensive carbon emission reduction guidance and evaluation system to provide carbon emission reduction guidance and governance effectiveness evaluation for enterprises involved in carbon emission reduction control.

Carbon emission reduction rating is required, so that enterprises can make corresponding carbon emission reduction investment according to their expected rating. Of course, a corresponding penalty mechanism for carbon emissions is of equal importance. Enterprises that fail to meet the requirements of carbon emission reduction must be fined, and the amount of the fine should be large enough, at least greater than the benefit due to undermined carbon emission reduction. Only in this way, can we eliminate the "speculative behavior" of enterprises and achieve effective market equilibrium.

Under a decentralized administrative system and an assessment mechanism that relies on economic growth, local governments may sacrifice the environment for economic growth. This inference has become a controversial topic both in theory and practice. Under an assessment mechanism that relies on economic growth, local governments have motivation to relax carbon emission reduction regulations for larger liquidity, and local decentralization provides local governments with strong incentives to stand out in the inter-regional political and financial competition by rapidly developing the local economy, making carbon emission reduction regulation a game tool between local governments and enterprises, and thus resulting in an imbalance in carbon emission reduction and a distortion in resource allocation. This reminds us that to achieve the desired carbon emission reduction control, we also need the following requirements:

1 The central government should monitor and regulate local governments. In addition to clarifying the goals of local governments in terms of economic growth and carbon emission reduction, the central government should also adjust the institutional arrangements related to the assessment of local government, gradually reduce the weight of GDP in the assessment, and appropriately increase the weight of carbon emission reduction in the assessment of local governments.
2 Local governments should clarify the goals and measures for economic growth and carbon emission reduction and publicize them to the society. In addition, local governments should make appropriate investments in the research and development of carbon emission reduction technology and provide guidance to enterprises, and clarify the evaluation system and punishment mechanism for carbon emission reduction of enterprises.

11.4 Evolutionary game analysis of local governments' carbon emission reduction dilemma

Although the above studies have gone through a process of continuous improvement and deepening ranging from conceptual introduction, static game with complete information, static game with incomplete information, to dynamic game with incomplete information, the core concept of the analysis is "equilibrium". The concept of equilibrium is usually interpreted in two ways: one is the rationalist interpretation, and the other is the "mass-action interpretation" (Kainan Huang , 2009). The above studies all belong to the former interpretation, that is, the interpretation under the classical game theory "paradigm", which has three limitations:

1 The "individual game" assumption ignores the mass action and focuses on the interaction of action strategies between two participants. Even if there are multiple participants, they are often simplified to two different categories of participants in developing the model without considering the interaction among multiple individuals and between individuals and groups. However, in reality, carbon emission reduction is a national and a multi-subject behavior, and individuals imitate each other.
2 The "complete knowledge" assumption. Assuming that game participants have complete knowledge to participate in the game and understand the strategic benefit as well as the ability to comprehensively use all the knowledge in a full and complete way when making strategic choices. However, in reality, the participants have limited knowledge. Neither local governments, enterprises, or individuals know all the knowledge related to the carbon emission reduction game nor can they memorize all the knowledge accurately, let alone use of the knowledge in a full and effective manner.
3 The "perfect rationality" assumption, that is, the participants have "complete knowledge". They are consistently pursuing maximized interests and able to make the optimal choice for their maximized good in any uncertain condition. However, in reality, the participants' knowledge is incomplete, their ability to process knowledge is limited, and sometimes they may not be completely self-centered. Therefore, the carbon emission reduction action of local governments also involves "limited rationality". It can be concluded that the game analysis of carbon emission reduction requires research on the concept of "equilibrium" in another aspect of the "mass-action interpretation" as well as further research with the help of evolutionary game theory.

11.4.1 Analysis of game assumption

Evolutionary game theory is different from traditional static game theory and dynamic game theory in some aspects. The study objective of evolutionary game theory is a group composed of multiple participants rather than individuals, and its study purpose is to investigate the dynamic changes in the size of different groups and the dynamic evolution of strategic choices rather than comparison of the strategic benefit among individuals. In evolutionary game theory, the conclusion of the study focuses on explaining why the group is in its current strategic state and how to adjust the policy to maximize the social welfare in the long run, and no researches on individual strategic equilibrium will be performed. The evolutionary game theory has something in common with the traditional static game theory and dynamic game theory. Evolutionary game research also requires a game analysis framework. That is, it also requires a description of premise and payment of the game. For this reason, the following assumptions are made for the evolutionary game model of inter-provincial carbon emission reduction behavior in this section:

1 Group structure assumption: We assume there are two groups of players in the inter-provincial carbon emission reduction game, namely the local government groups in the developed eastern region represented by Guangdong Province and Zhejiang Province (referred to as A) and the local government groups in the central and western regions represented by Anhui Province and Sichuan Province (referred to as B).
2 Strategy space assumption: Given the overall national carbon emission reduction target, local governments have sufficient room for technological fraud to obtain carbon emission allowances. By comprehensively weighing their own interests, the set of actions that local governments can choose is assumed to be D = (fraud D1, self-discipline D2).[3]
3 The bounded rationality assumption: The carbon emission reduction behavior of both local government groups is "bounded rational". That is, there is no need to assume that the payment function is the common knowledge of the game players in traditional static and dynamic games, and the players may not even know their own benefit payment level.
4 Myopic behavior assumption: Since there is no "perfect knowledge" and "perfect rationality" assumption, local governments are all "bounded rational". They do not believe that their current strategic choices will have a significant impact on the future strategic choices of other local governments and they do not care whether other local governments will make the same strategic adjustments like they do. Moreover, the influence of current interests on the local governments' strategic choices is much greater than the influence of future interests on their strategic choices.
5 Policy inertia assumption: Under a complex and uncertain carbon emission reduction environment, local governments will follow the behavior logic of "learning, trying, adapting, and developing" to choose carbon emission reduction behavior. Under the assumptions of incomplete information, empirical learning lag time, strategy adjustment costs, and bounded rationality, there is an obvious inertia in the strategy distribution chosen by local government groups. That is, the strategy adjustment of local government groups is gradual.

Under the above basic assumptions and targets of the local governments in carbon emission reduction and economic growth, a local government can respond quickly to carbon emission allowances or carbon emission reduction policies of other local governments. The government can compete with other local governments for corporate investment resources or to directly obtain higher economic growth by actively striving for more carbon emissions allowance or relaxing carbon emission reduction control. For a specific local government, the different strategic choices and benefit of local governments in the game at different levels of economic development are described as follows:

1 When both economically developed regions and economically backward regions choose the self-discipline strategy, each will obtain benefit from environmental improvement, but will suffer certain losses due to constraints on economic development. Both sides will obtain corresponding benefit according to their own economic development and environment feature at R_1 and R_2, respectively.
2 When an economically backward region adopts a fraud strategy while an economically developed region adopts a self-discipline strategy, the economically backward region will obtain additional economic development benefit from fraud strategy, but at the same time suffer environmental losses, which are less than the additional economic development benefit. After the benefit is offset by losses, the net benefit from the fraud strategy in the economically backward region is G_2. On the one hand, the economically developed region will obtain the benefit from environmental improvement. On the other hand, it will suffer economic development losses as well as environmental losses due to excessive carbon emissions in the economically backward regions. It is assumed that the comprehensive net loss in all aspects is F_1. Therefore, the benefit obtained from fraud strategy in the economically backward region is $R_2 + G_2$, while the benefit in the economically developed region is $R_1 - F_1$.
3 When an economically developed region adopts a fraud strategy while an economically backward region adopts a self-discipline strategy, the economically developed region will obtain additional economic development benefit from fraud strategy, but at the same time suffer environmental losses, which are less than the additional economic development benefit. After the benefit is offset by losses, the net benefit from the fraud strategy in the economically developed region is G_1; The economically backward region will not obtain the additional economic development benefit, but it will suffer environmental losses F_2 due to excessive carbon emissions in the economically developed regions. Therefore, the benefit obtained from fraud strategy in the economically developed region is $R_1 + G_1$, while the benefit in the economically backward region is $R_2 - F_2$.
4 When both economically developed regions and economically backward regions choose the fraud strategy, each will obtain benefit from economic development, but will suffer certain losses due to the impact on the economic environment. Assuming that regulatory penalties from the central government are not taken into account and the economic development benefits from fraud strategy are not only greater than the losses caused by environmental damage, but also greater than the benefit when both sides adopt self-discipline strategies. That is, compared

Table 11.10 Game matrix of local governments' carbon emission reduction strategies

Economically backward region A	*Economically developed region B*			
	Fraud strategy		*Self-discipline strategy*	
Fraud strategy	$R^1 + E^1$	$R^2 + E^2$	$R^1 - F^1$	$R^2 + G^2$
Self-discipline strategy	$R^1 + G^1$	$R^2 - F^2$	$R^1 + R^2$	

with the benefit when both sides adopt the self-discipline strategy, both sides obtain an excess benefit. The excess benefit of economically developed regions and economically backward regions according to their own economic development and environment feature are E_1 and E_2, respectively. That is, the benefit from fraud strategy in economically developed regions is $R_1 + E_1$ while the benefit from fraud strategy in economically backward regions is $R_2 + E_2$.

According to the above strategy choice and benefit analysis, the carbon emission reduction behavior of a specific local government can be expressed as the game matrix in Table 11.10.

11.4.2 Analysis of strategy fitness

In general, the evolutionary process of evolutionary game theory consists of two major mechanisms: one is the selection mechanism that favors some categories and the other is the mutation mechanism that produces diversity (Weibull, 2006). Among them, the selection mechanism is used to test the fitness of the group strategy. The so-called fitness of the strategy can be simply interpreted as the growth rate of the number of populations adopting the strategy after each game. The mutation mechanism is used to test the stability of the evolutionary game equilibrium. In the specific evolutionary game analysis, the strategy fitness of the players is often tested first and then the stability of the evolutionary game equilibrium is tested. In evolutionary game theory, the replicator dynamics equation proposed by Taylor and Jonker (1978) is the most widely used model of strategy fitness analysis based on the selection mechanism. Its core idea is that if the fitness of a strategy is higher than the average fitness of the group, this strategy will be chosen by more and more participants in the group. Otherwise, this strategy will be abandoned by more and more participants in the group. The central role of the replicator dynamics equation is to model the evolution of the proportion of population with different strategy choices over time.

First, for the local governments in an economically developed region, assuming that the proportion of local governments adopting fraud strategies for carbon emission reduction is p and the proportion of local governments adopting self-discipline strategies for carbon emission reduction is 1-p. For the local governments in an economically backward region, assuming that the proportion of local governments adopting fraud strategy for carbon emission reduction is q and the proportion of local governments adopting self-discipline strategies for carbon emission reduction is 1-q. First, p is regarded as a function of time t. Then, in the economically developed region, the growth rate for the probability of local governments adopting the fraud strategy for carbon emission reduction can be expressed by the replicator dynamics equation as:

$$\frac{\mathrm{d}p}{\mathrm{d}t} = p\left[E(D_1) - \bar{E}\right] \tag{11.13}$$

Wherein $E(D_1)$ is the fitness of local governments in economically developed regions that adopt the fraud strategy; $E(D_2)$ is the fitness of local governments in economically developed regions that adopt the self-discipline strategy; and $\bar{E}$ is the average fitness of local governments in economically developed regions. According to Table 11.10, we have:

$$E(D_1) = q(R_1 + E_1) + (1-q)(R_1 - F_1) \tag{11.14}$$

$$E(D_2) = q(R_1 + G_1) + (1-q)R_1 \tag{11.15}$$

$$\bar{E} = pE(D_1) + (1-p)E(D_2)\cdots \tag{11.16}$$

Substituting Equation (11.16) into Equation (11.13), we get:

$$\frac{\mathrm{d}p}{\mathrm{d}t} = p\left[E(D_1) - pE(D_1) - (1-p)E(D_2)\right] \tag{11.17}$$

Then, substituting Equations (11.14) and (11.15) into Equation (11.17), we get:

$$\mathrm{d}p / \mathrm{d}t = p(1-p)(qE_1 - qG_1 + qF_1 - F_1) \tag{11.18}$$

Similarly, in the economically backward region, the proportion of the local governments that adopt the fraud strategy for carbon emission reduction is q, which is also regarded as a function of time t. Then, in the economically backward region, the growth rate for the probability of local governments adopting the fraud strategy for carbon emission reduction can be expressed by the replicator dynamics equation as:

$$\frac{\mathrm{d}q}{\mathrm{d}t} = q\left[U(G_1) - \bar{U}\right] \tag{11.19}$$

Wherein $U(G_1)$ is the fitness of local governments in economically backward regions that adopt the fraud strategy; $U(G_2)$ is the fitness of local governments in economically backward regions that adopt the self-discipline strategy; and $\bar{U}$ is the average fitness of local governments in economically backward regions. Also, according to Table 11.10, we have:

$$U(G_1) = p(R_2 + E_2) + (1 - p)(R_2 - F_2) \tag{11.20}$$

$$U(G_2) = p(R_2 + G_2) + (1 - p)R_2 \tag{11.21}$$

$$\bar{U} = qU(G_1) + (1 - q)U(G_2) \tag{11.22}$$

Substituting Equation (11.22) into Equation (11.19), we get:

$$\frac{\mathrm{d}q}{\mathrm{d}t} = q\left[U(G_1) - qU(G_1) - (1 - q)U(G_2)\right] \tag{11.23}$$

Then, substituting Equations (11.20) and (11.21) into Equation (11.23), we get:

$$\frac{\mathrm{d}q}{\mathrm{d}t} = q(1 - q)(pE_2 - pG_2 + pF_2 - F_2) \tag{11.24}$$

So far, the analysis of strategy fitness of local governments' voluntary carbon emission reduction can be expressed by differential equations (11.18) and (11.24).

$$\left.\begin{aligned} \mathrm{d}p/\mathrm{d}t &= p(1 - p)\left[q(E_1 - G_1 + F_1) - F_1\right] \\ \mathrm{d}q/\mathrm{d}t &= q(1 - q)\left[p(E_2 - G_2 + F_2) - F_2\right] \end{aligned}\right\} \tag{11.25}$$

The equation set shows that the rate at which a strategy is adopted in the population is positively related to the extent to which the fitness of adopting this strategy is higher than the average fitness of the population over time; the rate at which a strategy is abandoned in the population is positively related to the extent to which the fitness of adopting this strategy is lower than the average fitness of the population. In other words, in evolutionary game theory, the imitation probability of a player is negatively related to the size of the population. The larger the proportion of the group is in the entire population, the smaller the probability of imitating the strategy within the population will be. The smaller the proportion of the group is in the entire population, the greater the probability of imitating the strategy within the population will be. The imitation probability of the player is positively related to the fitness of the group being imitated. If the fitness of a new strategy is high, it will be chosen by more and more participants. Otherwise, this strategy may be phased out gradually. Through the entire evolutionary game analysis, we conclude that strategies with higher fitness gradually replace strategies with lower fitness, while strategies with lower fitness are gradually replaced by strategies with higher fitness over time. This is also the case for carbon emission reduction behavior among local governments.

11.4.3 Analysis of strategy stability

The ultimate goal of evolutionary game analysis is the study of "evolutionarily stable strategy" (ESS), which is the most basic equilibrium concept in evolutionary game models proposed by Smith and Price. In the so-called ESS, if every individual in a group adopts the same strategy, then in the state of natural development, there will not be a strategy with mutation characteristics that would cause the individuals in the group change their original strategy. The group strategy is stable and inviolable. The core idea is that the ESS can resist disturbance or "lock" the stable state, so that it is impossible for the small mutant group to invade this group, that is, when a local government's strategy selection ratio p or q deviates from the equilibrium state $\hat{p}$ or $\hat{q}$, the replicator dynamic mechanism can still make the current local government's strategy selection ratio p or q restore to the equilibrium state $\hat{p}$ or $\hat{q}$. In the process of mathematical calculations of game equilibrium, it is required that $\mathrm{d}p/\mathrm{d}t > 0$ when $p > \hat{p}$ due to the invasion of mutation strategy. Similarly, if $q > \hat{q}$, then $\mathrm{d}q/\mathrm{d}t > 0$ is also required. Otherwise, when $p < \hat{p}$ due to the invasion of mutation strategy, $\mathrm{d}p/\mathrm{d}t < 0$ is required. Similarly, if $q < \hat{q}$, then $\mathrm{d}q/\mathrm{d}t < 0$ is also required; when $p = \hat{p}$ or $q = \hat{q}$, and $\hat{p}$ or $\hat{q}$ is an equilibrium point under the ESS, then it is required that $\mathrm{d}p/\mathrm{d}t = 0$ or $\mathrm{d}q/\mathrm{d}t = 0$, and the second order derivative of p or q with respect to time t is less than zero.

According to the method proposed by Friedman, for population dynamic evolutionary games behavior described by a differential equation, the local stability conditions of its strategic equilibrium point can be calculated and analyzed by constructing the Jacobian matrix. The above-mentioned Jacobian matrix of the differential equations consisting of Equations (11.18) and (11.24) is:

$$J = \begin{bmatrix} (1-2p)\left[q(E_1-G_1+F_1)-F_1\right] & p(1-p)(E_1-G_1+F_1) \\ q(1-q)(E_2-G_2+F_2) & (1-2q)\left[p(E_2-G_2+F_2)-F_2\right] \end{bmatrix} \quad (11.26)$$

The determinant of matrix J is:

$$\begin{aligned} \det(J) = {} & (1-2p)\left[q(E_1-G_1+F_1)-F_1\right](1-2q)\left[p(E_2-G_2+F_2)-F_2\right]- \\ & p(1-p)(E_1-G_1+F_1)q(1-q)(E_2-G_2+F_2) \end{aligned} \quad (11.27)$$

The trace of matrix J is:

$$\mathrm{tr}(J) = (1-2p)\left[q(E_1-G_1+F_1)-F_1\right]+(1-2q)\left[p(E_2-G_2+F_2)-F_2\right] \quad (11.28)$$

According to the analysis of the stable points of the Equation set (11.25), the system has five local equilibrium points. Using the local stability analysis method of the Jacobian matrix, the stability analysis of these five equilibrium points is carried out by Equations (11.26), (11.27), and (11.28), and the

Table 11.11 Local stability analysis results of local governments' carbon emission reduction strategies

Balance point	*det (J)*	*det (J) symbol*	*tr (J)*	*tr (J) symbol*	*Local stability*
$p = 0, q = 0$	F_1F_2	+	$-F_1 - F_2$	−	ESS
$p = 0, g = 1$	$(E_1 - G_1)F_2$	+	$E_1 - G_1 + F_2$	+	Unstable
$p = 1, q = 0$	$(E_2 - G_2)F_1$	+	$E_2 - G_2 + F_1$	+	Unstable
$p = 1, q = 1$	$(E_1 - G_1)(E_2 - G_2)$	+	$-E_1 + G_1 - E_2 + G_2$	−	ESS
$p = F_2/(E_2 + F_2 - G_2)$ $q = F_1/(E_1 + F_1 - G_1)$	$\frac{F_1F_2(E_1 - G_1)(E_2 - G_2)}{(E_1 + F_1 - G_1)(E_2 + F_2 - G_2)}$	+	0		Saddle point

calculation results shown in Table 11.11 can be obtained. The calculation results given in Table 11.11 can also be converted into a strategy stability trend graph, as shown in Figure 11.9.

As shown in Table 11.11, there are five local equilibrium points in the above-mentioned local governments' strategy selection for carbon emission reduction. Among them, there are two local equilibrium points corresponding to points *O* (0, 0) and *O*″ (1, 1) in Figure 11.9, respectively. That is, both economically developed regions and economically backward regions adopt self-discipline strategies or fraud strategies. The other three local equilibrium points include a saddle point *D* (*p*, *q*) and two unstable local equilibrium points *A* (1, 0) and *B* (0, 1). The so-called saddle point is a singular point, which is unstable along the unstable local equilibrium points *A* and *B* and stable along the stable local equilibrium points *O* and *O*″.

Based on the analysis in Table 11.11, the long-term dynamic evolution trend of the two local governments' group game strategy selection is shown in Figure 11.9. The local equilibrium points *O* and *O*″ of the two evolutionary stabilization strategies as well as the two unstable local equilibrium points *A* and *B* forms a square area. Connected by the two unstable local equilibrium points *A* and *B*, the resulting diagonal divides the square *OAO*″*B* into two areas, where the shaded area is assumed to be *X* and the blank area is assumed to be *Y*. Taking the diagonal line connecting the local equilibrium points *O* and *O*″ of the two evolutionary stable strategies as a reference, the arc-shaped arrow line represents the convergence trend of the local government's group strategy. Then, according to the analysis of the above evolutionary game, it can be concluded that in both an economically developed area and an economically backward area, the initial state of the carbon emission reduction strategy of the two regional groups will directly determine the result of the long-term evolution and stability strategy of the carbon emission reduction behavior of the two regional groups. When the

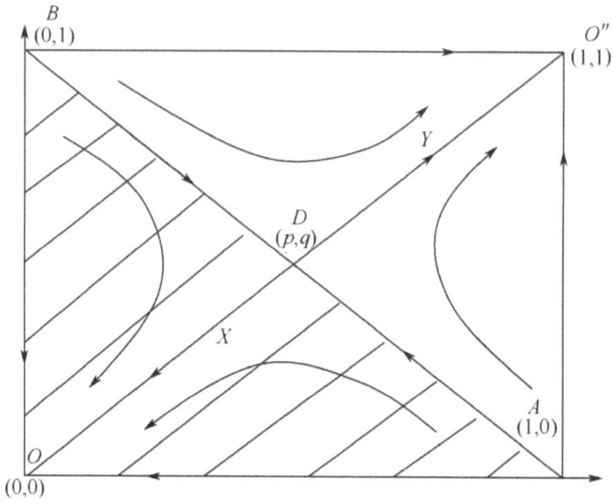

Figure 11.9 Strategy stability trend graph based on natural selection

initial state of the strategy of the two regional groups is in the blank area *Y*, the strategy of the local government group will converge to point *O″* (1, 1). That is, all regions will adopt the carbon emission reduction fraud strategy. When the initial state of the strategies of the two regional groups is in the shaded area *X*, the strategy combination of the local government groups will converge to point *O* (0, 0). That is, all regions will adopt the self-discipline strategy for carbon emission reduction.

11.4.4 Main conclusions

An important goal of theoretical research is to realize the guiding significance of policy making. Evolutionary game analysis is not only closer to reality in terms of game assumptions, but also more intuitively describes the strategy selection mechanism and strategy equilibrium evolution trend with groups as research objects. The results of the study show that when a certain amount of economically developed areas choose carbon emission reduction fraud strategies, economically backward areas also tend to choose fraud strategies for carbon emission reduction. When the proportion of economically developed regions choosing the fraud strategy for carbon emission reduction is below a certain number, the economically backward regions tend to choose the self-discipline strategy for carbon emission reduction. However, from the current reality of carbon emission reduction in China, economically developed regions should undertake more carbon emission reduction obligations. Therefore, the proportion of economically developed regions choosing fraud strategies for carbon emission reduction to make economically backward regions tend to choose the fraud strategy for carbon emission reduction should be smaller than that of economically backward regions choosing the fraud strategy for carbon emission reduction to make economically developed regions tend to choose the fraud strategy for carbon emission reduction. On the contrary, the proportion of economically developed regions choosing the self-discipline strategy for carbon emission reduction to make economically backward regions tend to choose the self-discipline strategy for carbon emission reduction should be greater than that of economically backward regions choosing the self-discipline strategy for carbon emission reduction to make economically developed regions tend to choose the self-discipline strategy for carbon emission reduction.

The above research results also show that although the two different types of local government groups will also affect the final result of the evolutionary game through continuous learning and strategy adjustment during the entire stable trend evolution process, the initial state of the strategies of the two different types of local government groups is more decisive to the final result of the evolutionary game. As shown in Figure 11.9, a diagonal line formed by connecting two unstable local equilibrium points A and B divides the square $OAO''B$ into two different initial states for the strategies. This will lead to the long-term evolution results under two distinctly different strategies, the self-discipline strategy and the fraud strategy, for carbon emission reduction adopted by both local governments.

The long-term evolution results of two completely different carbon emission reduction strategies for local government groups are brought about by the above-mentioned two different initial states of local government group strategies. This implies that by adjusting the initial state of local government group strategies, the ideal long-term evolution result of local government group strategy is possible. As shown in Figure 11.9, if the area of the shaded area X can be increased and the area of the blank area Y can be reduced by adjusting the policy, the chance of the long-term evolution of the game reaching the equilibrium point O (0, 0) of the evolutionary stable strategy will increase. That is, the chance that both local government groups tend to adopt self-discipline strategy for carbon emission reduction will increase. The specific policy measures include:

1. Increase the benefits of economically backward regions adopting self-discipline strategy for carbon emission reduction and the loss of economically developed regions adopting the fraud strategy for carbon emission reduction, so that the proportion of economically backward regions adopting the self-discipline strategy for emission reduction will increase and the proportion of economically developed regions adopting the fraud strategy for carbon emission reduction will decrease.
2. Increase the benefits of the self-discipline strategy for carbon emission reduction in economically developed regions and increase the loss of economically backward regions adopting the fraud strategy for carbon emission reduction. In this way, the proportion of economically developed regions adopting the self-discipline strategy for carbon emission reduction will increase, while the proportion of economically backward regions adopting the fraud strategy for carbon emission reduction will decrease.

3 Lower the benefits of economically developed regions and economically backward regions adopting the fraud strategy for carbon emission reduction, so that fewer of them will adopt fraud strategies for carbon emission reduction at the same time. As an ideal state, if the benefits of both local government groups adopting carbon emission reduction fraud strategies are reduced to 0, both local groups will adopt the self-discipline strategy for carbon emission reduction, which is also the long-term evolutionary result of the game.

It is worth noting that economically developed regions should bear more carbon emission reduction responsibilities. In the above-mentioned policy regulation, the benefits reduced for adopting fraud strategy for carbon emission reduction in economically developed regions should be greater than those in economically backward regions; the benefits increased for adopting self-discipline strategy for carbon emission reduction in economically backward regions should be greater than those in economically developed regions; the losses increased for adopting fraud strategy for carbon emission reduction in economically developed regions should be greater than those in economically backward regions. In addition, the above analysis does not consider the situation of central government regulation and a unified carbon market. In the event of central government regulation and a unified carbon market, the quota allocation mechanism will become an important means of adjusting the income matrix of the players, which will affect the initial state of the players and ultimately affect the realization of the long-term equilibrium outcome of the evolutionary games.

Notes

1 Data collated from China Carbon Emissions Trading Website: http://www.tanpaifang.com/.
2 The economic meanings of atmospheric pollution and carbon emissions are the same in this section, unless otherwise specified. Sometimes, in order to express the generality of the problem, atmospheric pollution is often used to replace carbon emissions, but the ideas and conclusions of the research are equally applicable to carbon emissions.
3 This action set can also be simply assumed to be fraud allowances, no fraud allowances. Considering the generality of the study, it is assumed that (fraud, self-discipline) action set can encompass more carbon emission reduction issues. The analysis is consistent in both scenarios.

References

Fudenberg, D., Tirole, J. *Game theory*. MIT Press, 1991.
Huang Kainan. Development of cognitive rationality and evolutionary economics methodology. *Institutional Economics Research*, 2009, 01: 1–25.
Taylor, P.D., Jonker, L.B. Evolutionary stable strategies and game dynamics. *Mathematical Biosciences*, 1978, 40(1–2): 145–156.
Weibull, J., Salomonsson, M. Natural selection and social preferences. *Journal of Theoretical Biology*, 2006, 239(1): 79–92.
Wang Wenju. *Economic game theory*. Higher Education Press, 2010.

Part IV

Carbon emissions trading game and mechanism analysis

12 Game analysis on the initial allocation of carbon emission rights

12.1 The main methods of the initial allocation of carbon emission rights

The initial allocation of carbon emission rights means that the government, by means of issuing emission licenses, sets the upper limit of carbon dioxide that market participants are allowed to emit, and manufacturers who have obtained the license then have the right to emit the corresponding amount of carbon dioxide. As carbon emission rights are of value, owners of licenses actually obtain a corresponding amount of assets.

The initial allocation of carbon emission rights is the foundation of carbon trade. The key to the initial allocation lies in fairness and effectiveness so as to achieve a reasonable allocation of carbon dioxide emissions. At present, it is generally acknowledged that the initial allocation of carbon emission rights can be divided into three main methods: full free by the government, public auction, and the mixed allocation method combining the two (Wei Lu and Liqin Cui, 2003).

12.1.1 Full free

Full free refers to the practice that government administrators allocate carbon emission rights in accordance with relevant standards, and manufacturers are not required to pay for it. The full free method can be further divided into two types: one is based on exogenous criteria of the manufacturer and the other is output-based allocation (Boemare and Quirion, 2002).

The allocation based on manufacturer's exogenous criteria means that under the total carbon emission control index, government administrators allocate carbon emission rights based on manufacturer's benchmarking or grandfathering, such as acid rain program in the US, while output-based allocation is a relative allocation method where under the total carbon emission control index, government administrators allocate carbon emission rights based on the actual production level or carbon dioxide emissions of manufacturers. The government allocates carbon emission rights

DOI: 10.4324/9781003388500-16

of the manufacturer according to its current output and carbon emission standards per unit of output (for example, 1 ton of carbon emission for every 1 kWh of electricity generated), and EU's carbon emissions trading mechanism make references to the output-based allocation method.

The advantage of full free is that it is more acceptable by manufacturers and its implementation in practice is more likely to be smoother. Instead of increasing the cost of the manufacturer, this method brings an asset, which can be sold in the market when needed, to the manufacturer. However, some researchers bring forward disadvantages of full free method. In 2002, Cramton and Kerr (2002) put forward that full free method would lead to benefit loss. From the perspective of allocation effect, shareholders of emission rights occupy all the scarcity rents, while the public fails to get corresponding compensation. In the long run, full free also tends to reduce the production capacity of enterprises in general and hinder competition to a certain extent.

12.1.2 Public auction

The public auction, which may determine price and resource ownership and realize allocation, is of great application value in the initial allocation stage of carbon trade. There are two major reasons for adopting the auction method: (1) buyers understand the value of carbon emission rights better than sellers, and the price can be determined through auctions, and (2) according to the principle of "Openness, fairness, equality, success of highest-price-offer", the auction helps to optimize the allocation of carbon emission rights and drive carbon emission rights to the manufacturer with the highest bid price. In short, public auction possesses the basic function of revealing transaction information and cutting back on transaction costs.

So far, the public auction of carbon emission rights is generally performed in the form of sealed-bid auction and open ascending auction (see Chapter 15 for details). Researchers believe that the sealed-bid auction is not the best way for carbon emissions auction. On the contrary, due to the more transparent price disclosure procedure, open ascending auction has its advantages over sealed-bid auction. Yet, the mature theoretical foundation and rich practical experience of sealed-bid auction still make it the most used auction method in practice, and it is widely adopted in carbon trade in Europe and the US.

From the perspective of theoretical research, a view prevails among scholars that public auction method is a more suitable way for allocation, because public auction has higher allocation efficiency. But public auction would usually make the cost grow for manufacturers, so it is not recommended in the initial period of carbon trade. Cramton and Kerr (2002), Parry and Pizer once analyzed strengths and weaknesses of full free and public auctions in terms of income, cost, and efficiency, and they concluded that public auctions have its relative advantages, but manufacturers are more likely to accept full free method at the beginning of the establishment of the carbon trade system.

12.1.3 Mixed method

The mixed method refers to the combination of full free and public auction in the allocation of carbon emission rights. The overwhelming consensus among many researchers is that at the beginning of carbon trade, full free is able to strengthen the acceptance and participation of manufacturers. And then different time periods can be designed to gradually whittle down the proportion of full free and scale up that of auctions, till the auction method completely dominates the market. Among all of these steps, design of the proportion of full free as well as the number of transitional stage is the pitfall of the mixed allocation method. Currently, the mixed allocation method is adopted in the relatively mature European Union Emissions Trading Scheme (ETS). Generally speaking, the central government first selects high energy consumption and high emission enterprises for pilot projects, such as thermal power, coke, iron and steel, and papermaking enterprises. During the trial period, at least 95% of the carbon emission rights allocated by the government to these enterprises are free and the remaining quota can be obtained by auction. When it comes to the second implementation period, the proportion of full free method will be cut to 90% and then gradually lowered in the following stages till zero.

The mixed allocation method is a transitional dynamic process to adjust policy variables, which avoids both the efficiency loss caused by full free method and the negative resistance of manufacturers to the auction method. Thus, the mixed allocation is an allocation model that is more recommended both in theory and practice.

Comparison of the above three allocation methods shows that public auction is the optimal allocation method from the perspective of efficiency (Fullerton and Metcalf, 2001). The auction method is conducive to stimulating manufacturers to realize energy conservation and emission reduction and to update technology. Meanwhile, this method would encourage emerging enterprises to participate in carbon trade.

However, at the beginning of the construction of the carbon emission rights trading market, full auction helps little in the promotion of carbon emission rights trading. On the contrary, the mixed allocation method, which combines advantages of full free and public auction, is the current mainstream mode of carbon emission rights allocation and should be adopted by China's carbon trade. Moreover, in the initial period of China's current carbon emission trading, in order to attract manufacturers to participate in the transaction, the main allocation method should be full free (the proportion can reach 95% based on the experience of ETS). In the future, as carbon emission rights trading matures and grows in size, the proportion of full free should be gradually reduced and that of auction method continuously increased.

12.2 Negotiation game analysis on carbon emission rights allocation quota

As an important component of the primary market of carbon emission rights trade, the initial allocation of carbon emission rights is related to the direct interests of all players, including regions and manufacturers. The goal of players is to maximize their own utility, while quota constraints of carbon emission rights will constrain their process of maximizing the utility. Therefore, players lack the motivation to participate in the initial allocation of carbon emission rights, and the government administrators are required to formulate the final allocation plan.

In full free of carbon emission rights by government administrators, given that the total carbon emission target is settled, manufacturers (industries or regions) will try their best to obtain more allocation quotas for themselves from the perspective of maximizing utility. Generally speaking, manufacturers (industries or regions) will negotiate on the allocation quota of carbon emission rights. Thus, there would be a game pattern among manufacturers (industries or regions), including many typical game phenomena, like Prisoner's Dilemma, Chicken Game, Boxed Pigs Game, and Stag Hunt Model. The following detailed analysis is an example of the allocation quota negotiation among manufacturers in conjunction with Palfrey and Rosenthal model (Palfrey and Rosenthal, 1989; Fudenberg and Tirole, 1991).

12.2.1 Establishment of negotiation game model

Suppose two manufacturers, $i = 1, 2$, negotiate on the allocation of carbon emission rights and each manufacturer's decision is to cooperate or not to cooperate with the government's allocation plan. Suppose if only one manufacturer chooses to cooperate with the government, then the government's allocation plan is passed, and both manufacturers can receive R unit of profits; if no manufacturer chooses to cooperate, the government allocation plan needs to be adjusted, and each manufacturer will receive 0 unit of payment. Assuming that the cost of each manufacturer to cooperate with the government is c_i, then the benefit matrix of this game is shown in Figure 12.1.

		Manufacturer 2	
		Cooperate	Do not Cooperate
Manufacturer 1	Cooperate	$R\ c,\ R\ c$	$R\ c,\ R$
	Do not Cooperate	$R\ R\ c$	$0, 0$

Figure 12.1 Negotiation Game

Assuming that the benefits of a successful allocation plan are the common knowledge of manufacturers and the cost for each manufacturer to choose cooperation is private information. That is, the cost c_i represents the type of manufacture i. Among them, it is common knowledge that c_i follows a uniform distribution on $[c, \overline{c}]$ and its distribution function is $P(\cdot)$ and $c < R < \overline{c}$.

12.2.2 Game model solution

This is a static game under incomplete information. A pure strategy $a_i(c_i)$ of this game can be regarded as a function from $[\underline{c}, \overline{c}]$ to $\{0,1\}$, wherein 0 means that the manufacturer chooses not to cooperate in the allocation and 1 means that the manufacturer chooses to cooperate in the allocation.

The payoff function of manufacturer i is:

$$u_i(a_i, a_j, c_i) = R \cdot \max(a_1, a_2) - a_i c_i \quad (i = 1,2)$$

The expected utility function of manufacturer i is:

$$E_i = p_j u_i(a_i, 1, c_i) + (1 - p_j) u_i(a_i, 0, c_i)$$

Wherein p_j represents the probability for manufacturer j to choose cooperation in the equilibrium state.

So, manufacturer i will choose strategy $a_i^*(\cdot)$ to maximize its expected utility $\max_{a_i} E_i$.

When $R - c_i > p_j \cdot R$, manufacturer i will choose to cooperate, that is, when $c_i < R(1 - p_j)$, $a_i^*(c_i) = 1$. When $R - c_i < p_j \cdot R$, manufacturer i will choose not to cooperate, that is, when $c_i > R(1 - p_j)$, $a_i^*(c_i) = 0$. This indicates that there is such a split point c_i^* that when $c_i \in [\underline{c}, c_i^*]$ (requiring $\underline{c} < c_i^*$), manufacturer i will choose to cooperate. Similarly, there is such a c_j^* that when $c_j \in [\underline{c}, c_j^*]$, manufacturer j will choose to cooperate.

Because:

$$p_j = \text{prob}(\underline{c} \le c_j \le c_j^*) = P(c_j^*) = \frac{c_j^* - \underline{c}}{\overline{c} - \underline{c}}$$

Similarly:

$$p_i = \frac{c_i^* - \underline{c}}{\overline{c} - c}$$

Therefore, the equilibrium point should satisfy the equation set:

$$\begin{cases} R - c_i^* = \dfrac{c_j^* - \underline{c}}{\bar{c} - \underline{c}} R \\ R - c_j^* = \dfrac{c_i^* - \underline{c}}{\bar{c} - \underline{c}} R \end{cases}$$

Solution is:

$$c_i^* = c_j^* = \frac{R^2\bar{c} - R(\bar{c} - \underline{c})^2 - R\underline{c}(\bar{c} - \underline{c})}{R^2 - (\bar{c} - \underline{c})^2}$$

Therefore, the Bayesian Nash equilibrium of this game is:

When $c_1 \leq \dfrac{R^2\bar{c} - R(\bar{c} - \underline{c})^2 - R\underline{c}(\bar{c} - \underline{c})}{R^2 - (\bar{c} - \underline{c})^2}$, manufacturer 1 will choose to cooperate; otherwise, it will not cooperate.

When $c_2 \leq \dfrac{R^2\bar{c} - R(\bar{c} - \underline{c})^2 - R\underline{c}(\bar{c} - \underline{c})}{R^2 - (\bar{c} - \underline{c})^2}$, manufacturer 2 will choose to cooperate; otherwise, it will not cooperate.

12.2.3 Game equilibrium analysis

1. If $\begin{array}{l} \underline{c} < c_1 \leq \dfrac{R^2\bar{c} - R(\bar{c} - \underline{c})^2 - R\underline{c}(\bar{c} - \underline{c})}{R^2 - (\bar{c} - \underline{c})^2} \\ \underline{c} < c_2 \leq \dfrac{R^2\bar{c} - R(\bar{c} - \underline{c})^2 - R\underline{c}(\bar{c} - \underline{c})}{R^2 - (\bar{c} - c)^2} \end{array}$, both manufacturers will choose to cooperate.
2. If $\begin{array}{l} \underline{c} < c_1 \leq \dfrac{R^2\bar{c} - R(\bar{c} - \underline{c})^2 - R\underline{c}(\bar{c} - \underline{c})}{R^2 - (\bar{c} - \underline{c})^2} \\ \dfrac{R^2\bar{c} - R(\bar{c} - \underline{c})^2 - R\underline{c}(\bar{c} - \underline{c})}{R^2 - (\bar{c} - \underline{c})^2} < c_2 \leq \bar{c} \end{array}$, manufacturer 1 will cooperate.
3. Generally, when the strength of the manufacturers participating in the allocation of carbon emission rights is quite mismatched (assuming the strength of manufacturer 2 is relatively weak), Boxed Pigs Game would come into being very easily.

   In this case, "not cooperate" is the dominant strategy for manufacturer 2 and the final Nash equilibrium is (cooperate, not cooperate), namely manufacturer 1 with stronger strength chooses to cooperate in the government's allocation plan, while manufacturer 2 with weaker strength, which chooses not to cooperate, also shares the benefits of the allocation scheme. It is a typical "free-rider" behavior.

The "free-rider" phenomenon is mainly caused by an unfair payment and strategic structure, driven by two major factors: (1) the atmospheric environment is public and is featured with non-excludability of consumption, and (2) in collective behaviors, it is difficult to discern individual contributions, responsibilities, and benefits. In this way, the allocation of carbon emission rights and the sequence of participation in trading form a pattern of Boxed Pigs Game. On the grounds of fairness and efficiency, strong manufacturers would require weaker manufacturers to participate in the allocation and trading of carbon emission rights, while weaker manufacturers tend to require stronger manufacturers to act first according to the principle of "common but differentiated responsibilities". Government administrators can refer to the concept of Nash equilibrium to trial and promote carbon emission trading when designing the allocation plan.

4 If $\begin{matrix} \dfrac{R^2\overline{c} - R(\overline{c} - \underline{c})^2 - R\underline{c}(\overline{c} - \underline{c})}{R^2 - (\overline{c} - \underline{c})^2} < c_1 \leq \overline{c} \\ \dfrac{R^2\overline{c} - R(\overline{c} - \underline{c})^2 - R\underline{c}(\overline{c} - \underline{c})}{R^2 - (\overline{c} - \underline{c})^2} < c_2 \leq \overline{c} \end{matrix}$, both manufacturers will choose not to cooperate. This can be regarded as a "prisoner's dilemma" among manufacturers.

If both manufacturers choose to cooperate, both parties will get the benefit of $R - c_i$ units; if they choose not to cooperate, both parties will receive 0 unit of benefit; if one party cooperates and the other does not cooperate, the benefit of the cooperating party is $R - c_i$ units, which is c_i units lower than that of the non-cooperating party. At this moment, for both manufacturers, choosing not to cooperate is their dominant strategy, and the final equilibrium of the dominant strategy is (not cooperate, not cooperate). This is actually an inefficient result and the Pareto optimality (cooperate, cooperate) cannot be achieved.

Both manufacturers insist that if one party is the only one responding to the government's call and adopts a cooperative attitude to negotiate the allocation of carbon emission rights while the other party does not cooperate, it will have no impact on the allocation policy and will lead to a great loss of the party's utility. In contrast, if the other party adopts a cooperative attitude and the party does not cooperate, it will not only have no decisive impact on the allocation policy, but also enhance the party's utility. Therefore, each manufacturer has its motive to refuse cooperation, which will inevitably lead to a "tragedy of the commons". That is to say, if each manufacturer rationally pursues the maximization of its own utility, the allocation of carbon emission rights quota under cooperative emission reduction cannot be achieved.

12.2.4 Other situations

The negotiation games under incomplete information are shown above, and there may also be Chicken Game and Stag Hunt Game in the actual negotiation state.

1 Chicken Game. Two evenly matched manufacturers are likely to have a chicken game in the negotiation on carbon emission rights allocation quotas. Assuming that the manufacturer's strategy choice is "cooperate" or "not cooperate", the chicken game will have two pure strategy Nash equilibrium (cooperate, not cooperate) or (not cooperate, cooperate), and they are both Pareto optimal. The Pareto sub-optimal result becomes (cooperate, cooperate), that is, both manufacturers choose to cooperate and obtain corresponding benefits, while (not cooperate, not cooperate) is the result of Pareto ineffectiveness, leading to a loss at both sides. To prevent extremely poor efficiency (not cooperate, not cooperate), the mechanism design of administrators becomes extremely important.

   In the era of globalization, "common development" is the rational choice for human beings. A chicken-game-style ending should be a choice or rotation between (cooperate, not cooperate) or (not cooperate, cooperate). The sub-optimality outcome should be (cooperate, cooperate) rather than irrational (not cooperate, not cooperate). It can be seen from the payoff matrix that there are problems of benefit distribution and benefit compensation in the chicken game. Administrators should consider the principle of fairness when designing the mechanism and give corresponding policy support to the party who chooses to cooperate.

2 Stag Hunt Game. During the negotiation process of the carbon emission rights allocation quota, the two manufacturers may also show efforts to cooperate or respond in a general way and then the so-called stag hunt game appears. Assuming that the manufacturer's strategy choice is "strive" or "general", there would be two pure strategy Nash equilibriums in this game: (strive, strive) and (general, general). Among them, (strive, strive) is a Pareto equilibrium and (general, general) is risk-dominated equilibrium. At this moment, there is no serious deviation between individual interests and collective interests, and the two are basically consistent. That is to say, the allocation of carbon emission rights and the sharing of emission reduction tasks can be achieved through the division of labor and cooperation among individuals.

   Due to the consistency of individual rationality and collective rationality, in the game, more attention is likely to be paid by players to absolute benefits (common interests) than relative benefits, and the main goal is to make the "cake" bigger and achieve Pareto efficiency equilibrium. However, due to the dependency of the player's strategy, it is easier to achieve (general, general) equilibrium from the perspective of risk, which is Pareto sub-optimal. Hence, the key to the success of the cooperation of players lies in avoiding risks, so that the promises and behaviors of players are able to be in a state of mutual guarantee. This is related to the opportunism motivation of the players, the uncertainty of the environment, the high transaction costs, and other factors. Thus, administrators should consider the influence of reputation and information on game efficiency when formulating the allocation mechanism.

12.2.5 Specific recommendations[1]

At present, the construction of carbon trade market in China faces the first headwind that initial allocation of carbon emission rights between regions is hard to put in place. This section believes that the principle of "common but differentiated responsibilities" should be followed during the allocation. Due to differences in resource endowments and policies in China, a vast territory, the economic development level, and industrial structure of various regions are unevenly developed. For example, the three provinces in the northeastern of China are developed in heavy industry, the southwest region mainly focuses on agricultural industry, and the coastal areas are more developed than the inland areas. Therefore, when formulating allocation policies, the government should set the allocation quota of carbon emission rights in combination with objective factors, such as the economic scale, energy structure, and industrial structure.

Developed regions have relatively larger historical carbon emissions and are obliged to take more responsibility for emission reduction, but there is little room for emission reduction given their low energy consumption. However, although less developed areas have larger spaces for emission reduction and lower cost in emission reduction, they enjoy the demands and rights to realize economic advancement. Therefore, the "prisoner's dilemma" in the allocation of carbon emission rights can be coordinated by carrying out carbon trade between two areas, especially with the help of the successful experience of the clean development mechanism. Developed regions help less developed areas implement emission reductions by funding and offering technology, and at the same time, sustainable development in less developed areas and emission reduction targets in developed regions can be achieved, resulting in a win-win situation.

Second, allocation pilot areas need to be established first and then gradually expanded to the whole country. It is practicable to first select areas (industries) or representative regions with high energy consumption and high emissions as "pioneers" in the allocation of carbon emission rights. By accumulating allocation experience of carbon emission right permits and promoting it to the whole nation, "free-rider" phenomenon in allocation can be avoided effectively.

Finally, the government should advocate the low carbon concept and guide manufacturers to form a cooperative awareness of carbon emission rights allocation. Only when manufacturers realize the asset nature of carbon in the future and the potential and advantages of the carbon trade market will they actively participate in the cooperation. In this way, in the event of the carbon emission quota allocation issue, their cooperation and overall awareness would go a long way in avoiding the above difficulties, and then Pareto efficiency equilibrium is able to be achieved.

12.3 Dynamic consistency analysis of carbon emission rights allocation policy

So far, the initial allocation of carbon emission rights in the international carbon trade market is mainly subject to full free method. The full free can facilitate operation and improve the participation of manufacturers. However, it is hard to ensure the fairness, justice, and efficiency of allocation under this mode. According to international experience, the initial allocation of carbon emission rights is mainly based on the output and carbon emissions of manufacturers. However, the government does not understand the real output of manufacturers or the marginal cost of carbon emission reduction, and most information comes from the manufacturer's report. Due to the incompleteness and asymmetry of information, it is very easy for manufacturers to falsely report carbon emissions, which brings difficulties to the allocation. Therefore, when designing allocation policies, government departments should pay more attention to motivate manufacturers to "speak the truth" and should reasonably allocate the proportion of their carbon emission quota to their total emissions, so as to help them achieve balanced development between production and emission reduction.

In conjunction with Stackelberg's dynamic game model, this section adopts the method of game theory analysis and focuses on the dynamic consistency of allocation policy. For sake of urging manufacturers to report their real carbon emissions and of enhancing the efficiency of policy implementation, the section discusses how government administrators should design the distribution policy of carbon emission rights under full free method and provides suggestions for the policy construction of full free.

12.3.1 Game model establishment

If there are n carbon emission manufacturers and one government administrator in an area, the administrator's goal is to design a reasonable allocation policy to determine the carbon emission quota of each manufacturer, and the manufacturer's decision-making goal is how to report its own carbon emissions. Since manufacturers have the motive to falsely report their carbon emissions, the allocation policy designed by the administrator should enable manufacturers to truthfully report their total carbon emissions.

Assume that administrators and manufacturers have signed a contract in advance.

Suppose the carbon emissions reported by manufacturers are recorded as $g_i\,(i=1,2,\ldots,n)$; the allocation of carbon emission rights determined by administrator is represented by the proportional coefficient $\alpha_i\,(i=1,2,\ldots,n)$ of the carbon emissions reported by each manufacturer, obviously $0<\alpha_i<1$. The remaining carbon emissions are reduced by the manufacturers themselves and the total carbon emissions reduced by each manufacturer is $G=\sum_{i=1}^{n}(1-\alpha_i)g_i$.

Let the budget revenue of the carbon emission rights obtained by each emission manufacturer be:

$$R_i = p\alpha_i g_i\,(i=1,2,\ldots,n)$$

Wherein p is the market price of unit carbon emission rights.

Let the administrator's utility function[2] be denoted as:

$$U_g=\sum_{i=1}^{n}\beta_i \ln(\alpha_i g_i)$$

Wherein $\beta_i\,(0<\beta_i<1)$ is the weighting coefficient and $\sum_{i=1}^{n}\beta_i=1$

The administrator's strategy is to choose the appropriate α_i to maximize its own utility, namely:

$$\max_{\alpha_i} U_g=\max_{\alpha_i}\sum_{i=1}^{n}\beta_i \ln(\alpha_i g_i) \tag{12.1}$$

$$s.t.\sum_{i=1}^{n}(1-\alpha_i)g_i \geq \Delta G$$

Wherein ΔG is the total amount of carbon emission reduction determined by government administrator, the weighting coefficient β_i represents the policy tendency of administrator to allocate carbon emission rights and represents the preference level of administrator to manufacturers.

If $\beta_i \neq \beta_j\,(i,\,j=1,2,\ldots,n)$, it means that the administrator implements a non-equalitarianism policy and offers allocation policy support to different manufacturers in a differentiated way; otherwise, it is an equalitarianism policy, that is, to each manufacturer, the allocation policy support difference is the smallest.

The utility function of each manufacturer is the budget revenue of carbon emission rights minus the declaration cost, which is recorded as:

$$U_{fi} = p\alpha_i g_i - C_i(g_i)(i = 1,2,\ldots,n)$$

Wherein $C_i(g_i)$ represents the declaration cost of the ith manufacturer. Each manufacturer will declare as many carbon emission amounts as possible, so the government administrator will set some systems to restrain over declaration, such as imposing a fine or producing reputational damage. Therefore, the manufacturer's strategy is how to report carbon emissions g_i to administrator to maximize its own utility, that is:

$$\max_{g_i} U_{fi} = \max_{g_i} p\alpha_i g_i - C_i(g_i) \tag{12.2}$$

Suppose the declaration cost function is a monotonically increasing convex function, and it means that the marginal cost of declaration increases with the increase of carbon emissions, which is consistent with the emission reduction idea of "polluter pays, and excessive emissions result in heavy penalties". Without loss of generality, let $C_i(g_i) = \frac{c_i}{2} g_i^2$. Wherein c_i represents the declaration cost coefficient. The smaller the c_i, the smaller the declaration cost, and then the stronger the emission reduction level of the enterprise. Generally speaking, $c_i \neq c_j(i \neq j)$, even if the carbon emissions are the same due to the different social benefits, the emission reduction levels of manufacturers would also be different.

12.3.2 Solution analysis of different time series game models

Under full free, there are usually two ways to set carbon emission rights quota. For the first method, government administrators set the allocation quota for every manufacturer at first, and manufacturers are allowed to report their carbon emission amounts, and then administrators would adjust the allocation quota (hereinafter referred to as policy 1). For the second method, manufacturers report carbon emission amounts at the beginning and government administrators would determine the allocation quota (hereinafter referred to as policy 2). In conjunction with Stackelberg Model, this section will respectively analyze the above-mentioned two situations and then comment both allocation policies.

12.3.2.1 Model 1: Situation where government administrators act first, manufacturers act later

If the government administrators act first, that is, in the first stage of the game, the administrators first decide the allocation proportion α_i of each manufacturer and each emission manufacturer will act then after observing α_i.

In the second stage, all manufacturers would report their own carbon emissions g_i at the same time.

By backward induction, we first solve the reaction function of each manufacturer in the second stage, namely:

$$\max_{g_i} U_{fi} = \max_{g_i} p\alpha_i g_i - \frac{c_i}{2} g_i^2$$

We solve its first-order condition to get the manufacturer's reaction function:

$$g_i^{(1)} = \frac{p\alpha_i}{c_i} (i = 1,2,\ldots, n) \tag{12.3}$$[3]

We substitute Equation (12.3) into the first stage, namely Equation (12.1), to solve the manufacturer's optimal decision, namely:

$$\max_{\alpha_i} U_g = \max_{\alpha_i} \sum_{i=1}^{n} \beta_i \ln\left(\alpha_i g_i^{(1)}\right)$$

$$s.t. \sum_{i=1}^{n} (1-\alpha_i) g_i^{(1)} \geq \Delta G$$

Since the constraints are linear functions, the constraint specifications are automatically satisfied.

The Lagrangian function is constructed as follows:

$$L(\alpha_i, \lambda) = \sum_{i=1}^{n} \beta_i \ln\left(\alpha_i \frac{p\alpha_i}{c_i}\right) - \lambda\left[-\sum_{i=1}^{n} (1-\alpha_i)\frac{p\alpha_i}{c_i} + \Delta G\right]$$

Then the optimal solution should satisfy the following first-order conditions:

$$\frac{\partial L}{\partial \alpha_i} = \frac{2\beta_i}{\alpha_i} + \lambda \frac{p(1-2\alpha_i)}{c_i} = 0 \tag{12.4}$$

$$\sum_{i=1}^{n} (1-\alpha_i)\frac{p\alpha_i}{c_i} - \Delta G \geq 0 \tag{12.5}$$

$$\lambda\left[-\sum_{i=1}^{n} (1-\alpha_i)\frac{p\alpha_i}{c_i} + \Delta G\right] = 0 \tag{12.6}$$

$$\lambda \geq 0 \tag{12.7}$$

Wherein $i = 1, 2, \ldots n$.

This system of equations is solved in two cases:

1 If $\lambda = 0$, then equation (12.4) does not hold, so the system of equations has no solution.

2 If $\lambda > 0$, then from equation (12.4) we get:

$$\frac{\alpha_i(1-2\alpha_i)}{\beta_i c_i} = \frac{\alpha_j(1-2\alpha_j)}{\beta_j c_j}(i \neq j,\ i,\ j = 1,2,\ldots,n) \tag{12.8}$$

By solving the above simultaneous equations, we get the optimal solution $\alpha_i^{*(1)}$ and then $g_i^{*(1)}$. Since this result does not affect the subsequent analysis, it will not be specifically calculated here.

Therefore, [the administrator chooses the allocation quota $\alpha_i^{*(1)}$, the manufacturer chooses to report $g_i^{*(1)}$] is the perfect Nash equilibrium of the subgame of this game.

At the same time, it can be seen from formula (12.3) that the carbon emission amount truthfully reported by manufacturers is an increasing function of the carbon emission rights allocation quota α_i and the unit price p of carbon emission rights, as well as a decreasing function of the declaration cost coefficient c_i. This indicates that larger allocation proportionality coefficient, higher unit price of carbon emission rights, and smaller declaration cost coefficient of manufacturers contribute to larger carbon emission amounts reported by manufacturers.

12.3.2.2 Model 2: Situation where manufacturers act first, government administrators act later

If the administrators, based on the carbon emissions g_i declared by the manufacturers, determine the proportionality coefficient α_i of the carbon emissions that each manufacturer deserves, this game becomes the situation where the first stage is manufacturers' action and the second stage is administrators' action. This section will solve the subgame perfect Nash equilibrium.

By backward induction, we first solve the optimal response function of the administrator in the second stage:

$$\max_{\alpha_i} U_g = \max_{\alpha_i} \sum_{i=1}^{n} \beta_i \ln(\alpha_i g_i)$$

$$s.t. \sum_{i=1}^{n} (1-\alpha_i) g_i \geq \Delta G$$

Since the constraints are linear functions, the constraint specifications are automatically satisfied.

The Lagrangian function is constructed as follows:

$$L(\alpha_i, \lambda) = \sum_{i=1}^{n} \beta_i \ln(\alpha_i g_i) - \lambda\left[-\sum_{i=1}^{n}(1-\alpha_i) g_i + \Delta G\right]$$

Its first-order optimal condition is:

$$\frac{\partial L}{\partial \alpha_i} = \frac{\beta_i}{\alpha_i} - \lambda g_i = 0 \tag{12.9}$$

$$\sum_{i=1}^{n} (1-\alpha_i) g_i - \Delta G \geq 0 \tag{12.10}$$

$$\lambda \left[-\sum_{i=1}^{n} (1-\alpha_i) g_i + \Delta G \right] = 0 \tag{12.11}$$

$$\lambda \geq 0 \tag{12.12}$$

Wherein $i = 1, 2, \ldots n$.

This system of equations is solved in two cases.

1 If $\lambda = 0$, then Equation (12.9) does not hold, so the system of equations has no solution.
2 If $\lambda > 0$, then from Equation (12.9) we can get:

$$\frac{\alpha_i g_i}{\beta_i} = \frac{\alpha_j g_j}{\beta_j} (i \neq j, i,\ j = 1,2,\ldots,n) \tag{12.13}$$

We solve the above simultaneous equations to get the administrator's response function:

$$\alpha_i^{(2)} = \beta_i + \beta_i \frac{\left(\sum_{i \neq j} g_j - \Delta G \right)}{g_i} \tag{12.14}$$

Then we substitute formula (12.14) in the first stage, namely formula (12.2), to solve the optimal decision of the manufacturer:

$$\max_{g_i} U_{fi} = \max_{g_i} p\alpha_i^{(2)} g_i - \frac{c_i}{2} g_i^2$$

From the first-order condition, we can get:

$$g_i^{*(2)} = \frac{p}{c_i} \beta_i \tag{12.15}$$

We substitute Equation (12.15) into Equation (12.14) to obtain $\alpha_i^{*(2)}$.

Therefore, [the manufacturer chooses to report $g_i^{*(2)}$, the administrator chooses the allocation quota $\alpha_i^{*(2)}$] is the perfect Nash equilibrium of the subgame of this game.

From formula (12.14), it can be seen that the allocation ratio selected by administrator is an increasing function of the weighting coefficient β_i and the other manufacturers' declaration amount $g_j(i \neq j)$, as well as a decreasing function of the self-declaration amount g_j. This indicates that the higher the administrator's preference levels for the manufacturer, the greater the proportion of the manufacturer's share. Meanwhile, each manufacturer creates a positive external effect on other manufacturers, which reduces the enthusiasm of manufacturers to truthfully report their emissions.

12.3.3 Dynamic consistency analysis

The dynamic consistency of policy[4] is the capability to maintain a policy optimal in both the formulation stage and the execution stage under the premise that no new information appears. If the policy is optimal only in the formulation stage, it is dynamically inconsistent.

Comparison between the above two game models with different time series shows that Model 1 can be regarded as a situation where administrators no longer adjust the allocation quota as administrators first determine the allocation ratio, and manufacturers then report carbon emissions; and Model 2 can be seen as a simulated situation of policy 2, or a situation in which administrators adjust the allocation quota as manufacturers report carbon emissions first and then administrators determine the allocation ratio. Therefore, integration of Model 1 and Model 2 leads to the simulated situation of policy 1.

The administrators in policy 1 adjust the allocation quota, as the initial allocation quota does not meet the requirements of dynamic consistency, and it is not a perfect Nash equilibrium of the subgame. The specific analysis is as follows.

Integrating Model 1 and Model 2, given that the administrator has set the allocation ratio $\alpha_i^{(1)}$ in advance, if the manufacturer believes that the administrator abides by the contract, the optimal reporting amount is $g_i^{(1)} = \frac{p\alpha_i^{(1)}}{c_i}$.

It can be seen from Model 2 that the first-order optimal conditions for administrators after the fact should satisfy formula (12.13), namely:

$$\frac{\alpha_i g_i}{\beta_i} = \frac{\alpha_j g_j}{\beta_j}$$

After substituting $g_i^{(1)}$ into the equation, we get:

$$\frac{\alpha_i^{(1)2}}{c_i\beta_i} = \frac{\alpha_j^{(1)2}}{c_j\beta_j}(i \neq j, i, j = 1,2,\ldots,n) \tag{12.16}$$

The administrator's prior first-order optimal condition satisfies formula (12.8), namely:

$$\frac{\alpha_i^{(1)}\left(1-2\alpha_i^{(1)}\right)}{\beta_i c_i}=\frac{\alpha_j^{(1)}\left(1-2\alpha_j^{(1)}\right)}{\beta_j c_j}\left(i\neq j, i, j=1,2,\ldots,n\right) \tag{12.17}$$

If the allocation ratio $\alpha_i^{(1)}$ satisfies the requirement of dynamic consistency, it must satisfy both Equations (12.16) and (12.17), and there are the following two cases.

1 If the administrator adopts an egalitarianism policy, that is, $\beta_i=\beta_j\left(i,j=1,2,\ldots,n\right)$, the dynamic consistency of the policy can be achieved only when $c_i=c_j$. Since c_i describes the declaration cost of the manufacturer, which represents the manufacturer's emission reduction level, and the situation of $c_i=c_j$ would not occur generally. Under this situation $\alpha_i^{(1)}$ does not meet the requirements of dynamic consistency. That is to say, assuming that the manufacturer believes in the administrator's promise, but the administrator is not motivated to abide by the contract, naturally, the manufacturer will also anticipate the administrator's behavior, and will not believe the administrator's prior commitment. So manufacturers will inevitably act first. The requirement of dynamic consistency is only met when the allocation proportion $\alpha_i^{(2)}$ is adopted. To keep the $\alpha_i^{(1)}$ satisfactory to the requirements of dynamic consistency, a constraint mechanism that restricts administrator from changing the prior agreement at will must be established.

   At the same time, under the egalitarianism policy, $\alpha_i g_i=\alpha_j g_j$ can be obtained from formula (12.13), indicating that the carbon emissions allocated to each manufacturer are equal, which is obviously unreasonable, and will reduce motivation of manufacturers with high emissions but low emission reduction level in truthful report.

   In addition, if administrators do not keep their promises and violate prior agreements, they will also lose their "pioneer advantage". Assuming that administrators set the allocation ratio α_i^*, it can be known from the formula (12.14) that $\alpha_i^*>\beta_i$. If the administrator acts first, the declaration amount of the manufacturer can be obtained from the formula (12.3) as $g_i^{(1)}=\frac{p}{c_i}\cdot\alpha_i^*$; if administrators violate the prior agreement, the declared amount of the manufacturer is $g_i^{(2)}=\frac{p}{c_i}\beta_i$, and $g_i^{(1)}>g_i^{(2)}$, which indicates that the breach of contract by the administrators reduces the enthusiasm of the manufacturer to declare the real emissions.

2 If the administrator adopts a non-egalitarianism policy, that is, $\beta_i\neq\beta_j\left(i, j=1,2,\ldots,n\right)$.In this case, if $\beta_i c_i=\beta_j c_j$ and $\alpha_i^{(1)}=\alpha_j^{(1)}$ are satisfied at the same time, dynamic consistency of policy 1 can be achieved.

Among them, $\beta_i c_i = \beta_j c_j$ indicates that administrators would favor more when making allocation policies towards manufacturers that have stronger emission reduction level, lower reporting cost, and better reputation; $\alpha_i^{(1)} = \alpha_j^{(1)}$ indicates that the government will implement the same allocation ratio (which is in line with many current pollution emission policies) for all manufacturers.

From the above analysis, it can be seen that government administrators should pay attention to the following two points when designing the full free policy of carbon emission rights:

First, the administrators establish the allocation quota on the basis of the manufacturer's prior report. This allocation policy is dynamic and consistent. However, the above analysis shows that the declared amount of each manufacturer will create positive external effects on other manufacturers, which reduces the enthusiasm of manufacturers to truthfully report carbon emissions. At this time, the government must monitor the actual carbon emissions of manufacturers, which is in line with the current allocation policy in the EU emissions trading system. Such policy requires manufacturers to report the demand for carbon emissions, and then receive the verification of an independent verification agency before the quota of their carbon emission rights is allocated.

Second, if the administrators set the initial allocation quota of the carbon emission rights of each manufacturer in advance, in order to ensure the dynamic consistency of the allocation policy, attention should be paid to the implementation process of the allocation policy: ① The administrators must strictly abide by the prior agreement and not adjust allocation quota arbitrarily. Measures such as publicizing the allocation quota and formulating specific restraint systems can be taken to prevent administrators from breaching the contract afterwards. ② Administrators should set the same allocation quota, and should not set different allocation quotas because of the different carbon emission declarations of manufacturers, otherwise the implementation of emission reduction would be hindered. A same allocation ratio quota will help stimulate the enthusiasm of manufacturers to declare real carbon emissions, and is conducive to the realization of administrators' emission reduction goals. ③ Administrators has the responsibility to put an end to egalitarianism policy, and give more allocation policy supports to manufacturers with strong emission reduction capabilities and good reputation, which will help to stimulate the enthusiasm of manufacturers to actively reduce emissions.

12.4 Summary

This chapter introduces and compares the characteristics and allocation efficiency of three methods of initial allocation of carbon emission permits, namely full free, public auction and mixed allocation methods. With reference to the current international mature carbon emission rights allocation methods, the chapter concludes that in the initial period of China's carbon trade market, full free should be the main method, supplemented by a small-share auction allocation method.

At the first beginning, this chapter analyzes the negotiation dilemma of the allocation of carbon emission rights, and points out that in the current allocation of carbon emission rights in China, there will be games like Boxed Pigs Game, Prisoner's Dilemmas, Chicken Games, and Stag Hunt Model among regions, industries, and manufacturers. Then, the chapter proposes the principle of "common but differentiated responsibilities" for the allocation, and highlights the necessity to set a reasonable allocation quota of carbon emission rights. In addition, relevant allocation schemes should be trialed and then gradually promoted so as to effectively prevent the "free-rider" phenomenon in allocation. At last, the government should advocate the low carbon concept and guide manufacturers' awareness of cooperation in the allocation of carbon emission rights.

Under full free method, the setting of carbon emission rights allocation quota is usually realized by two methods. In the first method, the government administrators set the allocation quota of each manufacturer in advance, and then the manufacturers report their own carbon emission amounts, and finally the administrators adjust the quota. In the second method, the manufacturers report the carbon emissions in advance, and then the government administrators set the allocation quota. Also, dynamic consistency is an important indicator to test the effectiveness of government policies.

This chapter mainly analyzes the above allocation policies from the perspective of policy dynamic consistency, and draws the following conclusions:

First, government administrators are recommended to use the allocation policy where manufacturers report the required carbon emissions in advance, and then administrators formulate an allocation strategy for the proportion of carbon emission rights. This is in line with the dynamic consistency requirements of the policy. However, it would reduce the enthusiasm of manufacturers to truthfully report carbon emissions. Therefore, the government must strictly monitor the carbon emissions actually produced by manufacturers.

Second, if the government administrators set the initial allocation quota of the carbon emission rights of each manufacturer in advance, in order to ensure the dynamic consistency in the implementation of the allocation policy, the administrators must ensure that the allocation quota is the same and not adjusted arbitrarily. Meanwhile, the egalitarianism policy tendency must be eradicated, and more policy support should be given to manufacturers with strong emission reduction capacity and good reputation.

As a matter of fact, the allocation of carbon emission rights plays a crucial role in the operation of carbon trade. Instead of designing the allocation mechanism of carbon emission rights from the perspective of efficiency and fairness, this chapter analyzes allocation policies of carbon emission rights in terms of dynamic consistency. In the future, in-depth research on the optimal design of the allocation mechanism of carbon emission rights may continue.

Notes

1 Nie Li. On the mechanism construction of China's carbon trading market. *Modernization of Management*, 2012, 6: 55–57.
2 Since any monotonic transformation of the cobb–douglas utility function represents the same preference relationship, its logarithmic form is taken.
3 The superscript (1) represents Model 1, similarly (2) represents Model 2.
4 Zhou Jing, Sheng Zhaohan, He Jianmin. An analysis on the dynamic consistency of enterprise group policies based on dynamic game. *Journal of Management Sciences in China*, 2000, 6: 49–53.

References

Boemare, C., Quirion, P. Implementing greenhouse gas trading in Europe lessons from economic literature and international experiences. *Ecological Economics*, 2002, 43: 213–230.

Cramton, P., Kerr. S. Tradable carbon permit auctions: how and why to auction not grandfather. *Energy Policy*, 2002, 30: 333–345.

Fudenberg, D., Tirole, J. *Game theory*. Cambridge, MA: MIT Press, 1991.

Fullerton, D, Metcalf, G. Environmental controls, scarcity rents, and pre-existing distortions. *Journal of Public Economics*, 2001, 80: 249–267.

Lu Wei, Cui Liqin. Analysis on initial allocation model of tradable emission rights. *Chinese Journal of Environmental Management*, 2003, 5(22): 8–9.

Palfrey, T.R., Rosenthal, H. Underestimated probabilities that others free ride: an experimental test. Mimeo, California Institute of Technology and Carnegie-Mellon University, 1989.

13 Game analysis on carbon emissions trading price

13.1 Theoretical analysis on the factors affecting carbon emissions trading price

The trading prices discussed in this chapter are trading prices in the circulation market of carbon emission rights. The circulation market of carbon emissions rights is a secondary market for carbon emission rights trading, which is the core link of the carbon trading market. The essence of carbon emissions rights circulation is to share the responsibility of carbon dioxide emissions reduction effectively. As the first element of trading, the price of carbon emission rights is mainly affected by supply, demand, and market factors.

13.1.1 Supply and demand factors affecting the price of carbon emission rights[1]

Firms obtain carbon emission allowances allocated in the primary market. Thus, in the circulation of the secondary market, manufactures must weigh the marginal value of carbon emission rights to decide whether to achieve the goal of constraining carbon emission rights through their own emissions reduction or through market transactions. If the cost of reducing emissions by firms is higher, manufactures will lower reducing emissions and buy carbon emission rights; if the cost of reducing emissions by firms is lower, it will reduce more emissions and sell carbon emission rights. Through trading, an equilibrium price for carbon emission rights is achieved in the circulation market.

In a market with perfect competition, as shown in Figure 13.1, let the total carbon emission rights issued by the government at a certain stage (that is, the allowable carbon dioxide emissions) be denoted by G^*. Because the total amount of carbon emissions is constant over a period of time, the total supply curve of carbon emission rights is a straight vertical line denoted by S_0. The aggregate demand curve is denoted as D, which represents the total cost of emissions reduction. The y coordinate of the point of intersection between the aggregate supply curve S_0 and the aggregate demand curve D

DOI: 10.4324/9781003388500-17

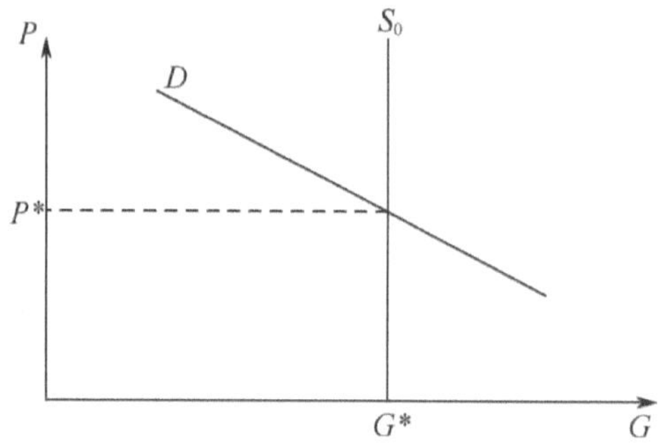

Figure 13.1 Equilibrium price under perfect competition

is the equilibrium price p^* in the carbon emissions trading market. Since the supply curve is perfectly inelastic, the price of carbon emission rights is determined by the position of the demand curve. The position of a demand curve is determined by the marginal abatement costs for firms. Firms with high emission reduction costs are willing to pay more for buying carbon emission rights, while firms with low emission reduction costs are willing to sell carbon emission rights, and finally a transaction is made. At this time, the marginal abatement costs of all firms are equal to the equilibrium price in the carbon emissions trading market.

13.1.1.1 Main supply factors affecting the price of carbon emission rights

The main factors affecting the supply of carbon emission rights include the allocation quota of carbon emission rights and the trading rules of carbon emission rights.

1 The allocation quota of carbon emission rights.
2 The allocation quota of carbon emission rights is the maximum carbon dioxide emissions that market participants are allowed to emit during the agreed emissions reduction trading period. The price of carbon emission rights is determined by the proportion of the allocated quota to the actual carbon emissions of market participants. If the quota is relatively smaller than the participants' actual carbon emissions, the demand will increase, and the price of carbon emission rights will rise; if the quota is relatively larger than the participants' actual carbon emissions, the demand will decrease, and the price of carbon emission rights will fall. In the European Union, for example, the National Allocation Plan (NAP) for European carbon emission rights in which all EU member states participate determines the allocation quota for each participating country.

The allocation plan is developed every few years, which has become the most important factor affecting supply in the long run.

3 Rules for carbon emissions trading.
4 The rules for carbon emissions trading affect the supply of carbon emission rights, which is mainly reflected in trading projects (Clean Development Mechanism [CDM] and Joint Implementation [JI]) and banking and borrowing systems.

Since the carbon emissions saved by CDM projects and JI projects established in the Kyoto Protocol can also be converted into the supply of carbon emission rights.

These two types of projects have also become factors affecting the supply of carbon emission rights. In theory, the more supply of carbon emission rights from these two types of projects, the lower the price; conversely, the less the supply, the higher the price. Due to the relatively small market scale of CDM projects and JI projects, they have little impact on the supply and price of carbon emission rights at the current stage. However, there is uncertainty in the future.

"Banking" means that the current surplus of carbon emission rights for market participants can be saved to the next period; "borrowing" means that market participants are allowed to use the carbon emission rights of the future period. Theoretically, if the banking system in the current period reduces the supply of carbon emission rights, the price of carbon emission rights will rise; if the borrowing system in the current period increases the supply of carbon emission rights, the price of carbon emission rights will fall. From the administrator's point of view, the banking and borrowing systems of carbon emission rights can prevent fluctuations in the price of carbon emission rights and therefore improve market efficiency. However, due to inconvenient supervision, uncertainty, and risk, the EU emissions trading system prohibits the banking and borrowing of carbon emission rights at the first stage.

13.1.1.2 The main demand factors affecting the price of carbon emission rights

The demand for carbon emission rights is reflected in the estimation of expected carbon emissions, which is mainly affected by factors such as economic growth, marginal abatement costs, and expectations on future prices for carbon emission rights.

1 Economic growth

   Most studies show that economic growth leads to an increase in carbon emissions. Under constraints on total carbon emissions, if the total supply of carbon emissions remains unchanged, the increase in demand for carbon emissions will shift the demand curve *D* upward and the price of carbon emission rights will increase; conversely, the price will decrease.

2 Marginal abatement costs
3 Marginal abatement costs are mainly determined by low-carbon technologies. Long-term marginal abatement costs are usually determined by low-carbon energy equipment and technology investments; short-term marginal abatement costs and demand for carbon emissions are mainly affected by unpredictable energy prices and demand, such as short-term price fluctuations of oil, natural gas, and coal, which affect the price of carbon emission rights. In addition, studies have shown that factors such as extreme weather can also cause fluctuations in energy demand and therefore affect the price of carbon emission rights. Since the majority of carbon dioxide emissions are related to the use of fossil energy, the only way to achieve short-term emission reduction is the transition of marginal abatement costs from high carbon to low carbon. If fossil energy can only be replaced by another fossil energy with higher carbon content, the increase in its price in the short term will lead to an increase in the demand for carbon emissions, thereby increasing the price of carbon emission rights.
4 Expectation factors
5 Expectations of the future price of carbon emission rights will affect the price of carbon emission rights in the current period. The future price of carbon emission rights depends mainly on market supply and demand situation and changes in demand. The dynamic efficiency of the carbon trading market will gradually reduce the marginal abatement cost, while the carbon dioxide emission reduction set by the government authority shows an increasing trend. The decrease in marginal abatement costs will reduce the demand for carbon emission rights trading, while the increase in carbon dioxide emission reductions will reduce the supply of carbon emission rights. In this way, market participants have different expectations on the price changes in carbon emission rights due to different expectations on emission reduction technologies and total emission reductions. If market participants expect the price of carbon emission rights to rise in the future, they will store a certain amount of carbon emission rights for future sales through allowance banking projects, which will lead to a reduction in the supply of carbon emission rights in the current period and an increase in the price; on the contrary, if market participants expect that the price of carbon emission rights will decrease in the future, they will reduce the purchase of carbon emission rights in the current period, resulting in an increase in supply and a decrease in price.

13.1.2 Market transaction factors that affect the price of carbon emission rights

In actual transactions, the conditions of zero transaction cost, a large number of buyers and sellers, and complete information required by a perfectly competitive market cannot be satisfied. Therefore, transaction costs and market powers will have an impact on the trading price of carbon emission rights in an imperfect competition market.

13.1.2.1 Transaction costs

Incomplete information, frictions, and inactive transactions are common in the carbon emissions trading market, which creates transaction costs.

As for the definition of transaction costs, new institutional economists have different interpretations. The first view is that transaction costs are the fees paid for acquiring, protecting, and transferring property rights; the second view is that transaction costs are the costs for the operation of the economic system; and the third view regards all costs other than those in the Robinson's world as transaction costs. Coase (1960) theorized that transactions via market mechanisms incur cost, and he believed that transaction costs include four aspects:

(1) The activity cost of finding and determining an appropriate trade price
(2) The cost of determining the responsibility of the contractor
(3) Risk costs related to accepting the contract
(4) The cost of engaging in market trade

Transaction costs can be divided into market transaction costs, management transaction costs, and political transaction costs, where market transaction costs include search and information costs, bargaining and decision-making costs, policing, and enforcement costs; management transaction costs include the cost of establishing, maintaining, and changing the organizational structure, operating costs, information costs, transportation costs of goods and services; and political transaction costs include the cost of establishing, maintaining, and changing the system of formal and informal political organizations and operating costs of the political system. At the same time, it is not easy to measure the transaction cost, but such cost can be replaced by the difference between the selling price and the purchase price of products in the market.

The transaction cost is a key factor determining the success of carbon emission trading. Gangadharan (2000) studied the emissions trading market in Los Angeles in 1994 and found that the transaction cost had a significant impact on the initial emissions trading, with 32% of the emissions trading failed due to high transaction costs. Both Stavins's (1995) and Cason and Gandgadharan's (2003) research works show that in emissions trading, the presence of transaction costs makes the marginal administrative costs of the firm not equal to the market price of emissions, which affects the efficiency of emissions trading, and thereby makes actual emissions trading much less than the theoretical value. Generally, the high transaction costs are mainly caused by the technical problems in emissions reduction and the unreasonable emissions trading system. The transaction cost will increase the total cost in emission reduction of firms, thereby reducing the possibility of emissions trading.

Figure 13.2 shows the impact of transaction costs on carbon emissions trading and the trading price. The horizontal axis represents carbon emissions and the vertical axis represents marginal abatement costs. The curves MC_A and MC_B represent the marginal cost curves of two firms A and B, respectively. When the transaction cost is zero, the equilibrium point of the transaction is E. At this time, the marginal abatement costs of the manufactures A and B are equal and the transaction volume is G_0. If there is a transaction cost, assuming that the trading volume is G_2 when the transaction occurs, then firm A sells the carbon emissions $(G_2 - G_1)$ at the unit price $\underline{P}$ (the carbon emission in the initial state is denoted as G_1), and the firm B buys the carbon emissions at the unit price $\overline{P}$. $\overline{P} - \underline{P}$ is the transaction cost per unit of carbon emission rights. At this time, compared with the equilibrium price P, the abatement cost will increase by $(\overline{P} - \underline{P})(G_2 - G_1)$, which is the square area in the figure. At the same time, the existence of transaction cost prevents the transaction where the marginal abatement cost differences between firms are less than the transaction costs.

13.1.2.2 Market power

In the actual carbon emissions trading, it is very likely that large-scale firms or monopolies affect the price of carbon emission rights through their

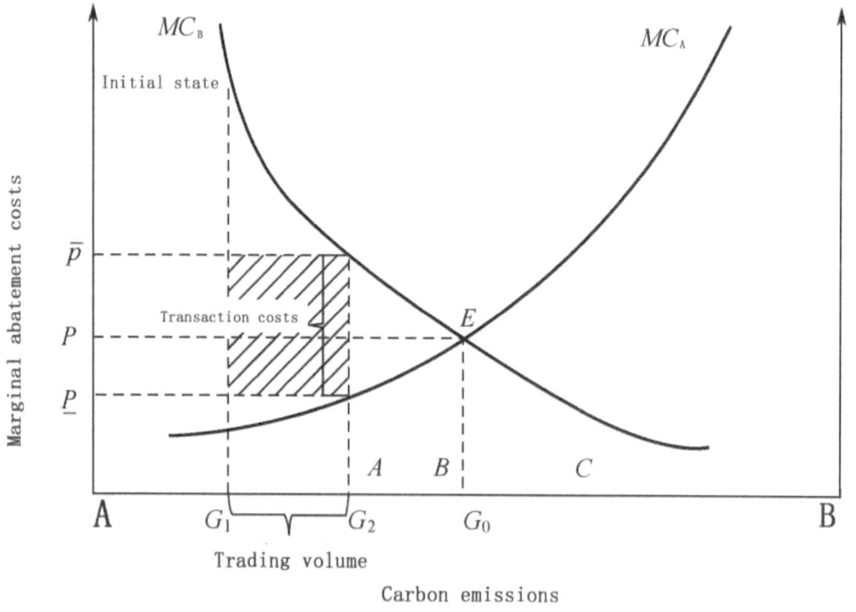

Figure 13.2 Effects of transaction costs on transaction prices

own buying and selling behavior, which is the so-called market power. The influence of these firms on the price of carbon emission rights is mainly manifested in two scenarios: the first scenario is the profit maximization goal, that is, the firm wants to minimize the abatement cost and the cost of purchasing carbon emission rights; the second scenario is the goal of exclusivity, that is, firms use prices to prevent other firms from entering the carbon emissions trading market.

Figure 13.3 illustrates the impact of market power on the price of carbon emission rights. Assuming there is a monopoly firm in the market that obtains more carbon emission rights in the initial allocation, it will affect the price of carbon emission rights through buying and selling behavior. As shown in Figure 13.3, the horizontal axis represents the amount of carbon emission rights and the vertical axis represents the price of carbon emission rights. Firms will choose the supply G' of carbon emission rights where MC is equal to MR to maximize their own profits, then the market price of unit carbon emission rights is P', which is higher than the market price P under perfect competition. As can be seen from the figure, in a monopoly situation, the deviation of the supply and price of carbon emission rights from the perfectly competitive market equilibrium depends on the slope of the monopolist's marginal cost curve.

If a monopolist firm wants to prevent other firms from entering the carbon emissions trading market, it will bank carbon emission rights. As shown in Figure 13.4, the firm does not provide the remaining carbon emission rights, which will greatly reduce the supply of carbon emission rights, and

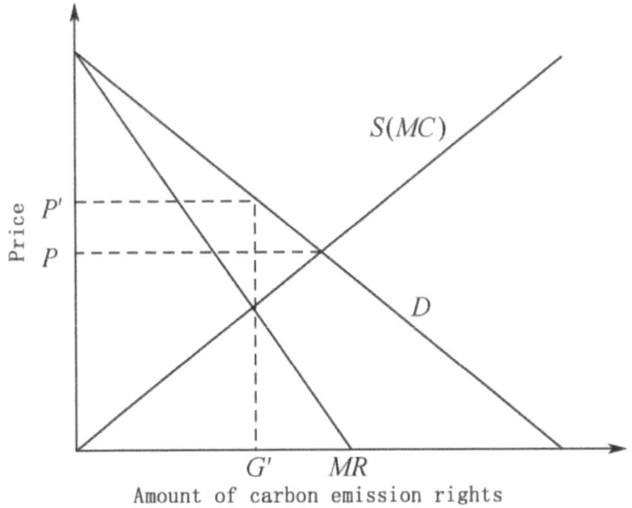

Figure 13.3 The first scenario of the influence of market power: profit maximization

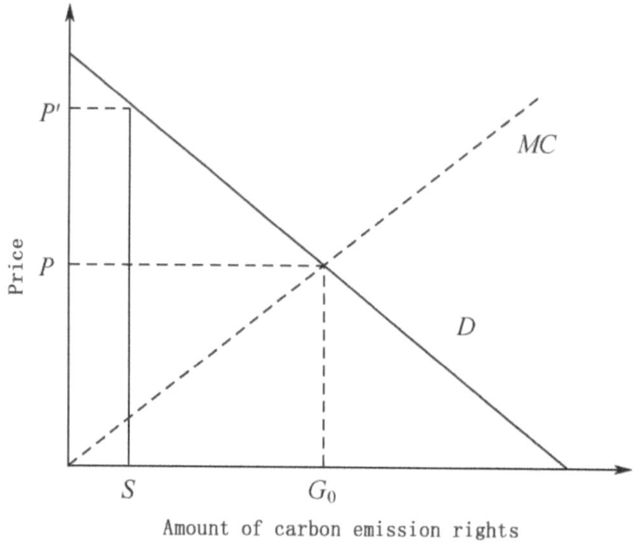

Figure 13.4 The second scenario of the influence of market power: exclusivity

therefore increase the price of carbon emission rights, and ultimately reduce the efficiency of carbon emissions trading.

13.2 Bargaining game analysis on prices of directly purchased carbon emission rights

At present, China's carbon emissions trading lack a perfect price guidance system. For example, the most popular CDM project in China lacks reasonable price guidance, resulting in the transaction price of carbon emissions trading in China being far lower than the average level of the international carbon trading market. Therefore, the research on the bargaining behavior of prices of carbon emission rights under direct purchasing behavior may provide suggestions for the construction of China's carbon trading market and the management of prices of carbon emission rights.

The model in this section is based on the direct purchasing behavior among firms. Since the price of carbon emission rights is greatly affected by multiple market factors, firms usually sign contracts to eliminate the price fluctuations of carbon emission rights. In the process of contracting, both buyers and sellers negotiate on the price of carbon emission rights. This section adopts the idea of Rubinstein bargaining model to establish a bargaining model for the price of carbon emission rights under direct purchasing behavior and analyzes the bargaining process between buyers and sellers with incomplete information. The low transaction price of CDM projects in China is explained and corresponding policy suggestions are proposed in this section.

13.2.1 Establishment of bargaining game model

It is assumed that in the carbon emissions trading market, both buyers and sellers tend to complete transactions by signing contracts. In order to make a transaction, both parties mainly negotiate on the unit price of carbon emission rights and the amount of carbon emission rights. Assuming that the amount q of carbon emission rights traded is a fixed value, both parties only bargain over the unit price p of carbon emission rights.

Assuming ω_b and ω_s represent the buyers' and sellers' expectations on the unit price of carbon emission rights in the future, respectively, if $\omega_b < \omega_s$, the buyer's expectation on the price of carbon emission right is less than that of the seller, no transaction can be made. If $\omega_b \geq \omega_s$, the transaction is possible. Therefore, the conclusion of the contract mainly depends on the buyers' and the sellers' expectations on the unit price of carbon emission rights in the future. In this section, the bargaining process of both parties under the condition of $\omega_b \geq \omega_s$ is mainly studied.

We suppose ω_b and ω_s are both private information, that is, ω_b represents the type of buyers while ω_s represents the type of sellers, and both ω_b and ω_s obey a uniform distribution between a and b.

In the negotiation process, the bids of both parties are not simultaneous. Often, one party offers a price and the other party chooses to accept or reject it. In the event of rejection, the other party may give another price for further negotiation until the end of the negotiation (Myerson, 2001). Moreover, both the buyers and the sellers can learn in bargaining process (Shiyu Xie, 2002).They will estimate the other party's expectation on the price of carbon emission rights according to the other party's bid and behaviors, that is, the seller will offer a price p_s first and the buyer will revise its initial estimate on ω_s. ω_s will be considered to obey a uniform distribution on the interval [a, p_s].

Suppose this is an n-stage bargaining game (n is an exogenous variable) and the seller and the buyer take turns making bids. The seller offers a price p_1^s at the first stage and the buyer chooses to accept or reject. If the buyer accepts, the negotiation ends, and the seller's benefit is $\left(p_1^s - \omega_s\right)q$, while the buyer's profit will be $\left(\omega_b - p_1^s\right)q$. If the buyer rejects, the game enters the second stage, where the buyer offers a price p_1^b, and the seller chooses to accept or reject. If the seller accepts, the negotiation ends. Since the negotiation is concluded at the second stage, both parties will lose corresponding profits. Let δ_s and δ_b be the discount factors of the seller and the buyer, respectively ($0 < \delta_s < 1, 0 < \delta_b < 1$), then the seller's profit is $\delta_s\left(p_1^b - \omega_s\right)q$ and the buyer's profit is $\delta_b\left(\omega_b - p_1^b\right)q$. If the seller rejects, the game enters the third stage. Both parties take turns offering prices until the nth stage of the game.

The structure of the game depends on the parity of n. If n is an odd number, then the seller offers a price $p^s_{\frac{n+1}{2}}$ at the nth stage, and the negotiation

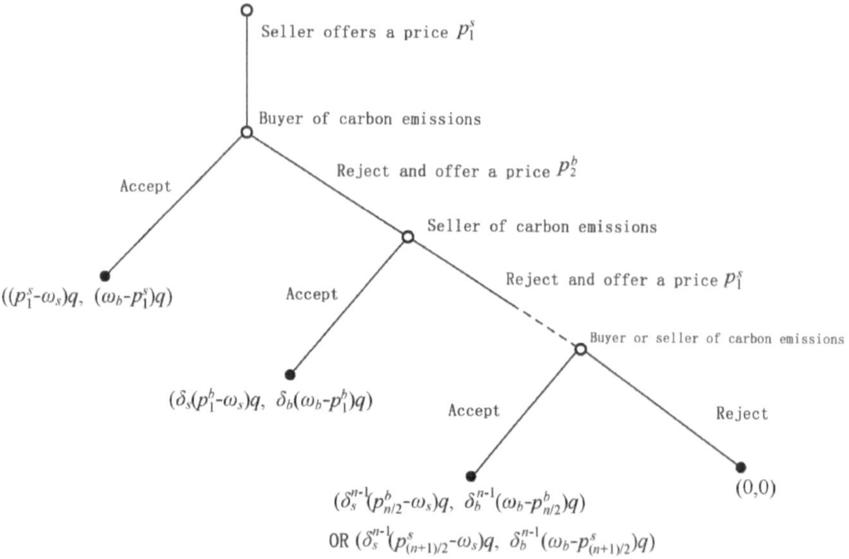

Figure 13.5 Extended form representation of the n-stage bargaining game

ends whether the buyer accepts or not. If the buyer accepts, the seller's profit is $\delta_s^{n-1}\left(p_{\frac{n+1}{2}}^s-\omega_s\right)q$ and the buyer's profit is $\delta_b^{n-1}\left(\omega_b-p_{\frac{n+1}{2}}^s\right)q$. If the buyer rejects, both parties get zero profits. If n is an even number, the buyer offers a price $p_{\frac{n}{2}}^b$ at the nth stage, and the negotiation ends whether the seller accepts or not. If the seller accepts, then the seller's profit is $\delta_s^{n-1}\left(p_{\frac{n}{2}}^b-\omega_s\right)q$ and the buyer's profit is $\delta_b^{n-1}\left(\omega_b-p_{\frac{n}{2}}^b\right)q$. If the seller rejects, both parties get zero profits.

The expanded form of this game is shown in Figure 13.5.

13.2.2 Game model solution

13.2.2.1 Two-stage bargaining game with $n = 2$

Assuming the probability of the buyer accepting the price proposed by the seller is p_{ba} at the first stage of negotiation, the probability of the buyer rejecting the proposed price at the first stage but the seller accepting it at the second stage is p_{br}; the probability of the seller accepting the price proposed by the buyer at the second stage of negotiation is p_{sa} and the probability of the seller rejecting the buyer's proposed price is p_{sr}.

In terms of the seller's strategic choice at the second stage (assuming that the buyer rejects the seller's proposed price at the first stage), since there is no opportunity for subsequent bargaining, the seller gets zero profit if he chooses to reject, and if the seller chooses to accept, the profit will be $\delta_s\left(p_1^b-\omega_s\right)q$. As long as $\delta_s\left(p_1^b-\omega_s\right)q \geq 0$, the seller will certainly choose to accept, that is:

$$p_1^b \geq \omega_s \tag{13.1}$$

Next, we solve the buyer's proposed price at this stage. The buyer knows the seller's selection criteria at this stage (that is Equation (13.1), and the buyer judges that the seller's expectation on the price of carbon emission right is in line with the uniform distribution on the interval $\left[a, p_1^s\right]$. Therefore, the buyer's proposed price p_1^b should satisfy the following equation:

$$\max_{p_1^b}\left[\delta_b\left(\omega_b-p_1^b\right)qp_{sa}+0p_{sr}\right] \tag{13.2}$$

Wherein:

$$p_{sa}=p\left\{p_1^b \geqslant \omega_s\right\}=\frac{p_1^b-a}{p_1^s-a}$$

$$p_{sr}=p\left\{p_1^b < \omega_s\right\}=\frac{p_1^s-p_1^b}{p_1^s-a}$$

Substituting them into Equation (13.2), and we have:

$$\max_{p_1^b}\left[\delta_b\left(\omega_b-p_1^b\right)q\frac{p_1^b-a}{p_1^s-a}\right] \tag{13.3}$$

From the first-order condition, we get:

$$p_1^b=\frac{a+\omega_b}{2} \tag{13.4}$$

Thus, the seller's profit is $\frac{\delta_s q}{2}\left(a+\omega_b-2\omega_s\right)$ and the buyer's profit is $\frac{\delta_b q}{2}\left(\omega_b-a\right)$.

At the first stage, if the buyer accepts the seller's proposed price at the first stage, the profit is $\left(\omega_b-p_1^s\right)q$. As long as $\left(\omega_b-p_1^s\right)q \geq \frac{\delta_b q}{2}\left(\omega_b-a\right)$, that is, when $\omega_b \geq \frac{2p_1^s-\delta_b a}{2-\delta_b}$, the buyer will choose to accept the proposal. The seller also knows the buyer's decision-making process, so the seller's proposed price p_1^s at the first stage should satisfy:

$$\max_{p_1^p}\left[\left(p_1^s-\omega_s\right)qp_{ba}+\frac{\delta_s q}{2}(a+\omega_b-2\omega_s)\,p_{br}\right] \tag{13.5}$$

Wherein:

$$p_{ba}=p\left\{\omega_b\geq\frac{2p_1^s-\delta_b a}{2-\delta_b}\right\}=\frac{2\left(b-p_1^s\right)-\delta_b(b-a)}{(2-\delta_b)(b-a)}$$

$$p_{br}=p\left\{\omega_b<\frac{2p_1^s-\delta_b a}{2-\delta_b}\right\}p_{sa}=\frac{2\left(p_1^b-a\right)}{(2-\delta_b)(b-a)}$$

Substituting them into Equation (13.5), and we have:

$$\max_{p_1^s}\left[\left(p_1^s-\omega_s\right)q\frac{2\left(b-p_1^s\right)-\delta_b(b-a)}{(2-\delta_b)(b-a)}+\frac{\delta_s q}{2}(a+\omega_b-2\omega_s)\frac{2\left(p_1^b-a\right)}{(2-\delta_b)(b-a)}\right]$$

From the first-order condition, we get:

$$p_1^s=\frac{(2-\delta_b)(b-a)+2\omega_s+2a}{4} \tag{13.6}$$

To sum up, the perfect Bayesian Nash equilibrium of this game is:

At the first stage, the seller offers a price $p_1^s=\frac{(2-\delta_b)(b-a)+2\omega_s+2a}{4}$. If the buyer's expectation is $\omega_b\geq\frac{2p_1^s-\delta_b a}{2-\delta_b}$, then the buyer accepts the offer p_1^s; otherwise, the buyer rejects the offer and the negotiation enters the second stage.

At the second stage, the buyer offers a price $p_1^b=\frac{a+\omega_b}{2}$. If the seller's expectation is $\omega_s\leq p_1^b$, then the seller accepts the offer p_1^b; otherwise, the offer is rejected and the negotiation ends.

13.2.2.2 Three-stage bargaining game with n = 3

Assuming the probability of the buyer accepting the price proposed by the seller is p_{ba} at the first stage of negotiation, the probability of the buyer rejecting it at the first stage but the seller accepting the proposed price at the second stage is p_{br}; the probability of the seller accepting the price proposed by the buyer at the second stage of negotiation is p_{sa} and the probability of the seller rejecting at the second stage but the buyer accepting the proposed price at the third stage is p_{sr}; the probability of the buyer accepting the seller's proposed price at the third stage of negotiation is p_{ba}' and the probability of the buyer rejecting the seller's proposed price at the third stage is p_{br}'.

In terms of the buyer's strategic choice at the third stage (assuming that the seller rejects the buyer's proposed price at the second stage), since there is no opportunity for subsequent bargaining, the buyer gets zero profit if he chooses to reject. If the buyer chooses to accept, the profit will be $\delta_b^2\left(\omega_b - p_2^s\right)q$. As long as $\delta_b^2\left(\omega_b - p_2^s\right)q \geq 0$, the buyer will certainly choose to accept, that is:

$$p_2^s \leq \omega_b \tag{13.7}$$

Next, we solve the seller's proposed price at this stage. The seller knows the buyer's selection criteria at this stage [that is Equation (13.7)], and the seller judges that the buyer's expectation on the price of carbon emission rights is in line with the uniform distribution on the interval $\left[p_1^b, p_1^s\right]$. Therefore, the seller's proposed price p_2^s should satisfy the following equation:

$$\max_{p_2^s}\left[\delta_s^2\left(p_2^s - \omega_s\right)qp'_{ba} + 0\,p'_{br}\right] \tag{13.8}$$

Wherein:

$$p'_{ba} = p\left\{p_2^s \leq \omega_b\right\} = \frac{p_1^s - p_2^s}{p_1^s - p_1^b}$$

$$p'_{br} = p\left\{p_2^s > \omega_b\right\} = \frac{p_2^s - p_1^b}{p_1^s - p_1^b}$$

Substituting them into Equation (13.8), and we have:

$$\max_{p_2^s}\left[\delta_s^2\left(p_2^s - \omega_s\right)q\frac{p_1^s - p_2^s}{p_1^s - p_1^b}\right] \tag{13.9}$$

From the first-order condition, we get:

$$p_2^s = \frac{p_1^s + \omega_s}{2} \tag{13.10}$$

Thus, the seller's profit is $\frac{\delta_s^2 q}{2}\left(p_1^s - \omega_s\right)$ and the buyer's profit is $\frac{\delta_b^2 q}{2}\left(2\omega_b - p_1^s - \omega_s\right)$.

In terms of the seller's strategic selection at the second stage, if the seller accepts the buyer's proposed price at the second stage, the profit is $\delta_s\left(p_1^b - \omega_s\right)q$. As long as $\delta_s\left(p_1^b - \omega_s\right)q \geq \frac{\delta_s^2 q}{2}\left(p_1^s - \omega_s\right)$, the seller will choose to accept the proposal, that is:

$$\omega_s \leq \frac{2p_1^b - \delta_s p_1^s}{2 - \delta_s} \tag{13.11}$$

The buyer also knows the seller's decision-making process, and the buyer judges that the seller's expectation on the price of carbon emission right is in line with the uniform distribution on the interval $\left[a, p_1^s\right]$. Therefore, the buyer's proposed price p_1^b at the second stage should satisfy:

$$\max_{p_1^b}\left[\delta_b\left(\omega_b - p_1^b\right)q \cdot p_{sa} + \frac{\delta_b^2 q}{2}\left(2\omega_b - p_1^s - \omega_s\right) \cdot p_{sr}\right] \tag{13.12}$$

Wherein:

$$p_{sa} = p\left\{\omega_s \le \frac{2p_1^b - \delta_s p_1^s}{2-\delta_s}\right\} = \frac{2\left(p_1^b - a\right) - \delta_s\left(p_1^s - a\right)}{\left(2-\delta_s\right)\left(p_1^s - a\right)}$$

$$p_{sr} = p\left\{\omega_s > \frac{2p_1^b - \delta_s p_1^s}{2-\delta_s}\right\} \cdot p'_{ba} = \frac{2\left(p_1^s - p_2^s\right)}{\left(2-\delta_s\right)\left(p_1^s - a\right)}$$

Substituting them into Equation (13.12), and we have:

$$\max_{p_1^b}\left[\begin{array}{l}\delta_b\left(\omega_b - p_1^b\right)q\dfrac{2\left(p_1^b - a\right) - \delta_s\left(p_1^s - a\right)}{\left(2-\delta_s\right)\left(p_1^s - a\right)} + \\ \dfrac{\delta_b^2 q}{2}\left(2\omega_b - p_1^s - \omega_s\right)\dfrac{2\left(p_1^s - p_2^s\right)}{\left(2-\delta_s\right)\left(p_1^s - a\right)}\end{array}\right] \tag{13.13}$$

From the first-order condition, we get:

$$p_1^b = \frac{2a + 2\omega_b + \delta_s\left(p_1^s - a\right)}{4} \tag{13.14}$$

Therefore, the seller's profit is:

$$\frac{\delta_s q}{4}\left[2a + 2\omega_b + \delta_s\left(p_1^s - a\right) - 4\omega_s\right]$$

The buyer's profit is:

$$\frac{\delta_b q}{4}\left[2\omega_b - 2a - \delta_s\left(p_1^s - a\right)\right]$$

At the first stage, if the buyer accepts the price proposed by the seller, the profit will be $\left(\omega_b - p_1^s\right)q$ as long as:

$$\left(\omega_b - p_1^s\right)q \ge \frac{\delta_b q}{4}\left[2\omega_b - 2a - \delta_s\left(p_1^s - a\right)\right]$$

The buyer will choose to accept the offer, that is:

$$\omega_b \geq \frac{(4-\delta_b\delta_s)\,p_1^s - a\delta_b(2-\delta_s)}{4-2\delta_b} \tag{13.15}$$

The seller also knows the buyer's decision-making process, so the seller's proposed price p_1^s at the first stage should satisfy:

$$\max_{p_1^s}\left\{\left(p_1^s-\omega_s\right)qp_{ba}+\frac{\delta_s q}{4}\left[2a+2\omega_b+\delta_s\left(p_1^s-a\right)-4\omega_s\right]p_{br}\right\} \tag{13.16}$$

Wherein:

$$\begin{aligned} P_{ba} &= p\left\{\omega_b \geq \frac{(4-\delta_b\delta_s)\,p_1^s - a\delta_b(2-\delta_s)}{4-2\delta_b}\right\} \\ &= \frac{(4-2\delta_b)b-(4-\delta_b\delta_s)\,p_1^s + a\delta_b(2-\delta_s)}{(4-2\delta_b)(b-a)} \end{aligned}$$

$$\begin{aligned} P_{br} &= p\left\{\omega_b < \frac{(4-\delta_b\delta_s)\,p_1^s - a\delta_b(2-\delta_s)}{4-2\delta_b}\right\}\cdot p_{sa} \\ &= \frac{(4-\delta_b\delta_s)\left[2\left(p_1^b-a\right)-\delta_s\left(p_1^s-a\right)\right]}{(4-2\delta_b)(b-a)} \end{aligned}$$

Substituting them into Equation (13.16), and we have:

$$\begin{aligned} \max_{p_1^s}\{&\left(p_1^s-\omega_s\right)q\frac{(4-2\delta_b)b-(4-\delta_b\delta_s)\,p_1^s + a\delta_b(2-\delta_s)}{(4-2\delta_b)(b-a)} \\ &+\frac{\delta_s q}{4}\left[2a+2\omega_b+\delta_s\left(p_1^s-a\right)-4\omega_s\right] \\ &\frac{(4-\delta_b\delta_s)\left[2\left(p_1^b-a\right)-\delta_s\left(p_1^s-a\right)\right]}{(4-2\delta_b)(b-a)}\} \end{aligned} \tag{13.17}$$

From the first-order condition, we get:

$$\begin{aligned} p_1^s = &\frac{4(2-\delta_b)(b-a)}{(4-\delta_b\delta_s)\left(4+\delta_s^3\right)}+\frac{a\left(\delta_s^3-2\delta_s^2+2\right)}{4+\delta_s^3}+\frac{2\left(1+\delta_s^2\right)}{4+\delta_s^3}\omega_s \\ &+\frac{\delta_s^2}{4+\delta_s^3}\left(p_1^b-\omega_b\right) \end{aligned} \tag{13.18}$$

To sum up, the perfect Bayesian Nash equilibrium of this game is:

At the first stage, the seller offers a price $p_1^s = \frac{4(2-\delta_b)(b-a)}{(4-\delta_b\delta_s)(4+\delta_s^3)} + \frac{a(\delta_s^3 - 2\delta_s^2 + 2)}{4+\delta_s^3} + \frac{2(1+\delta_s^2)}{4+\delta_s^3}\omega_s + \frac{\delta_s^2}{4+\delta_s^3}(p_1^b - \omega_b)$. If the buyer's expectation is $\omega_b \geq \frac{(4-\delta_b\delta_s)p_1^s - a\delta_b(2-\delta_s)}{4-2\delta_b}$, then the buyer accepts the offer p_1^s. Otherwise, the offer will be rejected and the negotiation will enter the second stage.

At the second stage, the buyer offers a price $p_1^b = \frac{2a + 2\omega_b + \delta_s(p_1^s - a)}{4}$. If the seller's expectation is $\omega_s \leq \frac{2p_1^b - \delta_s p_1^s}{2-\delta_s}$, then the seller accepts the offer p_1^b; otherwise, the offer is rejected and the negotiation enters the third stage.

At the third stage, the seller offers a price $p_2^s = \frac{p_1^s + \omega_s}{2}$. If the buyer's expectation is $\omega_b \geq p_2^s$, the buyer accepts the offer p_2^s; otherwise, the offer is rejected and the negotiation ends.

By analogy, a perfect Bayesian Nash equilibrium for any given $n < \infty$ can be obtained. Similarly, the bargaining game in which the buyer offers a price in advance can be solved.

13.2.3 Analysis and recommendations of game equilibrium

1 In the two-stage bargaining game, it can be concluded from Equations (13.4) and (13.6) that:

$$\frac{\partial p_1^s}{\partial \omega_s} = \frac{1}{2} > 0, \frac{\partial p_1^b}{\partial \omega_b} = \frac{1}{2} > 0$$

In the three-stage bargaining game, it can be obtained from Equations (13.10), (13.14), and (13.18) that:

$$\frac{\partial p_2^s}{\partial \omega_s} = \frac{1}{2} > 0, \frac{\partial p_1^b}{\partial \omega_b} = \frac{1}{2} > 0, \frac{\partial p_1^s}{\partial \omega_s} = \frac{2(1+\delta_s^2)}{4+\delta_s^3} > 0$$

This shows that the offers of both parties are increasing functions of their own price expectations. If their expected prices are higher, the offers will be higher; otherwise, if their expected prices are lower, the offers will be lower. The price expectations of both parties mainly depend on two main factors: the understanding of the transaction status and real-time offers in the carbon trading market, and the invested cost, such as the cost in the application of low-carbon technology and transaction expenses.

2 In the two-stage bargaining game, from Equation (13.6), we conclude that:

$$\frac{\partial p_1^s}{\partial \delta_b} = -\frac{b-a}{4} < 0$$

In the three-stage bargaining game, we have:

$$\frac{\partial p_1^s}{\partial \delta_b} = \frac{4(\delta_s - 2)}{(4 - \delta_b \delta_s)^2} < 0$$

This suggests that the seller's offer is a decreasing function of the buyer's discount factor. Higher δ_b indicates lower cost and high level of patience of the buyer as well as lower offer of the seller.

From Equation (13.14), we have:

$$\frac{\partial p_1^b}{\partial \delta_s} = \frac{p_1^s - a}{4} > 0$$

This suggests that the buyer's offer is an increasing function of the seller's discount factor δ_s. Lower δ_s indicates higher cost and low level of patience of the seller as well as lower offer of the buyer. The discount factor is mainly affected by factors such as market efficiency, transaction costs, and transaction awareness.

3 In the two-stage bargaining game, from Equation (13.6), we conclude that:

$$\frac{\partial p_1^s}{\partial (b-a)} = \frac{2-\delta_b}{4} > 0$$

In the three-stage bargaining game, from Equation (13.18), we conclude that:

$$\frac{\partial p_1^s}{\partial (b-a)} = \frac{4(2-\delta_b)}{(4-\delta_b\delta_s)(4+\delta_s^3)} > 0$$

This suggests that the seller's offer is an increasing function of (*b*-*a*). The smaller the (*b*-*a*) is, the lower the seller's offer will be; conversely, the larger the (*b*-*a*) is, the higher the seller's offer will be. The (*a*, *b*) is a prediction interval of both parties based on the real-time bidding in the carbon emissions trading market. If the transparency of the carbon trading market is higher and the information is more complete, the distance between *a* and *b* will be larger; otherwise, the distance between *a* and *b* will be smaller.

From Equations (13.14) and (13.10), we conclude that:

$$\frac{\partial p_1^b}{\partial p_1^s} = \frac{\delta_s}{4} > 0, \frac{\partial p_2^s}{\partial p_1^s} = \frac{1}{2} > 0$$

It shows that the offers of both parties are increasing functions of the seller's first offer. That is, the final transaction price depends on the price of the first bidder. Therefore, the bargaining transaction of carbon emission rights is characterized by the first-mover advantage, and the first mover has the upper hand.

According to the above game models, in project transactions, the current transaction price of carbon emission rights in China is not only affected by negotiation skills, such as the first-mover advantage of offer, and the level of patience in negotiation, but also by the construction level of the carbon trading market, such as the incomplete information of the carbon trading market, market supervision (trading rules, systems), application of low-carbon technologies, and trading awareness and low-carbon idea of buyers and sellers.

Take CDM project transactions in China as an example. First of all, although many CDM project transactions have been completed successfully in China, most of them are initiated by buyers abroad through voluntary negotiations. These buyers are scattered in various industries and cities, so they have the first-mover advantage of transactions and the initiative in carbon pricing.

Second, China's current situation of productivity, energy structure, and development stage determine that most enterprises in China adopt high-carbon production mode, and the low-carbon technologies relatively lag behind. Meanwhile, Chinese enterprises generally lack the awareness of carbon trading, and they haven't recognized that carbon emission rights are financial assets. Therefore, Chinese enterprises generally have low price expectations and ignore the cost factors in the transaction (because many enterprises involved in CDM project transactions in China believe that they can make profits if the transaction is successful, and they have nothing to lose if the transaction is not successful), so buyers abroad will push down the price even lower (lower than the expected market price).

Last but not least, China's CDM market is fragmented, neither open nor transparent, and the majority of enterprises have little knowledge of the carbon market, which results in information asymmetry and incompletion. The large information gap puts Chinese enterprises in a weaker negotiating position, which causes the final transaction price of CDM projects in China far lower than the price in the international carbon emissions trading market, and Chinese enterprises suffer losses. Therefore, the Chinese government has to set a minimum price for CDM projects to regulate the transactions.

Therefore, in the carbon emissions trading process, China must speed up the construction of a unified and open carbon trading market, which incorporates both project transaction and allowance transaction. Although pilot carbon emissions trading markets have been set up in seven provinces and municipalities in China, these markets are scattered and isolated, and the trading rules vary among markets, which have prevented many large cross-regional enterprise groups from joining the market. It affects the enthusiasm of enterprises to participate in the trading. The establishment of the unified and open carbon emission trading market can improve the transparency of the carbon emissions trading market, build a fair trading platform for traders, and establish effective information channels, which is conducive to reducing transaction costs, maintaining the stability of the price of carbon emission rights, establishing effective channels of transaction information, and improving trading efficiency.

At the same time, we should enhance the publicity of the low-carbon concept and raise enterprises' awareness of carbon emissions trading. In the future, carbon will be an asset. Enterprises should alter the outdated production characterized by high carbon emissions and high energy consumption and improve the initiative and motivation for trading. Only in this way can enterprises develop. In addition, both parties will have higher expectations of the price of carbon emission rights, which is conducive to the healthy development of the price of carbon emission rights.

13.3 Research on the pricing of carbon emission rights under the influence of market power

13.3.1 Significance of research

Among the factors that affect the price of carbon emission rights, market power is very likely to occur in the development of the carbon trading market. For example, in the establishment of an international carbon market after the signing of the Kyoto Protocol, market power has emerged as an important factor affecting prices. The carbon dioxide emissions targets specified in the first phase (1997–2012) of the implementation of the Kyoto Protocol were based on the emissions levels in 1997, and the five-year development led to changes in the economic circumstances of all participating countries, making their respective carbon emissions also different from emissions targets. For example, the economic transition in Russia, Ukraine, and other countries has led to economic stagnation, making their carbon emissions much lower than the 1997 baseline levels. Therefore, these countries will have more surplus emissions rights. Some scholars have pointed out that these countries will not reduce emissions; instead, they will try to get more emission rights to trade, so as to monopolize the carbon trading market.

Similar problems exist in the establishment of carbon emissions trading market in China. At present, government has issued policy recommendations to speed up the establishment of carbon emissions trading markets in China. The pilot carbon trading scheme has been launched in seven provinces and municipalities, including Shenzhen, and it is gradually being promoted nationwide. An outstanding problem in this process is that the speed of economic development, technology level, and characteristic industries vary greatly among regions in China. The southeastern coastal regions of China are more economically developed, while the central and western regions of China are relatively economically backward; some regions are dominated by heavy industry, while some are dominated by agriculture. These differences also result in demands for carbon emissions and emission reduction potentials varying among regions. In addition, the direction and speed of economy are inconsistent with the expectations in some regions, resulting in a large gap between the carbon emissions cap set currently and the actual amount of carbon emissions in a few years. Similar situations are also common among industries and firms. For example, some firms (with high capacity for emissions reduction) will have surplus carbon emission rights, while other firms (with low capacity for emissions reduction) will suffer from severe shortage of carbon emission rights. For firms with insufficient carbon emission rights, in order to maintain production and increase profits, they must purchase the corresponding amount of carbon emission rights in the carbon trading market; otherwise, they will face high fines. In this case, firms with surplus carbon emission rights will become the sellers in the market, and they will also join forces to manipulate the market price. The largest buyer or buyer alliance with insufficient carbon emission rights among the firms will also become the most powerful market participants in bargaining with sellers, thereby controlling the market prices.

Generally, there are two types of firms that have market power. One is the sellers who own a large number of carbon credits for carbon emission rights in the carbon trading market and the other is the buyers who need a large share of carbon credits for carbon emission rights in the carbon trading market. Behavior will exert control over the market price of carbon emission rights. Government administrators should regulate the firms who control the market, so as to maintain a normal and stable transaction price, which is important for the design and management of the carbon trading market.

Few studies have been conducted on the impact of the market power of carbon market participants on the price of carbon emission rights. The real market is full of friction. It is an imperfectly competitive market where the surplus carbon emissions usually lead to market failure. If the surplus carbon emissions are concentrated in the hands of one market participant to a certain extent, it will inevitably form market power and lead to monopoly. So, what are the sources of market power? How to limit market power? Studies in this section are conducted mainly from the perspective of government regulators. We analyze the main factors of market power that affects the price of carbon emission rights, and the conditions of market power. We propose regulatory measures to control manufactures with market power.

13.3.2 Establishment and solution of game model

Referring to the Maeda model (2003), a game model for the carbon trading market with a large number of firms is constructed, which aims to analyze the pricing structure of carbon emission rights and provide conditions of market power. The design of the carbon trading market with a large number of firms is to create a competitive market.

The main difference between the model in this section and the Maeda model is that the Maeda model assumes two pricemakers, whereas the model in this section assumes only one pricemaker, since on principle, there is only one pricemaker through the comparison of market power.

The Maeda model assumes that each signatory has no emission reduction constraints and has a similar cost structure, which is obviously not consistent with reality. The model in this section assumes that each firm has to achieve the emissions reduction targets set by the regulator in advance through performing the emissions reduction task, and each firm has different emission reduction level. This assumption has more practical significance for the regulators to formulate policies.

13.3.2.1 Description and assumptions of the model

Assuming there are n firms in carbon trading market in China, wherein firm 1 is the "pricemaker" and the remaining n-1 firms are "price-takers". The so-called pricemaker refers to the firm with the ability to manipulate the price of carbon emission rights in the marketplace by manipulating the supply and demand level of carbon emission rights; the so-called price-taker refers to the firm who accepts the price of carbon emission rights.

In addition, the market also satisfies the following assumptions:

Assumption 1: The number of firms in the carbon market n is large enough.

Assumption 2: G^* denotes the total amount of carbon dioxide emissions set by China x_i; ($i = 1,2,\ldots n$) denotes the emissions reduction of firm i; y_i denotes the carbon emissions required for actual production; g_i denotes the number of carbon emission license held; the sum of carbon emission rights in the market is in line with the total emission target set by the government, namely $\sum_{i=1}^{n} g_i = G^*$.

Assumption 3: The carbon emission rights of the current period are not allowed to be saved to the next period. For firm i, if $y_i - g_i > 0$, it means that the carbon emission rights of firm i are insufficient, so it needs to reduce emissions or buy carbon emission rights. If $y_i - g_i < 0$, it means that the carbon emission rights of firm i are sufficient and the amount of carbon emission rights saved exceeds the amount of carbon emissions in actual production. Therefore, the surplus carbon emission rights can be sold.

Assumption 4: The carbon emissions trading volume of firm i is denoted as t_i. If $t_i > 0$, it means the corresponding amount of carbon emission rights have been bought; if $t_i < 0$, it means the corresponding amount of carbon emission rights have been sold. Since all firms are involved in the transactions, the market maintains a supply and demand equilibrium, that is $\sum_{i=1}^{n} t_i = 0$.

Assumption 5: The abatement cost function of firm i is denoted as $C_i(x_i) = \frac{c_i}{2} x_i^2$, wherein c_i is the abatement cost coefficient, which represents abatement levels of the firm.

Assumption 6: For writing convenience, we denote:

$$Y_k = \sum_{i=k}^{n} y_k ; C_k = \left(\sum_{i=k}^{n} c_k^{-1} \right)^{-1}$$

13.3.2.2 Equilibrium price of carbon emission rights in a perfectly competitive market

In a perfectly competitive market, all firms make trade-offs between trading and emissions reduction. Let the unit price of carbon emission rights in the market be p, the optimal decision of each firm should minimize the cost of emissions reduction, that is:

$$\min_{x_i > 0; t_i} \; p t_i + \frac{c_i}{2} x_i^2$$
$$s.t. \; y_i - g_i - x_i - t_i \le 0$$

Since the constraint function is a linear function, the constraint qualification is automatically satisfied.

Establish the Lagrangian function:

$$L(x_i, t_i, \lambda) = p t_i + \frac{c_i}{2} x_i^2 - \lambda(-y_i + g_i + x_i + t_i)$$

The first-order necessary conditions should satisfy:

$$\frac{\partial L}{\partial x_i} = c_i x_i - \lambda = 0 \tag{13.19}$$

$$\frac{\partial L}{\partial t_i} = p - \lambda = 0 \tag{13.20}$$

$$y_i - g_i - x_i - t_i \le 0 \tag{13.21}$$

$$\lambda(y_i - g_i - x_i - t_i) = 0 \tag{13.22}$$

$$\lambda \geq 0 \tag{13.23}$$

The following two situations are discussed:

If $\lambda = 0$, then from Equation (13.19), we have $x_i = 0$, which is inconsistent with the condition, so it is discarded.

If $\lambda > 0$, then the solution is:

$$x_i^* = \frac{p}{c_i}$$

$$t_i^* = y_i - g_i - \frac{p}{c_i}$$

Also, in the event of market clearing, then $\sum_{i=1}^{n} t_i = 0$, so we have:

$$\sum_{i=1}^{n}\left(y_i - g_i - \frac{p}{c_i}\right) = 0$$

Therefore, the equilibrium price in a perfectly competitive market is:

$$p^c = C_1\left(Y_1 - G^*\right) = \frac{c_1 C_2}{c_1 + C_2}\left(Y_1 - G^*\right) \tag{13.24}$$

Since:

$$\frac{\partial p^c}{\partial c_i} = C_1^{-2} c_i^{-2}\left(Y_1 - G^*\right) > 0$$

The market equilibrium price p^c is an increasing function of the marginal abatement cost of firm i. The higher the marginal abatement cost, the higher the equilibrium price.

13.3.2.3 The price of carbon emission rights under the influence of market power

If firm 1 in the market has absolute market power, it becomes the price decider and the rest of the firms are price followers. Assuming that the decision-making behavior of firm 1 leads to the market price of carbon emission rights as p^m, by backward induction, we solve the decision-making behavior of the price-taker:

$$\min_{x_i > 0; t_i} p^m(t_1)t_i + \frac{c_i}{2}x_i^2$$
$$s.t.\ \ y_i - g_i - x_i - t_i \leq 0 \left(i = 2, 3, \ldots, n\right)$$

The solution process is similar to that of Model 1, so we will not repeat it, and we get:

$$x_i^*(t_1) = \frac{p^m(t_1)}{c_i} \quad (i = 2,3,\ldots, n)$$

$$t_i^* = y_i - g_i - \frac{p^m(t_1)}{c_i}$$

With the market clearing condition $\sum_{i=1}^{n} t_i = 0$, the equilibrium price at this time is:

$$p^m(t_1) = C_2\left(t_1 + Y_2 - G^* + g_1\right)$$

Then, we solve the decision-making behavior of manufacture 1, that is:

$$\begin{aligned}&\min_{x_1>0;t_1} \ p^m(t_1)t_1 + \frac{c_1}{2}x_1^2\\ &s.t. \ y_1 - g_1 - x_1 - t_1 = 0\\ &p^m(t_1) = C_2\left(t_1 + Y_2 - G^* + g_1\right)\end{aligned}$$

Then we have:

$$\min_{t_1} U_1 = \min_{t_1} C_2\left(t_1 + Y_2 - G^* + g_1\right)t_1 + \frac{c_1}{2}\left(y_1 - g_1 - t_1\right)^2$$

From the first-order condition, we have:

$$t_1 = \frac{c_1(y_1 - g_1) - C_2\left(Y_2 - G^* + g_1\right)}{2C_2 + c_1}$$

Thus, the market price is:

$$p^m = \frac{C_2 c_1}{2C_2 + c_1}(y_1 - g_1) + \frac{C_2(1 - C_2)}{2C_2 + c_1}\left(Y_2 - G^* + g_1\right) \tag{13.25}$$

This is the price of carbon emission rights under the influence of market power.

13.3.2.4 Analysis of the impact of market power on the price of carbon emission rights

Denote the total emissions reduction as $\Delta G = Y_1 - G^*$ and denote the emissions reduction of firm i as $\Delta g_i = y_i - g_i$, then Equation (13.24) becomes:

$$p^c = \frac{c_1 C_2}{c_1 + C_2}\Delta G$$

Equation (13.25) becomes:

$$p^m = \frac{C_2 c_1}{2C_2 + c_1} \Delta g_1 + \frac{C_2(1 - C_2)}{2C_2 + c_1}(\Delta G - \Delta g_1)$$

Thus:

$$\frac{p^m}{p^c} = \frac{(c_1 + C_2)(c_1 + C_2 - 1)}{c_1(2C_2 + c_1)} \frac{\Delta g_1}{\Delta G} + \frac{(c_1 + C_2)(1 - C_2)}{c_1(2C_2 + c_1)} \tag{13.26}$$

If the number of firms n in the market is very large, then:

$$\lim_{n \to \infty} C_2 = \lim_{n \to \infty} \left(\sum_{i=2}^{n} c_i^{-1} \right)^{-1} = 0$$

Therefore, $C_2 \cong 0$ and Equation (13.26) can be expressed as:

$$\frac{p^m}{p^c} \cong \frac{\Delta g_1}{\Delta G} + \frac{1}{c_1}\left(1 - \frac{\Delta g_1}{\Delta G}\right) \tag{13.27}$$

Denote:

$$\frac{p^m}{p^c} = \alpha, \frac{\Delta g_1}{\Delta G} = \delta(0 < \delta < 1)$$

Wherein δ represents the ratio of the emission reduction allowance of firm 1 to the total emission reduction allowance of the market, then Equation (13.11) can be expressed as:

$$\alpha \cong \delta + \frac{1}{c_1}(1 - \delta) \tag{13.28}$$

From this Equation, it can be concluded that the market power of firm 1 is related to the ratio of its emission reduction allowance to the total emission reduction allowance in the market and its emission reduction level. The analysis is as follows:

1 If $c_1 = 1$, then $\alpha \cong 1$, that is, $p^m \cong p^c$. It suggests that firm 1 does not have market power, and the market is equivalent to a completely competitive market.
2 If $0 < c_1 < 1$, then $\alpha > 1$, that is, $p^m > p^c$. It suggests that firm 1 has market power, and the price of emission rights is higher than the equilibrium price under perfect competition.

   In this case:

$$\frac{\partial \alpha}{\partial \delta} = 1 - \frac{1}{c_1} < 0$$

The smaller δ is, the larger α is, and that is, the smaller the proportion of emissions reduction shared by firm 1, the stronger its market power. Also:

$$\frac{\partial \alpha}{\partial c_1} = -c_1^{-2}(1-\delta) < 0$$

The smaller c_1 is, the larger α is, that is, the higher the level of emissions reduction of firm 1, the stronger its market power.

3 If $c_1 > 1$, then $\alpha < 1$, that is, $p^m < p^c$. It suggests that firm 1 has market power, and the price of emission rights is lower than the equilibrium price under perfect competition.

In this case:

$$\frac{\partial \alpha}{\partial \delta} = 1 - \frac{1}{c_1} > 0$$

The smaller ∂ is, the smaller α is, that is, the smaller the proportion of emissions reduction shared by firm 1, the stronger its market power is. Also:

$$\frac{\partial \alpha}{\partial c_1} = -c_1^{-2}(1-\delta) < 0$$

The larger c_1 is, the smaller α is, that is, the lower the level of emissions reduction of firm 1, the stronger its market power.

13.3.3 Model evaluation and policy recommendations

13.3.3.1 Evaluation of model findings

Hahn (1984) proved that when there is market power, the price of emissions may be above or below the market price, which is consistent with the conclusion in this section. In Hahn's paper, Q_1^* is the amount of emission rights of firms that have market power in a competitive market. If the amount of emission rights initially allocated to a firm is less than Q_1^*, then the firm will set a price that is lower than the equilibrium price under competition conditions. If the amount of emission rights initially allocated to a firm is greater than Q_1^*, the price of emission rights set by the firm will be higher than the competitive level. Through numerical analysis, Hahn found that the effect of the former monopolistic behavior is weaker than that of the latter. He also asserted that "the relative importance of monopoly and monopolistic behavior can be very sensitive to changes in parameters". In this respect, the conclusion of this section, Equation (13.28), is consistent with his conclusion.

In contrast, Tietenberg (1985) mentioned the unimportance of the initial allocation of emission rights, which is contrary to the conclusion of this section. The price equation established in this model shows that the initial allocation of carbon emission rights determines the emission reduction credits of firms, which, in turn, affects the price deviation.

The advantage of the Equation (13.28) presented in this section is that it is simple and easy to describe, but the disadvantage is that when using it to estimate the market price and price deviation affected by market power, we must estimate the marginal abatement cost of firms and confirm the proportion of emission reduction allowances among firms. Since the marginal abatement cost of a firm is usually private, it is costly for government regulators to get the information, which complicates the regulation to a certain extent.

13.3.3.2 Policy recommendations

For government authorities, it is very important to strengthen the ability to predict market prices and prevent market powers. According to the conclusion established by the model in this section, the government authority can estimate the market price of carbon emission rights of a firm that has market power according to Equation (13.25), and point out that the influence of the firm with market power on the equilibrium price is mainly reflected in two factors according to Equation (13.28): the ratio of its emission reduction allowance to the total emission reduction allowance in the market and its level of emissions reduction.

More importantly, according to Equation (13.28), the government can effectively avoid the impact of firms who have market power on the price of carbon emission rights through the formulation of systems and policies. According to the above analysis, we can conclude that for monopolies with high level of emissions reduction, the government should reduce the carbon emission allowance allocated to them, so as to increase their emissions reduction quotas; for monopolies with low level of emissions reduction, the government should encourage them to improve the level of emissions reduction and increase its emissions reduction quota so as to reduce its impact on market prices.

To sum up, first, the government should pay attention to the initial allocation of carbon emission rights in the process of managing the market price of carbon emission rights, since the efficiency of the initial allocation of carbon emission rights directly affects the trading price and the formation of market power in the carbon market. Second, the promotion of emission reduction technologies is conducive to the balanced development of the carbon trading market. The government can improve the level of emissions reduction of large-scale firms with high energy consumption through technical support, policy support, and other incentives, which brings the carbon trading price closer to the equilibrium price.

13.4 Summary

This chapter first analyzes the supply and demand of the carbon trading market as well as the impact of transaction costs and market power on the price of carbon emission rights from a theoretical perspective.

Next, the chapter focuses on the low transaction price of CDM projects in the current carbon trading market in China, establishes a bargaining model of direct purchase behavior in carbon trading for research, and draws the following conclusions:

First, the offers of both parties are increasing functions of their own expected price of carbon emission rights. The higher the expected price, the higher the offer; on the contrary, the lower the expected price, the lower the offer.

Second, the seller's offer in the transaction is a decreasing function of the buyer's discount factor, while the buyer's offer is an increasing function of the seller's discount factor; at the same time, the seller's offer is affected by the transparency of the real-time trading market. The more complete the market information, the higher the market transparency and the higher the seller's offer.

This chapter focuses on the influence of market power on the transaction price of carbon emission rights, establishes the transaction pricing equation under market power, and points out that the influence of the monopolies' market power on the equilibrium price is mainly reflected in two factors: the ratio of the emission reduction allowance of monopolies to the total emission reduction allowance in the market and the level of emissions reduction.

If a monopoly's level of emissions reduction is relatively high or the proportion of emissions reduction is relatively small, it will reflect in the fact that the supplier of carbon emission rights has market dominance, making the price of carbon emission rights higher than the equilibrium price under perfect competition; if a monopoly's level of emissions reduction is low or the proportion of emissions reduction is low, it will be manifested in the fact that the demander of carbon emission rights has market dominance, making the price of carbon emission rights lower than the equilibrium price under perfect competition.

The issue of pricing in the carbon trading market has always been a hot topic of research, and further explorations can be made on the risk characteristics and bargaining power of both parties in the future.

Note

1 Shen Manhong, Zhao Liqiu. Theoretical discussion on emission rights pricing. *Zhejiang Social Sciences*, 2012, 5: 26–30.

References

Cason, T.N., Gandgadharan, L. Transactions cost in tradable permit markets: an experimental study of pollution market designs. *Journal of Regulation Economics*, 2003, 23: 145–165.

Coase, R. The problem of social cost. *Journal of Law and Economics*, 1960, 3: 1–44.

Gangadharan, L. Transaction cost in pollution markets: an empirical study. *Land Economics*, 2000, 76: 601–614.

Hahn, F. *Equilibrium Macroeconomics*, Cambridge, MA: MIT Press, 1984.

Myerson R. B. *Game theory: analysis of conflict*. Translated by Yu Yin, Fei Jianping. Beijing: Economic Press China, 2001: 314–327.

Stavins, R. Transactions costs and tradable permits. *Journal of Environmental Management and Policy*, 1995, 29: 133–148.

Tietenberg, T. H. Emission Trading, An Exercise in Reforming Pollution Policy, Washington DC: Resources for the Future, 1985.

Xie Shiyu. *Economic game theory*. Shanghai: Fudan University Press, 2002: 286–290.

14 Analysis on the formation mechanism of carbon emissions trading

At this stage, due to the relatively backward production in China and an urgently needed restructuring in industries with high-carbon emission and high-energy consumption, there may be few buyers at the beginning of the carbon emission trading. The reasons are as follows: first, since we have no mandatory emission reduction targets or perfect regulations at the current stage, rational firms in pursuit of maximized interests will not consciously fulfill the targets. Second, because of the extensive growth of China, the marginal abatement costs of most firms are almost the same. In other words, it is unlikely to have remaining quotas of carbon emissions for firms and they have less motivation for carbon emission trading. Therefore, the development of carbon emissions trading in China, especially in its infancy, is in desperate need of guidance and regulation from the government.

The governmental regulation of carbon emission trading is the foundation for a smooth trading. At the beginning of carbon emission trading, it is necessary to strengthen the regulation of the trading; otherwise, the transaction will not be carried out normally. For example, the EU's emission trading mechanism has established strict governmental regulations and verification measures. In EU countries, if the actual carbon emission of the firm exceeds the rationed quota in the year and the firm does not purchase the corresponding quota in the carbon emission trading market, it will pay a fine, the price of which is much higher than the price of the unit carbon emission rights on the market in the same period. At the same time, the list of firms with excess emissions will be publicized, which is equivalent to an official criticism. Those firms, in the next year, must yield savings of carbon emission rights through emission reduction or purchase carbon emission rights to make up the difference in the previous year. Meanwhile, the government should foster the initiative of firms to participate in carbon emission trading. The proper incentive stems from the analysis of the internal motivation that can increase the willingness of firms to participate in the trading. With both the external government regulation and the internal initiative of firms to participate in the trading, we can better promote the formation and development of carbon emission trading under a two-way cooperation mechanism.

DOI: 10.4324/9781003388500-18

This chapter analyzes the game equilibrium between firms and the government on illegal emissions and makes suggestions for governmental regulation. In the meantime, internal factors that encourage firms to take part in carbon emission trading are pointed out in this chapter in order to analyze the impact of transaction costs on firms' willingness to participate in this trading. Through the establishment and analysis of the low-carbon technology transfer mechanism in carbon emissions trading, this chapter offers advice on increasing the enthusiasm of firms to participate in the trading.

14.1 Analysis on the role of governmental regulation

The carbon emission trading is based on the total amount control. If the firms, in a certain period, emit and trade in strict accordance with the carbon emission rights granted in an area and if they purchase the rights in the trading market and make up for the extra-quota carbon emissions according to the regulations, the harm to the environment caused by the carbon dioxide emissions in this area will always remain within a controllable range in this period. However, the ultimate goal of rational firms is to maximize their own profits. When the amount of carbon emission rights of a firm is far from meeting the needs of production and emission, illegal emissions, or emissions in violation of the relevant system of carbon emissions trading will be tempting to the firm, as such behavior, compared with participating in carbon emissions trading, is a cost-free method. However, illegal emissions will lead to environmental degradation and bring huge negative effects to the society.

Obviously, this is not what the government administrative department wants. In order to control illegal emissions, the administrative department must design a series of regulations to supervise the emission behavior of firms. Once emission violations are detected, severe punishment must be taken against the firm, just like the EU's carbon emission trading supervision system. Therefore, firms will face certain risks when choosing emission violations, thereby decreasing the possibility of such behaviors and improving their engagement in carbon emissions trading. The punishment includes huge fines, a notice of criticism, or even suspended production for rectification. The fines levied on firms can be used to remediate the environmental destruction caused by emission violations or used for the construction and management of the carbon emissions trading market.

14.1.1 Analysis of the game background

For the government, the representative of the public, the benefits obtained by advocating the carbon emission trading are multiple, including ecological benefits, social benefits, and economic benefits. Also, the benefits are of sociality in the long run. For firms, the entity in the economic operation of the entire carbon emissions trading market, this trading will reduce the cost of emission reduction and improve the reduction efficiency, so enterprises will be motivated to participate in it. But at the same time, the enterprises are rational and focus more on the current interests in pursuit of maximized profits. In the early stage of carbon emission trading, influenced by the imperfect market mechanism and the "speculative psychology", firms with excess emissions lack the enthusiasm and self-consciousness to purchase carbon emission rights through trading. Hence, government leadership and supervision are required. Once the government takes corresponding regulatory measures, firms and the government will start a game around their respective interests.

14.1.2 Establishment of the regulation game model

14.1.2.1 Assumptions of the strategy space in the game

1. Firms which commit illegal emissions are rational in pursuit of maximized utility. However, what the government pursues is the maximization of the comprehensive utility of the society, including utility in economy, ecology, environment, and other sectors.
2. The government can take two types of measures: strengthened regulation and deregulation based on the emission violations of firms. Strengthened regulation requires the government to pay the costs of regulation. At the same time, the government will impose a fine on firms which violate regulations.
3. There are two solutions for such firms, namely participating in carbon emissions trading to purchase carbon emission rights (referred to as "participation in trading") or illegal emission. Firms participating in the trading need to pay corresponding costs such as transaction fees.
4. As long as the government conducts inspections, the illegal emissions of the firm will be detected, and concealment does not exist.
5. Firms that violated the regulations will be criticized in a circulated notice.

14.1.2.2 Variable assumptions in the game model

1. Suppose the utility of the firm's emission violations is U_1 and the transaction cost in the trading is C_1. At the same time, firms participating in the trading will be encouraged to update low-carbon technologies and reduce production costs, which will increase a certain amount of utility $(\Delta U, \Delta U > 0)$ in the current period.
2. Suppose the government obtains utility (U_2) under deregulation and pays a cost of regulation and supervision (C) when strengthening regulations. Since the government will benefit from the firms participating in trading, suppose the comprehensive social utility is S. Under the strengthened regulations, the government imposes a fine of F on the firms that violate the regulations. The loss of reputation brought by the public notice of criticism for the firms is denoted as L.

14.1.2.3 The payoff matrix of the game

The payoff matrix of the game is built based on the above assumptions, as shown in Figure 14.1.

1 $C_1 - \Delta U > 0$, affected by the cost of carbon emissions trading and the lag of technical incentives, the implementation cost of participating firms is greater than the benefit.
2 $F > C$, the fines imposed on firms for illegal emissions are greater than the inspection costs of the government, which ensures the feasibility of the government to strengthen regulations.
3 $F + L > C_1 - \Delta U$, under the government's strengthened regulation, the profit of the firm's illegal emission is less than that of the trading, which ensures the enthusiasm of the firm in the carbon emission trading.

If any one of condition (2) or (3) is not satisfied, the Nash equilibrium of this game will be illegal emission of firms and deregulation from the government or illegal emission of firms and strengthened regulation from the government. In this circumstance, buying carbon emission rights through trading cannot be realized and trading cannot be carried out.

14.1.3 Game model solution

Upon examination of this payoff matrix, it is easy to know that there is no pure strategy Nash equilibrium in the game (see arrows in Figure 14.1). Thus, we will solve the mixed strategy Nash equilibrium. Suppose the probability of firms participating in the trading is P and the probability of the government to strengthen regulation is q.

For the government, given the probability distribution (p, 1-p) of the firm's strategy, the expected profit of the government's strengthened regulation is:

$$\pi_g(p, 1) = p \cdot (U_2 - C + S) + (1 - p) \cdot (U_2 - C + F)$$

Firm	Government	
	strengthen regulation (q)	deregulation (1-q)
Participate in transactions (p)	U_1-C_1+ΔU, U_2-C+S	U_1-C_1+ΔU, U_2+S
Illegal emissions (1-p)	U_1-F-L,U_2-C+F	U_1,U_2

Figure 14.1 Payoff Matrix

The expected profit of the government's deregulation is:

$$\pi_g(p,0)=p\cdot(U_2+S)+(1-p)\cdot U_2$$

Solve $\pi_g(p,1)=\pi_g(p,0)$, we get:

$$p^*=\frac{F-C}{F} \tag{14.1}$$

For the firm, given the probability distribution (*q*, 1-*q*) of the government's strategy, the expected profit of the firm's participating in trading is:

$$\pi_f(1,q)=q\cdot(U_1-C_1+\Delta U)+(1-q)\cdot(U_1-C_1+\Delta U)$$

The expected profit of the firm's illegal emissions is:

$$\pi_f(0,q)=q\cdot(U_1-F-L)+(1-q)\cdot U_1$$

Solve $\pi_f(1,q)=\pi_f(0,q)$, we get:

$$q^*=\frac{C_1-\Delta U}{F+L} \tag{14.2}$$

The mixed strategy Nash equilibrium of this game is $\left[\left(p^*,1-p^*\right),\left(q^*,1-q^*\right)\right]$, which means that the probability for the firm to participate in the transaction isp^* and the probability for the government to strengthen regulation is q^*.

14.1.4 Analysis of the game equilibrium

If the probability for firms to participate in trading is higher than p^*, the government will relax regulation since the expected benefit of deregulation is greater than that of strengthened regulation. If the probability for the government to regulate firms is higher than q^*, the firms will take an active part in the transaction since the expected benefit of participation in trading is greater than that of illegal emissions. Therefore, in order to promote the carbon emission trading, the government's regulatory design should increase p^*, the probability of firms participating in the transaction, and reduce q^*, the probability of strengthened regulation, so as to improve the Pareto efficiency of the whole society.

Equations (14.1) and (14.2) show that:

1 Increased fine *F* helps to increase the probability of the firm to participate in the transaction (p^*) and reduce the probability of strengthened regulation from the government (q^*). A larger *F* indicates a stricter punishment from the government. The firm will be more motivated to participate in the transaction after being constrained by the punishment.

As a result, the government will relax the regulation. But at the same time, we must also be wary of the government inaction due to the benefit gained from the fine.

2 Reducing the government's regulatory inspection cost (C) helps to increase the probability of the firm to participate in the transaction (p^*). It shows that the lower the regulation and inspection cost of the government is, the stronger the credibility of the regulation turns. It will increase the initiative of the firm to participate in the transaction.
3 Reducing the transaction cost of firms to take part in the trading (C_1) helps to decrease the probability of strengthened regulation from the government (q^*). The lower the transaction cost of firms is, the higher the enthusiasm of firms to participate in carbon emission trading becomes. As a result, the government will relax the regulation.
4 The probability of strengthened regulation from the government (q^*) decrease as the utility brought by low-carbon technologies (ΔU) rises. As the low-carbon technologies produce more utilities for firms, firms will be promoted to actively participate in transactions. As a result, the government will relax the regulation.
5 The increase of L, the loss of reputation, helps to reduce the probability of strengthened regulation from the government (q^*). This impact on reputation may reduce the illegal emissions of firms and encourage those firms to participate in the trading. As a result, the government will relax the regulation.

To sum up, fines and impact on reputation can be used as effective regulatory methods to ensure the smooth development of carbon emissions trading. Increasing fines and expanding influence on reputation can effectively regulate the behavior of firms and ensure that firms participate in carbon emissions trading. Therefore, in order to improve the efficiency of supervision, the government must make efforts to reduce the cost of regulation.

At the same time, the root of the active participation of firms in trading, the formation of the carbon emissions trading, and a higher activity level of the trading lies in two internal factors: the reduction of transaction costs and the learning and transfer of low-carbon technologies for firms. The next two sections will mainly focus on these two factors and propose corresponding suggestions.

14.2 Analysis of the impact of transaction costs

New institutional economics believes that the transaction cost hinders or even prevents the formation of markets. The transaction cost refers to the cost used to make use of the economic system. It can be seen as the operating cost of the system (Coase, 1994). In the implementation of carbon emission trading, considering transaction costs in reality, firms driven by individual rationality will decide their own optimal emissions, the number of carbon emission rights that need to be purchased, reduction of emissions through technologies, and the amount of carbon dioxide emitted illegally according to the government's regulatory strategy in order to maximize their own utility.

Through establishing a model of behavioral decision of firms facing situations, including participation in trading, reduction of emissions with technologies, and illegal emissions when they are under governmental regulation, this section analyzes the main factors that affect firms' decision-making and points out the impact of transaction costs on firms' willingness to participate in transactions, and then offers specific suggestions to reduce transaction costs.

14.2.1 Establishment of game modell

Suppose there are n firms in the carbon emission trading market; the government allocates carbon emission rights to each firm in the primary market and denotes the allocated carbon emission rights license by l_i^0 (given that the allocated amount is less than the actual production need). After that, each firm conducts production according to the reality. If the carbon emission quota is insufficient, the enterprise can obtain it through other ways, including buying on the market, emissions reduction with technologies, or illegal emissions.

The government administrative department will punish the firm i due to its illegal emissions. The regulation is designed as follows: when monitoring those firms, set the amount of illegal emission to be v_i; the monitoring level is denoted by $\alpha_i(v_i)(0 < \alpha_i \le 1)$. $\alpha_i(v_i)$ is the function of illegal emissions v_i, and it satisfies $\alpha_i'(v_i) > 0$, $\alpha_i''^{(v_i)} > 0$ and $\alpha_i(0) > 0$, which means that the monitoring level increases with the amount of illegal emissions and that the marginal monitoring level increases by degrees. Moreover, even if there are no illegal emissions, the government should also conduct supervision. At this time, although the cost of the government administrative department is relatively high, the supervision over the firm's illegal emissions is more comprehensive.

Fines levied on firms violating the regulations are denoted as $F_i(v_i)$ and a notice of criticism will be issued. The corresponding reputation loss brought by the notice is denoted by $L_i(v_i)$, and $F_i'(v_i) > 0$, $F_i''(v_i) > 0$, $F_i(0) = 0$, $L_i'(v_i) > 0$, $L_i''(v_i) > 0$, $L_i(0) = 0$. This shows that both fines and reputation losses are increasing functions of illegal emissions. The larger the illegal emissions are, the heavier fines and reputational loss become. Meanwhile, the amount of the marginal fine and the marginal reputational loss increase progressively.

Assumption 1: The profit obtained by the firm due to e_i units of carbon emissions without monitoring is $B_i(e_i)$, $B_i'(e_i) > 0$, and $B_i''(e_i) < 0$. It indicates that the profit of the firm increases with carbon emissions and that the marginal profit decreases by degrees.

Assumption 2: The transaction price of unit carbon emission rights in the trading market is p.

Assumption 3: The number of carbon emission rights the firm i dealt in the trading is t_i, and the function of transaction cost is denoted by $T_i(t_i)$ and $T_i'(t_i) > 0$. It indicates that the transaction cost is an increasing function of the trading volume. The larger the trading volume is, the higher the transaction cost turns.

Assumption 4: The carbon emission reduced through technology by the firm i is denoted as x_i and the function of emission reduction cost is denoted as $C_i(x_i)$.

Assumption 5: When the monitoring level is 100%, namely $\alpha_i = 1$, the cost paid by the government administrative department is C.

Assumption 6: The disutility to the society caused by v_i units of illegal emissions by the firm i is $D(v_i)$.

Assumption 7: The number of carbon emission rights that firms dealt in the market is t_i, and the value of t_i could be positive or negative. When $t_i > 0$, it means that the firm buys carbon emission rights. When $t_i < 0$, it means that the firm sells carbon emission rights.

Assumption 8: $p, B(e), D(v), T(t), C, C(x), F(v), L(v)$ are common knowledge of the firm and the administrative department.

Assumption 9: Once the government administrative department inspects the firm, it will be able to find out whether the firm emits in private or not. If the firm does violate regulations concerning emissions, the actual emissions will be definitely found out.

Assumption 10: Both government administrative departments and firms are risk-neutral.

14.2.2 Game model solution

In practice, the goal of the administrative department is to minimize the environmental impact caused by the illegal emissions of firms. However, if the management cost is too large, the department will be overburdened and the loss will outweigh the gain. Assuming that the goal of the department is to minimize the sum of the cost of monitoring mechanisms and environmental destruction resulted from illegal emissions, the utility function of the government management department is:

$$U_g = \sum_{i=1}^{n}\left[C\alpha_i(v_i) + D(v_i)\right] - \sum_{i=1}^{n}\alpha_i(v_i)F_i(v_i)$$

The purpose in decision-making of firms is to weigh their own carbon emissions e_i, the number of carbon emission rights dealt in market transactions t_i, and the volume of illegal emissions v_i under the supervision and regulation of the government so as to realize maximized utility. The utility function of the firm is:

$$U_f = B_i(e_i) - pt_i - T_i(|t_i|) - C_i(x_i) - \alpha_i(v_i)[F_i(v_i) + L_i(v_i)]$$

Assuming that the goal of government administrator is to determine the monitoring level $\alpha_i(v_i)$. Based on the government's monitoring mechanism, firms make decisions on the quota of carbon emissions for their own production, participation in trading, and illegal emissions.

First, we solve the optimal decision of the firm through backward induction, namely:

$$\max_{e_i,\, t_i,\, x_i} U_f = \max_{e_i,\, t_i,\, v_i} B_i(e_i) - pt_i - T_i(|t_i|) - C_i(x_i) - \alpha_i(v_i)[F_i(v_i) + L_i(v_i)]$$

$$s.t.\ t_i + l_i^0 + x_i + v_i = e_i, v_i \geq 0$$

From the first-order condition, we get:

$$\frac{\partial U_f}{\partial e_i} = B_i'(e_i) - \alpha_i'(v_i)[F_i(v_i) + L_i(v_i)] - \alpha_i(v_i)[F_i'(v_i) + L_i'(v_i)] = 0 \tag{14.3}$$

$$\begin{aligned}\frac{\partial U_f}{\partial t_i} = &-p - T_i'(|t_i|)|t_i|' + \alpha_i'(v_i)[F_i(v_i) + L_i(v_i)] + \\ &\alpha_i(v_i)[F_i'(v_i) + L_i'(v_i)] = 0\end{aligned} \tag{14.4}$$

$$\frac{\partial U_f}{\partial x_i} = -C_i'(x_i) + \alpha_i'(v_i)[F_i(v_i) + L_i(v_i)] + \alpha_i(v_i)[F_i'(v_i) + L_i'(v_i)] = 0 \tag{14.5}$$

Since the objective function is a strictly convex one and the constraints are linear, by solving Equations (14.3), (14.4), and (14.5) and operating the equation system simultaneously, we can get the only optimal response: $(e_i^*, t_i^*, x_i^*, v_i^*)$.

Then, considering the optimal response of the firm, the government administrative department selects the optimal monitoring level, that is:

$$\min_{\alpha_i} U_g = \sum_{i=1}^{n}[C\alpha_i(v_i^*) + D(v_i^*)] - \sum_{i=1}^{n}\alpha_i(v_i^*)F_i(v_i^*)$$

The optimal monitoring level can be obtained by setting a specific functional relationship. Since the following section mainly analyzes the decision-making behavior of firms, the solution of the optimal monitoring level is skipped.

14.2.3 Analysis on the decision-making behavior of the firm

Observing the three first-order conditional expressions (14.3), (14.4), and (14.5) of the firm's optimal decision, we draw the following conclusions:

1 When the enterprise participates in the carbon emission trading and does not conduct illegal emissions, that is, $v_i = 0$, plug it into Equation (14.4) and we get:

$$p+T_i'(|t_i|)|t_i|' = \alpha_i(0)\left[F_i'(0)+L_i'(0)\right] \tag{14.6}$$

By Equation (14.6), it can be inferred that when $p+T_i'(|t_i|)|t_i|' \leq \alpha_i(0)\left[F_i'(0)+L_i'(0)\right]$, firms will participate in carbon emissions trading instead of choosing illegal emissions. When $p+T_i'(|t_i|)|t_i|' > \alpha_i(0)\left[F_i'(0)+L_i'(0)\right]$, firms will choose illegal emissions. This shows that the firm's decision on illegal emissions depends on the market price of carbon emission rights, the transaction costs, and the policy of punishment implemented by the government.

2 Operate Equations (14.3), (14.4), and (14.5) simultaneously, we get:

$$p+T_i'(|t_i|)|t_i|' = B_i'(e_i) \tag{14.7}$$

$$p+T_i'(|t_i|)|t_i|' = C_i'(x_i) \tag{14.8}$$

It can be inferred that the firm's optimal production emissions and emission reduction through technologies rely on the unit price and marginal transaction cost of carbon emission rights, irrelevant of the regulatory strategy set by the government.

When $t_i > 0$, $|t_i|' = 1$, there is $p+T_i'(|t_i|) = B_i'(e_i) = C_i'(x_i)$.

From Equation (14.4), we can know that when $p+T_i'(|t_i|) \leq B_i'(e_i) = C_i'(x_i)$, firms choose to buy carbon emission rights. At this time, they will increase emissions from production and decrease emission reduction through technologies.

When $t_i < 0$, $|t_i|' = -1$, there is $p-T_i'(|t_i|) = B_i'(e_i) = C_i'(x_i)$.

From Equation (14.4), we can know that when $p-T_i'(|t_i|) \geq B_i'(e_i) = C_i'(x_i)$, the firm will sell carbon emission rights. At this time, firms will reduce emissions from production and increase more emissions through technologies.

When $p-T_i'(|t_i|) < B_i'(e_i) < p+T_i'(|t_i|)$, firms will not participate in carbon emission trading.

It shows that the willingness of firms to participate in carbon emission trading is related to the market price of carbon emission rights, marginal transaction costs, and the original marginal profit of firms. When the marginal profit of the firm is greater than the sum of the price of carbon emission rights and the marginal transaction cost, the firm chooses to buy carbon emission rights; when the marginal profit of the firm is less than the difference between the price of carbon emission rights and the marginal transaction cost, the firm chooses to sell carbon emission rights.

To sum up, the behavior choice of firms in carbon emission trading (participation in trading, emission reduction through technologies, or illegal emissions) mainly depends on external factors such as the market price of carbon emission rights, transaction costs, and governmental regulations and policies. When both the level of governmental supervision and the current market price is confirmed, the reduction of transaction costs will ensure the activity of the carbon emission trading market and will further reduce the basic supervision level of the government and improve the efficiency of governmental regulation.

At the same time, the willingness of firms to participate in trading is directly related to the size of transaction costs. The expression $p - T_i'(|t_i|) < B_i'(e_i) < p + T_i'(|t_i|)$ shows that the increase of marginal transaction cost reduces both the incentives of firms to participate in trading and the efficiency of carbon emission trading market.

14.2.4 Suggestions on reducing the transaction cost of carbon emission rights2

The above analysis shows that the transaction decision-making behavior of firms is directly affected by the transaction costs of the carbon emissions trading. Higher transaction cost means lower participation of enterprises, and firms are more likely to choose illegal emissions, which leads to a more serious distortion of the market equilibrium, thereby severely affecting the establishment and operation of the carbon emissions trading market.

According to the Coase theorem, the transaction costs in carbon emission trading can be divided into two types: exogenous and endogenous transaction cost. Exogenous transaction cost, which refers to the loss of social welfare before carbon emission trading is carried out, mainly includes the following points: clear property rights of carbon emission rights; the establishment of carbon emission trading market and formulation of rules; setting of total carbon emissions and the quota of unit carbon emission; supervision over firms which produce emissions; and the cost of finding transaction information for firms in the trading.

Endogenous transaction cost refers to the loss of social welfare caused by the behavior of participants in carbon emissions trading. It mainly refers to illegal emissions and other opportunistic behaviors of firms by taking advantage of loopholes in carbon emission trading rules, imperfect monitoring systems, and high costs of government supervision. Such opportunistic behavior will lead to high endogenous costs in the carbon emissions trading market, making firms less motivated to participate in the transaction.

The transaction costs that affect the decision-making behavior of firms mainly include the cost to formulate trading rules in the carbon emission trading market, the cost to supervise over firms which create emissions, and the cost for firms to search for transaction information in the trading. To reduce the transaction cost in the implementation of carbon emissions trading, the following points can be considered:

First, clarify the property rights of carbon emission rights and make the rights become commodities in order to conduct trading normally and achieve the optimal allocation of resources.

Second, speed up the construction of the market system of carbon emissions trading and formulate reasonable trading rules. Meanwhile, clarify the types of carbon emissions trading and determine transaction fees.

Third, establish a unified and complete carbon emission trading platform to effectively reduce the cost of collecting information for trading entities and improve the operating efficiency of the market.

Fourth, establish and improve the auction mechanism for carbon emission trading, and use the form of auction to allocate and trade carbon emission rights in a reasonable way and effectively reduce transaction costs.

Fifth, establish and improve the monitoring and supervision system for firms' carbon emissions to make sure the carbon emissions trading runs smoothly.

14.3 Analysis of low-carbon technology transfer mechanism

The formation of carbon emissions trading and market activity largely hinges on the difference of marginal abatement cost and capabilities of emission reduction of the participants. Only with different marginal abatement costs can we promote the formation of carbon emissions trading and improve the efficiency of carbon emissions trading. Studies have shown that a bigger difference in the marginal abatement cost among potential participating firms in the carbon emission trading market will bring about a higher probability of transactions. It means that a greater difference in the marginal abatement cost among firms is more conducive to the establishment and effectiveness of the carbon emissions trading market (Lei Chen and Shiqiu Zhang, 2005). With the extensive growth in China, it is difficult for firms to differ in emission reduction levels, resulting in the lack of supplies of carbon emission rights. Therefore, the learning and transfer of low-carbon technologies is the driving force to build the carbon emission trading. Only when there are differences in emission reduction levels and abundance or shortage of carbon emission rights among firms can the trading happen. Therefore, the overall emission reduction target of China can be realized.

At the same time, the current carbon emission trading in China is mainly focused on the CDM project. As the trading volume is rising dramatically, we should also be clearly aware of the severe situation of low-carbon emission reduction. The CDM project requires buyers in developed countries to provide technology and funds for developing countries, and the savings in carbon emission rights can offset their emission reductions. Concerning the current implementation in China, the transaction on both sides is more concentrated on funds. Yet, the transfer of technology has not been realized, which is unfavorable to our firms in the transaction. This section will use the Holmstrom-Milgrom Model of Principal-Agent to analyze the main factors affecting low-carbon technology transfer and promote the healthy development of carbon emissions trading.

14.3.1 Establishment of game model[3]

Suppose that buyers and sellers trade around the low-carbon technology transfer in carbon emissions trading projects. The buyer, as the demander of low-carbon technology, proposes to learn the other party's low-carbon technology. In return, the buyer pays the carbon footprint saved by the low-carbon technology to the seller according to a certain proportion.

Assumption 1: The low-carbon technology stock owned by the seller is T. In the short term, T is a continuous constant and can be sold separately.

Assumption 2: The willingness of sellers to transfer low-carbon technology is α $(0 < \alpha < 1)$. α represents the proportion of the transferred technology in the original technology stock T, and α cannot be observed. Therefore, the amount of low-carbon technology finally transferred by the seller is $\Delta T = \alpha T$.

Assumption 3: The buyer of the low-carbon technology could absorb all transferred low-carbon technologies and convert them into output and save a certain amount of carbon emissions (Y).

Assumption 4: According to the capability theory, knowledge determines capability and capability determines output. Thus, supposing that Y, the carbon footprint saved, is a function of low-carbon technology T, that is, $Y = f(T)$. For the sake of convenience, it is assumed that the carbon footprint saved is a linear function of low-carbon technology, that is, $Y = T + \theta$, wherein θ, representing the exogenous uncertainty, is a normally distributed random variable with mean value of zero and variance of σ (Xiaogang He, 2002). After the buyer absorbs the low-carbon technology, the carbon emission saved is denoted by $\Delta Y = \Delta T + \theta$.

Assumption 5: The buyer pays a proportion of carbon emissions saved to the seller of low-carbon technology as a reward, and the proportion is β, thus the buyer pays $C = \beta \Delta T = \alpha \beta T$.

Assumption 6: The buyer is risk-neutral because it actively seeks out low-carbon technologies. The utility function of the seller is characterized by the constant and absolute risk aversion, namely $U_s = -e^{-\rho w}$, wherein ρ is the absolute risk-averse measurement, w is the actual money income, and the seller's cost of risk is $\frac{\rho \beta^2 \sigma^2}{2}$.

Assumption 7: The cost function of the buyer to absorb technology is $C_b(\Delta T)=\frac{1}{2}b_b\Delta T^2=\frac{1}{2}b_b(\alpha T)^2$. The cost function for the seller to transfer technology is $C_s(\Delta T)=\frac{1}{2}b_s\Delta T^2=\frac{1}{2}b_s(\alpha T)^2$, wherein $b_b>0$ and $b_s>0$ are the cost coefficient of the buyer and the seller respectively.

14.3.2 Solution for the game model

Since the buyer is risk-neutral, the expected utility of the buyer is:

$$EU_b=\Delta T-C-C_b(\Delta T)=\alpha(1-\beta)T-\frac{1}{2}b_b(\alpha T)^2$$

Since the seller is risk-averse, at this time, the expected utility of the seller is equivalent to the certainty equivalence, that is, the mean value of stochastic income minus the cost of risk, so the expected utility of the seller is:

$$EU_s=C-C_s(\Delta T)-\frac{\rho\beta^2\sigma^2}{2}=\alpha\beta T-\frac{1}{2}b_s(\alpha T)^2-\frac{\rho\beta^2\sigma^2}{2}$$

If we denote the level of the seller's revenue reserve by $\overline{w}$, the seller's participation in the technology transfer transaction must satisfy the participation constraint (*IR*), in other words, the expected utility of the seller to participate in the transaction cannot be less than its revenue reserve, that is, $EU_s\geq\overline{w}$, so:

$$\alpha\beta T-\frac{1}{2}b_s(\alpha T)^2-\frac{\rho\beta^2\sigma^2}{2}\geq\overline{w}(IR)$$

In this model, through the decision-making in the value of decision β, the buyer prompts the seller to decide the value of α to realize the transfer of low-carbon technology in order to obtain maximum utility.

Therefore, the maximum expected utility of the seller is:

$$\max_{\alpha} EU_s=\max_{\alpha}\left[\alpha\beta T-\frac{1}{2}b_s(\alpha T)^2-\frac{\rho\beta^2\sigma^2}{2}\right]$$

From the first-order condition, we get:

$$\alpha=\frac{\beta}{b_sT}(IC)$$

This is the seller's incentive constraint (*IC*).

At this time, the optimal decision of the buyer is:

$$\max_{\beta} EU_b=\max_{\beta}\left[\alpha(1-\beta)T-\frac{1}{2}b_b(\alpha T)^2\right]$$

$$s.t.\ (IR)\alpha\beta T-\frac{1}{2}b_s(\alpha T)^2-\frac{\rho\beta^2\sigma^2}{2}\geq\bar{w}$$

$$(IC)\alpha=\frac{\beta}{b_sT}$$

At this point, it is unnecessary for the buyer to pay the seller more than $\bar{w}$, so the participation constraint is as follows:

$$\beta T-\frac{1}{2}b_s(\alpha T)^2-\frac{\rho\beta^2\sigma^2}{2}=\bar{w}$$

Plug it into the objective function, and we have:

$$\max_{\beta}\left[\frac{\beta}{b_s}-\frac{\rho\beta^2\sigma^2}{2}-\frac{1}{2}b_b\left(\frac{\beta}{b_s}\right)^2-\frac{1}{2}b_s\left(\frac{\beta}{b_s}\right)^2-\bar{w}\right]$$

From the first-order condition, we get:

$$\beta=\frac{b_s}{b_s\rho\sigma^2+b_s+b_b}$$

Thereby:

$$\alpha=\frac{1}{\left(b_s\rho\sigma^2+b_s+b_b\right)T}$$

Then the amount of transferred technology is:

$$\Delta T=\alpha T=\frac{1}{b_s\rho\sigma^2+b_s+b_b}$$

14.3.3 Analysis and suggestions of the solution for the model

From

$$\frac{\partial\beta}{\partial b_s}=\frac{b_b}{\left(b_s\rho\sigma^2+b_s+b_b\right)^2}>0$$

We know that β in the optimal contract is an increasing function of b_s, indicating that with a higher cost of tech transfer for the seller, the buyer must increase the value of β in order to encourage the seller to generate the same level of technology transfer.

From

$$\frac{\partial \beta}{\partial b_b} = -\frac{b_s}{\left(b_s \rho \sigma^2 + b_s + b_b\right)^2} < 0,$$ we can know that β in the optimal contract

is a decreasing function of b_b, indicating that a smaller β is expected out of the optimal risk as the cost of the buyer's absorption of technology rises.

From

$$\frac{\partial \beta}{\partial \rho} = -\frac{b_s^2 \sigma^2}{\left(b_s \rho \sigma^2 + b_s + b_b\right)^2} < 0; \frac{\partial \beta}{\partial \sigma^2} = -\frac{b_s^2 \rho}{\left(b_s \rho \sigma^2 + b_s + b_b\right)^2} < 0,$$ we can know

that β in the optimal contract is a decreasing function of ρ, σ^2, indicating that the more risk-averse the seller is, the greater the variance of technology transfer is, the higher the cost of risk for the buyer becomes, and a smaller β is expected out of the optimal risk.

Similarly, the amount of transferred technology ΔT is a decreasing function of b_s, b_b, ρ, σ^2, which means that the greater the cost of both the buyer and the seller is, the higher the seller's risk aversion becomes. And it means not only a greater variance of technology transfer but a lower amount of technology transferred in the end. In this process, the cost of the buyer is relatively high, which will reduce the seller's remuneration, thereby reducing the technology transfer volume of the seller.

Therefore, in the current carbon emission trading, especially the trading of CDM projects, the government administrative department can promote the transfer of low-carbon technologies through the following measures to differentiate the marginal abatement cost of firms, strengthen the supply and demand of carbon emission rights, and expand the capacity of the carbon emissions trading market so as to promote the enthusiasm of firms to participate in carbon emissions trading.

First, we should build a unified platform for carbon emissions trading. Therefore, we can improve information sharing on trading, enhance mutual trust and cooperation, and reduce the risk aversion of the seller.

Second, we should simplify the technology transaction process through specific policies and systems to effectively reduce the transaction cost of the tech transfer between the two sides. It can be seen that with a great reduction of b_s, the cost of technology transfer of the seller is beneficial to the technology buyers. It not only reduces the payment to the seller, but also increases the volume of technology transfer.

Third, we should enhance our capability to absorb the technology. In this regard, we can optimize the knowledge structure of technical personnel through training and improve the capability of firms to learn and absorb technology so as to reduce the cost of technology absorption.

Fourth, we should create an efficient channel for the transformation of technological achievements. Therefore, we can reduce the uncertainty of technology transfer, strengthen the output of technology transfer, and bolster the motivation of firms to actively learn low-carbon technologies.

In short, the learning and introduction of low-carbon technologies is a prerequisite for the formation of a carbon emissions trading market. The introduction of low-carbon technologies brings differences in the marginal abatement cost among firms, thereby promoting the building of carbon emission trading market. In turn, participating in the carbon emission trading also encourages firms to reduce emissions and increases their initiatives to learn low-carbon technologies. This virtuous circle is beneficial to the improvement of the carbon emission trading system.

14.4 Summary

The governmental regulation of carbon emissions trading is the foundation for the development of carbon emissions trading. Compared with participating in carbon emission trading, illegal emission is an attractive method for firms as it is cost-free. However, illegal emissions will inevitably bring serious negative effects to environmental governance and social benefits. To reduce this disutility, the government must regulate illegal emissions. This chapter first analyzes the main factors that can increase the enthusiasm of firms to participate in transactions and reduce governmental regulation by establishing a regulation game model between firms and the government. Then this chapter analyzes the transaction cost, an important factor affecting the participation of firms in carbon emission trading. The transaction cost seriously restricts the trading efficiency of carbon emission rights. Among them, the focus is on the impact of transaction costs on corporate transaction behavior and violations, and relevant suggestions for saving transaction costs are put forward.

Since the formation of carbon emission trading is based on the differences in emission reduction levels among firms, the greater the difference in the marginal abatement cost of carbon emissions is, the higher the transaction costs will be saved, which indicates that the transaction is more likely to occur, and it is more conducive to the establishment of the carbon emission trading market and improvement of the efficiency. However, the increase of marginal abatement cost depends on the introduction and learning of low-carbon technologies. In the end, this chapter discusses the low-carbon technology transfer mechanism which affects carbon emissions trading, analyzes the main factors in technology transfer, and provides effective incentives for the formation of carbon emissions trading.

In conclusion, this chapter makes the following suggestions.

First, we should strengthen the regulatory capacity of the government and design a scientific and effective monitoring and supervision system. The government is the "principal" with information inferiority, while the enterprise is the "agent" with private information. Due to this information asymmetry between the government and firms, the government must strengthen the monitoring and supervision over the firm's carbon emissions. For example, it can design a scientific monitoring system for carbon emissions to grasp the real carbon emissions of firms or establish strict supervision mechanisms and laws and regulations to restrain the illegal emission behavior of firms. At the same time, the government should also accept supervision from firms, and set up a performance assessment system to reduce the cost of the governmental regulation, and make the government regulation more transparent.

Second, we should reduce the transaction cost of carbon emission rights and promote the formation of the carbon emission trading market. The existence of transaction cost seriously restricts the construction of the trading. Since the relationship between endogenous and exogenous transaction costs of carbon emission trading is considered to be a counterbalance paradox, to build a perfect carbon emission trading system, it is necessary to reduce the total cost of carbon emission trading. Specifically, carbon emission rights must be clarified, specific rules for the trading must be formulated, a unified carbon emissions trading market must be created, and scientific and strict monitoring and supervision systems must be developed.

Third, we should strengthen investment in low-carbon technology and create an incentive mechanism to support firms to learn and introduce low-carbon technology. The development and use of low-carbon technologies is the prerequisite for the development of carbon emission trading in China. China is a resource-consuming country and its extensive growth leads to a small difference in marginal abatement cost among firms, which is harmful to the development of carbon emissions trading. The government should boost the confidence and motivation of firms to learn and introduce low-carbon technologies through technical and financial supports and other effective measures. The government should make efforts to provide an efficient channel for the transformation of technologies so that firms will feel the real benefit of low-carbon technologies and have an enduring motivation to learn and introduce such technologies.

The research in this chapter emphasizes on microscopic analysis, and in-depth researches can be conducted on the design of governmental regulation and incentive mechanism under incomplete information as well as the method to improve the efficiency of market transactions in the future.

Notes

1 Chen Dehu, Li Shoude, Jiang Fu. An analysis on firm's behavior and government's control in emissions trading market. *Systems Engineering*, 2004, 3: 44–46.
2 Hu Min. An analysis on the operation mechanism of emissions trading markets based on transaction cost theory. *Theoretical Investigation*, 2006, 5: 83–85.
3 Dai Jun, Sheng Zhaohan. Modeling and research on the transaction mechanism of the enterprise's internal knowledge market. *Forecasting*, 2004, 4: 19, 48–51.

References

Chen Lei, Zhang Shiqiu. Micro game analysis on enterprise behaviors in emission trading. *Acta Scientiarum Naturalium Universitatis Pekinensis*, 2005(11): 926–934.
Coase, R.H. El problemadelcoste social//De la economíaambiental a la economíaecológica. Icaria, 1994: 65–124.
He Xiaogang. Sustainable competitive advantage: an explanation of resource-based view. *Nankai Business Review*, 2002, 5(4): 32–37.

15 Analysis of auction mechanism for carbon emissions trading

15.1 Auction mechanism of carbon emission rights

15.1.1 Comparison of auction mechanisms of carbon emission rights

The units of carbon emission rights are the same, and they can be substituted for each other, so the auction of carbon emission rights is deemed as the auction of multiple homogeneous items. From the current experience, the international multiple homogeneous items auction mainly has two forms: the sealed-bid auction and the ascending auction.

15.1.1.1 Sealed-bid Auction

In a sealed-bid auction, each bidder submits a demand schedule to the auctioneer simultaneously and independently to indicate his or her price demand function. The auctioneer aggregates these data into an aggregate demand curve and the price corresponding to the intersection of the aggregate demand curve and the aggregate supply curve is the clearing price. All bidders whose bid price is higher than this price will be accepted and all demands at the clearing price point will be allocated proportionately, while bids below the clearing price will be rejected (Figure 15.1).

Sealed-bid auctions can be divided into three types: uniform price auctions, discriminatory price auctions, and Vickrey auctions. Comparing these three types, Ausubel and Cramton (1996) pointed out that in uniform price auctions and discriminatory price auctions, bidders would try their best to conceal the value of the auction object by various complicated methods, so as to make their bids lower than the true value. This differential bidding behavior leads the two auction methods to be not fully effective. In a Vickrey auction, the highest bidder gets the auction item at the second highest price. In private value auctions, a Vickrey auction reduces the concealment behavior of bidders. It is a dominant strategy that each bidder bids according to the real demand curve, which can overcome the ineffectiveness of the other two auction methods. But in practice, it is difficult to execute Vickrey auctions. Cramton and Kerr (2002) argued that when no significant

DOI: 10.4324/9781003388500-19

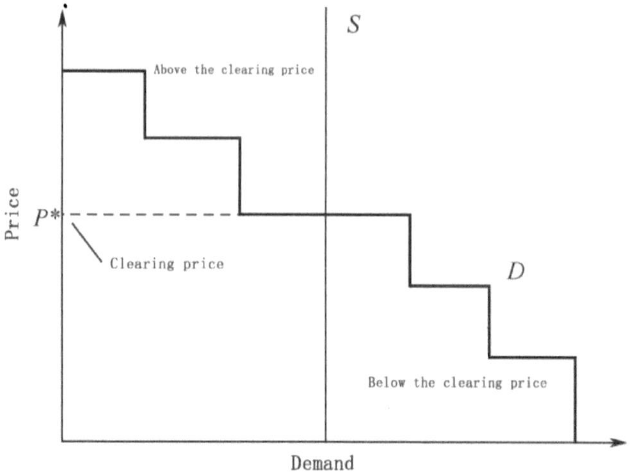

Figure 15.1 Schematic diagram of a sealed-bid auction

market power exists, the efficiency of a uniform price auction is close to that of a Vickrey auction. Moreover, since small bidders in a uniform price auction can profit from the large bidders' concealing their true valuations, the enthusiasm of smaller bidders to participate in the auction can be promoted. In practice, the single-pricing method is simple, feasible, and transparent, and is more popular among bidders.

15.1.1.2 Ascending auction

There are two specific types of auctions in an ascending auction: demanded schedules and ascending clock auctions. Demanded schedules can be viewed as multi-round sealed-bid auctions. In each round, demand curves are drawn according to demand schedules submitted by bidders to generate a clearing price. Then, successful bidders are determined and the next round begins. It should be noted that in each subsequent round, the number of bidders must be reduced. In an ascending clock auction, the current price is marked on the clock and bidders report the quantity demanded at that price. If the total demand exceeds the supply, the price is raised for the next round, until the demand is less than the supply, and the allocation price is determined.

Ascending auctions have many advantages over sealed-bid auctions, the most important of which is better process of price discovery. In the process of ascending auction, each bidder has the opportunity to raise his or her bid price every time, and finally the highest bidder wins the auction. For homogeneous items with common attributes of values, the bidder's valuation relies on the information of other bidders. An ascending auction provides the bidders with relatively transparent price through the process of bidding, which strengthens the confidence of the bidder in valuation. Bidders can adjust their demand based on price information. Ultimately, the bidder who really needs the subject matter wins the auction, so there is no fear of a "winner's curse".

The majority of scholars have shown that although an ascending auction performs better than a sealed-bid auction, the ascending auction has strict time and place restrictions and involves more difficulties in specific implementation. Therefore, the sealed-bid auction is not the best way to auction carbon emission rights. However, for government administrators, the first-price sealed-bid auction with relatively rich theoretical knowledge and practical experience is generally adopted.

15.1.2 Choice of auction mechanisms for carbon emission rights

This chapter mainly selects the first-price sealed-bid auction and the double auction to analyze the auction mechanism for carbon emissions trading.

At present, under the mainstream pricing mechanism of carbon emission rights auctions in Western countries, the highest bidder obtains carbon emission rights and pays the bids. This auction method has the characteristics of the first-price sealed-bid auction. Therefore, in studies of the behavior of bidders in carbon emission rights auctions, the first-price sealed-bid auction model can be used to illustrate the bidding strategies of firms participating in emission reductions. Section 15.2 of this chapter uses the first-price sealed-bid auction to study the auction of carbon emission rights. At the same time, since carbon emission rights is deemed as multiple homogeneous items, the multiple rounds of first-price sealed-bid auction are adopted.

Due to its "many-to-many" market structure, double auctions are more in line with the actual transaction and are widely used in many fields such as electricity, water rights, online auctions, and financial markets in the market transactions. Smith (1962), the "founding father of experimental economics", reveals in experiments that even with a small number of buyers and sellers and incomplete information about supply and demand, the double auction market can achieve the competitive equilibrium predicted by neoclassical economics, with high price discovery efficiency. Moreover, there is an equal supply-demand relationship between both buyers and sellers in double auctions, which can effectively solve the problems of conspiracy and hostile bids (Shulin Liu et al., 1998). Therefore, Section 15.3 of this chapter examines the linear bidding equilibrium of the double auction of carbon emissions trading.

15.1.3 Significance of carbon emission rights auction

The carbon emission rights auction is essential for the development of China's carbon trading markets.

From a macro perspective, the carbon emission rights auction is relatively fair and equitable, which can reduce disputes between regions, industries, and other interest groups caused by free allocation; the revenue from carbon emission rights auction can increase the fiscal revenue of the government, reduce social costs, and improve the governance efficiency of emissions reduction.

From a micro perspective, the carbon emission rights auction can provide a price signal for the carbon trading market, improve the allocation efficiency of carbon emission rights, and support the establishment of the carbon market; such auction is conducive to stimulating bidders to reduce emissions, learn low carbon technologies, and transform outdated production methods; such auction is also conducive to increasing participation in the carbon trading market, that is, both profitable firms with high marginal abatement costs and emerging firms can obtain carbon emission rights through the auction, which in turn improves the market efficiency of carbon emissions rights trading.

15.2 Multi-round first-price sealed-bid auction in carbon emissions trading

This section examines the multi-round first-price sealed-bid auctions in carbon emissions trading. In the auction, each firm participating in it only knows its own valuation of the carbon emission rights being auctioned rather than the valuations of other firms; thus, it is a game of incomplete information. Moreover, in the auction of carbon emission rights, the value of carbon emission rights varies among the firms, since the marginal abatement cost varies among the firms. Firms with high marginal abatement costs have higher valuation of carbon emission rights, while firms with low marginal abatement costs have lower valuation of carbon emission rights. Since the carbon emission rights auctions exhibit significant private value elements, an independent private value model is adopted in this section to describe the buyer's valuation of a unit of carbon emission rights.

15.2.1 Basic model of first-price sealed-bid auction of carbon emission rights

In a so-called first-price sealed-bid auction, all bidders bid on the auction items simultaneously and independently and submit sealed bids to the auctioneer. The auctioneer selects the highest bidder as the winner from all the bidders. The winner gets the item and pays the bid to the auctioneer. In this process, the bid is known only to the bidder, not to any other bidders, as it is private information.

With all the preconditions simplified, the basic model of the first-price sealed-bid auction for the unit of carbon emission rights is listed below.

15.2.1.1 Basic assumptions and factor analysis

Suppose there are n risk-neutral bidders (buyers) and one auctioneer (seller) in the carbon emission rights auction.

The value of the unit of carbon emission rights to the bidders is denoted by v_i, $i = 1,2,\dots, n$, and v_i is the private information of bidder i. Each bidder only knows his/her own private value v_i, but does not know the private value of others, $v_j(i \neq j)$. At the same time, there is common knowledge: v_i is a random variable distributed on $[\overline{v}, v]$, and the distribution function and the density function are $F_i(v)$ and $f_i(v)$, respectively.

Let b_i be the bid of bidder i. If the bidder i wins, he/she will obtain the net utility of carbon emission rights, v_i-b_i, then the expected revenue of bidder i is:

$$R_i = (v_i - b_i) \text{ prob } \{b_i \text{ is the highest price}\} = (v_i - b_i) F^{n-1}(t) \tag{15.1}$$

15.2.1.2 The optimal strategy for the bidder

Suppose the bidder's optimal strategy function is $b(v)$ and the bid $b(v)$ is a strictly increasing differentiable function of its value v,[1] which means that the optimal bid of the bidder with higher private value is strictly greater than that of the bidder with lower private value. The optimal strategy means that if the private valuation of an emission reduction firm is v and the bidding strategy is $b(v)$, the expected revenue will be the highest. Any other bid higher or lower than $b(v)$ will not yield the highest profit. Therefore, as long as the expression of $b(v)$ is found, the optimal bidding strategy is determined.

When the private value of the bidder is v, according to Equation (15.1), the expected revenue is maximized as:

$$\max_t R(v, t) = [v - b(t)] F^{n-1}(t) \tag{15.2}$$

The optimal solution should satisfy the first-order condition, $\frac{\partial R}{\partial t}|_{t=v} = 0$, that is:

$$-b'(v) F^{n-1}(v) + [v - b(v)](n-1) F^{n-2}(v) f(v) = 0 \tag{15.3}$$

Substituting the initial condition $b(v) = v$ into it, we get

$$b(v) = v - \frac{\int_{\underline{v}}^{v} F^{n-1}(t)\,dx}{F^{n-1}(v)} \tag{15.4}$$

wherein $v \in [\overline{v}, v]$.

It is easy to verify that $b(v)$ is a monotonically increasing function, which means that the higher the private value is, the higher the bid is. But the bid is always lower than the private value (hidden value). According to the first-price sealed-bid auction rules, the highest bidder, also the bidder with the highest private value, wins the carbon emission rights.

15.2.2 Improved multi-round first-price sealed-bid auction model for carbon emission rights

In most studies on auction theory, there are usually no restrictions on the purchasing power of the bidders. However, in practice, restricted by their own marginal abatement costs and capital, bidders often have to consider budget constraints on the amount of money invested in auctions. In addition, government administrators usually commission specialized agencies or carbon exchanges to auction carbon emission rights. After an auction concludes, exchanges usually charge a certain commission.

Therefore, the following section focuses on the influence of the commission and the bidder's budget constraint on the decision-making of traders in the multi-round first-price sealed-bid auction of carbon emission rights. Meanwhile, analysis on bidders' bidding strategies and expected revenue for auctioneers, bidders, and exchanges will also be emphasized.

15.2.2.1 Establishment of a multi-round first-price sealed-bid auction model

An auctioneer auctions a total of Q carbon emission rights with first-price sealed-bid auction method through carbon exchanges. At the same time, n ($n \geq 2$) risk-neutral bidders simultaneously submit a sealed bid. The bid is the combination of the unit price (p_i) and the purchased quantity (q_i) of carbon emission rights, wherein $p_i > 0$, $q_i > 0$, $i = 1, 2, \ldots, n$. After the seal is opened, the highest bidder gets the carbon emission rights at the price and quantity according to his/her bid. The other bidders get nothing at this round and they enter the next round of the first-price sealed-bid auction along with the remaining carbon emission rights, and this process will be repeated until all carbon emission rights are sold.

To make the above model easier to solve, the following assumptions are made.

Assumption 1: Let the value of the unit of carbon emission right to the bidder be $v_i, i = 1, 2 \ldots, n$. v_i is the private information of bidder i; each bidder only knows his/her own private value v_i, but does not know the private values of others $v_j \left(i \neq j\right)$. Meanwhile, there is common knowledge that $v_i$obeys a uniform distribution on (0,1).

Assumption 2: If an auction concludes, the bidder will pay the exchange a commission in proportion of $k(0 < k < 1)$ to the unit transaction price.

Assumption 3: Let the budget (that is, the available capital in the auction) of bidder i be $C_i, i = 1, 2, \ldots, n$. C_i is the private information of bidder i. At the same time, there is common knowledge that $Qp_i \geq C_i \geq (1+k)\, p_i q_i, i = 1, 2, \ldots, n$, indicating that the bidder's bound funds cannot purchase all carbon emissions. In the above formula, $p_i = p_i\left(v_i\right) \geq 0$ is the unit price offered by bidder i, which is a strictly increasing differentiable function of the valuation (v_i) for unit of carbon emission right. As bidders' private information is different, their bids are different. For buyers, the game is symmetric. Therefore, $p_i(v_i) = p_j(v_j)$.

In the auction process, each bidder's strategy is a combination of the price (p_i) and the quantity (q_i) determined according to his/her own estimate for carbon emission rights and the judgment of other bidders' estimate for carbon emission rights. The process is actually a static Bayesian Game for bidders.

15.2.2.2 Comparative analysis with the benchmark model

The benchmark model is the basic model for studying auctions, and many important auction models are derived by changing its basic assumptions. Table 15.1 clearly shows the difference between the model in this section and the benchmark model.

Table 15.1 Comparison of the differences between the model in this section and the benchmark model

Content for comparison		*Model*		
Benchmark model		*Model in this section*	*Same/different*	
Basic assumptions	Auction quantity	Single item	Multiple homogeneous items	Different
	Risk attitude of buyers and sellers	Risk neutral	Risk neutral	Same
	Buyer symmetry	Symmetric (estimation obeying the same distribution)	Symmetric (estimation obeying the same distribution)	Same
	Value model	Independent private value model	Independent private value model	Same
	Final payment	Bid	Product of unit price and quantity	Different
	Cooperativeness of bidders	Non-cooperative game	Non-cooperative game	Same
	Transaction fees	No commission	Commission needed	Different
Other conditions	Bidder's objective	Expected utility maximization	Expected utility maximization	Same
	Contents of bidders' offer	Price	Unit price and quantity	Different
	Budget constraint	No constraint	Constraint	Different

Specifically, the differences between the model in this section and the benchmark model are as follows:

1 The model in this section studies the auction of carbon emission rights, which is categorized as a multiple homogeneous items auction. This auction is different from the single-item auction studied in the benchmark model.
2 The model in this section studies the multiple homogeneous items auction of carbon emission rights, so the final payment is the product of the bidder's unit price and the purchased quantity. The benchmark model studies single-item auctions, so the final payment is the bidder's bid.
3 The model in this section will produce transaction costs, which means that bidders pay a commission to the exchange, which is different from the basic assumption in the benchmark model. According to the auction law, auctions should be conducted by a special auction house, so an auction house takes a portion of commission from the auction. The model in this section introduces third party carbon exchanges in transactions and examines the bidding strategy of the bidders when the percentage of the commission is constant.
4 The model in this section studies the auction of the multiple homogeneous items of carbon emission rights. Therefore, two elements are included in the bid: one is the auction price of the unit of carbon emission rights and the other is the quantity of carbon emission rights purchased at this price. This is different from the benchmark model, where a bidder only offers the price of the auction item.
5 The model in this section takes the bidder's budget constraints into account, supposing the bidder's bidding funds have an upper limit, which is restricted by his/her purchasing power. However, budget constraints are not taken into account in the benchmark model.

15.2.2.3 Model solution

First, we solve the bidding strategy of the bidders in the first round of auction. In the first round, the expected utility of bidder i is:

$$\pi_i = \left[v_i - (1+k)p_i\right]q_i \prod_{j \neq i} \text{prob}\left\{p_j < p_i\right\}(i = 1,2,\ldots,n)$$

By symmetry, considering the equilibrium bidding strategy of bidder i, we have:

$$p_i(v_i) = p^*(v_i)(i = 1,2,\ldots,n)$$

In this case, the probability that $p_j < p_i$ is:

$$\text{prob}\left\{p_j < p_i\right\} = \text{prob}\left\{p^*(v_j) < p_i\right\} = \text{prob}\left\{v_j < p^{*-1}(p_i)\right\}$$

Supposing $\Phi(p_i) = p^{*-1}(p_i)$ and v_i obeys the uniform distribution on (0,1), we derive that:

$$\text{prob}\{p_j < p_i\} = \text{prob}\{v_j < \Phi(p_i)\} = \Phi(p_i)$$

Thus, the expected utility of bidder i is:

$$\pi_i = \left[v_i - (1+k)p_i\right] q_i \Phi^{n-1}(p_i)(i = 1,2,\ldots,n)$$

And C_i as the budget of bidder i, satisfies $C_i \geq (1+k)p_i q_i$, and thus $q_i \leq \frac{C_i}{(1+k)p_i}$.

And if p_i is constant, the larger the q_i is, the larger the expected revenue π_i is. Therefore, according to the principle of expected utility maximization, we have $q_i = \frac{C_i}{(1+k)p_i}$.

In this case, the expected utility function of bidder i is:

$$\pi_i = \left[v_i - (1+k)p_i\right] \frac{C_i}{(1+k)p_i} \Phi^{n-1}(p_i)$$

that is:

$$\pi_i = \left[\frac{v_i}{(1+k)p_i} - 1\right] C_i \Phi^{n-1}(p_i)$$

It can be seen that the amount of C_i only affects the expected utility π_i and does not affect the value of the bid p_i.

Solve the equation: $\max_{p_i} \pi_i = \max_{p_i} \left[\frac{v_i}{(1+k)p_i} - 1\right] C_i \Phi^{n-1}(p_i)$

1 If $n > 2$, then from the first-order condition, we have:

$$\frac{\partial \pi_i}{\partial p_i} = C_i \left[-\frac{v_i}{(1+k)p_i^2}\right] \Phi^{n-1}(p_i) +$$
$$C_i \left[\frac{v_i}{(1+k)p_i} - 1\right](n-1)\Phi^{n-2}(p_i)\Phi'(p_i) = 0$$

that is:

$$\left[-\frac{v_i}{(1+k)p_i^2}\right]\Phi(p_i) + \left[\frac{v_i}{(1+k)p_i} - 1\right](n-1)\Phi'(p_i) = 0 \quad (15.5)$$

Since in the equilibrium case, $p_i = p^*(v_i)$, $\Phi(p_i) = p^{*-1}\left[p^*(v_i)\right] = v_i$. Substituting it into Equation (15.5), we get:

$$\left[-\frac{\Phi(p_i)}{(1+k)\,p_i^2}\right]\Phi(p_i)+\left[\frac{\Phi(p_i)}{(1+k)\,p_i}-1\right](n-1)\Phi'(p_i)=0$$

Solving the above differential equation, we get:

$$p_i^* = \frac{1}{1+k}\cdot\frac{n-2}{n-1}v_i\,(i=1,2,\ldots,n) \tag{15.6}$$

and then:

$$q_i^* = \frac{n-1}{n-2}\cdot\frac{C_i}{v_i}(i=1,2,\ldots,n) \tag{15.7}$$

Therefore, the equilibrium bidding strategy of bidder i in the first round of auction is:

$$\left\{\left(p_1^*, q_1^*\right), \left(p_2^*, q_2^*\right), \ldots, \left(p_n^*, q_n^*\right)\right\}$$

For the other rounds, the above derivation still holds, except that the number of participants (n) needs to be adjusted.

2 If $n = 2$, the expected utility of bidder i is:

$$\max_{p_i} \pi_i = \max_{p_i}\left[\frac{v_i}{(1+k)\,p_i}-1\right]C_i\Phi(p_i)$$

Its first-order condition is:

$$\left[-\frac{v_i}{(1+k)\,p_i^2}\right]\Phi(p_i)+\left[\frac{v_i}{(1+k)\,p_i}-1\right]\Phi'(p_i)=0$$

Similarly, substituting $\Phi(p_i) = p^{*-1}\left[p^*(v_i)\right] = v_i$ to solve the differential equation, we get:

$$p_i^* = \frac{1}{1+k}\cdot\frac{v_i}{\ln v_i}$$

Since $v_i \in (0,1]$, p_i^{**} is a monotonically decreasing function of v_i, which is inconsistent with the assumption. Therefore, there is no Bayesian equilibrium.

To sum up, in a multi-round first-price sealed-bid auction, for the number of bidders $n(n > 2)$, the optimal bid of the bidders in the first round is $\left\{\left(p_1^*, q_1^*\right), \left(p_2^*, q_2^*\right), \ldots, \left(p_n^*, q_n^*\right)\right\}$, wherein the optimal bid for bidder i is $\left(p_i^*, q_i^*\right)=\left(\frac{1}{1+k}\cdot\frac{n-2}{n-1}v_i, \frac{n-1}{n-2}\cdot\frac{C_i}{v_i}\right)$, $i=1,2,\ldots,n$. This conclusion can be applied to the other rounds of auction, in turn.

In this case, the expected revenue of bidder i is:

$$\pi_i=\left[\frac{v_i}{(1+k)\,p_i}-1\right]C_i\Phi^{n-1}\left(p_i\right)=\frac{C_i}{n-2}v_i^{n-1} \tag{15.8}$$

The expected revenue of the auctioneer is:

$$\pi_s=E\left(p_i^*q_i^*\right)=\frac{C_i}{1+k} \tag{15.9}$$

The expected revenue of the exchange is:

$$\pi_m=E\left(kp_i^*q_i^*\right)=\frac{kC_i}{1+k} \tag{15.10}$$

15.2.2.4 Equilibrium Analysis

1. By analyzing the bidding strategies of the bidders [Equations (15.6) and (15.7)], the following conclusions can be drawn: the bid price is uncorrelated to the bidder's budget constraints, but is only correlated to the valuation of the unit of carbon emission rights to the bidder $\left(v_i\right)$, the commission coefficient required for the transaction (k) as well as the number of bidders (n). Among them, the bid price increases with the valuation of the unit of carbon emission right to the bidder $\left(v_i\right)$, that is, the larger v_i is, the higher the bidder's bid becomes. And the highest bidder gets the corresponding carbon emission rights. This is consistent with the improved allocation efficiency of carbon emission rights. The bid price increases as the number of bidders n increases. When $n\to\infty$, $p_i^*\to v_i$, which indicates that when the number of bidders tends to infinity, the auctioneer gets almost all of the estimated values of bidders. The bid price is a decreasing function of the commission coefficient k and increases as the value of k decreases.

   The number of bids is uncorrelated to the percentage of commission charged by the exchanges, but is correlated to the budget constraint $\left(C_i\right)$, the valuation of the unit of carbon emission rights to the bidder$\left(v_i\right)$, and the number of bidders (n). That is, the number of bids increases as the budget constraint C_i rises, decreases as the bidder's valuation v_i rises, and decreases as the number of bidders n increases.
2. Through analyzing the expected revenue of all parties [Equations (15.8)–(15.10)], the following conclusions can be drawn: from Equation (15.8), it can be concluded that the expected revenue of the bidder increases as the budget constraints C_i rise, increases as the bidder's valuation v_i rises, and decreases as the number of bidders n increases. It can

be concluded from Equations (15.9) and (15.10) that the revenue of both the auctioneers and the exchanges is correlated to the bidder's budget constraint C_i and the commission coefficient k. In addition, the revenue of both parties increases as the budget constraint C_i rises. With the increase of the commission coefficient k, the revenue of the exchanges rises, while the revenue of the auctioneers decreases.

In conclusion, the derivation above proves that under the restrictions of budget constraints and commissions, the bidder's bid is affected by the percentage of commission, but is not affected by the budget constraints. That is, the bidders' financial strength does not affect their bidding process; the number of bids is limited by their own budget constraints. The expected revenue of both the exchanges and the auctioneers is affected by the percentage of commission and the budget constraints.

Furthermore, in the process of carbon emission rights auction, if an emission firm obtains an amount of carbon emission rights (q_i) through bidding, the carbon dioxide disposal cost of the same amount of emission reduction (q_i) will be saved. We denote the value of the cost by $\Delta C = (v_i - p_i)q_i$, wherein v_i, the valuation of carbon emission rights by emission firms is equivalent to the average abatement cost of the carbon dioxide for the same amount of emission reduction q_i.

Through the auction, the carbon emission rights flow to the firms with the highest emission reduction costs, and the emission reduction is undertaken more by the firms with lower emission reduction costs and thus reducing the total social cost of emission reduction and improving the efficiency of emission reduction management.

15.3 Double auctions in carbon emissions trading

In the transaction of homogeneous items, double auctions are preferred over the traditional auction featured with a "one-to-many" market structure. For instance, Nasdaq Commodities and the Chicago Mercantile Exchange have adopted different forms of the double auction mechanism, since the double auction adopts a "many-to-many" market structure, which is similar to the real trading market. In the auction, the sellers ask a price, the buyers bid, and the auctioneers select the transaction price to clear the market. All sellers who ask less than that transaction price sell their items and all buyers who bid more than the transaction price buy the items. As a result, the total supply of auction items is equal to the total demand at the transaction price. Since both the parties involved in the auction are under incomplete information, both parties are faced with a series of complex decision-making processes, for example in deciding how to offer and whether to accept the bid or not.

This section establishes a double auction model in carbon emissions trading by combining the constrained Zero-Intelligence model and the double auction model of Chatterjee and Samuelson, in order to provide bidding strategies for the auction mechanism and the negotiated direct purchase transactions between both parties in the carbon emissions trading.

15.3.1 Benchmark pricing model for double auction

The benchmark pricing model for double auctions, also the Zero-Intelligence model, was invented by Gode and Sunder. The Zero-Intelligence model can be divided into two specific forms: constrained Zero-Intelligence and unconstrained Zero-Intelligence, depending on the constraints on the bids of both parties.

Assuming that the highest bid allowed in the double auction market is o_{max} and that the lowest bid is o_{min}, b_i denotes the bid of the *i*th bidder, v_i denotes the valuation of the auction item by the *i*th bidder. The offering price of the *i*th auctioneer is denoted by s_i and the cost of the *i*th auctioneer is denoted by c_i.

The constrained Zero-Intelligence model requires that the bidder's bid in a transaction cannot be higher than his/her estimated price for the auction item, and the auctioneer's offer cannot be lower than its cost, otherwise the bid will be considered invalid. The mathematical description is: a uniform distribution of b_i in $\left[o_{min} v_i\right]$; a uniform distribution of s_i in $\left[c_i, o_{max}\right]$.

The unconstrained Zero-Intelligence model has no constraints on the bids of both parties in the auction, and its mathematical description is: the uniform distribution of b_i in $\left[o_{min}, o_{max}\right]$; the uniform distribution of s_i in $\left[o_{min}, o_{max}\right]$. The prices of both parties can be any value that is evenly distributed between the lowest and the highest prices in the market. The bidder's price can be higher than his/her estimated price of the auction item $(b_i > v_i)$ and the auctioneer's price can be lower than the cost $(s_i < c_i)$.

Gode and Sunder found that the constrained Zero-Intelligence model represents bounded rational individuals in the market and the unconfined Zero-Intelligence model represents irrational individuals in the market. In double auctions, whether market participants are rational or not, the market eventually manifests collective rationality, and the ultimate market efficiency is higher than 90%.

15.3.2 Improved double auction model for carbon emission rights

15.3.2.1 Modeling

Suppose that a firm (the demander /buyer) in the carbon trading market wants to purchase Q units of carbon emission rights and a firm (the supplier/ seller) can provide the same units of carbon emission rights, thus a double auction happens between the two sides. And the success of the auction depends on the bids of both parties. In this process, the government acts as the designer of the price mechanism. It sets a reasonable transaction price according to the bids of both parties.

Suppose that the production cost (or the value of the goods to the seller) for the seller to provide Q units of carbon emission rights is $c \in [\underline{c}, \overline{c}]$, and the value of such carbon emission rights to the buyer is $v \in [\underline{v}, \overline{v}]$, and $\overline{v} > c$, wherein v and c are the private information of the buyer and the seller, that is not known to the other party. However, the distributions of c and v are common knowledge: v is uniformly distributed in $[\underline{v}, \overline{v}]$ c is uniformly distributed in $[\underline{c}, \overline{c}]$.

The government stipulates that both buyers and sellers submit a bid simultaneously. The seller's bid is denoted by p_s and the buyer's bid is denoted by p_b. If $p_s > p_b$, the transaction will be rejected; if $p_s \le p_b$, both parties will trade at the transaction price $p = kp_s + (1-k)\,p_b (0 < k < 1)$.

The seller's utility function is denoted as:

$$U_s = \begin{cases} kp_s + (1-k)\,p_b - c, & \text{if } p_s \le p_b \\ 0, & \text{if } p_s > p_b \end{cases}$$

The buyer's utility function is denoted as:

$$U_b = \begin{cases} v - \left[kp_s + (1-k)\,p_b\right], & \text{if } p_s \le p_b \\ 0, & \text{if } p_s > p_b \end{cases}$$

The parameter k in the transaction price reflects the degree of government administrators' support to buyers and sellers. The bigger (smaller) k is, the more (less) utility the seller obtains.

This is a static game with incomplete information. Both parties of the transaction decide their own bidding strategies, where p_s is a function of c and p_b is a function of v.

15.3.2.2 Model solution

According to the above description, when the following two conditions hold, the combination strategy $\left[p_s^*(c), p_b^*(v)\right]$ is the Bayesian Nash equilibrium of this game.

Condition 1: For all $\in [\underline{c}, \overline{c}]$, $p_s^*(c)$ is the solution to the following optimization problem:

$$\max_{p_s} \left\{kp_s + (1-k)\,E\left[p_b(v) \middle| p_b(v) \ge p_s\right] - c\right\} \cdot \text{prob}\left\{p_b(v) \ge p_s\right\} \quad (15.11)$$

Wherein $E\left[p_b(v) \middle| p_b(v) \ge p_s\right]$ represents the seller's expected bid of the buyer when the buyer's bid is higher than the seller's asking price.

Condition 2: For all $v \in [\underline{v}, \overline{v}], p_b^*(v)$is the solution to the following optimization problem:

$$\max_{p_b}\left\{v-\left[(1-k)\,p_b+kE\left[p_s(c)\,\middle|\,p_b\geq p_s(c)\right]\right]\right\}\cdot \text{prob}\left\{p_b\geq p_s(c)\right\} \quad (15.12)$$

Wherein $E\left[p_s(c)\,\middle|\,p_b\geq p_s(c)\right]$ represents the buyer's expected asking price of the seller when the buyer's bid is higher than the seller's asking price.

Although there are many Bayesian Nash equilibriums in this game, in 1983, Myerson and Satterthwaite proved that when the valuations of both parties obey the uniform distribution, the expected revenue of the participants from the linear equilibrium strategies of the double auction is higher than that from any other Bayesian Nash equilibrium. Therefore, in this section, the situation in which both buyers and sellers adopt the linear bidding equilibrium strategies are studied.

Supposing that the linear bidding strategies of buyers and sellers are as follows:

$$\begin{cases} p_s(c)=\alpha_s+\beta_s c \\ p_b(v)=\alpha_b+\beta_b v \end{cases}$$

Because of the uniform distribution of v in $\left[\underline{v},\,\overline{v}\right]$, we have the uniform distribution of p_b in $\left[\alpha_b+\beta_b v,\alpha_b+\beta_b\overline{v}\right]$, thereby:

$$\begin{aligned}\text{prob}\left\{p_b(v)\geq p_s\right\}&=\text{prob}\left\{\alpha_b+\beta_b v\geq p_s\right\}=\text{prob}\left\{v\geq\frac{p_s-\alpha_b}{\beta_b}\right\}\\ &=\frac{\beta_b\overline{v}-p_s+\alpha_b}{\beta_b\left(\overline{v}-\underline{v}\right)}\end{aligned} \quad (15.13)$$

$$E\left[p_b(v)\,\middle|\,p_b(v)\geq p_s\right]=\frac{\dfrac{1}{\beta_b\left(\overline{v}-v\right)}\displaystyle\int_{p_s}^{\alpha_b+\beta_b\overline{v}}x\,dx}{\text{prob}\left\{p_b(v)\geq p_s\right\}}=\frac{\beta_b\overline{v}+\alpha_b+p_s}{2} \quad (15.14)$$

Substituting Equations (15.13) and (15.14) into Equation (15.11), which represents the seller's objective function (i.e., condition 1), we get:

$$\max_{p_s}\left[kp_s+(1-k)\frac{\beta_b\overline{v}+\alpha_b+p_s}{2}-c\right]\cdot\frac{\beta_b\overline{v}-p_s+\alpha_b}{\beta_b\left(\overline{v}-\underline{v}\right)}$$

From the first-order condition, we get:

$$p_s=\frac{k}{k+1}\beta_b\overline{v}+\frac{k}{k+1}\alpha_b+\frac{1}{k+1}c \quad (15.15)$$

It can be concluded that if the buyer chooses a linear strategy, then the seller's optimal response is also linear.

Similarly, because of the uniform distribution of c in $[\underline{c}, \overline{c}]$, we have the uniform distribution of p_s in $[\alpha_s + \beta_s \underline{c}, \alpha_s + \beta_s \overline{c}]$, thereby:

$$\text{prob}\{p_b \geq p_s(c)\} = \text{prob}\{p_b \geq p_s(c)\} = \text{prob}\left\{c \leq \frac{p_b - \alpha_s}{\beta_s}\right\}$$
$$= \frac{p_b - \alpha_s - \underline{c}\beta_s}{\beta_s(\overline{c} - \underline{c})} \tag{15.16}$$

$$E[p_s(c) | p_b \geq p_s(c)] = \frac{\frac{1}{\beta_s(\overline{c} - c)} \int_{\alpha_s + \beta_s \underline{c}}^{p_b} x dx}{\text{prob}\{p_b \geq p_s(c)\}} = \frac{p_b + \alpha_s + c\beta_s}{2} \tag{15.17}$$

Substituting Equations (15.16) and (15.17) into Equation (15.12), which represents the buyer's objective function (i.e., condition 2), we get:

$$\max_{p_b} \left\{ v - \left[(1-k) p_b + k \frac{p_b + a_s + \underline{c}\beta_s}{2}\right] \cdot \frac{p_b + a_s + \underline{c}\beta_s}{\beta_s(\overline{c} - \underline{c})} \right\}$$

From the first-order condition, we get:

$$p_b = \frac{k-1}{k-2} c\beta_s + \frac{k-1}{k-2} \alpha_s - \frac{1}{k-2} v \tag{15.18}$$

For combined Equations (15.15) and (15.18), the solution to the equilibrium linear strategies is:

$$p_s^*(c) = \frac{1}{k+1} c + \frac{k}{2}\left(\overline{v} + \frac{1-k}{k+1} c\right)$$
$$p_b^*(v) = \frac{1}{2-k} v + \frac{1-k}{2}\left(\underline{c} + \frac{k}{2-k} \overline{v}\right)$$

15.3.2.3 Equilibrium Analysis

1 Constraint condition for transactions. Under the equilibrium linear strategy, only if $p_s \leq p_b$, that is

$$v \geq \frac{2-k}{k+1} c + \frac{k}{2} \overline{v} - \frac{(1-k)(2-k)}{2(k+1)} \underline{c} \tag{15.19}$$

the transaction can take place.

Also, according to the constraint condition of constrained Zero-Intelligence model, when $p_s(c) < c$, that is, $c > \frac{k+1}{2}\left(\overline{v} + \frac{1-k}{k+1} c\right)$, the transaction does not happen. When $p_b(v) > v$, that is, $v < \frac{2-k}{2}\left(\underline{c} + \frac{k}{2-k}\overline{v}\right)$, the transaction does not happen either.

2 Utility analysis of buyers and sellers in equilibrium. Based on the bids of both parties, the government determines the transaction price as follows:

$$p^E = kp_s^*(c) + (1-k)p_b^*(v) = \frac{k}{k+1}c + \frac{1-k}{2-k}v + \frac{k}{2(2-k)}\overline{v} + \frac{1-2k}{2}\underline{c}$$

1 When the carbon emissions trading takes place, the buyer's utility is:

$$U_b = v - p^E = \frac{1}{2-k}v - \frac{k}{k+1}c - \frac{k}{2(2-k)}\overline{v} - \frac{1-2k}{2}\underline{c}$$

From Equation (15.19), we have:

$$U_b \geq \frac{1-k}{k+1}(c-c) + \frac{k^2}{1+k}c > 0$$

Therefore, under the linear equilibrium strategy, the buyer's utility is improved compared with the situation that the carbon emission trading is not achieved.

2 But for the seller, when the carbon emissions trading is completed, the utility is:

$$U_s = p^E - c = \frac{-1}{k+1}c + \frac{1-k}{2-k}v + \frac{k}{2(2-k)}\overline{v} + \frac{1-2k}{2}c$$

Since it is unknown whether U_s is a positive value or a negative value, the seller's utility may not be improved when the transaction is completed.

If $U_s > 0$, we get:

$$v \geq \frac{2-k}{(1-k)(1+k)}c + \frac{k}{2(1-k)}\overline{v} - \frac{(1-2k)(2-k)}{2(1-k)}c \tag{15.20}$$

Further combining Equations (15.19) and (15.20), we assume:

$$\frac{2-k}{k+1}c + \frac{k}{2}\overline{v} - \frac{(1-k)(2-k)}{2(k+1)}c \geq \frac{2-k}{(1-k)(1+k)}c$$
$$+\frac{k}{2(1-k)}\overline{v} - \frac{(1-2k)(2-k)}{2(1-k)}\underline{c}$$

We get:

$$c \le \frac{k(k+1)}{2-k}\bar{v} - \frac{3k-1}{2}\underline{c}$$

If we denote $c_0 = \dfrac{k(k+1)}{2-k} - v - \dfrac{3k-1}{2}\underline{c}$, then if $c \le c_0$, the seller's utility is improved in the case of Equation (15.19); if $c > c_0$, the seller's utility is improved in the case of Equation (15.20).

Also:

$$\frac{\partial c_0}{\partial k} = \frac{-k^2+4k+2}{(2-k)^2}\bar{v} - \frac{3}{2}\underline{c} > \frac{3}{2}(\bar{v} - \underline{c}) > 0 \left(k \geqslant \frac{1}{2}\right)$$

Therefore, the government should increase the support to the seller, so that the ex-post utility of both sellers and buyers can be improved when the transaction is completed.

It is clear that the completion of a transaction under the linear equilibrium strategy will definitely increase the utility of buyers, while it is uncertain for sellers. In order to improve the ex-post utility of the seller, the government should provide more support for the seller to increase the seller's enthusiasm to participate in double auctions and then achieve Pareto improvement in the efficiency of carbon emissions trading.

15.4 Summary

The auction mechanism plays an important role in the allocation and circulation markets of carbon emissions trading because of its functions in revealing information and reducing agency costs. In the development of carbon emission rights trading in China, we should learn from mature markets abroad to choose auction methods for carbon emission rights and then design and pilot the method based on the characteristics of our own market. This chapter focuses on the first-price sealed-bid auction method and the double auction method.

Based on the basic model of first-price sealed-bid auction, this chapter designs a multi-round first-price sealed-bid auction model that considers bidders' budget constraints and the commission that bidders pay to exchanges. Studies show that bidders' bids are affected by the amount of the commission they pay, but not affected by their budget constraints, that is, bidders' financial strength does not affect the bidding process; the number of bids is limited by their own budget constraints. At the same time, when the budget constraints increase, the expected revenue of the bidders, the sellers, and the exchanges increase. However, as the commission coefficient rises, the revenue of the exchanges increases, and the revenue of the auctioneer decreases.

Since the double auctions are widely used in the real market of multiple homogeneous items, this chapter expands it on the basis of the constrained Zero-Intelligence model and the double auction model of Chatterjee and Samuelson, and develops a new double auction model, in which the values of buyers and sellers obey the uniform distribution and the transaction price reflects the administrator's preference. Such model is developed to solve the linear bidding equilibrium strategies.

Regarding the auction mechanism design for carbon emission rights, conditions in the model can be further relaxed. For example, the study on the bidding strategy can be taken under the conditions that the bidder is risk-averse, their behavior is asymmetric, and their value model is an associated value model or a common value model. Also, the study can discuss the establishment of a "many-to-many" double auction model based on the "one-to-one" double auction.

Note

1 Differentiability is a technical assumption, with the strictly increasing coming from maximized behavior.

References

Ausubel, L.M., Cramton, P. Demand reduction and inefficiency in multiple-unit auctions. Working Paper, 1996.

Cramton, P., Kerr, S. Tradeable carbon permit auctions: How and why to auction not grandfather. *Energy Policy*, 2002, 30: 333–345.

Liu Shulin, Wang Shouyang, Li Jianqiang. Several mathematical models for bidding and auctions. *Journal of Management Sciences in China*, 1998, 1(2): 11–16.

Myerson, R.B., Satterthwaite, M. Efficient mechanisms for bilateral trading. *Journal of Economic Theory*, 1983, 29: 265–281.

Smith, V.L. An experimental study of competitive market behavior. *Journal of Political Economy*, 1962, 70 (3): 111–137.

Index

Note: **Bold** page numbers refer to tables, *italic* page numbers refer to figures and page numbers followed by "n" refer to end notes.